P9-AFT-855

DATE DUE

			PRINTED IN U.S.A.

Authors & Artists for Young Adults

ISSN 1040-5682

Authors & Artists for Young Adults

VOLUME 28

Thomas McMahon
Editor

The Gale Group

DETROIT • SAN FRANCISCO • LONDON • BOSTON • WOODBRIDGE, CT

Riverside Community College
MAR '99   Library
4800 Magnolia Avenue
Riverside, CA 92506

REFERENCE
PN1009.A1 A88
Garrett, Agnes.
Authors & artists for young
adults.

Thomas McMahon, *Editor*

Joyce Nakamura, *Managing Editor*
Hal May, *Publisher*

Diane Andreassi, Carol Brennan, Ken Cuthbertson, Mary Gillis, Cathy Goldstein,
Kevin S. Hile, J. Sydney Jones, Marie J. MacNee, Tom Pendergast, Nancy Rampson,
Jon Saari, Gerard J. Senick, Tracy J. Sukraw, Diane Telgen, Kathleen Witman,
Sketchwriters/Contributing Editors

Victoria B. Cariappa, *Research Manager*
Cheryl L. Warnock, *Project Coordinator*
Patricia Tsune Ballard, Wendy K. Festerling, *Research Assistants*

Susan M. Trosky, *Permissions Manager*
Maria L. Franklin, *Permissions Specialist*
Sarah Chesney, Edna Hedblad, Michele Lonoconus, *Permissions Associates*

Mary Beth Trimper, *Production Director*
Cindy Range, *Production Assistant*

Randy Bassett, *Image Database Supervisor*
Gary Leach, *Graphic Artist*
Robert Duncan, Michael Logusz, *Imaging Specialists*
Pamela A. Reed, *Imaging Coordinator*

While every effort has been made to ensure the reliability of the information presented in this publication, Gale Research Inc. does not guarantee the accuracy of the data contained herein. Gale accepts no payment for listing; and inclusion in the publication of any organization, agency, institution, publication, service, or individual does not imply endorsement of the editors or publisher. Errors brought to the attention of the publisher and verified to the satisfaction of the publisher will be corrected in future editions.

The paper used in this publication meets the minimum requirements of
American National Standard for Information Sciences—Permanence Paper
for Printed Library Materials, ANSI Z39.48-1984.

This publication is a creative work fully protected by all applicable copyright laws, as well as by misappropriation, trade secret, unfair competition, and other applicable laws. The authors and editors of this work have added value to the underlying factual material herein through one or more of the following: unique and original selection, coordination, expression, arrangement, and classification of the information.

All rights to this publication will be vigorously defended.
Copyright (c) 1999 by Gale Research
27500 Drake Rd.
Farmington Hills, MI 48331-3535

All rights reserved including the right of reproduction in whole or in part in any form.

Library of Congress Catalog Card Number 89-641100
ISBN 0-7876-2071-8
ISSN 1040-5682

10 9 8 7 6 5 4 3 2 1

Printed in the United States of America

Authors and Artists for Young Adults

NATIONAL ADVISORY BOARD

A five-member board consisting of teachers, librarians, and other experts on young adult literature was consulted to help determine the contents of *Authors and Artists for Young Adults*. The members of the board for this volume include:

Donald J. Kenney
Associate Dean of Administrative Services, Virginia Tech, member of Young Adult Library Services Association and Assembly on Literature of Adolescents

Nancy Reich
Coordinating Field Librarian, Los Angeles United School District Library Services, chair of Popular Paperbacks for Young Adults committee, Young Adults Library Services Association, 1998

Esther R. Sinofsky
Coordinating Field Librarian, Los Angeles United School District Library Services, member of Young Adult Library Services Association

Caryn Sipos
Librarian, Young Adults Services, King County (WA) Library System, member of board of directors, Young Adult Library Services Association

Authors and Artists for Young Adults

TEEN BOARD ADVISORS

A number of teen reading boards were consulted to help determine series' content. The teen board advisors for this volume include:

Terry Christner
Children's librarian, and advisor for young adult programming and young adult board at the Hutchinson Public Library in Kansas

Joan Eisenberg
Children's librarian and advisor to the "Bookies" reading group at the Cambridge Public Library in Massachusetts

Francisco Goldsmith
Senior librarian for Teen Services, and advisor to "Feedback," a teen advisory group, at the Berkeley Public Library in California

Jesse Warren
Children's and young adult library assistant, and young adult advisory board director at the Boulder Public Library in Colorado

Authors and Artists for Young Adults

TEEN BOARD

The staff of *Authors and Artists for Young Adults* wishes to thank the following young adult readers for their teen board participation:

Berkeley Public Library:

Stephanie Andrews

Rachel Bloom

Rebecca Brewer

Dora Hsia

Janice Kao

Cheung Ki

Albert Kung

Eleanor Kung

Stephanie Li

Brian Louie

Jascha Pohl

Aletheia Price

Betsy Shyn

Alex Tsai

Hutchinson Public Library:

Nathan Christner

Gretchen Gier

Lauri Hume

Mary Johnston

Sarah Johnston

Elizabeth Rankin

Elizabeth Richardson

Jordan Vieyra

Kristen Walker

Cambridge Public Library:

Mabrouka Boukraa

Adrian Danemayer

Cristina Groeger

Lena Groeger

Ana Riedlmayer-Munroe

Joanna Rifkin

Boulder Public Library:

Jonathan Beall

Andrew Bond

Alonit Cohen

Jenny Dowe

Tiernan Doyle

Ariel Goldstein

Nicholas Grzenda

Asa Henderson

Shandra Jordan

Jess Lundie

Tony Richards

Contents

Introduction

Authors and Artists for Young Adults is a reference series designed to serve the needs of middle school, junior high, and high school students interested in creative artists. Originally inspired by the need to bridge the gap between Gale's *Something about the Author,* created for children, and *Contemporary Authors*, intended for older students and adults, *Authors and Artists for Young Adults* has been expanded to cover not only an international scope of authors, but also a wide variety of other artists.

Although the emphasis of the series remains on the writer for young adults, we recognize that these readers have diverse interests covering a wide range of reading levels. The series therefore contains not only those creative artists who are of high interest to young adults, including cartoonists, photographers, music composers, bestselling authors of adult novels, media directors, producers, and performers, but also literary and artistic figures studied in academic curricula, such as influential novelists, playwrights, poets, and painters. The goal of *Authors and Artists for Young Adults* is to present this great diversity of creative artists in a format that is entertaining, informative, and understandable to the young adult reader.

Entry Format

Each volume of *Authors and Artists for Young Adults* will furnish in-depth coverage of twenty to twenty-five authors and artists. The typical entry consists of:

—A detailed biographical section that includes date of birth, marriage, children, education, and addresses.

—A comprehensive bibliography or filmography including publishers, producers, and years.

—Adaptations into other media forms.

—Works in progress.

—A distinctive essay featuring comments on an artist's life, career, artistic intentions, world views, and controversies.

—References for further reading.

—Extensive illustrations, photographs, movie stills, cartoons, book covers, and other relevant visual material.

A cumulative index to featured authors and artists appears in each volume.

Compilation Methods

The editors of *Authors and Artists for Young Adults* make every effort to secure information directly from the authors and artists through personal correspondence and interviews. Sketches on living authors and artists are sent to the biographee for review prior to publication. Any sketches not personally reviewed by biographees or their representatives are marked with an asterisk (*).

Highlights of Forthcoming Volumes

Among the authors and artists planned for future volumes are:

T. A. Barron	John Jakes	Nick Park
Cherie Bennett	Francisco Jimenez	Jackson Pollack
Robert Bloch	Laurie R. King	Tom Robbins
Olive Ann Burns	Rudyard Kipling	Neil Simon
Judith Ortiz Cofer	Trudy Krishner	Mary Stewart
Robin Cook	Stephen Lawhead	Sheri S. Tepper
Edwidge Danticat	Spike Lee	Vincent van Gogh
Julie Dash	Lois Lowry	Joan D. Vinge
Harlan Ellison	Morgan Llywelyn	Will Weaver
Charles Ferry	Jess Mowry	Connie Willis
Daniel Hayes	Edvard Munch	Oprah Winfrey
John Hersey	Phyllis Reynolds Naylor	Tad Williams

Contact the Editor

We encourage our readers to examine the entire *AAYA* series. Please write and tell us if we can make AAYA even more helpful to you. Give your comments and suggestions to the editor:

BY MAIL: The Editor, *Authors and Artists for Young Adults*, 27500 Drake Rd., Farmington Hills, MI 48331-3535.

BY TELEPHONE: (800) 347-GALE

Sherman Alexie

book of fiction; named one of *Granta* literary magazine's Best of Young American Novelists, 1996; American Book Award, 1996, and International IMPAC Dublin Literary Award nomination, 1997, both for *Reservation Blues*.

■ Personal

Born October 7, 1966, in Spokane, WA; son of Sherman Joseph and Lillian Agnes (Cox) Alexie; married, c. 1994; wife's name, Diane; children: one son. *Education:* Attended Gonzaga University, 1985-87; Washington State University, B.A., 1991

■ Addresses

Home—Seattle, WA. *Office*—P. O. Box 376, Wellpinit, WA 99040.

■ Career

Writer.

■ Awards, Honors

Washington State Arts Commission, poetry fellow, 1991; National Endowment for the Arts, fellow, 1992; winner of Slipstream's fifth annual chapbook contest, 1992, for *I Would Steal Horses*; citation winner, PEN/Hemingway Award, and Great Lakes Colleges Association Award, both for *The Lone Ranger and Tonto Fistfight in Heaven* as best first

■ Writings

The Business of Fancydancing: Stories and Poems, Hanging Loose Press, 1992.
I Would Steal Horses (poems), Slipstream, 1992.
First Indian on the Moon (poems), Hanging Loose Press, 1993.
The Lone Ranger and Tonto Fistfight in Heaven (short stories), Atlantic Monthly Press, 1993.
Old Shirts & New Skins (poems), UCLA American Indian Studies Center, 1993.
Water Flowing Home (poems), Limberlost Press, 1994.
Seven Mourning Songs for the Cedar Flute I Have Yet to Learn to Play (poems), Whitman College Press, 1994.
Reservation Blues (novel), Atlantic Monthly Press, 1995.
Indian Killer, Atlantic Monthly Press, 1996.
The Summer of Black Widows, Hanging Loose Press, 1996.
Smoke Signals (screenplay; based on the short stories in *The Lone Ranger and Tonto Fistfight in Heaven*), ShadowCatcher Entertainment/Miramax, 1998.

Contributor to *The Most Wonderful Books: Writers on Discovering the Pleasures of Reading,* edited by

Michael Dorris and Emilie Buchwald, 1997; contributor of articles and reviews to *New York Times, Ploughshares,* and *Seattle Weekly,* among other periodicals.

■ Sidelights

Sherman Alexie admits he was once a "good" Indian, his term for a person of Native American heritage who does his best to assimilate into mainstream North American society. It drove him to drink, and then to write, and with the latter act he found his own particular brand of salvation. A major theme of Alexie's poetry and fiction is the destructiveness of the dominant white culture upon the Indian world, which is then rendered rudderless and confused. Much of the grist for

Alexie paints a grim picture of life on a Native American reservation in this 1993 collection of tales.

these ideas and incidents comes from life as he witnessed it growing up on the Spokane Reservation. "His work offers a devastating and deeply human portrait of contemporary Indian life," wrote Doug Marx in *Publishers Weekly.* At the age of just thirty-one, Alexie landed a first in the annals of American cultural history with his screenplay for *Smoke Signals,* based on a collection of his short stories. *Smoke Signals* was the first feature film to be written, directed, and acted by Native Americans.

Alexie once explained to a journalist that he did not scheme to become a writer so that he could "set the world straight about the Indian experience," as he told Terry Lawson in the *Detroit Free Press.* Rather, he only hoped to "reclaim my own story. Oh, and to get revenge. I'm big on revenge," the writer added. Born on the Spokane Reservation in Washington state in 1966, Alexie's father was a Coeur d'Alene, and the Spokane ancestors on his mother's side were forcibly removed by U.S. Cavalry forces in 1858 to make way for white settlers. Eight hundred of the Spokanes' horses were slaughtered as well. A legacy of economic deprivation for Native Americans manifests itself well into the twentieth century, and one marker of this is infant mortality rates. Alexie himself was born with hydrocephaly, or excess fluid in the cranium, a very serious condition. His parents were informed that surgery was possible, but the infant might not survive it, or if he did, would probably be mentally retarded. Yet Alexie did survive, and surprised everyone with his strong, intellectually curious personality, even at an early age. As a toddler, he has said, he knew he would be famous. "I was smart, and I knew it," he told Lawson in the *Detroit Free Press* interview. "I didn't know what I would be good at, had no idea really."

Still, Alexie suffered seizures until the age of seven, and had to take strong drugs like lithium to control them. Because of his health problems, he was excluded from many of the strenuous activities that are rites of passage for young Indian males in Wellpinit, the reservation's sole town. "I was a total geek, which automatically made me an outcast, so in order to succeed I had to be smarter than everybody else," Alexie told Marx in *Publishers Weekly.* "I was fierce in the classroom, I humiliated everybody and had my nose broken five times after school for being the smart kid." By the time he was twelve and had read the en-

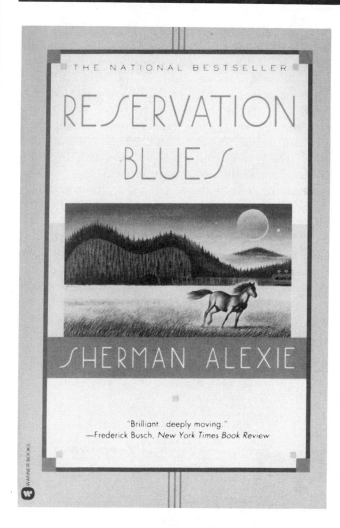

In this 1995 novel, Thomas-Build-the-Fire's musical career soars after he receives an unusual guitar from a former blues musician.

tire library at his reservation school, it was clear to Alexie he needed a greater challenge. So in 1981 he transferred to a school in Spokane, where he was the only student of official Native heritage. There he excelled in both academics and—surprisingly—in athletics, becoming a standout basketball player for the Reardan High Indians, a name whose irony was not lost on the rest of his family. He was also class president, and the achievements won him a scholarship to a Roman Catholic college in the area, Gonzaga University.

Alexie enrolled in Gonzaga's pre-med curriculum, but was overwhelmed by the grotesqueries in anatomy classes. He switched to law, but found that unpleasant as well. He also started drinking. Depressed, he found some solace in literature

classes and the canon of English-language poets, which he initially approached as "anthropology," as he explained to Marx in *Publishers Weekly:* "I didn't see myself in them," he said of writers like Walt Whitman and William Butler Yeats, ". . . and then I realized that the poems *weren't* just about white people. They were about everybody. I also realized that the poets were outcasts, too." Alexie dropped out of Gonzaga after two years, but despite his severe drinking did manage to enroll at Washington State University. There he took a writing class taught by Alex Kuo, a published poet, who lent his student an anthology titled *Songs of This Earth on Turtle's Back.* The book changed his life, especially a line from an Adrian C. Louis poem, "Elegy for the Forgotten Oldsmobile": "O Uncle Adrian! I am in the reservation of my own mind." The line had such an impact upon Alexie that "I started crying," he recalled in the interview with Marx. "That was my whole life."

Literary Beginnings

Alexie began reading the work of other Native American writers and then writing himself. His first collection, *I Would Steal Horses*, was published in 1992, and a literary career picked up steam rapidly from that point on. The Brooklyn, New York-based Hanging Loose Press published his second collection, *The Business of Fancydancing,* that same year; three other books by Alexie would be issued in 1993 alone. Writing in the *Dictionary of Literary Biography,* Susan B. Brill described *The Business of Fancydancing* as "stories and poems about reservation life—a life of alcoholism, commodity food, broken families, and a pervasive racism. . . ." The work sold very well—over 10,000 copies—and Alexie turned to writing full-time. He quit college three credits short of a degree (Washington State awarded him a bachelor's in 1995 after he had published several books), and even more portentously, decided to quit drinking. Soon he was well-known in contemporary literary circles for invoking laughs at his readings. "I get high, I get drunk off of public readings," Alexie said to Marx in *Publishers Weekly.* "I'm good at it. It comes from being a debater in high school, but also, crucially, it comes from the oral tradition of my own culture."

Life in Wellpinit and Alexie's own hardships continued to provide inspiration for his work. In his 1993 collection of verse, *First Indian on the Moon,* he writes about his sister and her husband who died in a house fire, so deeply asleep from alcohol they didn't hear the smoke alarm. Yet there are also frequent flashes of love and humor in his works. "Comic moments appear suddenly and unexpectedly on this harsh landscape, so that irony twists despair into a peculiar kind of faith," remarked Carl Bankston III in the *Bloomsbury Review* about Alexie's style. Though he had experimented with the short-story format before, *The Lone Ranger and Tonto Fistfight in Heaven,* published in 1993, was his first fully developed collection of prose works. In one of the short stories, a father and son take a short trip into Spokane. Both are diabetic, and as Brill explained in the *Dictionary of Literary Biography,* "government-subsidized commodity food is one of the signs of Indian America that appear throughout Alexie's writing—a sign of particular significance to the writer, whose diabetes manifests the effects of his childhood diet." In these stories Alexie introduced characters who would appear in later works, most notably Thomas Builds-the-Fire and Victor Joseph.

Another tale in *The Lone Ranger* chronicles the self-abuse of a former high school hoops star who has turned to alcohol. In this piece, Alexie sums up what it means to be "Indian" (a term he does not find objectionable) in North America in the 1990s: ". . .it's almost like Indians can easily survive the big stuff. Mass murder, loss of language and land rights. It's the small things that hurt the most. The white waitress who wouldn't take an order, Tonto, the Washington Redskins." After three more collections of poetry, including 1994's *Seven Mourning Songs for the Cedar Flute I Have Yet to Learn to Play,* Alexie expanded the characters of *The Lone Ranger* into a full-fledged novel, *Reservation Blues.* Its plot begins with the sudden appearance of a renowned bluesman on the reservation, who brings with him a guitar allegedly possessing otherworldly powers. The instrument was given to him in a deal he once made with "the Gentleman," and now he wants to get rid of it. Thomas takes it off his hands and forms an R&B act called Coyote Springs. Success, groupies from Spokane, and a record deal arrive in quick

Smoke Signals, released in 1998, is based on the short stories in *The Lone Ranger and Tonto Fistfight in Heaven.*

succession, but things also go awry, and badly. In a critique of the work for *People*, Pam Lambert termed *Reservation Blues* a "high-flying, humor-spiked tale of culture and assimilation." A *Publishers Weekly* critic found it "hilarious but poignant, filled with enchantments yet dead-on accurate with regard to modern Indian life."

Alexie's next work and second novel, *Indian Killer*, offered far less amusement. Published by Atlantic Monthly Press in 1996 (by this point in his career, Alexie also had well-known literary agent Morgan Entrekin behind him), *Indian Killer* proceeds to the city of Seattle, where a gruesome serial killer is scalping white men and leaving owl feathers—a death symbol for the indigenous peoples of the Northwest—near the corpses. An antagonistic local radio host fans the flames among Seattle's more impressionable, racist citizens, and the city's indigent Indian men soon become the target of violent retaliatory attacks. Some begin to suspect a quiet construction worker named John Smith of the murders. Smith is Indian, but was adopted into a white family as a baby; the dislocation he feels from his culture extends so far that he begins to become clearly dislocated from society and any sense of human community at all as an adult.

Other characters in the novel offer Alexie a chance to skewer pop culture and the academic world's depiction of Indians as wise and deeply spiritual. A novelist in *Indian Killer* named Jack Wilson, who becomes involved in trying to solve the killing spree, falsely claims Indian blood and writes popular detective fiction featuring sagacious sleuth Aristotle Little Hawk. Another character butts heads with a Native Studies professor at her college, at one point telling him, "I'm not some demure little Indian woman healer talking spider this, spider that."

Alexie faced some criticism for *Indian Killer* for both the gruesome subject matter and the lampooning of Native-loving non-Natives. "This is sad and eloquently written," assessed *Time*'s John Skow. "It is also ugly." Skow found Alexie's novel "septic with what clearly seems to be his own unappeasable fury." *New York Times Book Review* writer Richard E. Nicholls was more charitable in his assessment. "It's difficult not to make 'Indian Killer' sound unrelievedly grim," noted Nicholls, who explained that Alexie was skilled at injecting mordant humor into the proceedings. "It's also

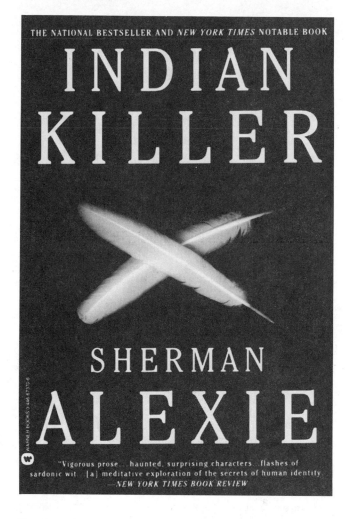

THE NATIONAL BESTSELLER AND *NEW YORK TIMES* NOTABLE BOOK

INDIAN KILLER

SHERMAN ALEXIE

"Vigorous prose...haunted, surprising characters...flashes of sardonic wit...[a] meditative exploration of the secrets of human identity."
—*NEW YORK TIMES BOOK REVIEW*

Tensions between whites and Native Americans rise in this 1996 novel when a serial killer thought to be Native American terrorizes Seattle.

difficult not to make the novel seem more angry than reflective," Nicholls continued, "But Sherman Alexie is too good a writer. . . . His vigorous prose, his haunted, surprising characters and his meditative exploration of the sources of human identity transform into a resonant tragedy what might have been a melodrama in less assured hands."

Controversial Author

Alexie's success has not brought him enthusiastic acclaim back in Wellpinit, either. He has endured criticism from the Native community itself. A librarian at the Salish-Kootenai College on the Spokane Reservation, Mikki Samuels, explained to Timothy Egan in the *New York Times Magazine* that

If you enjoy the works of Sherman Alexie, you may also want to check out the following books and films:

Dee Brown, *Bury My Heart at Wounded Knee*, 1970.
Michael Dorris, *A Yellow Raft in Blue Water*, 1987.
James Welch, *The Indian Lawyer*, 1990.
Powwow Highway, an independent film starring A Martinez, 1989.

"what people on the reservation feel is that he's making fun of them. It's supposed to be fiction, but we all know who he's writing about. He has wounded a lot of people." Alexie's response is to attribute some of the complaints to reservation politics, which are similar to small-town politics, but does concede that some of the blame lies on himself—"I was as mouthy and opinionated as a kid as I am now," he told Egan. Outside the Native community and in the greater literary one, Alexie has also made enemies for his involvement or instigation of literary feuds.

Alexie continued to write poetry, give readings, and contemplate offers from Hollywood producers interested in turning his fiction into feature films. Since 1993 and the success of *The Lone Ranger* short stories, he had listened to pitches for movie ideas that planned to leave him out of the writing process altogether. One scheme even wanted to erase the Indian heritage of the characters altogether. Yet a combination of luck and perseverance eventually yielded production funds, a deal with Miramax, and the 1998 release of *Smoke Signals*. Chris Eyre, a filmmaker of Cheyenne-Arapaho heritage, had read Alexie's *Lone Ranger* stories and simply called up the author himself one day; they found financing for its paltry $1.7 million budget via the Seattle multimedia firm that had once taken a chance on *sex, lies, and videotape*, one of the first commercially successful independent films.

Alexie penned the screenplay himself and was insistent that his characters be played by Native actors. His doggedness resulted in the first commercial feature film written, directed, and acted by a Native American cast and crew—but "the film is so relaxed about its characters, so much at home in their world, that we sense it's an inside job," wryly noted Chicago *Sun-Times* film critic Roger Ebert. The action opens on July 4, 1976, when much of America celebrated the Bicentennial with great hoopla; Victor Joseph and Thomas Builds-the-Fire are children. That night, a fire destroys the latter's house, killing his parents, but the head of the Josephs, Arnold, saves Thomas. As they grow into young adulthood, Thomas and Victor are not especially close. "Thomas, much like Alexie himself when he grew up on the Spokane reservation, is a storyteller ignored by the rest of the tribe," explained Egan in the *New York Times Magazine*.

Victor learns that his father, whose alcoholism eventually drove him far away from his family, has died, and Thomas offers to pay for the bus trip to Arizona to retrieve the ashes if he can come along too. Victor dislikes the talkative Thomas, but acquiesces. The taciturn Victor considers Thomas far too influenced by media and pop culture representations of Native heritage, such as the film *Dances with Wolves*. Thomas is well aware of the ironies of the situation. "The only thing more pathetic than an Indian on TV," he says at one point to Victor, "is an Indian watching an Indian on TV." Their road trip to Arizona is naturally a journey of self-discovery, but they also manage to do what they are supposed to do: bring Arnold's ashes back and scatter them near the falls of the Spokane River.

Alexie also co-produced *Smoke Signals* and composed some of the music for its soundtrack. *Time* writer Jeffrey Ressner compared him to Spike Lee. Alexie relished the idea of becoming so influential—"Spike didn't necessarily get films made as much as he inspired filmmakers to believe in themselves," Alexie said. "That's what's going to happen here. These 13-year-old Indian kids who've been going crazy with their camcorders will finally see the possibilities." He is set to direct the film version of *Indian Killer* beginning in late 1998. "The one thing I learned making 'Smoke Signals' is that the myth of the director is just waiting to be punctured," Alexie told Lawson in the *Detroit Free Press* with characteristic fervor. "You will never see the words 'A Film by Sherman Alexie' on anything like that on any movie I'm ever involved with."

Alexie lives in Seattle with his wife and their son, and has no plan to forsake his writing career for more lucrative artistic involvements. The first member of his family not to live on the Spokane Reservation, his fame sometimes makes it difficult to visit his parents. "My friends are happy to see me," he said to Egan. "My enemies are not."

■ Works Cited

Bankston, Carl III, review of *First Indian on the Moon, Bloomsbury Review,* May/June, 1994, p. 15.

Brill, Susan B., "Sherman Alexie," *Dictionary of Literary Biography,* Volume 175: *Native American Writers of the United States,* Gale, 1997, pp. 3-10.

Ebert, Roger, review of *Smoke Signals, Sun-Times* (Chicago), July 7, 1998.

Egan, Timothy, "An Indian without Reservations," *New York Times Magazine,* January 18, 1998, pp. 16-19.

Lambert, Pam, review of *Reservation Blues, People,* May 8, 1995, p. 35.

Lawson, Terry, "An American Indian Writer Gets His Revenge," *Detroit Free Press,* July 5, 1998, pp. 1E, 6E.

Marx, Doug, "Sherman Alexie: A Reservation of the Mind," *Publishers Weekly,* September 30, 1996.

Nicholls, Richard E., review of *Indian Killer, New York Times Book Review,* November 24, 1996.

Review of *Reservation Blues, Publishers Weekly,* May 1, 1995, p. 42.

Ressner, Jeffrey, "They've Gotta Have It," *Time,* June 29, 1998.

Skow, John, review of *Indian Killer, Time,* October 21, 1996.

■ For More Information See

BOOKS

Contemporary Literary Criticism, Volume 96, Gale, 1997, pp. 1-18.

PERIODICALS

Chicago Tribune, September 27, 1993.

Los Angeles Times Book Review, June 18, 1995, p. 2.

New Yorker, May 10, 1993.

New York Times Book Review, October 11, 1992; October 17, 1993; July 16, 1995, p. 9.

New York Times Magazine, October 4, 1992.

People, October 28, 1996, p. 42.

USA Today, July 23, 1998, p. 2D.*

—Sketch by Carol Brennan

Jennifer Armstrong

puppy raiser for Guiding Eyes for the Blind. *Member:* Society of Children's Book Writers and Illustrators, Saratoga County Arts Council.

■ Personal

Born May 12, 1961, in Waltham, MA; daughter of John (a physicist) and Elizabeth (a master gardener; maiden name, Saunders) Armstrong; married James Howard Kunstler (a writer). *Education:* Smith College, B.A., 1983. *Hobbies and other interests:* Gardening, teaching, music, reading.

■ Addresses

Home—Saratoga Springs, NY. *Electronic mail*—JMA@aol.com. *Agent*—Susan Cohen, Writers House, 21 West 26th St., New York, NY 10010.

■ Career

Cloverdale Press, New York City, assistant editor, 1983-85; freelance writer, 1985—; teacher. Girl Scout leader, 1987-89; Smith College recruiter, 1990—; leader of writing workshops. Literacy Volunteers of Saratoga, board president, 1991-93;

■ Awards, Honors

Best Book Award, American Library Association (ALA), and Golden Kite Honor Book Award, Society of Children's Book Writers and Illustrators, both 1992, for *Steal Away;* Notable Book Citations, ALA, 1992, for *Steal Away* and *Hugh Can Do.*

■ Writings

Steal Away (novel), Orchard Books, 1992.
Hugh Can Do, illustrated by Kimberly Root, Crown, 1992.
Chin Yu Min and the Ginger Cat, illustrated by Mary GrandPre, Crown, 1993.
That Terrible Baby, illustrated by Susan Meddaugh, Tambourine Books, 1994.
Little Salt Lick and the Sun King, illustrated by Jon Goodell, Crown, 1994.
The Whittler's Tale, illustrated by Valery Vasiliev, Tambourine Books, 1994.
Black-Eyed Susan, illustrated by Emily Martindale, Crown, 1995.
King Crow, illustrated by Eric Rohmann, Crown, 1995.

Wan Hu Is in the Stars, illustrated by Barry Root, Tambourine, 1995.

The Snowball, illustrated by Jean Pidgeon, Random House, 1996.

Patrick Doyle Is Full of Blarney, illustrated by Krista Brauckmann-Towns, Random House, 1996.

The Dreams of Mairhe Mehan (novel), Knopf, 1996.

Sunshine, Moonshine, Random House, 1997.

Foolish Gretel, illustrated by Bill Dodge, Random House, 1997.

Mary Mehan Awake (novel), Knopf, 1997.

Pockets, illustrated by Mary GrandPre, Crown, 1998.

Shipwreck at the Bottom of the World: The Extraordinary True Story of Shackleton and the Endurance, Crown, 1999.

MIDDLE GRADE FICTION; "PETS, INC." SERIES

The Puppy Project, Bantam, 1990.

Too Many Pets, Bantam, 1990.

Hillary to the Rescue, Bantam, 1990.

That Champion Chimp, Bantam, 1990.

YOUNG ADULT FICTION; "WILD ROSE INN" SERIES

Bridie of the Wild Rose Inn, Bantam, 1994.

Ann of the Wild Rose Inn, Bantam, 1994.

Emily of the Wild Rose Inn, Bantam, 1994.

Laura of the Wild Rose Inn, Bantam, 1994.

Claire of the Wild Rose Inn, Bantam, 1994.

Grace of the Wild Rose Inn, Bantam, 1994.

YOUNG ADULT FICTION; UNDER PSEUDONYM JULIA WINFIELD

Only Make-Believe (part of "Sweet Dreams" series), Bantam, 1987.

Private Eyes (part of "Sweet Dreams" series), Bantam, 1989.

Partners in Crime (part of "Private Eyes" series), Bantam, 1989.

Tug of Hearts (part of "Private Eyes" series), Bantam, 1989.

On Dangerous (part of "Private Eyes" series), Bantam, 1989.

■ Sidelights

In a 1997 essay that she wrote for the *Something about the Author Autobiography Series* (*SAAS*) the versatile and prolific children's author Jennifer Armstrong mused, "It occurs to me that there is a popular cliché in our culture: for there to be Real Art, there must be Suffering. Yet I never suffered at all really." This perceived dearth of creative tension in her life at times has caused Armstrong to stop and wonder about her ability to sustain a successful literary career. Yet, like Eeyore, the resident pessimist in Winnie the Pooh's charmed world, Armstrong always seems to make do. In fact, she more than *makes do*; Armstrong has enjoyed considerable success, garnering critical praise, winning numerous awards, and attracting a wide readership. She deals with topical themes and issues that interest her in the hope that will also appeal to her young readers. "More and more these days I see people—grown up people—trying to control what kids can see and do and read," Armstrong once told *Something about the Author*. "I know teachers and librarians who scorn the mass market books which I wrote and still write, and insist on giving kids exclusively 'good' books. But adults have access to a variety of fiction, and I think all kinds of fiction have to be available to kids so that they can make their own decisions about what they enjoy."

Armstrong grew up in a safe, comfortable home environment, where she felt secure and content. Both of her parents were professionals; her father was a physicist, her mother a master gardener. The couple and their two daughters lived in a big house in the country; young Jennifer's life there was filled with pets, music lessons, travel, and carefree summers spent at camp. Lest anyone get the idea that Armstrong has led a totally idyllic life, with tongue firmly in-cheek she has hastened to reveal the real "facts." Writing in *SAAS*, Armstrong observed, "Careful readers [will] notice . . . [that] I am assuming my work is Real Art." She then explained, "I did have *some* suffering. I dropped a large rock on my bare foot once, and to this day I have a deformed toenail as a result; I learned very late how to ride a bike, and until I did, my inability caused frequent attacks of horrific embarrassment; I was unable to hang onto nice things without wrecking or staining or ruining them; my mother would not let me pierce my ears until I was sixteen; I was held at bay by a large, fierce, barking dog once as I walked to my piano lesson."

Armstrong more than made up for any perceived or real shortcomings with a boundless inventiveness. "My imagination was always an unwieldy one, and I had a dreamy romantic temperament even as a child," she recalled in *SAAS*. Armstrong was a born storyteller. It was during a year in Switzerland, when she was still in first grade, that she announced to her family that she intended to become an author, although she still had no idea how to go about doing so. "My small school practiced 'whole language,'" she wrote, "even though it hadn't been invented yet. I had beautiful blue notebooks with smooth blank white paper for each subject: science, spelling, nature, reading, and so on. Each book was supposed to be filled up with stories, reports, pictures, and observations. One of my first literary triumphs was a story about Simba the baby elephant. . . . Simba is in the jungle one day when a leopard jumps down on him from a tree. Simba's screams bring his mother

charging to the rescue." Even in this story, Armstrong sees evidence of her "suffering-free" childhood. She noted that "This now strikes me as the story of a confident and happy child. No matter what wicked biting toothy creatures lived in the jungle, there was a capable parent within earshot all the time to bail out the kid."

Back home in South Salem, New York, Armstrong honed her imagination, practicing a self-acted "TV show," in the fields behind her house. There, she related in *SAAS*, she "pretended to be the hero or heroine of a dramatic saga. I made up a mournful theme song for the show and practiced those fake-surprised expressions that used to be common in the opening credits of TV programs in the 1960s. Then I would proceed to have adventures, taking all the parts. . . . I never tried to entice anyone else into my TV game: it was strictly a one-girl show." Armstrong, who never minded being alone, was unknowingly teaching herself the art of storytelling.

Future adventures came when she emulated the main character in *Harriet the Spy* (a favorite literary character in her youth) by writing notes about her sister, her family, and other local characters. When her sister found the notebook, which mainly featured her own idiosyncrasies, Armstrong decided to move on to another form of writing. In elementary school, she and her best friend would write long notes to each other. Armstrong spent her evenings reading these notes and writing back. She told *SAAS*, "I saved shopping bags full of these letters until after college, when I had to admit to myself that whatever delightful prose they contained must be lost forever, because I could not bear to read through pounds and pounds of paper on such subjects as braces, gym class, who had gotten her period, who had picked his nose in class, and dinner."

Poetry Prefaced Suffering

By the time that she reached high school, Armstrong had discovered a new form of literary expression. She found that writing poetry allowed her to *act* as though she was suffering. Since she had schoolgirl crushes on one boy after another, none of whom returned her affections, Armstrong was understandably depressed. "But even then," she commented in *SAAS*, "I realized it was an amateur suffering, not really full-fledged tragedy.

Susie's attempts to revive her mother's depressed spirits fail until some unexpected guests visit their Dakota prairie home in this 1995 novel.

I listened to a lot of Joni Mitchell albums and imagined myself truly suffering someday like Joni."

Armstrong continued to dream of becoming an author during her college days, when she again tried to prod to life the agonized artist in herself. "While I was waiting patiently for the Suffering to commence," she related, "I took a job in publishing in New York City." The work turned out to more mundane than exciting; she ended up typing a lot of letters and calling for messengers. However, because Armstrong's employer published both adult and children's books, she also got an insider's education into how the literary world works. The experience proved invaluable.

Convinced that she was ready to begin her own long-planned career as a writer, in mid-1985, Armstrong quit after just a year and a half on the job. She went to work as a freelance writer. "It sounds ridiculously overconfident," she admitted in her *SAAS* essay. "But you see, the Suffering had never happened, so I wasn't conditioned to expect things to go wrong. I was conditioned to expect things to go right. They did go right." Armstrong found work as a ghostwriter for a mass market juvenile book. However, like most fledgling writers, she secretly had more lofty aspirations. "At twenty-three, I considered the writing I was doing for kids to be a temporary thing," she confessed to *SAAS*, "something to do *until I got good enough to write for adults.*"

In retrospect, Armstrong realizes that she was not being fair to the market or to the audience that she now writes for almost exclusively. "Now when I encounter this assumption, that writing children's books is somehow preparatory to something larger and more important, I want to slap the person who has suggested it. I have come to realize that there is a hypocritical bias, in our youth-enchanted culture, against children; anyone who works for children . . . must be doing it out of some lack of ambition, some failure of will or fortitude," she related in *SAAS*.

Writing mass market books kept her going until she realized that she wanted something more. Armstrong was soon ready for a greater challenge than writing a book using stock characters and situations. Her first original book was a 1992 novel called *Steal Away*. "The original spark of an idea for [it] is lost somewhere in the murk of my

memory, but I do remember that I wanted very much to write an adventure story about girls. I also wanted to write a historical novel," Armstrong mused in *SAAS*. She came up with a plot about an orphaned Vermont girl named Susannah, who goes to live with her Uncle in the south and is given her own slave, Bethlehem. Both girls feel entrapped, and so they run away together.

Stolen Moments

"In the beginning, this was a very simple idea. I began by writing it in Susannah's voice, but that didn't work. I then tried alternating chapters between Susannah's voice and Bethlehem's, and that didn't work either. I was struggling for a way to tell this story, and unconsciously, I think, struggling for a way to make it a bigger story," she told *SAAS*. Finally, Armstrong hit upon the idea of adding another narrator to the story: Susannah's granddaughter, Mary. She was satisfied with this, so she sent off a sample to her agent, who loved it. A meeting with editor Dick Jackson from Orchard Books prompted her to answer some questions about the narrative. Then she felt like she had a real plan for her work.

However, there was still much more to do. She told *SAAS* that "understanding my novel was one thing; writing it was another. It was very hard to write, and I became very anxious about writing in Bethlehem's voice. I was writing this novel when the first signs of political correctness were rearing their ugly mugs, and I was sure someone was going to jump on me for writing as a black slave. So I did exhaustive research, even going so far as to study language patterns of West Africa. . . . Finally Dick Jackson called me and said, 'Just write it.' So I put down the books and steeled myself to face the computer. And I wrote *Steal Away.*"

Although writing the book was difficult, Armstrong managed to hold it together. "When I was done, I felt very smug. I huffed on my fingernails and polished them against my shirt. Dick read the manuscript and said I had a lot of work to do. A terrific editor makes all the difference of course, and Dick's meticulous editing and hard questions helped me get this novel into shape. When it finally came out, the reviews were almost universally excellent and went straight to my head," she told *SAAS*.

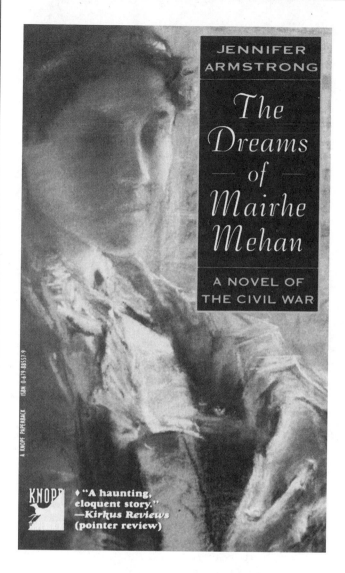

Mairhe Mehan finds herself scared and alone in Washington, D.C., after her brother enlists as a Union soldier in the Civil War and her ailing father returns to Ireland.

Elizabeth S. Watson, in *Horn Book*, wrote glowingly about Armstrong's characters, concluding that the book is a "moving, thought-provoking novel that will be accessible to middle-school age children and of interest to older students as well." Reviewer Hazel Rochman of *Booklist* praised the strength of Armstrong's narrative, and commented that "she weaves a strong story of doubt and guilt as well as courage."

Armstrong also worked on several picture books during this period, including *Hugh Can Do* (1992) and *Chin Yu Min and the Ginger Cat* (1993). How-

ever, Armstrong told *SAAS* that "my editor at Crown, although very fond of my picture books . . . kept urging me to write more novels." It was a lengthy drive to Minnesota as well as her discovering a fact about early pioneers that triggered her next story. She had read in *Audubon* magazine that people moving to the western plains had brought canaries along to remind them of eastern songbirds. After thinking about it for a while, her idea germinated into an outline for a novel. "I also decided that I wanted to set myself a particular challenge—to write a novel whose action spanned only twenty-four hours," she told *SAAS*.

The Wide Open Prairie

The solution Armstrong devised was to write the book as a series of stories told by the main character, Susie, as well as other characters. Susie's family has moved to the prairie and is living in a sod house. While Susie loves the open skies and prairies, her mother is becoming increasingly depressed. "Susie's job in this novel is literally to help her mother be born, or to resurrect her, to bring her up out of the hole in the earth where she is hiding and let her take the wide world into her arms. Susie actually does it, I am glad to say, with the help of the Icelanders and the canary, who came along just in time," Armstrong related in *SAAS*.

Black-Eyed Susan (1995) was well received by critics. Elizabeth S. Watson, writing in *Horn Book*, called the work "a highly readable text that is almost poetic at times." Reviewer Margaret B. Rafferty commented in the *School Library Journal* that *Black-Eyed Susan* has remarkably realistic and satisfying characters. Armstrong's book "is readable and evocatively re-creates the time and place," she concluded.

After the success of *Black-Eyed Susan*, Armstrong was ready to write another novel. Ken Burns's documentary on the Civil War was being aired on PBS, and watching it gave Armstrong the idea for another story. "Two things jumped out at me while I watched *The Civil War*," Armstrong related in *SAAS*. "One was that the U.S. Capitol was being fitted with a new dome. The physical symbol of the Union was being rebuilt *even as the Union itself was being pulled to pieces*. If that is not fodder for the imagination, I don't know what is. The second item that jumped out at me during

If you enjoy the works of Jennifer Armstrong, you may also want to check out the following books and films:

Paul Fleischman, *Bull Run*, 1993.
Irene Hunt, *Across Five Aprils*, 1965.
Jackie French Koller, *The Primrose Way*, 1992.
Patricia MacLachlan, *Sarah, Plain and Tall*, 1986.
Elizabeth George Speare, *The Sign of the Beaver*, 1983.
Friendly Persuasion, a film starring Gary Cooper, 1956.

the documentary was this: there were regiments on both sides of the war composed entirely of Irish immigrants."

The story she imagined featured Mairhe Mehan, an Irish barmaid who is concerned about the safety of her brother Mike, who is fighting for the Union army. Additionally, Mairhe's father cannot take the stress of the war, and he goes back to Ireland. Mairhe tries to make enough money to buy her brother out of his service, but fails; he is killed in the war. Interwoven with the narrative are Mairhe's powerful dreams about the war and about her lost brother. *School Library Journal* reviewer Connie Parker described *The Dreams of Mairhe Mehan* as "a tightly woven story that is deeply meaningful, yet accessible to teen readers." A *Publishers Weekly* reviewer praised the book as being "remarkable for its artistry and the lingering musicality of its language."

Suffering Surfaces

"In writing *The Dreams of Mairhe Mehan*, I did Suffer at last!," Armstrong told *SAAS*. "I suffered so much I felt physically sick every day as I worked on it. . . . In order to recover from writing this book, I had to take a train to Hudson Bay to look for polar bears. And on the way, I thought of a sequel." This book, *Mary Mehan Awake*, picks up Mary's story as she struggles to recover from the loss of her beloved brother. Her friend Walt Whitman, the real-life poet, finds work for her as a servant to a kind upstate New York couple. Mary, whose senses have been dulled by

her distress, comes awake sensually in the chapters of the book. She meets a war veteran, Henry, who has been deafened by cannon fire in the war. As they both heal, they also fall in love. Marie Wright, in the *School Library Journal*, described the book as "a wonderful story about love, dreams, and renewal, written in beautiful prose."

Although it may not qualify as actual artistic *suffering*, Armstrong has expressed disdain for critics who would silence the writer's voice or chide them for not having experienced everything they write about. "I have learned that some critics will not allow writers to be writers," she remarked in *SAAS*. "By that I mean that there is a widely held belief that only an African American can write the African American experience, only a Native American can retell Native American tales, and so on." Armstrong has stated that she feels that this is destructive to creativity. "If I am not allowed to imagine anything beyond my own experience, you will simply have to put up with more stories from me about my dogs and favorite trees."

Armstrong remains unfazed by critics, and she continues to produce imaginative high quality tales for young readers. In addition to her other works, she has written a series of books about members of a family who live in the Wild Rose Inn in Marblehead, Massachusetts. This series spans several centuries and is filled with a wealth of historical detail. Armstrong herself lives in a heritage setting, in the hilly, wooded setting of Saratoga Springs, New York, where she rides her bike and walks on her daily errands. The 1820s cottage that she calls home is inhabited by several dogs who keep her company when she writes.

■ Works Cited

Armstrong, Jennifer, comments in *Something about the Author*, Volume 77, Gale, 1994, pp. 5-8.

Armstrong, Jennifer, essay in *Something about the Author Autobiography Series*, Volume 24, Gale, 1997, pp. 1-15.

Review of *The Dreams of Mairhe Mehan*, *Publishers Weekly*, July 8, 1996, p. 84.

Parker, Connie, review of *The Dreams of Mairhe Mehan*, *School Library Journal*, October, 1996, p. 144.

Rafferty, Margaret B., review of *Black-Eyed Susan*, *School Library Journal*, October, 1995, p. 132.

Rochman, Hazel, review of *Steal Away, Booklist,* February 1, 1992, p. 1019.

Watson, Elizabeth S., review of *Steal Away, Horn Book,* May-June, 1992, p. 339.

Watson, Elizabeth S., review of *Black-Eyed Susan, Horn Book,* March-April, 1996, p. 193.

Wright, Marie, review of *Mary Mehan Awake, School Library Journal,* January, 1998, p. 108.

■ For More Information See

ON-LINE

Jennifer Armstrong answers questions for teachers at Web site located at http://www.randomhouse.com (September 18, 1998).

Interview with Jennifer Armstrong at http://www.amazon.com (December 22, 1998).

PERIODICALS

Booklist, October 1, 1990, p. 344; March 15, 1994, p. 1341; June 1, 1994, p. 1801; January 1, 1997, p. 842; December 1, 1997, p. 615.

Bulletin of the Center for Children's Books, March, 1992, p. 173; December, 1997, pp. 116-7.

Horn Book, November-December, 1997, pp. 675-6.

Kirkus Reviews, July 15, 1992, p. 917; December 1, 1998, p. 1730.

Kliatt, November, 1998, p. 10.

Publishers Weekly, March 24, 1989, p. 73; July 13, 1990, p. 55; June 29, 1992, p. 62; December 6, 1993, p. 74; July 10, 1995, p. 58; October 19, 1998, p. 78; January 25, 1999, p. 97.

School Library Journal, June, 1989, p. 125; July, 1990, p. 74; February, 1992, p. 85; October, 1992, p. 78; October, 1998, p. 86.

Voice of Youth Advocates, August, 1992, p. 165.*

—Sketch by Nancy Rampson

Melvin Burgess

■ Personal

Born April 25, 1954, in Twickenham, Surrey, England; son of Christopher (an educational writer) and Helen Burgess; married to Avis von Herder (marriage ended); married to Judith Liggett; children: Oliver von Herder, Pearl Burgess. *Politics:* Left.

■ Addresses

Home—4 Hartley St., Garby, Lancashire BB8 GNL, England.

■ Career

Writer. *Member:* Society of Authors.

■ Awards, Honors

Carnegie Medal runner-up, British Library Association, 1991, for *The Cry of the Wolf,* and 1993, for *An Angel for May;* Carnegie Medal, British Library Association, and *Guardian* Prize for Children's Fiction, both 1997, both for *Junk.*

■ Writings

The Cry of the Wolf, Andersen (London), 1990, Tambourine Books, 1992.

Burning Issy, Andersen, 1992, Simon & Schuster, 1994.

An Angel for May, Andersen, 1992, Simon & Schuster, 1995.

The Baby and Fly Pie, Andersen, 1993, Simon & Schuster, 1996.

Loving April, Andersen, 1995.

Earth Giant, Andersen, 1995, Putnam, 1997.

Tiger, Tiger, Andersen, 1996.

Junk, Andersen, 1996, published in the U.S. as *Smack,* Holt, 1998.

Kite, Andersen, 1997.

Copper Treasure, A & C Black, 1998.

■ Work in Progress

City of Light, a novel.

■ Sidelights

British writer Melvin Burgess has combined fantasy with gritty realism in a succession of critically-acclaimed young adult novels which are unsettling and controversial. In *Junk*, his best known work, and in several other books, Burgess deals with troubled characters on the fringe of society who are struggling to come to grips with the world and their place in it. In his writing, Burgess has revealed a perspective that is hard-edged and sometimes dark. As he once told *Something about the Author* (*SATA*), "My books are about *anything* that interests me, but they really all have this in common—they are life seen from the underside, not (usually) from the top."

Burgess was born into a middle class family living in Twickenham, Surrey, just southwest of Lon-

don, but grew up in nearby Sussex and Berkshire counties. He recalled in a 1998 interview with Brangien Davis of Amazon.com that he was not much of a student. "I was no good at school—no confidence at all, but reading and, later on, writing were things I was always good at," Burgess said. He enjoyed the books of British authors Mervyn Peake (1911-1960) and George Orwell (1903-1950), and of the German poet-dramatist Bertolt Brecht (1898-1956). "I think the writer who influenced me most was . . . Brecht—his poetry rather than his plays—marvelous!" Burgess told Davis. "There's a line of his: 'The simplest possible words and your heart must be broken.' I'd like to write like that!"

Inspired by Brecht and his other favorites, Burgess began to dream of being a writer when he was a teenager. Having decided that in order to write well "you need to have lived at least three different lives and been at least three different people," as he told *SATA*, Burgess spent the late 1960s and early 1970s hanging out on the streets of central London. For a time, he joined friends living as a squatter in abandoned buildings, where blaring rock music, sex, and illegal drugs were central aspects of the desultory lifestyle. "A lot of people I was close to had heroin problems," Burgess recalled in an interview with Kit Alderdice of *Publishers Weekly*. (Among them was his own brother, who eventually died of Hodgkins disease.) Not surprisingly, during this formative period of his life, Burgess's efforts to write proved futile. He spent six years experimenting with fiction techniques until finally it occurred to him what he was doing wrong. "It wasn't until I started seriously thinking about plot that I got anywhere," he told Brangien Davis.

Ecological Thriller Takes Root

Burgess settled down in the early 1980s. He married for the first time, and he and his wife opened a marbling business. Burgess continued to dream of becoming a writer, but it was not until 1990 that his debut novel was published. That book, an ecological thriller called *The Cry of the Wolf*, may at first glance seem like an unusual story to be written by a young man who'd come of age in the big city of London. However, the novel actually reflects Burgess's own left-wing, green-oriented outlook on life. *Cry of the Wolf* is about what happens when a ten-year-old boy named

Ten-year-old Ben inadvertently threatens the lives of a pack of wolves when he reveals their whereabouts to a wolf hunter in this 1990 novel.

Ben inadvertently endangers a rare pack of wolves who live in the forest near his home on a farm in Surrey. Ben reveals the pack's existence to a mysterious stranger identified only as "the Hunter." The man sets out with his crossbow to win fame by hunting down and killing the last seventy wild wolves in England; he very nearly succeeds before he, too, is destroyed.

"This is indeed a powerful first novel, and sinister too," noted a reviewer in the *Junior Bookshelf*. Susan Oliver of *School Library Journal* agreed. *Cry of the Wolf* is "a dramatic and horrifying tale of the tragedy of extinction," she wrote. However, a critic from *Kirkus Reviews* was less impressed. "The cumulative brutality here lends the story a certain raw power . . . in the end, nobody wins: the Hunter's death, though slow and painful, comes too late," wrote the reviewer. "There's more food for confusion than thought in this savage hunt and its ambiguous outcome."

Elements of fantasy that were present in *The Cry of the Wolf* echo through Burgess's next two novels, both of which were backward-looking tales and both of which were published in 1992. *Burning Issy,* set in the seventeenth century, is about a young orphan woman named Issy, who is accused of witchcraft after she becomes involved with both black and white witches. Issy, who has been badly burned in a fire when she was a girl, eventually realizes that she incurred her wounds when she almost died alongside her mother, a convicted witch who was burned at the stake. Helen Turner of *Voice of Youth Advocates* praised *Burning Issy* as "a riveting exploration into some dark corners of history." Linda Newbery of *School Librarian* wrote that Burgess has an uncanny imagination and that *Burning Issy* unearths "timeless questions about persecution and hatred;" and the idea that the earth god must thrive "'or the world will begin to die' is only too relevant today."

The other Burgess novel published in 1992 was *An Angel for May.* The novel is a poignant time-travel story about Tam, a distraught twelve-year-old boy who spends his days rambling around the English countryside in the wake of his parents' divorce. Tam's adventures begin when he meets a strange bag lady named Rosey. The woman transports him fifty years into the past—to the time of the Second World War. There he meets a young retarded girl named May, and the pair become friends. May and Tam help each

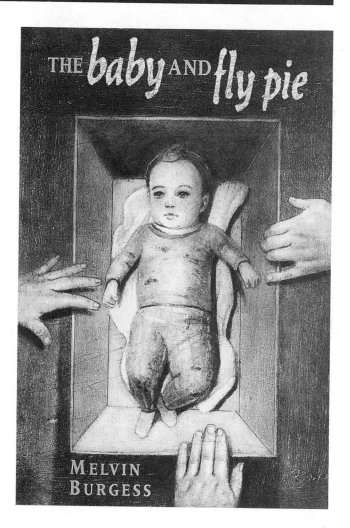

Fly Pie, an orphaned teen living in future London, and his two friends become surrogate parents after they intercept a baby from would-be kidnappers.

other make some sense of their troubled lives. Merri Monks of *Booklist* praised *An Angel for May* as "a story of courage, moral development, friendship and love." A reviewer for the *Junior Bookshelf* wrote, "Melvin Burgess hits the right note throughout, never stressing the tragedy but leaving the reader to put [a] personal gloss on the facts. It is all beautifully done. . . ."

Burgess moved from the past into the near future with his next book, an Orwellian novel called *The Baby and Fly Pie.* The book's enigmatic title comes from the story's two main characters: Fly Pie is a teenage orphan who survives on London's mean streets by scavenging as a "Rubbish Kid." The Baby is the kidnapped daughter of a wealthy family. When the kidnapper dies, Fly Pie and his friend Sham discover the baby. The street kids are then faced with a decision of whether to take the child home to her parents or to try to collect the ransom. Reviewers were sharply divided in their reaction to the novel. A reviewer for the *Junior Bookshelf* described the novel as "strong meat for early teenagers." Anne O'Malley of *Booklist* was among those who liked *The Baby and Fly Pie*. "The stunning characterizations, fascinating scenario, well-plotted, virtually non-stop action and mounting suspense pull the reader right in from start to tragic end," she wrote. Deb Palmer of *Voice of Youth Advocates* had a very different opinion. "This is a chilling, bleak story set in a harsh, unfriendly world. Both the title and the cover art are unappealing. I cannot see teens willingly picking up this book," she stated.

Burgess returned to familiar territory for his next two novels, both of which were published in England in 1995. Again he dealt with characters trapped on the margins of society. *Loving April* is a novel about the relationship that develops between a misunderstood deaf girl and a divorced woman and her son, who settle in the deaf girl's village in hopes of starting their lives over. A reviewer for the *Junior Bookshelf* gave *Loving April* only tepid praise and concluded with a disapproving mention of the fact that "There is no conventionally happy ending." The second Burgess novel published in 1995 was a fairy tale fantasy called *The Earth Giant*. It is a story about what happens when a girl named Amy discovers a frozen female giant whose body is unearthed when a tree is toppled by a violent storm. "Whatever the plausibility of the cryogenic background, within its parameters the implications are handled skillfully without outraging credulity," a reviewer in the *Junior Bookshelf* commented.

Burgess's next book, *Tiger, Tiger*, was reminiscent of his very first novel, *The Cry of the Wolf*, in that it focused on the plight of endangered animals. The plot deals with a Chinese businessman's efforts to turn the Yorkshire countryside into an animal safari park. Some of the animals in the park are rare Siberian tigers, a species of large cats which is reputed to possess magical powers. When one of the female tigers escapes, she encounters some children from a nearby village; the magical relationship that develops between the beast and the humans is at the root of Burgess's story. Reviewer Linda Newbery of *School Librarian* called *Tiger, Tiger* an "absorbing and exciting

novel." Another reviewer, writing in the *Junior Bookshelf*, noted, "The adroit combination of fact and fantasy is expertly managed with no concession to the tenderhearted."

Novel of the Decade?

Turning from the plight of Siberian tigers to the perils of street kids struggling to survive in an equally strange world, Burgess wrote his 1996 novel *Junk*. (When the book subsequently appeared in the U.S., publisher Henry Holt changed the title to *Smack* to avoid it being confused with another recent novel with the word junk in the title, and for idiomatic reasons; "junk," the British slang word for heroin, means trash or other worthless stuff to American ears.) The book, based on

This work, which many critics consider to be Burgess's best, is based on the author's late brother's experiences as a heroine addict.

Burgess's own late brother's experiences as a heroin addict, is considered his best. It is also his most controversial. *Junk*, which has been favorably compared to the popular 1993 novel *Trainspotting* by Scottish writer Irvine Welsh, is a dark, unflinching look at life and drug use among English teens living on the streets. Burgess explained to Brangien Davis of Amazon.com. that *Junk* and *Trainspotting* are dealing with very different cultural groups, ". . . *Trainspotting* with a very deprived part of Edinburgh, and [*Junk*] with middle-class dropouts in the wealthy southwest of England. The culture is very different, except for the presence of heroin, which of course has the same kind of effect on any group of people in terms of their personalities and relationships."

Set in the 1980s, *Junk* tells the story of a girl named Gemma and her boyfriend Tar, two fourteen-year-olds who run away to Bristol. There they become swept up in the twilight netherworld of squatters, punk culture, and heroin use. The events of the four years Gemma and Tar spend living on the streets are recounted in shifting first-person accounts from the lips of Gemma, Tar, and other assorted characters. "Using many different voices, letting everyone tell their own story in their own words, allowed the twisted voice of heroin itself to come through," Burgess told Julia Eccleshare of *Publishers Weekly*. The story the narrators tell is anything but happy; it chronicles how the innocent, idealistic young people from the book's opening pages are gradually transformed into hardcore drug addicts; the results are inevitable: Gemma turns to prostitution to support her habit, while Tar becomes a petty street thief.

Junk caused a sensation when it was published, both in England and in the U.S. Paradoxically, on the one hand, Burgess was chided by squeamish critics for the bleakness and the intensity of his description of street life, and on the other by cynics who charged that he had made Gemma and Tar's initial experiences with heroin seem too glamorous and fun. The author defended himself on both charges. "As for people who say [*Junk* is] too racy, I'd say that this is all about trust. There are people who cannot bring themselves to trust their own children. I think it's sad," Burgess told Brangien Davis. "As for the other argument you often hear, about children growing up too quickly and so on . . . well, that's already happened. This is the age of television, and television keeps no secrets."

If you enjoy the works of Melvin Burgess, you may also want to check out the following books and films:

Anonymous, *Go Ask Alice*, Aladdin, 1998.
Margaret Buffie, *The Warnings*, 1988.
David Klass, *California Blue*, 1994.
Trainspotting, a film starring Ewan McGregor, 1996.

Apparently most readers and critics sided with Burgess, for *Junk* won two of Britain's most prestigious literary awards: the Carnegie Medal and the Guardian Prize for fiction. The reaction to *Junk* by a reviewer in *Books For Keeps* was typical: "This is a complex . . . and tremendously powerful story that the teenage readers I lent it to found troubling, fascinating and recognizable." Peter Hollindale of *School Librarian* had much the same reaction: "*Junk* is not bibliotherapy but no adolescent reader can fail to see from it the scale and consequences of the seemingly small and tempting step to heroin from other substances. A compelling, brutally informative and important novel."

School Library Journal reviewer Alison Follos agreed with her British counterparts. "It's a slap in the face, and, vicariously a hard-core dose of the consequences of saying 'yes,'" Follos said. Cathi Dunn MacRae of *Voice of Youth Advocates* was even more enthusiastic in her praise for Burgess's book. "[*Smack*] is the YA novel of the decade," she wrote. But not everyone agreed on the book's merits. A *Horn Book* reviewer voiced the minority opinion when she panned *Smack* for being too slow to get moving. She wrote, "*Go Ask Alice* junkies looking for a quick fix" will be disappointed, especially if they're expecting the "action and snappy, surreal humor" of *Trainspotting*. "Ultimately and disappointingly, *Smack* fails to score a hit," she added. Despite the hot and cold reviews, *Junk* (and *Smack*) were popular at the bookstores and had been sold to publishers in seventeen countries as of early 1998, according to *Publishers Weekly*.

■ Works Cited

Alderdice, Kit, "A Hotly debated Novel Crosses the Atlantic," *Publishers Weekly*, February 16, 1998.

Review of *An Angel For May, Junior Bookshelf*, February, 1993, pp. 26-27.

Review of *The Baby and Fly Pie, Junior Bookshelf*, April, 1994, p.64.

Burgess, Melvin, comments in *Something about the Author*, Volume 96, Gale, 1998.

Review of *The Cry of the Wolf, Junior Bookshelf*, February, 1991, pp. 29-30.

Review of *The Cry of the Wolf, Kirkus Reviews*, October 15, 1992, p. 1307.

Davis, Brangien, "Hooked on Smack," Amazon. com interview with Melvin Burgess located at http://www.amazon.com (1998).

Dunn, Cathi MacRae, review of *Smack, Voice of Youth Advocates*, February, 1998, pp. 358-59.

Review of *The Earth Giant, Junior Bookshelf*, August, 1996, p. 146.

Eccleshare, Julia, "Letter From London," *Publishers Weekly*, August 18, 1997, p. 25.

Follos, Alison, review of *Smack, School Library Journal*, May, 1998, p. 138.

Hollindale, Peter, review of *Junk, School Librarian*, May, 1997, p. 99.

Review of *Junk, Books for Keeps*, May, 1997, p. 27.

Review of *Loving April, Junior Bookshelf*, August, 1995, p. 142-43.

Monks, Merri, review of *An Angel For May, Booklist*, May 1, 1995, pp. 1571-72.

Newbery, Linda, review of *Burning Issy, School Librarian*, November, 1992, pp. 156-57.

Newbery, Linda, review of *Tiger, Tiger, School Librarian*, August, 1996, p. 117.

Oliver, Susan, review of *The Cry of the Wolf, School Library Journal*, September, 1992, p. 250.

O'Malley, Anne, review of *The Baby and Fly Pie, Booklist*, May 15, 1996, p. 1586.

Palmer, Deb, review of *The Baby and Fly Pie, Voice of Youth Advocates*, August, 1996, p. 154.

Review of *Smack, Horn Book,* May/June, 1998, p. 340.

Review of *Tiger, Tiger, Junior Bookshelf*, August, 1996, pp. 153-54.

Turner, Helen, review of *Burning Issy, Voice of Youth Advocates*, April, 1995, p. 19-20.

■ **For More Information See**

PERIODICALS

Booklist, October 15, 1992, p. 428.

Bulletin of the Center for Children's Books, July, 1995, pp. 378-79; May, 1996, pp. 294-95.

Horn Book, March-April, 1995, p. 192; September-October, 1998, pp. 590-91.

Junior Bookshelf, June, 1992, pp. 117-18.

Kirkus Reviews, October 1, 1997, p. 1529.

Kliatt, July 1998, p. 4.

New York Times Book Review, November 15, 1998, p. 36.

Observer, March 30, 1997, p. 17.

Publishers Weekly, October 19, 1998, p. 31; November 2, 1998, pp. 50-51.

School Librarian, May, 1993, p. 59.

School Library Journal, December, 1994, p. 106; June, 1995, p. 108.

—Sketch by Ken Cuthbertson

Chuck Close

■ Personal

Born July 5, 1940, in Monroe, WA; married Leslie Rose, 1967; children: Georgia Molly, Maggie Sarah. *Education:* Attended Everett Community College, 1958-60; University of Washington, B.A., 1962; attended Yale Summer School of Art and Music, 1961; Yale University, B.F.A., 1963, M.F.A., 1964; attended Akademie der Bildenden Kunste, Vienna, 1964-65.

■ Addresses

Home—271 Central Park West, New York, NY 10024. *Studio*—75 Spring St., New York, NY 10012. *Agent*—Pace Gallery, 32 East 57th St., New York, NY 10022.

■ Career

Artist, 1966—. Instructor at University of Massachusetts, Amherst, 1965-67, School of Visual Arts, New York City, 1967-71, New York University, New York City, 1970-73, University of Washing-

ton, Seattle, 1970, and Yale Summer School of Art and Music, Norfolk, CT, 1971-72. *Exhibitions:* Close's first solo exhibition was at the University of Massachusetts Art Gallery, Amherst, in 1967; other notable displays of his work have included the 1970 group show "22 Realists" at the Whitney Museum, New York; *Recent Work,* Los Angeles County Museum of Art, 1971; Museum of Contemporary Art, Chicago, IL, 1972; Museum of Modern Art, New York, NY, 1973; San Francisco Museum of Modern Art, 1975; the 1968-1980 retrospective *Close Portraits,* Walker Art Center, Minneapolis, MN, 1980, and subsequently at the St. Louis Art Museum, Missouri, Museum of Contemporary Art, Chicago, and Whitney Museum, New York, all 1981; *Works on Paper,* Contemporary Arts Museum, Houston, TX, 1985; Fuji Television Gallery, Tokyo, Japan, 1985; Carnegie Museum of Art, 1995, Museum of Modern Art, New York City, 1998.

Close's works have been acquired for the permanent collections of the Museum of Modern Art, New York, NY; Metropolitan Museum of Art, New York, NY; Whitney Museum of American Art, New York; National Gallery of Art, Washington, DC; National Portrait Gallery, Washington, D.C.; Art Institute of Chicago; Solomon R. Guggenheim Museum, New York City; Tate Gallery, London, England; National Gallery of Canada, Ottawa; Neue Gallery, Aachen, Germany; Australian National Gallery, Canberra.

■ Awards, Honors

Fulbright Grant, 1964; National Endowment for the Arts Grant, 1973; elected member, American Academy and Institute of Arts and Letters, 1992.

■ Sidelights

Striking, large-scale portraits the artist himself simply refers to as "heads" established Chuck Close as an eminent American painter by the mid-1980s. But when he suffered a medical trauma that left him paralyzed and in a wheelchair, he assumed he would never be able to hold a brush again, let alone wield it with any finesse. However, Close—one of the most respected and genial of personalities inside the sometimes vicious New York art scene—recovered enough strength in his arms to begin painting again; since then his work has altered and expanded in a way that typically leaves viewers and reviewers stunned.

Perhaps the first painter in the history of art who has confined his subject matter to depictions of other contemporary artists, Close works on a monumental scale that has progressed from the superrealistic likenesses of the late 1960s to near-Impressionistic works of the Nineties that are veritable riots of color. His eight- or nine-foot canvases all begin from the same point of departure: a straightforward photograph, resembling a passport photo, driver's license, or even a police mug shot. Close then enlarges it and divides the image into a grid, which is then translated, square by square, onto canvas. "Against the fast click of the camera, he insists upon the slow time it takes to construct a face," wrote Mark Stevens of Close's body of work in *New York*. "We are always aware that even so, we cannot finally know these people; we must look at them through the powerful filters of process and artfulness."

Close was born in 1940 and spent the early years of his life in Monroe, Washington. Later his parents moved to Tacoma. There his mother taught piano, and his father, a sheet-metal worker and mechanical genius, spent his leisure time building fantastical toys at home, such as a pedal-powered Jeep, for his son. In school, however, Close had trouble from the start. As an adult, he came to realize he suffers from dyslexia—a type of learning disability that hinders the ability to read—and because of it, did poorly in school. Teachers described him as "lazy" and a "shirker" on his report cards; little was known about dyslexia and other learning disabilities during this era. Close did, however, display a talent for art—creative aptitude is often prevalent in dyslexics—and his parents encouraged him by giving him art supplies and paying for lessons. He recalled in an interview with *New York Times Magazine* writer Deborah Solomon that he used to scrutinize, with a magnifying glass, the illustrated magazine covers popular during the 1940s and 1950s, such as the *Saturday Evening Post*, "trying to figure out how paintings got made."

Close's life changed dramatically at the age of eleven when his father died. He and his mother moved to Everett, Washington. He continued to be a "slow learning" student, but came up with an unusual study method to help him make it through school: he would put a board across the bathtub, fill the tub with water, turn the light off, and use a flashlight to read each page aloud; the darkness and hot water helped him concentrate on the material until he absorbed it. It also took him half the night. He still drew avidly, however, and knew from an early age that he wanted to be an artist. "It was the first thing that I was good at, the first thing that really made me feel special," Close told Jan Greenberg and Sandra Jordan for their book *Chuck Close Up Close*. "I had skills the other kids didn't have. Art saved my life."

After high school, Close enrolled in Everett Junior College, which fortunately for him had a thriving art department. From there he went to the University of Washington, earning a B.A. in 1962, and then headed to Connecticut when he was accepted to the prestigious fine-arts program at Yale University. He received his B.F.A. in 1963 and a master's degree a year later. Here Close, having gained confidence though his art—as well as benefiting from a loosening of the cultural climate in North America that was bringing new forms of art, music, and literature into play—quickly became a well-liked figure in this insular, East-Coast art world. Many of his classmates at Yale's Graduate School of Art would go on to equal acclaim in the American art scene. Meanwhile, the popularity of the postwar American Abstract painters like Jackson Pollock and Willem de Kooning was giving way to the Pop Art of Andy Warhol and Roy Lichtenstein. Close and his young friends spent much time theorizing about where the form

To create *Big Self-Portrait* (acrylic on canvas, 1968), Chuck Close divided a large photo of himself into more than 57,000 squares, which he then reproduced, square-by-square, on a large canvas using an airbrush.

was going. "We all wanted to de-artify our work, to make something that didn't look like art," Simon Schama of the *New Yorker* quoted Close as saying. Like others, Close strove to create works that were free of "content," or utterly devoid of meaning, impervious to interpretation.

After Yale, Close went to Vienna for further study on a Fulbright scholarship, then returned and accepted a teaching post at the University of Massachusetts. Even after, in a sense, having realized his childhood dream—to earn a living creatively—it was a difficult period. "Amherst is farther from New York than it looks on a map," he joked to Solomon in the *New York Times Magazine*. He did, however, meet his wife when she took one of his painting classes as a first-year student, and he and Leslie Rose wed in 1967 and moved to New York City. At the time, Close was painting in a style similar to de Kooning, an artist whose work many young painters revered at the time, but knew he had to find his own path. At Amherst, he had already experimented with large-scale figurative work (*Big Nude*, a twenty-foot painting of a woman in black and white, dates from this era), and after moving to an unheated loft in the then-rough, uncool area of SoHo with his new wife, Close got rid of his brushes and picked up some new tools instead. These included a camera, which he used to photograph himself head-on, and an airbrush, which he then used to literally reproduce the black-and-white image on a huge canvas after enlarging the photo and dividing it into over 57,000 squares. He painted each square, one by one, onto the canvas.

That work became *Big Self-Portrait* (1968), done in varying shades of black, white, and gray, and it "remains among his most memorable," opined Solomon, "capturing him as an archetypal Cool Dude." Response from his fellow mavericks in SoHo—he and Leslie had quickly become habitués of the Factory, Andy Warhol's aluminum-foil plastered studio/party place—was positive, and Close began to use the same method to paint his friends. By 1970 he had eight "heads," as he called them, and was invited to exhibit them in a solo show at New York's Bykert Gallery. The Whitney Museum of American Art bought one of the pieces, a portrait of the composer Philip Glass, and Close's career took off.

Close was working in a movement called Photorealism, which strove to render the subject in a style that came as close to actual photography as possible, though it used traditional artistic methods. Close and artists Richard Estes and Duane Hanson would become the most well-known names associated with Photorealism. By breaking down the photograph into tiny squares, then translating those minuscule, seemingly unrelated fragments onto a canvas, Close was working in a way that was a reflection of his dyslexia and how he learned to absorb information by reading one page at a time in the bathtub. "Almost every decision I've made as an artist is an outcome of my particular learning disorders," Close told Greenberg and Jordan in *Chuck Close Up Close*. "I'm overwhelmed by the whole. How do you make a big head? How do you make a nose? I'm not sure! But by breaking the image down into small units, I make each decision into a bite-sized decision."

By the early 1970s, however, Close was already looking for further challenges. He began using color photography, devising a way to actually imitate that process itself in his art. In the darkroom, film is developed using a method that reads and mimics the three primary colors in the color spectrum—red, yellow, and blue. Close began to paint one image three times over on the same canvas, three monochromatic paintings of these hues superimposed upon one another. "When I get to the last color, yellow, you can't see the pigment come out of the air brush—it's like waving a magic wand in front of the picture, and the purple eye becomes brown," Close explained to Robert Hughes in *Time* in 1981. "It's really quite wonderful; there are a few kicks left in this racket after all, and that's one of them."

Close also found an unusual method to execute his oversized paintings: by rigging a forklift with a platform and a chair, and a rope that moved the platform vertically when he pulled on it, he could easily navigate the entirety of the massive canvas. He also installed a television on his platform to keep him company. Close's method of painting is painstaking, to say the least, and it takes him over a year to complete just one. Sometimes the titles of his works include the number of grid squares within it, as in *Robert, 104,072* (1973-74). The detail inside the grids was so precise that one of them, done of his father-in-law in 1971, was noticed by an opthamalogist when it hung on a museum wall; the doctor sent a message to Close that he thought one of the eyes

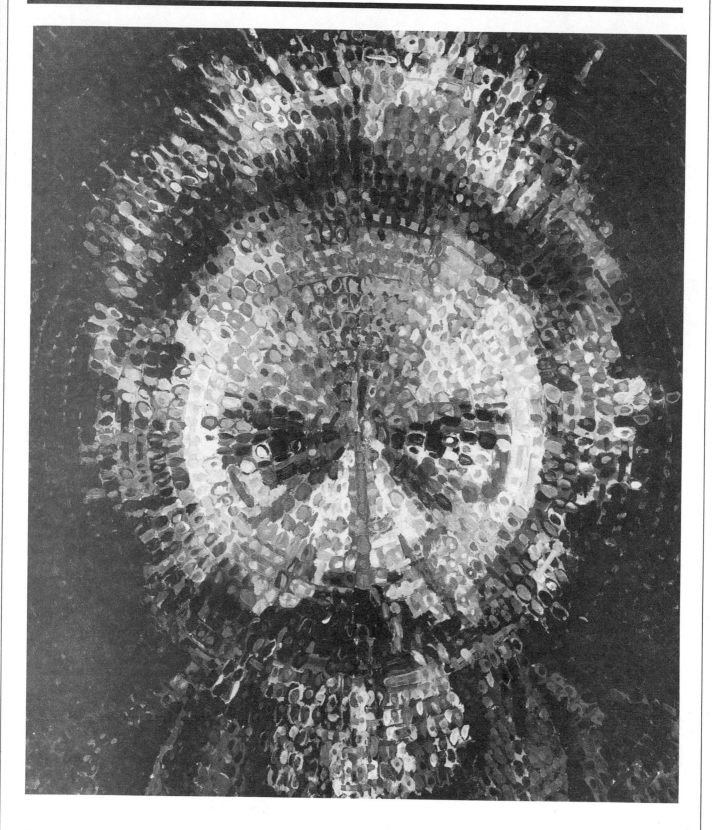

Fellow artist Lucas Samaris is the subject of *Lucas II,* completed in 1987.

displayed evidence of being pre-cancerous. Close's father-in-law went to his doctor and it was found to be true; the early detection had saved his sight.

Yet Close's work also presents an unusual problem in its final version, hung at an eminent New York gallery and stared at by champagne-quaffing denizens of the art scene. "Almost everyone has some trouble dealing with these nine-foot-high images of themselves," Close told Greenberg and Jordan in *Chuck Close Up Close.* "It's difficult for people to accept how they look." Many have even done something to change their appearance after being painted by Close, who does not consult the subject matter at all and does not accept commissions, or requests for a portrait from an individual. From the start, his subject matter has been his family and friends, and his list of comrades in the art world has grown to include some of the greatest names in late twentieth-century American art. Close has executed the likenesses of, among others, Roy Lichtenstein, Lucas Samaras, Cindy Sherman, Alex Katz, Eric Fischl, and William Wegman.

Later in his career Close began using a Polaroid camera that is literally the size of a small room. A company-owned lab in SoHo features one of these rare, expensive, large-format cameras that result in extremely dramatic, hyperreal imagery. Close explained his feelings about portraiture in an essay for *Contemporary Artists.* "If I were painting a tree," he wrote, "and it were a little too green or too red, no one but a botanist would know or care. I wanted to paint something that people cared about—a face contains very specific information that people can sense is either right or wrong." Close also wrote that he wanted to detach himself from his work as an artist. "I think of how all portraits by Rembrandt look like paintings by Rembrandt—that would seem to be a shortcoming of portraiture," he reflected.

But in December of 1988, Close's career as an artist seemed to end with what he calls "the event": he felt chest pain while at an award ceremony at the New York mayor's residence, and went to a hospital emergency room, where his wife caught up with him and witnessed a horrific seizure. Close had suffered an unusual medical occurrence, the collapse of a major artery along the spinal cord, and it left him paralyzed. He could not walk, let alone curl his fingers to even hold a brush. He spent much of 1989 at the Rusk

---

If you enjoy the works of Chuck Close, you may also want to check out the following:

The Photorealistic works of Duane Hanson and Richard Estes.
The photography of Cindy Sherman and William Wegman.
The Pop Art of Andy Warhol and Roy Lichtenstein.

Institute at New York University Medical Center, working in physical therapy several hours a day, and was able to regain the use of his upper arms. He began painting again by using a brush attached to his wrist with velcro.

There were rumors in the art world that Close's career was over, but near the end of 1991, his gallery, Pace, announced an upcoming show of recent work. Before his trauma, Close had already begun to depart from the exacting imagery of Photorealism and was painting in a looser style, but now he abandoned his monochrome technique and began painting each individual square almost as if it was its own separate painting. A definite oval of color was visible in each, but viewed from afar, the effect was spectacular. Those who wrote about his art have described these little ovals as, alternately, a lozenge, donut, bagel, jellybean, or even hot dog. "Seen close up, the slippery glowing shapes seem charged with organized energy, jostling against their containing grid," wrote Schama of this new period in an article on Close for the *New Yorker.* "They appear less like doughnuts than like cellular organisms in microscopic magnification, swimming in their nourishing culture and adhering to one another to generate new strings of life," Schama reflected. *New York* magazine's Mark Stevens was equally generous in his praise. "In the end, Close, whether intentionally or not, does what most important portrait painters do: He upholds the mystery of the flesh."

Close continued to paint and exhibit throughout the decade, and received numerous accolades, culminating in a Museum of Modern Art retrospective that opened in early 1998, an honor few living artists achieve. Yet there is division of opinion inside the art community over Close's work.

Eric, a 1990 portrait of Close's friend Eric Fischl, is shown here in progress in the artist's studio.

A 1992 oil painting of artist John Chamberlain, entitled *John*.

Jed Perl, the art critic for the *New Republic,* is one detractor; in writing about the MoMA show, Perl commented that Close's "billboard-scale portraits have a sideshow fascination," and elsewhere even went so far as to term it "highfalutin paint-by-numbers." Close, however, takes such criticism with his characteristic good humor. The *New York Times Magazine* writer Solomon interviewed artist Rackstraw Downes for her article on Close, and wrote that Downes recalled being at a panel discussion once in which one of the parties termed Close's work "boring." Close, reported Downes, responded drily, "You find them boring? How do you think I feel painting them?"

Close no longer uses the well-equipped forklift at his SoHo studio, but does have a mechanized trap door that allows him to work on just one section of the painting in progress at eye level. A quartet of nurses work in shifts at his home to help him, and he is famously reticent regarding the daily difficulties of being confined to a wheelchair, though he did tell Solomon that he still has dreams that he walks. In her *New York Times Magazine* profile, Solomon wrote of Close's exuberant personality that has made him one of the most respected and beloved figures in the New York art scene. "Affable, sociable and hopelessly untortured, he keeps up friendships with so many artists that he has been nicknamed, only half-jokingly, the Mayor of SoHo." He and Leslie, a landscape historian and writer, live on Central Park West and in Bridgehampton, and have raised two daughters. His works now fetch an estimated $400,000 each, but Close has said that his medical expenses consume much of his income.

Befitting such a pragmatic personality, Close is fond of dismissing the notion of "inspiration" in creative life. "Inspiration is for amateurs," he told the *New York Times Magazine*'s Solomon. "Some of the time you know you're cooking, and the rest of the time, you just do it." He also touched upon the same subject in discussing his work in the book *Chuck Close Up Close*. "If you wait for inspi-

ration, you'll never get anything done," he told Greenberg and Jordan. "The important thing is getting into a rhythm and continuing it. It makes for a very positive experience. Every day when I roll out of the studio and look over my shoulder, I say, 'That's what I did today.'"

■ Works Cited

Contemporary Artists, St. James Press, 1989.

Greenberg, Jan, and Sandra Jordan, *Chuck Close Up Close,* DK Ink, 1998.

Hughes, Robert, "Close, Closer, Closest," *Time,* April 27, 1981, p. 60.

Perl, Jed, "Death and Realism," *New Republic,* April 20, 1998, p. 25.

Schama, Simon, "Head Honcho," *New Yorker,* March 23, 1998, pp. 91-93.

Solomon, Deborah, "The Persistence of the Portraitist," *New York Times Magazine,* February 1, 1998, pp. 24-30, 52, 60, 66, 70-73.

Stevens, Mark, "Machine Dreams," *New York,* March 9, 1998, pp. 54-56.

■ For More Information See

BOOKS

Guare, John, *Chuck Close: Life and Work 1988-1995,* Thames and Hudson, 1995.

Lyons, Lisa, and Robert Storr, *Chuck Close,* Rizzoli International Publications, 1987.

PERIODICALS

Interview, November, 1995, p. 80.

New Yorker, February 24, 1992, pp. 76-78; January 15, 1996, p. 48.

New York Times, July 25, 1997.

Time, April 13, 1998, pp. 209, 211, 214, 216.

—*Sketch by Carol Brennan*

Sharon M. Draper

ence on English Leadership, Delta Kappa Gamma, Phi Delta Kappa, Women's City Club.

■ Awards, Honors

First prize, *Ebony Magazine* Literary Contest, 1991, for short story, "One Small Torch"; Coretta Scott King Genesis Award for an outstanding new book, American Library Association (ALA), 1995, for *Tears of a Tiger*; Best Book for Young Adults, ALA, Best Books, Children's Book Council and Bank Street College, Books for the Teen Age, New York Public Library, and Notable Trade Book in the Field of Social Studies, National Council for the Social Studies, 1995, for *Tears of a Tiger*, and 1998, for *Forged by Fire*; Coretta Scott King Genesis Award, ALA, 1998, for *Forged by Fire*. Outstanding High School English Language Arts Educator, Ohio Council of Teachers of English Language Arts, 1995; Midwest regional winner of the NCNW Excellence in Teaching Award, 1996; Governor's Educational Leadership Award from the Governor of Ohio, 1996; National Teacher of the Year, 1997.

■ Personal

Born in Cleveland, OH; daughter of Victor (a hotel manager) and Catherine (a gardener) Mills; married Larry E. Draper (an educator); children: Wendy, Damon, Crystal, Cory. *Education:* Pepperdine University, B.A.; Miami University (Oxford, OH), M.A.

■ Addresses

Office—2650 Highland Ave., Cincinnati, OH 45219. *Electronic mail*—TTYGER@aol.com.

■ Career

Junior- and senior-high school teacher, 1972—. Public speaker, poet, and author. *Member:* International Reading Association, American Federation of Teachers, National Board for Professional Teaching Standards (Board of Directors, 1995—), National Council of Teachers of English, Ohio Council of Teachers of English Language Arts, Confer-

■ Writings

FOR CHILDREN

Ziggy and the Black Dinosaurs, Just Us Books (East Orange, NJ), 1994.

Ziggy and the Black Dinosaurs: Lost in the Tunnel of Time, Just Us Books, 1996.

Ziggy and the Black Dinosaurs: Shadows of Caesar's Creek, Just Us Books, 1997.

FOR YOUNG ADULTS

Tears of a Tiger, Simon and Schuster, 1994.
Forged by Fire, Simon and Schuster, 1997.
Romiette and Julio, Simon and Schuster, 1999.
Jazzimagination, Scholastic, 1999.

OTHER

Also author of *Let the Circle Be Unbroken* (children's poetry), and *Buttered Bones* (poetry for adults). Contributor of poems and short stories to literary magazines, and of an award-winning essay, "The Touch of a Teacher," to *What Governors Need to Know About Education,* Center for Policy Research of the National Governor's Association.

■ **Sidelights**

Sharon Draper is a teacher and writer with a philosophy that guides her in how she teaches and what she writes. That philosophy is evident in her remarks to *Something About the Author (SATA)* about being honored as the 1997 National Teacher of the Year: "It is a wonderful honor, but also an awesome responsibility—to be the spokesperson and advocate for education in America. I was ready for this challenge, however, because I had been preparing for this work my entire life." Reading, teaching, and writing are all connected for Draper, who wanted to be a teacher since childhood. In an interview with Jon Saari for *Authors and Artists for Young Adults,* Draper said, "I was an avid reader. I read every single book in the elementary school library, all of them. I did not plan to be a writer until much, much later. I tell kids all the time that in order to be a good writer it is necessary first to be a good reader. You need some information in your head. Reading is input. Writing is output. You can't write without input.

"Reading should not be a painful experience," Draper said in the *AAYA* interview. Her experience teaching public school since 1972 has given her some definite ideas on the reading habits of teens. "I know what kids like—what they will read, and what they won't. Although I have nothing against Charles Dickens, many teenagers would rather gag than read him. Dickens wrote for his contemporaries—young people of a hundred and fifty years ago. American students might need to know about the world of London in the 1860s, but they would much rather read about their own world first. Not only will they read about recognizable experiences with pleasure, but they will also be encouraged to write as well."

Draper advises other teachers to read aloud the first chapter of *Tears of a Tiger* (her first young adult novel) to students and then put the book down. "The kids break their necks getting the book. They fight over who gets to read it next. If you can capture their attention very early in a

During a camping trip at Caesar's Creek State Park, the Black Dinosaurs become lost in woods supposedly inhabited by spirits.

book, then you'll be successful." From her own teaching experiences, Draper knows the obstacles teachers face in getting students to read. "I want them to enjoy what they are reading. I want them to learn from it, but I don't want them to know they are learning something in the process. The best learning is painless. If I get too didactic, teenagers will turn it off if they think I am preaching at them. I try not to do that."

Draper has firm ideas on how to cultivate an idea in fiction. "The idea grows as the characters develop, and it is a kind of combined effort with characters, idea, and theme. And that drives what the plot is going to be." A book evolves for Draper and is not a predetermined plan she sticks to. "It's not as if I have a preconceived notion, 'I am going to teach students about this particular goal and make a book about it.' Instead it's the other way around: The characters and plot drive the theme." Research has an essential place in the writing process. "If a writer wants reality and accuracy, research, even into seemingly insignificant things, is very important," she told Saari. "For example, in the third Ziggy book, which is called *Shadows of Caesar's Creek*, the kids go on a field trip to a placed called Caesar's Creek State Park, and there they meet up with Shawnee Indians that live in Ohio. In order to make it real and true I had to do the research. I spent time with the Shawnee Indians in Ohio. I spent several days at the park so that my writing had validity."

Given her commitment to teaching, Draper often must squeeze time out of her busy day by writing early in the morning or late at night after family members are in bed. Those odd times, though, provide the necessary ingredient for her creative work, which is "absolute silence, absolutely no interruptions for long periods of time. It's basically impossible, but that's what I need," she said to Saari.

In 1994 Draper began her "Ziggy" series, writing for a young audience about African American history and folklore. Ziggy and his friends call themselves the Black Dinosaurs, and they have a number of adventures that appeal to the younger reader. In the first book, *Ziggy and the Black Dinosaurs*, Draper set an entertaining tone that drew a positive response from readers and critics. In the second book, *Lost in the Tunnel of Time*, Ziggy and friends, on a field trip to the Ohio River, learn

A sequel to Draper's debut young adult novel *Tears of a Tiger*, this work received the Coretta Scott King Award in 1998.

about the Underground Railroad and the tunnels the slaves used to escape the South. In the third volume, *Shadows of Caesar's Creek*, Draper makes connections between African Americans and Native Americans.

YA Novels Win King Award

In the fall of 1994 Draper published the young adult novel, *Tears of a Tiger*, a story about Andy Jackson, an African-American youth who struggles to make sense of the death of his best friend, Robert, in an automobile accident in which Andy was the driver. Andy must live with his friend's last words: "Oh God, please don't let me die like this! Andy!" The two teenagers had been drinking beer with their friends Tyrone and B. J. in celebration of a victory by their high school basketball team. Tyrone and B. J. are able to move past the awful pain caused by the accident: Tyrone finds support from his girlfriend Rhonda, B. J. through religion. Andy, however, is racked with guilt, grief, and pain that does not subside with time.

Tears of a Tiger shows the difficulties in healing a damaged teenager. Andy's coach is understanding, as is his girlfriend, Keisha, despite Andy's frequent childish displays of bad behavior which work to mask his anguish. Neither, however, are available in the hour of his greatest need—the night he kills himself with a shotgun. Draper also places in her narrative characters who represent institutional attitudes confronting the young black male. In one episode, two teachers discuss how Andy's grief can't be all that serious since he is black. Andy also internalizes some ideas about himself that prevent him from realizing his full capabilities; for example, he thinks he cannot be successful academically because he is a basketball player. Merri Monks, writing in *Booklist*, observes that "Andy's perceptions of the racism directed toward young black males—by teachers, guidance counselors, and clerks in shopping malls—will be recognized by African American YAs."

"*Tears of a Tiger* is written for high school students—on their level, in their style, about their world," Draper told *SATA*. "The main characters are African American males, but it's written for all teenagers. The characters are just ordinary kids trying to get through high school. The book does not deal with drugs or gangs or sex. It does, however, deal with parents, girlfriends, and homework. It also discusses the problems of drinking and driving, racism and teen suicide."

Critics of *Tears of a Tiger* believe Draper effectively uses dialog to advance the story. Kathy Fritts, writing in the *School Library Journal*, points out that "the characters' voices are strong, vivid, and ring true. This moving novel will leave a deep impression." Furthermore, Draper's use of news stories, journal entries, homework assignments, and letters give the novel an immediacy that adds to its power. Although some critics fault Draper for a tendency to be preachy, most agree with

---

If you enjoy the works of Sharon M. Draper, you may also want to check out the following books and films:

James D. Forman, *The Big Bang*, 1989.
Walter Dean Myers, *Somewhere in the Darkness*, 1992.
Jacqueline Woodson, *I Hadn't Meant to Tell You This*, 1994.
Ordinary People, a film starring Timothy Hutton, 1980.

Monks, who remarks that the work's "characters and their experiences will captivate teen readers." In *Publishers Weekly*, a reviewer concludes that "the combination of raw energy and intense emotions should stimulate readers." Dorothy M. Broderick, critiquing the work in *Voice of Youth Advocates*, writes: "Suffice to say, not only is Draper an author to watch for, but that this is as compelling a novel as any published in the last two decades." Roger Sutton, writing in *The Bulletin of the Center for Children's Books*, states that "rather than a tidy summary of suicide symptoms and 'ways to help,' readers instead get a grave portrait of unceasing despair and a larger picture of how young African-American men like Andy get lost in a system that will not trust or reach out to them." *Tears of a Tiger* has received several national honors, including the Coretta Scott King Genesis Award.

Forged by Fire, the 1997 sequel to *Tears of a Tiger*, has a similar socially relevant nexus for the plot. Child sexual abuse and drug addiction replace suicide and racism, yet both books reach a tragic finality. Draper wrote the *Forged by Fire*'s first chapter as a short story, "One Small Touch," published in *Ebony*. The novel went on to win Draper her second Coretta Scott King Award.

Gerald Nickelby, the hero of this story, is a minor character in *Tears of a Tiger*—a friend of Robert. (The car accident and Robert's death are retold here). Gerald, at age three, is burned in a fire when left alone by his mother, Monique. After his hospital stay, Gerald is not returned to his mother. Instead he lives with his Aunt Queen, a loving and supportive woman. Six years later, Monique reenters Gerald's life after Aunt Queen dies. Monique has married Jordan Sparks, the father of Angel, Gerald's new half-sister. Gerald learns that Sparks has sexually abused Angel. Through the testimony of the children, Sparks is sent to prison. When Sparks returns six years later (Gerald is now fifteen), Monique, who indulges too much in drugs, lets him return to family life where he once again attempts to sexually harm Angel.

Tom S. Hurlburt, reviewing *Forged by Fire* in *School Library Journal*, assesses the book's impact this way: "There's no all's-well ending, but readers will have hope for Gerald and Angel, who have survived a number of gut-wrenching ordeals by relying on their constant love and caring for one another." Candace Smith, writing in *Booklist*, concludes that "Draper faces some big issues (abuse, death, drugs) and provides concrete options and a positive African American role model in Gerald."

Draper told *SATA:* "I feel very blessed that I have had so much success in such a short time. I hope that my books can continue to make a difference in the lives of young people."

■ Works Cited

Broderick, Dorothy M., review of *Tears of a Tiger, Voice of Youth Advocates*, February, 1995, p. 338.

Draper, Sharon M., comments in *Something about the Author*, Volume 98, Gale, 1998, pp. 49-50.

Draper, Sharon M., interview with Jon Saari for *Authors and Artists for Young Adults*, December 15, 1998.

Fritts, Kathy, review of *Tears of a Tiger, School Library Journal*, February, 1995, p. 112.

Hurlburt, Tom S., review of *Forged by Fire, School Library Journal*, March 1997, p. 184.

Monks, Merri, review of *Tears of a Tiger, Booklist*, November 1, 1994, p. 492.

Smith, Candace, review of *Forged by Fire, Booklist*, February 15, 1997, p. 1017.

Sutton, Roger, review of *Tears of a Tiger, Bulletin of the Center for Children's Books*, January, 1995, p. 164.

Review of *Tears of a Tiger, Publishers Weekly*, October 31, 1994, p. 64.

■ For More Information See

PERIODICALS

Booklist, November 1, 1994, p. 492; February 15, 1997, p. 1016.

Publishers Weekly, October 31, 1994, p. 64; March 25, 1996, p. 85; December 16, 1996, p. 61.

School Library Journal, March, 1995, p. 202; March, 1997, p. 184.

—Sketch by Jon Saari

T. S. Eliot

■ Personal

Born September 26, 1888, in St. Louis, MO; moved to England, 1914, naturalized British subject, 1927; died January 4, 1965, in London, England; buried in Westminster Abbey; son of Henry Ware (president of Hydraulic Press Brick Co.) and Charlotte Chauncey (a teacher, social worker and writer; maiden name Stearns) Eliot; married Vivien Haigh-Wood (a dancer), January, 1915 (divorced c. 1930; died, 1947); married (Esme) Valerie Fletcher (his private secretary before their marriage), 1957; children: none. *Education:* Attended Smith Academy (of Washington University), St. Louis, 1898-1905; Milton Academy, Milton, MA, graduated, 1906; Harvard University, B.A. (philosophy), 1909, M.A. (philosophy), 1910, graduate study, 1911-14 (his doctoral dissertation "Experience and the Objects of Knowledge in the Philosophy of F. H. Bradley," was accepted in 1916 but never presented for the degree; the dissertation was published in 1964 as *Knowledge and Experience in Philosophy of F. H. Bradley*); attended University of Paris (Sorbonne), 1910-11; studied in Munich, 1914; read philosophy at Merton, Oxford, 1914-15; also studied under Edward Kennard Rand, Irving Babbitt, and Alain Fournier, and attended courses given by Henri Bergson. *Politics:* Conservative ("royalist"). *Religion:* Church of England (Anglo-Catholic wing; confirmed, 1927; served as vestryman in a London church). (In his 1028 essay "For Lancelot Andrewes," Eliot called himself a "classicist, " "royalist, " and "Anglican." Later, in the work *After Strange Gods,* he regretted that declaration as "injudicious.")

■ Career

Harvard University, Cambridge, MA, assistant in philosophy department, 1913-14; teacher of French, Latin, mathematics, drawing, geography, and history at High Wycombe Grammar School, London, then at Highgate School, London, 1915-17; Lloyds Bank Ltd., London, clerk in the Colonial and Foreign Department, 1917-25; *The Egoist,* London, assistant editor, 1917-19; founder of the *Criterion* (literary quarterly), London, 1922, and editor, 1922-39 (ceased publication, at Eliot's decision, in 1939 because of the war and paper shortage); Faber and Gwyer Ltd. (publishers), later Faber & Faber Ltd., London, literary editor and member of the advisory board, 1925-65. Clark Lecturer at Trinity College, Cambridge, 1926; Charles Eliot Norton Professor of Poetry at Harvard University, six months, 1932-33; Page-Barbour Lecturer at University of Virginia, 1933; resident at Institute for Advanced Study at Princeton, 1948; Theodore Spencer Memorial Lecturer at Harvard University, 1950; lecturer at University of Chicago during the fifties;

lecturer at Library of Congress, at University of Texas, at University of Minnesota, and before many other groups. President of London Library, 1952-65. *Wartime Service:* None; was rejected by the U.S. Navy, 1918, because of poor health. *Member:* Classical Association (president, 1941), Virgil Society (president, 1943), Books Across the Sea (president, 1943-46), American Academy of Arts and Sciences (honorary member), Accademia dei Lincei (Rome; foreign member), Bayerische Akademie der Schoenen Kuenste (Munich; foreign member), Athenaeum, Garrick Club, Oxford and Cambridge Club.

■ Awards, Honors

Sheldon Travelling Fellowship for study in Munich, 1914; Dial award ($2,000), 1922, for *The Waste Land*; Nobel Prize for Literature, 1948; Order of Merit, 1948; Commander, Ordre des Arts et des Lettres; Officier de la Legion d'Honneur; New York Drama Critics Circle Award, 1950, for *The Cocktail Party* as best foreign play; Hanseatic Goethe Prize of Hamburg University, 1954; Dante Gold Medal (Florence), 1956; Ordre pour le Merite (West Germany), 1959; Emerson-Thoreau Medal of the American Academy of Arts and Sciences, 1959; honorary fellow of Merton College, Oxford, and of Magdalene College, Cambridge; honorary citizen of Dallas, TX; honorary deputy sheriff of Dallas County, TX; Campion Medal of the Catholic Book Club, 1963, for "long and distinguished service to Christian letters"; received President Johnson's award for distinguished contribution to American literature and public life. Honorary degrees: Litt.D., Columbia University, 1933, Cambridge University, 1938, University of Bristol, 1938, University of Leeds, 1939, Harvard University 1947, Yale University, 1947, Princeton University, 1947, Washington University, 1953, University of Rome, 1958, University of Sheffield, 1959 LLD., University of Edinburgh, 1937, St. Andrews' University, 1953, DLitt., Oxford University, 1948, University of London, 1950, DPhilos., University of Munich, 1959, Des L., University of Paris, 1959, Universite d'Aix-Marseille, 1959, University of Rennet, 1959.

■ Writings

POETRY

Prufrock, and Other Observations (contains eleven poems and a prose piece, "Hysteria"; the title poem, "The Love Song of J. Alfred Prufrock," was first published in *Poetry*, June, 1915; five other poems were originally published in *Catholic Anthology*, edited by Ezra Pound, 1915), The Egoist (London), 1917.

Poems by T. S. Eliot, Hogarth, 1919.

Ara Vos Prec (includes *Poems by T. S. Eliot*, above), Ovid Press (London), 1920, published in America as *Poems*, Knopf, 1920.

The Waste Land (first published in *Criterion*, first issue, October, 1922), Boni & Liveright, 1922.

Poems, 1909-1925 (contains all works cited above and "The Hollow Men"; earlier drafts and sections of "The Hollow Men" appeared in *Chapbook*, *Commerce*, *Criterion*, and *Dial*, 1924-25), Faber, 1925.

Journey of the Magi (one of the "Ariel Poems"), Faber, 1927.

Animula (one of the "Ariel Poems"), Faber, 1929.

Ash-Wednesday (first three parts originally published in French, American, and English magazines, respectively; Part 2, first published as "Salutation" in *Saturday Review of Literature*, was intended as another of the "Ariel Poems" and as a complement to *Journey of the Magi*; the publisher also intended to issue this part separately as a Christmas card), Putnam, 1930.

Marina (one of the "Ariel Poems"), Faber, 1930.

Triumphal March, Faber, 1931.

The Waste Land, and Other Poems, Harcourt, 1934.

Words for Music, [Bryn Mawr], 1935.

Collected Poems, 1909-1935, Harcourt, 1936.

A Song for Simeon (written in the 1920's; one of the "Ariel Poems"), Faber, 1938.

(With Geoffrey Faber, Frank Morley, and John Hayward) *Noctes Binanianae* (limited edition of twenty-five copies for the authors and friends; never reprinted), privately printed (London), 1939.

Old Possum's Book of Practical Cats, Harcourt, 1939.

East Coker, Faber, 1940.

Burnt Norton, Faber, 1941.

The Dry Salvages, Faber, 1941.

Later Poems, 1925-1935, Faber 1941.

Little Gidding, Faber, 1942.

Four Quartets (consists of *Burnt Norton, East Coker, The Dry Salvages,* and *Little Gidding*), Harcourt, 1943.

A Practical Possum, Harvard Printing Office, 1947.

Selected Poems, Penguin, 1948, Harcourt, 1967.

The Undergraduate Poems, Harvard Advocate (unauthorized reprint of poems originally published in the *Advocate*), 1949.

Poems Written in Early Youth, privately printed by Bonniers (Stockholm), 1950, new edition prepared by Valerie Eliot and John Hayward, Farrar, Straus, 1967.

The Cultivation of Christmas Trees (one of the "Ariel Poems"), Faber, 1954, Farrar, Straus, 1956.

Collected Poems, 1909-1962, Harcourt, 1963.

The Waste Land: A Facsimile of the Original Drafts, Including the Annotations of Ezra Pound, edited and with introduction by Valerie Eliot, Harcourt, 1971.

Inventions of the March Hare: Poems, 1909-1917, edited by Christopher Ricks, Harcourt, 1997.

Poetry also represented in anthologies.

PLAYS

Fragment of a Prologue, [London], 1926.

Fragment of the Agon, [London], 1927.

Sweeney Agonistes: Fragments of an Aristophanic Melodrama (provisionally titled "Wanna Go Home, Baby?" during composition; consists of two fragments cited above; first produced in New York at Cherry Lane Theater, March 2, 1952), Faber, 1932.

The Rock: A Pageant Play (a revue with scenario by E. Martin Browne and music by Martin Shaw; first produced in London at Sadler Wells Theatre, May 9, 1934), Faber, 1934.

Murder in the Cathedral (provisionally titled "Fear in the Way" during composition; first produced in an abbreviated form for the Canterbury Festival in the Chapter House of Canterbury Cathedral, June, 1935; produced in London at Mercury Theatre, November 1, 1935; first produced in America at Yale University, January, 1936; first produced in New York at Manhattan Theater, March 20, 1936), Harcourt, 1935.

The Family Reunion (often cited as a rewriting of the unfinished *Sweeney Agonistes;* first produced in London at Westminster Theatre, March 21, 1939; produced in New York at Phoenix Theater, October 20, 1958), Harcourt, 1939.

The Cocktail Party (provisionally titled "One-Eyed Riley" during composition; first produced for the Edinburgh Festival, Scotland, August, 1949; produced in New York at Henry Miller's Theater, January 21, 1950), Harcourt, 1950.

The Confidential Clerk (first produced for the Edinburgh Festival, August, 1953; produced in London at Lyric Theatre, September 16, 1953; produced in New York at Morosco Theater, February 11, 1954), Harcourt, 1954.

The Elder Statesman (first produced for the Edinburgh Festival, August, 1958; produced in

London at Cambridge Theatre, September 25, 1958), Farrar, Straus, 1959.

Collected Plays, Faber, 1962.

Plays also represented in anthologies.

PROSE

Ezra Pound: His Metric and Poetry (published anonymously) Knopf, 1917.

The Sacred Wood (essays on poetry and criticism), Methuen, 1920, 7th edition, 1950, Barnes & Noble, 1960.

Homage to John Dryden (three essays on seventeenth-century poetry), L. and V. Woolf at Hogarth Press, 1924, Doubleday, 1928.

Shakespeare and the Stoicism of Seneca (an address), Oxford University Press, for the Shakespeare Association, 1927.

For Lancelot Andrewes: Essays on Style and Order, Faber, 1928, Doubleday, 1929.

Thoughts After Lambeth (a criticism of the *Report* of the Lambeth Conference, 1930), Faber, 1931.

Charles Whibley: A Memoir, Oxford University Press, for the English Association, 1931.

Selected Essays, 1917-1932, Harcourt, 1932, 2nd edition published as *Selected Essays,* Harcourt, 1950, 3rd edition, Faber, 1951.

John Dryden, the Poet, the Dramatist, the Critic (three essays), T. & Elsa Holiday (New York), 1932.

The Use of Poetry and the Use of Criticism: Studies in the Relation of Criticism to Poetry in England (the Charles Eliot Norton lectures), Harvard University Press, 1933, 2nd edition, Faber, 1964.

Elizabethan Essays (includes *Shakespeare and the Stoicism of Seneca*), Faber, 1934, Haskell House, 1964.

After Strange Gods: A Primer of Modern Heresy (the Page-Barbour lectures), Harcourt, 1934.

Essays, Ancient and Modern (first published in part as *For Lancelot Andrewes*), Harcourt, 1936.

The Idea of a Christian Society (three lectures), Faber, 1939, Harcourt,1940.

Christianity and Culture (contains *The Idea of a Christian Society* and *Notes Towards the Definition of Culture*), Harcourt, 1940.

Points of View (selected criticism), edited by John Hayward, Faber, 1941.

The Classics and the Man of Letters (an address), Oxford University Press, 1942.

The Music of Poetry (lecture), Jackson (Glasgow), 1942.

Reunion by Destruction: Reflections on a Scheme for Church Union in South India (an address), Pax House (London), 1943.

What Is a Classic? (an address), Faber, 1945.

Die Einheit der europaischen Kultur, Carl Havel, 1946.

On Poetry, [Concord], 1947.

A Sermon, [Cambridge], 1948.

From Poe to Valery (first published in *Hudson Review*, 1948), privately printed for friends by Harcourt, 1948.

Milton (lecture), Cumberlege (London), 1948.

Notes Towards the Definition of Culture (seven essays; a few copies erroneously stamped *Notes Towards a Definition of Culture*), Harcourt, 1949.

The Aims of Poetic Drama, Galleon, 1949.

The Value and Use of Cathedrals in England Today, [Chichester], c. 1950.

Poetry by T. S. Eliot: An NBC Radio Discussion, [Chicago], 1950.

Poetry and Drama (the Theodore Spencer lecture), Harvard University Press, 1951.

American Literature and the American Language (an address and an appendix entitled "The Eliot Family and St. Louis," the latter prepared by the English Department at Washington University), Washington University Press, 1953.

The Three Voices of Poetry (lecture), Cambridge University Press, for the National Book League, 1953, Cambridge University Press (New York), 1954.

Selected Prose, edited by John Hayward, Penguin, 1953.

Religious Drama, House of Books (New York), 1954.

The Literature of Politics (lecture), foreword by Sir Anthony Eden, Conservative Political Centre, 1955.

The Frontiers of Criticism (lecture), University of Minnesota, 1956.

Essays on Elizabethan Drama (contains nine of the eleven essays originally published as *Elizabethan Essays*), Harcourt, 1956.

On Poetry and Poets (essays), Farrar, Straus, 1957.

Essays on Poetry and Criticism, introduction and notes in Japanese by Kazumi Yano, Shohakusha (Tokyo), 1959.

William Collin Brooks (an address), The Statist (London), 1959.

Geoffrey Faber, 1889-1961, Faber, 1961.

George Herbert, Longmans, Green, for the British Council and the National Book League, 1962.

Elizabethan Dramatists, Faber, 1963.

Knowledge and Experience in the Philosophy of F. H. Bradley (doctoral dissertation), Farrar, Straus, 1964.

To Criticize the Critic, and Other Writings (contains *From Poe to Valery*; *American Literature and the American Language*; *The Literature of Politics*; *The Classics and the Man of Letters*; *Ezra Pound: His Metric and Poetry*; and new essays), Farrar, Straus, 1965.

Prose also represented in anthologies.

OMNIBUS VOLUMES

The Complete Poems and Plays, 1909-1950, Harcourt, 1952.

CONTRIBUTOR

"A Dialogue on Poetic Drama," in *Of Dramatic Poesie* (edition of an essay by John Dryden), Etchells & Macdonald (London), 1928.

"The Place of Pater," in *The Eighteen-Eighties: Essays by Fellows of the Royal Society of Literature* (Eliot did not, however, hold the title F.R.S.L.), edited by Walter de la Mare, [Cambridge], 1930.

"Donne in Our Time," in *A Garland for John Donne*, edited by Theodore Spencer, Harvard University Press, 1931.

"Religion and Literature," in *The Faith That Illuminates*, edited by V. A. Demant, Centenary (London), 1935.

"Byron," in *From Anne to Victoria: Essays by Various Hands*, edited by Bonamy Dobree, Cassell, 1937.

(Author of text) *Britain at War* (pictorial essay), Museum of Modern Art (New York), 1941.

"Henry James," in *The Shock of Recognition*, edited by Edmund Wilson, Doubleday, 1943, reprinted as *On Henry James*, in *The Question of Henry James*, edited by F. W. Dupee, Wingate, 1947.

Peter Russell, editor, *Examination of Ezra Pound*, New Directions, 1950 (published in England as *Ezra Pound: A Collection of Essays*, Nevill, 1950).

"Andrew Marvell," in *Gedichte* (an edition of Marvell's poems), Karl H.Henssel Verlag, 1962.

"George Herbert," in *British Writers and Their Work* (periodical), number 4, University of Nebraska Press, 1964.

AUTHOR OF INTRODUCTION

Charlotte Chauncey Eliot, *Savonarola* (dramatic poem), R. Cobden Sanderson, 1926.

Seneca His Tenne Tragedies, Knopf, 1927, introduction reprinted as "Seneca in Elizabethan Translation," in *Eliot's Selected Essays*.

Wilkie Collins, *The Moonstone* (novel), Oxford University Press, 1928.

James B. Connolly, *Fishermen of the Banks*, Faber, 1928.

Edgar Ansel Mowrer, *This American World*, Faber, 1928.

Ezra Pound, *Selected Poems*, Faber, 1928.

Samuel Johnson, *London, a Poem [and] The Vanity of Human Wishes*, Etchells & Macdonald, 1930, introduction reprinted as "*Johnson's* London *and* "The Vanity of Human Wishes," in *English Critical Essays: Twentieth Century*, edited by Phyllis M. Jones, Oxford University Press, 1933.

G. Wilson Knight, *The Wheel of Fire: Essays in Interpretation of Shakespeare's Sombre Tragedies*, Oxford University Press, 1930.

Charles Baudelaire, *Intimate Journals*, translated by Christopher Isherwood, Random House, 1930, introduction reprinted as "Baudelaire," in *Eliot's Selected Essays*.

Pascal's Pensees, translated by W. F. Trotter, Dutton, 1931, introduction reprinted as "The Pensees of Pascal," in *Eliot's Selected Essays*.

Marianne Moore, *Selected Poems*, Macmillan, 1935.

Poems of Tennyson, Nelson, 1936, introduction reprinted as "In Memoriam," in *Eliot's Selected Essays*.

Djuna Barnes, *Nightwood* (novel), Harcourt, 1937, 2nd edition, Faber,1950.

(And compiler) *A Choice of Kipling's Verse*, Faber, 1941.

Charles-Louis Philippe, *Bubu of Montparnasse*, English translation by Laurence Vail and others, 2nd edition (not associated with first edition), Avalon, 1945.

Simone Weil, *The Need for Roots*, Putnam, 1952.

Literary Essays of Ezra Pound, New Directions, 1954.

Opada bhul (Oriya translation of some of Eliot's poems), P. C. Das, c.1957.

Stanislaus Joyce, *My Brother's Keeper*, edited by Richard Ellmann, Viking, 1958.

Paul Valery, *The Art of Poetry*, translated by Denise Folliot, Pantheon, 1958.

Ezra Pound, *Kabita* (Oriya translation of *Pound's Selected Poems*), translated by Jnanindra Barma, P. C. Das, 1958.

Hugo von Hofmannsthal, *Poems and Verse Plays*, edited by Michael Hamburger, Pantheon, 1961.

David Jones, *In Parenthesis* (novel), Viking, 1961.

John Davidson: A Selection of His Poems, edited by Maurice Lindsay, Hutchinson, 1961.

(And editor) *Introducing James Joyce* (selected prose), Faber, 1962.

Also author, between 1930 and 1941, of introductions to books of poems by Harry Crosby and Abraham Cowley; author, prior to 1952, of introduction to an edition of Mark Twain's *The Adventures of Huckleberry Finn*.

OTHER

(Translator) St. John Perse (pseudonym of Alexis Saint-Leger Leger) *Anabasis* (poem; published in a bilingual edition with the original French), Faber, 1930, revised edition, Harcourt, 1949.

(With George Hoellering) *Murder in the Cathedral* (screenplay based on Eliot's play), Harcourt, 1952.

The Letters of T. S. Eliot, Volume 1: 1898-1922, Harcourt, 1988.

Mr. Mistoffelees; with Mungojerrie and Rumpelteazer, Faber, 1990, Harcourt, 1991.

The Varieties of Metaphysical Poetry: The Clark Lectures at Trinity College, Cambridge, 1926, and *The Turnbull Lectures at the Johns Hopkins University*, 1933, Harcourt Brace (New York City), 1994.

Also lyricist for songs "For An Old Man," [New York], 1951, and "The Greater Light," [London], released in 1956, with music by David Diamond and Martine Shaw. A complete run of Eliot's periodical, *Criterion* (1922-1939), was published by Barnes & Noble, 1967. Also author under pseudonyms Charles Augustus Conybeare, Reverend Charles James Grimble, Gus Krutzch, Muriel A. Schwartz, J. A. D. Spence, and Helen B. Trundlett. Editor of the *Harvard Advocate*, 1909-1910. Member of the editorial boards of *New English Weekly*, *Inventario*, *Christian News-Letter*, and other periodicals. Contributor to periodicals.

■ Adaptations

"The Hollow Men" was set for baritone solo, male voice chorus, and orchestra, published by Oxford University Press, 1951; Stravinsky set sections of "Little Gidding" to music; *Murder in the Cathedral* was filmed in 1952, and Eliot wrote some new lines for the script and himself read the part of The Fourth Tempter, who is never seen on the screen; The Old Vic issued a recording of *Murder in the Cathedral* in 1953; *Sweeney Agonistes* was adapted into a jazz musical by John Dankworth for "Homage to T. S. Eliot"; *Old Possum's Book of Practical Cats* was adapted as the stage musical *Cats*, 1981.

A memorial service for Eliot at Westminster Abbey, February 4, 1965, was published as *Order of*

Service in Memory of Thomas Stearns Eliot, Hove Shirley Press (London), 1965. On June 14, 1965, a program entitled "Homage to T. S. Eliot" was presented at the Globe Theatre in London. To the program Igor Stravinsky contributed "Introitus," a new choral work written in Eliot's memory, and Henry Moore a huge sculpture entitled "The Archer." Andrei Voznesensky, Peter O'Toole, Laurence Olivier, and Paul Scofield recited. Poems read during the program were selected by W. H. Auden, and Cleanth Brooks contributed a brief narration.

Eliot's works have been translated into at least twenty-two languages. Harvard University has recorded his readings of "The Hollow Men," "Gerontion," "The Love Song of J. Alfred Prufrock," "Journey of the Magi," "A Song for Simeon, Triumphal March," "Difficulties of a Statesman," "Fragment of an Agon," and "Four Quartets." Eliot's readings of *The Waste Land,* "Landscapes I and II," and "Sweeney Among the Nightingales" have been recorded by the Library of Congress.

■ Sidelights

"In ten years' time," Edmund Wilson wrote in *Axel's Castle,* "Eliot has left upon English poetry a mark more unmistakable than any other poet writing in the English language." Recognized as the most imposing literary figure of his time—even at the time of his death—T. S. Eliot changed the way that his generation looked at literature. Through the media of poetry, drama, and criticism, he left an indelible mark on his contemporaries, and, consequently, on the future of English letters and beyond: his works have been translated into some twenty-two languages. While Eliot borrowed liberally from his predecessors and staunchly defended the importance of tradition, he is recognized as a genuine modernist who—with virtually no influence from his contemporaries—gave voice to distinctly modern themes. R. A. Scott-James noted in *Fifty Years of English Literature, 1900-1950* that Eliot "brought into poetry something which in this generation was needed: a language spare, sinewy, modern; a fresh and springy metrical form; thought that was adult; and an imagination aware of what is bewildering and terrifying in modern life and in all life. He has done more than any other [contemporary] English poet to make this age conscious of itself, and, in

being conscious, apprehensive." Jewel Spears Brooker expressed a similar assessment in *Dictionary of Literary Biography,* "Perhaps without having intended to do so, Eliot diagnosed the malaise of his generation and indeed of Western civilization in the twentieth century."

A man whose poetry sought to explore elusive subjects such as personal identity, fulfillment, and perception, Thomas Stearns Eliot was an enigmatic figure. Accused of being distant, condescending, unnecessarily obtuse and erudite, he was at the same time an affable individual who loved whoopee cushions and joke cigars, and was a devoted follower of Sherlock Holmes. Responding to a request for biographical information from his alma mater, Harvard University, Eliot wrote in 1935, "I prefer sherry (light dry) to cocktails. I . . . like such games as poker, rummy and slippery Ann for low stakes. I like certain very simple and humane kinds of practical joke. . . . I never bet, because I never win. . . . I like detective stories . . . and tend to fall asleep in armchairs." Stephen Spender noted the contradictory nature of Eliot's private and public selves: "Religiously, poetically and intellectually, this very private man kept open house. . . . Yet in spite of all this, he was sly, ironic, a bit cagey, a bit calculating perhaps, the Eliot whom Ezra Pound called 'old Possum.'"

During his lifetime and after, Eliot's work has had detractors. John Frederick Nims wrote in 1963, for instance, that Eliot "woos the lugubrious" and that his poems "are a bore, obtruding and exhorting, buttonholing us with 'Redeem the time' and so forth." V. S. Pritchett described Eliot as "a trim anti-Bohemian with black bowler and umbrella . . . ushering us to our seats in hell." But the overriding critical sentiment—both during Eliot's lifetime and in subsequent decades—has recognized the American expatriate as a key voice in modern American and English letters. Northrop Frye acknowledged Eliot's impact when he wrote: "A thorough knowledge of Eliot is compulsory for anyone interested in contemporary literature. Whether he is liked or disliked is of no importance, but he must be read."

Family History and Student Years

Eliot was born on September 26, 1888, in St. Louis, Missouri, the last of seven children born to Henry Ware Eliot, the wealthy president of the Hydraulic-Press Brick Company, and Charlotte Stearns. On both sides of his family, Eliot descended from prominent New Englanders. His ancestors included Puritan settlers of the original Massachusetts colonies—prominent clergymen and educators such as Charles William Eliot, a president of Harvard University, and three presidents of the United States: John Adams, John Quincy Adams, and Rutherford B. Hayes. Eliot's grandfather—William Greenleaf Eliot, a Unitarian minister and educator—moved the family from Boston to St. Louis, where he established the city's first Unitarian church. He also founded Washington University and Smith Academy, where both Eliot and his brother received their primary education.

The Waste Land, **a long, multi-voiced poem first published in 1922, is considered one of the masterpieces of twentieth-century poetry.**

Even after moving to St. Louis, Eliot's family maintained strong ties to the East. From the age of eight on, Eliot spent summers with his family on Cape Ann on the Massachusetts coast. The family's dual allegiance had a profound impact on the adult Eliot. Although acutely aware of a sense of family history, he was at the same time plagued by a feeling of deracination. He later recalled, in a 1928 preface, "The family guarded jealously its connections with New England; but it was not until years of maturity that I perceived that I myself had always been a New Englander in the South West, and a South Westerner in New England." Although well-to-do, Eliot's family remained in a run-down and unfashionable area of St. Louis, in deference to his widowed grandmother, who wanted to continue to live in the house her husband had built. The urban images of St. Louis made a profound impression on the young Eliot, who later recaptured the sights and sounds of the city in minute and tangible detail in his poetry. The author wrote in "The Influence of Landscape upon the Poet" (1960): ". . . for nine months of the year my scenery was almost exclusively urban, and a good deal of it seedily, drably urban at that." Encouraged by his mother, who exposed her children to literature, Eliot began to write poetry when he was about fourteen years old. In a 1959 interview with Donald Hall he admitted that he wrote this juvenile verse "under the inspiration of Fitzgerald's *Omar Khayyam,* [and I wrote] a number of very gloomy and atheistical and despairing quatrains in the same style, which fortunately I suppressed completely—so completely that they don't exist."

After graduating from Smith Academy in 1905, Eliot attended the Milton Academy in Massachusetts. The following year he entered Harvard University, where he studied French literature and ancient and modern philosophy in addition to Latin, Greek, and German. Already a scholar in the making, Eliot was reportedly so well read that he could correct his fellow students' misquotations from a wide range of works. During his three years as an undergraduate he also wrote for the *Harvard Advocate,* where he struck up what would become a lifelong friendship with poet Conrad Aiken. The *Advocate,* a prestigious breeding ground for poets and writers, first published some of Eliot's earliest poems. Eliot's studies at Harvard also exposed him to some of the day's foremost philosophers: Bertrand Russell and George Santayana were among his undergraduate professors.

Eliot later reported that during his undergraduate years he discovered, by chance, a book that would alter the course of his life. That book was Arthur Symon's *Symbolist Movement in Literature* (1899), which in turn introduced the young writer to the poetry of Jules Laforgue. Noted for its irony and symbolic expression, Laforgue's poetry helped Eliot find his own poetic voice. Eliot himself later confirmed, "The kind of poetry that I needed, to teach me the use of my own voice, did not exist in English at all; it was only found in French." The ironic commentator so characteristic of Eliot's early poems—such as "Preludes" and "The Love Song of J. Alfred Prufrock"—clearly mirrors the detached quality of Laforgue's poetry. Increasingly interested in things French, Eliot enrolled in a course in French literary criticism as a master's student at Harvard. His teacher, Irving Babbitt, would have a lasting impact on the young author's habit of mind: Babbitt's dedication to the classical virtues of reason, order, and proportion struck a chord with Eliot's quest for some kind of transcendent authority.

Having completed his M.A. in 1910, Eliot ventured to Paris, where he hoped to reinvent himself as an intellectual. He later explained the move to Donald Hall: "I had at that time the idea of giving up English and trying to settle down and scrape along in Paris, and gradually write in French." Eliot studied at the University of Paris (Sorbonne) for less than a year before deciding to return to the familiar halls of Harvard. Before leaving Paris, however, he formed a number of friendships and acquaintances that would influence his later intellectual life. Jacques Rivière, for instance, had a lasting impact on Eliot, who would later model his own literary review after the French editor's *Nouvelle Revue Française*. Returning to Harvard in 1911 as a graduate student in philosophy, Eliot took courses in symbolic logic and scientific method as well as two years of Sanskrit and Indian philosophy. After spending from 1911 to 1914 at Harvard, he began a year of study—sponsored by Harvard's Sheldon Traveling Fellowship—at Merton College, Oxford University. In England Eliot made the acquaintance of the American expatriate and poet Ezra Pound, whose friendship he would enjoy throughout his adult life.

A skeptic whose ideas were allayed by idealism, Eliot had been drawn to the philosophy of F. H. Bradley. While at Merton, he studied with Brad-

ley scholar Harold Joachim, and eventually wrote his dissertation on the British philosopher. Written between 1915 and 1916, the dissertation was hailed as the work of an expert by Harvard professor Josiah Royce. Eliot, however, was less effusive in later references to his thesis: responding to a 1935 alumnae update, he wrote that the dissertation "was accepted, I suppose, because it was unreadable." In fact, when the thesis was published years after Eliot had established himself as a poet and critic, he claimed, in the preface, to be perplexed by his own work. "Forty-six years after my academic philosophizing came to an end," he wrote, "I find myself unable to think in the terminology of this essay. Indeed, I do not pretend to understand it." Whether unfathomable or not, Eliot's dissertation was approved by Harvard, although World War I travel restrictions prevented Eliot from returning to Harvard to defend his thesis.

A Troubled Marriage and *The Lovesong of J. Alfred Prufrock*

While a student at Oxford, Eliot met the vivacious but troubled Vivien Haigh-Wood. The two were married on June 26, 1915, having met just months earlier. News of the wedding dismayed Eliot's family—so much so that the poet's father amended his will to exclude Vivien from inheritance should her husband precede her in death. The marriage took a heavy toll on both Vivien and Eliot, whose opposite temperaments proved to be incompatible. Stephen Spender noted "[Eliot's] first wife, who had been a dancer . . ., was gay, talkative, a chatter-box. She wanted to enjoy life, found Eliot inhibiting and inhibited, yet worshipped him. . . ." Months after the marriage, Bertrand Russell described Vivien: "She is a person who lives on a knife-edge, and will end as a criminal or a saint." Many critics have speculated that Eliot's early poetry—distrustful of sex and romance—reflects the strain of his troubled marriage (which has been documented in the movie *Tom and Viv*). Aldous Huxley once told Robert Craft that Vivien "was an ether addict, you know, and the house smelled like a hospital. All that dust and despair in Eliot's poetry is to be traced to this fact."

In the fall of 1915, after briefly returning to the United States to see his parents, Eliot accepted a teaching position at a boy's school in London. To save money, the couple accepted the offer of philosopher Bertrand Russell to share his modest two-bedroom flat. After four months rooming with Russell—whose motives have been questioned by some—the Eliots spent the following spring with Vivien's parents before settling into their own living quarters. Eliot spent two years teaching at High Wycombe Grammar School and Highgate Junior School prior to working at Lloyd's Bank—under the false pretense, he later claimed, of being a linguist. Of Eliot's term as a banker, Robert M. Adams noted in the *New York Review of Books*, "At a time when bohemianism was the order of the day, Eliot exaggerated his bank clerk's correctness—the bowler hat, the tightly rolled umbrella, the "four-piece suit" (as Virginia Woolf wickedly called it)."

Working full-time at the bank, Eliot labored after-hours for the *Egoist*, a periodical devoted to poetry and essays. Appointed to the position of assistant editor in June 1917, he produced numerous articles of literary criticism—articles that would become dogma to a generation of writers and critics. "The Lovesong of J. Alfred Prufrock," composed in 1914 and 1915 while Eliot was a Harvard student, was also published in the *Egoist* in 1917. At once disillusioned and nostalgic in tone, "Prufrock" captured the psychological and spiritual timbre of Eliot's contemporaries and of generations to follow. Modern in its concerns, the poem encapsulated the disillusionment and disenfranchisement of an unstable society that appeared to be destined for self-destruction.

The first lines of the poem set the stage for the narrator's inability to act: the evening is likened to "a patient etherised upon the table"; the streets are "half-deserted" and follow "like a tedious argument." These same streets lead insidiously to "an overwhelming question"—a question the speaker urges us not to ask. The narrator, who has been likened to a latter-day Hamlet, is forced to confront the fact that his life has been devoted to insignificant concerns. He admits, "I have measured out my life with coffee spoons." Convinced that his redemption lay in embracing some sort of decision and commitment, he finds that he is incapable of surmounting his fears. His question, "Do I dare/Disturb the universe?," requires no answer. Opting not to hazard a dare, the speaker concludes that he is "not Prince Hamlet, nor was meant to be"; rather, he is an "attendant lord" and "Almost, at times, the Fool."

Part of the genius of the poem lay in Eliot's ability vividly to capture physical and psychological landscapes. As novelist May Sinclair noted in a 1917 essay in the *Little Review*, Eliot is careful to present a city street, a drawing room, and the ordinary human mind *as they are*. Prufrock's thoughts are represented just as they are: "live thoughts, kicking, running about and jumping, nervily, in a live brain. . . . Mr. Eliot simply removes the covering from Prufrock's mind: Prufrock's mind, jumping quickly from actuality to memory and back again, like an animal, hunted, tormented, terribly and poignantly alive."

Clearly influenced by the poetry of Jules Laforgue and other French symbolists, "Prufrock" exhibited the unique stylistic techniques that would remain Eliot's poetic trademark throughout his career: open-ended in method, the poem elicits collaboration from the reader through the use of allusion, juxtaposition, and irony. Jewell Spears Brooker noted in *Dictionary of Literary Biography*: "The early-twentieth century shattering of shared meanings puts the artist in a situation analogous to that of Prufrock. Prufrock can never get beyond the corridors of his own mind, can never speak to the chattering abstractions who convert him into an abstraction. But Eliot did reach beyond his own mind. By using formal techniques which force the reader to do his part of art's labor, he had spoken to and has moved countless readers." Part of the reader's labor lies in deciphering the meaning of Eliot's highly allusive poem. Employing allusions as a means to layer texts, Eliot forces the reader to collaborate in "art's labor"—and to scrutinize the tradition from which his work arises. Brooker continued, "beneath Eliot's ironic love song, the perceptive reader cannot but hear the sentimental love songs of the nineteenth century; beneath Prufrock's debate with himself, the reader may discover the medieval debate of body and soul; beneath Prufrock's paralysis, that of Hamlet; beneath Prufrock's burial, that of Lazarus, beneath Prufrock's hell, Dante's inferno. The careful reader not only sees this complex layering of texts, but is literally forced to see with new eyes the entire tradition in which these texts exist."

By 1919 Eliot had begun writing articles for John Middleton Murry's *Athenaeum* and reviews for the *Times Literary Supplement*. (The latter, the thirty-one-year-old Eliot enthused in a letter to his mother, was considered to be 'the highest honour possible in the field of critical literature.') Eventually, however, the strain of his dual career as a banker and writer—coupled with grief over his father's death in January 1919 and guilt over his inability to cope with his wife's increasing mental instability—Eliot suffered a nervous breakdown in the fall of 1921. Frank Kermode noted in the *London Review of Books* that in September 1911, Eliot confided in John Quinn that he had felt "under the continuous strain of trying to suppress a vague but acutely intense horror and apprehension" and he admitted to Pound that he felt that mistakes that he made had been "largely the cause" of his wife's "present catastrophic state of health." On leave from the bank, Eliot spent October of 1921 with Vivien at a Margate resort. Leaving his wife in Paris, he traveled to Lausanne, Switzerland, where he sought refuge at the sanitarium of Roger Vittoz. From the sanitarium he wrote his brother that he was trying to learn "to use all my energy without waste, to be calm when there is nothing to be gained by worry, and to concentrate without effort." There, too, on the advice of doctors who urged him to write as therapy, he completed a long poem that reflected his own emotional turmoil.

The Wasteland

"April is the cruellest month, breeding/Lilacs out of the dead land, mixing/Memory and desire, stirring/Dull roots with spring rain": so begins what would be Eliot's most famous work. In a lecture delivered at his alma mater, Eliot later said of the poem, "To me it was only the relief of a personal and wholly insignificant grouse against life." The poem was a grouse, indeed, but it was much more than personal, and anything but insignificant. Many claimed that Eliot's complaint represented the disillusionment of a generation (a claim that the poet adamantly refused to accept). And as for the poem's significance, *The Wasteland* is universally recognized as the twentieth century's most influential poem. A blatant challenge to traditional definitions of poetry, Eliot's method was considered, in some circles, to be tantamount to a literary revolution.

Written mostly between 1921 and 1922, *The Wasteland* (whose title had been suggested by Vivien) was at once innovative and controversial. Divided into five apparently unrelated sections, the poem startled readers with its multiple narrators and layers of allusions and untranslated citations. Not

Critics believe that this 1943 work reflects Eliot's decision to join the Anglican church.

everyone knew what to make of it: the March 3, 1923 issue of *Time* magazine, for example, reported that the poem was an elaborate hoax cooked up by Eliot. Others, however, immediately recognized its brilliance. Ezra Pound, to whom Eliot had given a copy of the poem in January 1922, was convinced that the poem—although in need of revision at that time—was the work of a genius. "About enough, Eliot's poem," Pound once said, "to make the rest of us shut up shop." The final version of *The Wasteland* reflected many of Pound's suggested revisions, which substantially reduced its length. Published in England in October 1922 in the inaugural issue of the *Criterion* (a quarterly journal Eliot had convinced Lady Rothermere to finance) it appeared in the United States within one month, in the *Dial*, which rewarded the author with $2,000.

Eliot later explained to the *Paris Review* that he had written the poem in an effort to get something of his chest, and that "one doesn't know quite what it is that one needs to get off the chest until one's got it off." Influenced by recent studies in ethnology and psychology, Eliot acknowledged two profound influences in his critical notes *to The Wasteland:* author Jessie Weston, whose *From Ritual to Romance* attempts to find an antecedent that links all stories concerning the Holy Grail, and James Frazer's compendious work on religious history, *The Golden Bough* (published in twelve volumes from 1890 to 1915).

Two themes permeate Eliot's poem: the fragmented nature of the present and the meaning-filled continuity of tradition. Composed of five sections—"The Burial of the Dead," "A Game of Chess," "The Fire Sermon," "Death by Water," and "What the Thunder Said"—the poem is a montage of disjointed images, stockpiled allusions to hundreds of other texts, multiple voices, and various styles. Writing in *Dictionary of Literary Biography*, Michael Beehler explained the thematic significance of the fragmentation of Eliot's poem: "'These fragments I have shored against my ruins,' says the speaker near the end, striking a personal note within an impersonal cacophony of allusions, quotes, and echoes that left many readers stunned and baffled. The disorder of modern civilization and the shattered subjectivity of the individual soul constitute a waste land through which the speaker seeks for a redeeming word."

In spite of the difficulty posed by interpretation, the poem expresses hope that the dual themes of a fragmented present and unifying tradition will become integrated—separate yet complementary like two distinct musical themes. Integral to this process is the reader, whose collaboration is fundamental to Eliot's poem: the fragmentation and allusive quality of the poem force the reader into an active role. Brooker, writing in *Dictionary of Literary Biography*, cited Eliot's own words to explain his motive for soliciting audience collaboration: "Deprived of a shared mythic or religious frame, the modern artist was forced to come up with other means of unity, other grounds for collaboration with an audience." He had to find, as Eliot put it in his *Dial* review of James Joyce's *Ulysses*, "a way of controlling, of ordering, of giving a shape and a significance to the immense panorama of futility and anarchy which is contemporary history."

The Pope of Russell Square and "The Hollow Men"

Eliot returned to his job at Lloyd's, although Pound and other of his friends attempted to make it possible, financially, for him to get away from the bank to devote more time to his writing. The poet later claimed, however, that he preferred not to turn his entire attention to writing: asked whether the optimal career for a poet would involve only reading and writing, Eliot told Donald Hall, "No, . . . it is very dangerous to give an optimal career for everybody. . . . I feel quite sure that if I'd started by having independent means, if I hadn't had to bother about earning a living and could have given all my time to poetry, it would have had a deadening influence on me." Able to write productively for only three hours a day, he further claimed, "a poet must be deliberately lazy. One should write as little as one possibly can. I always try to make the whole business seem as unimportant as I can."

Beginning in 1922, the *Criterion* (whose title had also been provided by Vivien), became a major intellectual outlet for Eliot, who edited the journal until 1939. Responsible for selecting and commissioning works to appear in the journal, he provided a platform for such writers as T. E. Hulme, Wyndham Lewis, Charles Maurras, John Middleton Murry, Ezra Pound, Marcel Proust, Paul Valery, Virginia Woolf, and W. B. Yeats. Eliot wrote little poetry during this period, focusing instead on critical prose. His articles did much to shape the literary opinions of his contemporaries: he was largely responsible, for example, for the favorable reassessment of a number of authors, including Donne, Dryden, Marvell, and lesser-known Elizabethan dramatists. Milton and some of the Romantic poets, on the other hand, did not fare so well in Eliot's estimation (although he recanted a number of opinions, including his devaluation of Milton, in later criticism).

Eliot's role as an arbiter of literary taste was solidified in 1925 when he left the bank to assume a position on the board of directors at the London publishing house of Faber & Gwyer (later Faber & Faber). "This man who seemed so unapproachable," noted Stephen Spender, "was the most approached by younger poets—and the most helpful to them—of any poet of his generation." Spender further recalled that W. H. Auden once informed him that "of all the older writers with whom we had dealings, Eliot was the most consistently friendly, the least malicious, envious, and vain." Comfortably ensconced in a community of like-minded intellectuals, Eliot, who enjoyed a reputation as "the Pope of Russell Square," remained at Faber & Faber until the end of his life.

The same year that Eliot assumed the editorial directorship of Faber, "The Hollow Men" was published. Written in fragments over the course of two or three years, the poem, which appeared as a single piece in *Poems 1909-1925*, echoes the concerns and desperate tone of *The Wasteland*. The style, too, resembles that of a portion of the earlier poem: the water dripping song in "What the Thunder Said" (which Eliot once proclaimed to be the best part of *The Wasteland*). "The Hollow Men" revolves around four primary allusions: Joseph Conrad's *Heart of Darkness*, Dante's *Divine Comedy*, Shakespeare's *Julius Caesar*, and an event in English history—the Gunpowder Plot of 1605—in which Guy Fawkes was involved in a conspiracy to blow up the Houses of Parliament. A highly personal account of the pain and disappointment implicit in lost idealism, "The Hollow Men" is considered by some to be Eliot's most beautiful poem.

Eliot's burgeoning reputation as an intellectual led to his being invited, in 1926, to deliver the Clark Lectures at Trinity College, Cambridge. These lectures concerned themselves with Eliot's vision of literary history and articulated a number of critical terms which both informed his poetry and transformed the subsequent practice of literary criticism. Among the most celebrated is the notion of "dissociation of sensibility." Eliot employed the term, John Paul Pritchard noted in *Criticism in America*, "to indicate [an] inability to 'devour any kind of experience.'" Also critical to Eliot's literary vocabulary is the term "objective correlative"—denoting the situation, thing, or event which becomes, in essence, a formula for a particular emotion, as expressed through art.

Religious Conversion

Increasingly desirous of a public and regimented source of authority and system of belief, Eliot arrived at a decision to convert to the Anglican Church by a process of elimination. On June 29, 1927, he was baptized in a small church at Finstock near Oxford. In a 1932 article titled

---

If you enjoy the works of T. S. Eliot, you may also want to check out the following:

The poetry of W. H. Auden.
The works of poet Ezra Pound, one of the fathers of modernism.
The works of James Joyce, including *Dubliners*, 1914, and *A Portrait of the Artist as a Young Man*, 1916.

"Christianity and Communism," Eliot explained his need to embrace Christianity: "In my own case, I believe that one of the reasons [for being drawn to Christianity] was that the Christian scheme seemed to me the only one which would work . . . the only possible scheme which found a place for values which I must maintain or perish." Less than six months after his baptism, in November 1927, Eliot, who had enthusiastically embraced British culture, became a naturalized citizen.

Eliot's poetry, following his religious conversion, underwent significant change: the "Ariel Poems" (1927-1930), while stylistically consistent with Eliot's earlier verse, introduce a more blatant religious dimension to the poet's thematic concerns. The collection, which comprises *Journey of the Magi, A Song for Simeon, Animula*, and *Marina*, articulate both the hope and doubt of the religious convert. *Ash Wednesday*, published in 1930, was also explicitly Christian in inspiration. At once an expression of spiritual longing and a loss of hope, the poem—which posits the necessity of conversion—finds order in the Christian liturgy and the figure of Mary.

Eliot wrote little poetry in the years soon after the publication of *Ash Wednesday*. While continuing his editorial duties at Faber & Faber, he produced a number of essays and several plays. A highly sought-after lecturer—in spite of his condescending and aloof demeanor—he was appointed to the Charles Eliot Norton professorship of poetry at Harvard University in 1932-1933. Eliot, who had not returned to his native country for seventeen years, delivered a series of eight lectures at Harvard (published in 1933 as *The Use of Poetry and The Use of Criticism*) and elsewhere, including the University of California at Los Angeles, Princeton, Yale, and the University of Virginia. The extended trip to America did more to separate Eliot from his adoptive country: it initiated a formal separation from his wife, who showed no signs of regaining mental health.

Four Quartets

The publication of *Four Quartets,* Eliot's last major poem, brought to an end what had been a relatively unproductive poetic period. Published in 1943, this ambitious sequence comprised a collection of poems which had been written and issued in four volumes over a seven-year span beginning in 1935: "Burnt Norton" (1936), "East Coker" (1940), "The Dry Salvages" (1941), and "Little Gidding" (1942). Each of the sections is named for a landscape significant to the author. "Burnt Norton" refers to a country house in Gloucestershire where Eliot spent time during the summer of 1934 (accompanied by his American friend Emily Hale, a drama professor and amateur actress whom he had gotten to know at Harvard). East Coker is named after a village in Somersetshire which represented the ancestral home of the Eliot family (to which the poet's ashes were later returned). A dangerous cluster of rocks lo-

cated off the coast of Cape May, Massachusetts, where Eliot had spent summers with his family as a youth, is the physical inspiration of the "Dry Salvages" section. The final quartet, "Little Gidding" is named for a small village in Huntingdonshire. Having visited the village in 1936, the poet had been attracted to its seventeenth-century history, at which time Little Gidding had been comprised of a small group of Christians, led by Nicholas Ferrar, who gave up wealth and position to pursue simple lives of work and prayer.

Noted for its attention to sound and music, *Four Quartets* is a long meditation on a number of themes, most notably time and history. "To be conscious," the first section asserts, "is not to be in time"; but in the same section the poet declares "Only through time time is conquered." Brooker explained Eliot's paradoxical view of time in *Dictionary of Literary Biography:* "Whereas [Eliot's] earlier poems had been centered on the isolated individual, *Four Quartets* is centered on the isolated moment, the fragment of time which takes its meaning from and gives its meaning to a pattern, a pattern at once in time, continuously changing until the supreme moment of death completes it, and also out of time. Since the individual lives

This adaptation of *Murder in the Cathedral* starred John Westbrook as Thomas Becket.

and has his being only in fragments, he can never quite know the whole pattern, but in certain moments, he can experience the pattern in miniature."

While the poem concerns itself, like Eliot's earlier works, with the fragmented nature of man's existence, it expresses a certain optimism and confidence in a transcendent pattern which animates and gives meaning to this fragmentation. In short, it reflects the poet's conversion. Brooker noted the poem's explicitly Christian vision of time, and, ultimately, of the function of poetry: "This moment of sudden illumination, in and out of time, Eliot associates with the Word-made-flesh, the Incarnation; and also with the word-made-art, poetry. . . . Both idea and form issue ultimately from Eliot's new 'scheme,' the Christian religion; and his masterpiece, like Milton's is a theodicy, a vindication of the ways of God to man."

Eliot considered *Four Quartets* to be his best work—and in particular, the final section, "Little Gidding." He told Donald Hall: ". . . I'd like to think [the poems that comprise Four Quartets] get better as they go on. The second is better than the first, the third is better than the second, and the fourth is the best of all. At any rate, that's the way I flatter myself." Although some critics found the poem to be pretentious and poorly composed, most saw it as did the poet—as the pinnacle of Eliot's poetic career.

Final Years and Accolades

Although *Four Quartets* proved to be his swan song as a poet, Eliot continued to garner honors and awards for his position as a man of letters. In 1948 he was awarded the Nobel Prize for Literature "for his work as a trail-blazing pioneer of modern poetry"—an honor Eliot received with ironic satisfaction. Also that year he was awarded the Order of Merit, England's most coveted civilian honor, by George VI. Added to these honors were numerous international prizes in the humanities, including the Hanseatic-Goethe Prize in 1954 and the Dante Gold Medal in 1959, and honorary doctorates from prestigious universities, including Harvard. Eliot's popularity extended far beyond the ivory-tower domain. Crowds flocked to his lectures (the 14,0000-member audience in attendance at his 1956 lecture at the University of Minnesota is considered to be the largest crowd

ever to attend a lecture on literature). Popular magazines (such as *Time*, which ran a cover story on Eliot in March 1950), featured him as a celebrity. So popular was he that the American expatriate was made "Honorary Deputy Sheriff" of Dallas County, Texas.

Eliot's personal life had also undergone significant change beginning in the late 1940s. After years of illness and institutionalization, Vivien Eliot died in January 1947, freeing Eliot from what had been a devastating emotional burden. Two years later, a woman named Esme Valerie Fletcher entered his life, working as his secretary at Faber & Faber. In 1957, the sixty-nine year old Eliot married Valerie, nearly twenty years his junior. The marriage was a happy one. Robert Giroux recalled in the *Washington Post Book World*: "'Radiant' is not a word one would ordinarily apply to T. S. Eliot, yet it is an accurate description of the last eight years of his life, during his second marriage. More than once in those years I heard him say, 'I'm the luckiest man in the world.' I remember Tom and Valerie's arrival at the pier in Nassau: they came down the gangplank holding hands and beaming."

Following a period of illness, Eliot died of emphysema and related complications on January 4, 1965—before the November publication of his final collection of essays, *To Criticize the Critic and Other Writings* (the title essay of which examines the author's critical career). "Our age," concluded the poet's lengthy obituary in *Life* magazine, "beyond any doubt has been, and will continue to be, the Age of Eliot." Recognized as "The most influential English poet of his time" by the London *Times*, Eliot was honored even in death. On February 4, 1965, Eliot's memorial service was held at Westminster Abbey. On June 14 of that year, the Globe Theatre in London presented a program entitled "Homage to T. S. Eliot." During the program, poems—selected by W. H. Auden—were recited by Laurence Olivier, Peter O'Toole, Paul Scofield, and Andrei Voznesensky. Henry Moore contributed a large sculpture, "The Archer," to the program, while Igor Stravinsky dedicated a choral work, "Introitus," to Eliot's memory. In 1988, numerous conferences, publications, and other activities marked the centenary of Eliot's birth, indicating the continued significance of his literary contribution.

In spite of the magnitude of his fame, Eliot had remained unaffected by his notoriety. "He was, above all, a humble man," claimed the *Times* obituary; "firm, even stubborn at times, but with no self-importance; quite unspoilt by fame; free from spiritual or intellectual pride." Eliot himself once commented on his celebrity: "One seems to become a myth, a fabulous creature that doesn't exist. One doesn't feel any different. It isn't that you get bigger to fit the world, the world gets smaller to fit you."

"No! I am not Prince Hamlet, nor was meant to be;
Am an attendant lord, one that will do
To swell a progress, start a scene or two,
Advise the prince, no doubt, an easy tool,
Deferential, glad to be of use,
Politic, cautious, and meticulous;
Full of high sentence, but a bit obtuse;
At times, indeed, almost ridiculous—
Almost, at times, the Fool.

I grow old. . . I grow old. . .
I shall wear the bottoms of my trousers rolled.

Shall I part my hair behind? Do I dare to eat a peach?
I shall wear white flannel trousers, and walk upon the beach.
I have heard the mermaids singing, each to each.

I do not think that they will sing to me.

I have seen them riding seaward on the waves
Combing the white hair of the waves blown back
When the wind blows the water white and black.

We have lingered in the chambers of the sea
By sea-girls wreathed with seaweed red and brown
Till human voices wake us, and we drown."

T. S. Eliot, *The Love Song of J. Alfred Prufrock*

■ Works Cited

Adams, Robert M., "The Beast in the Jungle," *New York Review of Books*, November 10, 1988.

Beehler, Michael, "T. S. Eliot," *Dictionary of Literary Biography*, Volume 63: *Modern American Critics, 1920-1955*, Gale, 1988, pp. 98-122.

Brooker, Jewel Spears, "T. S. Eliot," *Dictionary of Literary Biography*, Volume 45: *American Poets, 1880-1945*, Gale, 1986, pp. 150-181.

Brooker, Jewel Spears, "T. S. Eliot Centennial: The Return of Old Possum," *Dictionary of Literary Biography Yearbook*, Volume 88, Gale, 1989.

Eliot, T. S., "Christianity and Communism," *Listener*, March, 1932.

Frye, Northrop, *T. S. Eliot*, Oliver & Boyd, 1963.

Giroux, Robert, "Remembering T. S. Eliot: Poet, Editor and Friend," *Washington Post Book World*, December 18, 1988, pp. 1, 11.

Hall, Donald, "The Art of Poetry, I: T. S. Eliot," *Paris Review*, Spring/Summer, 1959, republished in *Writers at Work*, second series (New York: Viking, 1963), pp. 91-110; and in Donald Hall, *Remembering Poets* (New York: Harper & Row, 1977), pp. 203-21.

Kermode, Frank, "Feast of St. Thomas," *London Review of Books*, September 29, 1988, pp. 3-6.

Pritchard, John Paul, *Criticism in America*, University of Oklahoma Press, 1956.

Scott-James, R. A., *Fifty Years of English Literature, 1900-1950*, Longmans, Green, 1951.

Sinclair, May, "'Prufrock and Other Observations': A Criticism," *The Little Review*, December, 1917.

Spender, Stephen, *T. S. Eliot*, Viking, 1975.

■ For More Information See

BOOKS

Ackroyd, Peter, *T. S. Eliot: A Life*, Simon & Schuster, 1984.

Aiken, Conrad, *A Reviewer's ABC*, World Publishing, 1958.

Albright, Daniel, *Quantum Poetics: Yeats, Pound, Eliot, and the Science of Modernism*, Cambridge University Press (New York), 1997.

Alvarez, A., *Stewards of Excellence*, Scribner, 1958.

Asher, Kenneth George, *T. S. Eliot and Ideology*, Cambridge University Press (New York City), 1995.

Austin, William James, *A Deconstruction of T. S. Eliot: The Fire and the Rose*, Edwin Mellen Press (Lewiston, NY), 1997.

Blalock, Susan E., *Guide to the Secular Poetry of T. S. Eliot*, G. K. Hall (New York City), 1996.

Bogard, Travis, and William I. Oliver, editors, *Modern Drama: Essays in Criticism*, Oxford University Press, 1965.

Bradbrook, Muriel, *T. S. Eliot*, revised edition, Longmans, Green, 1963.

Braybrooke, Neville, editor, *T. S. Eliot: A Symposium for His Seventieth Birthday*, Farrar, Straus, 1958.

Braybrooke, Neville, *T. S. Eliot*, Eerdmans, 1967.

Breit, Harvey, *The Writer Observed*, World Publishing, 1956.

Brooker, Jewel Spears, *Mastery and Escape: T. S. Eliot and the Dialectic of Modernism*, University of Massachusetts Press (Amherst), 1994.

Browne, E. Martin, *The Making of T. S. Eliot's Plays*, Cambridge University Press, 1969.

Childs, Donald J., *T. S. Eliot: Mystic, Son, and Lover*, St. Martin's (New York City), 1997.

Concise Dictionary of American Literary Biography: The New Maturity, 1929-1941, Gale, 1989.

Contemporary Literary Criticism, Gale, Volume 1, 1973, Volume 2, 1974, Volume 3, 1975, Volume 6, 1976, Volume 9, 1978, Volume 10, 1979, Volume 13, 1980, Volume 15, 1980, Volume 24, 1983, Volume 34, 1985, Volume 41, 1987, Volume 55, 1989, Volume 57, 1990.

Cooper, John Xiros, *T. S. Eliot and the Ideology of Four Quarters*, Cambridge University Press (New York City), 1995.

Dawson, J. L., *A Concordance to the Complete Poems and Plays of T. S. Eliot*, Cornell University Press (Ithaca), 1995.

Dictionary of Literary Biography, Gale, Volume 7: *Twentieth-Century American Dramatists*, 1981, Volume 10: *Modern British Dramatists, 1940-1945*, 1982, Volume 45: *American Poets, 1880-1945, First Edition*, 1986, Volume 63: *Modern American Critics, 1920-1955*, 1988.

Donoghue, Denis, *Modern British and American Verse Drama*, Princeton University Press, 1959.

Enig, Rainer, *Modernism in Poetry: Motivation, Structures, and Limits*, Longman, 1996.

Gardner, Helen, *The Art of T. S. Eliot*, Dutton, 1959.

Gordon, Lyndall, *Eliot's Early Years*, Oxford University Press, 1977.

Gordon, Lyndall, *Eliot's New Life*, Farrar, Straus, 1988.

Gregory, Elizabeth, *Quotation and Modern American Poetry: Imaginary Gardens with Real Toads*, Rice University Press (Houston), 1995.

Harwood, John, *Eliot to Derrida: The Poverty of Interpretation*, St. Martin's Press, 1995.

Headings, Philip R., *T. S. Eliot*, Twayne, 1964.

Howarth, Herbert, *Notes on Some Figures Behind T. S. Eliot*, Houghton, 1964.

Howe, Irving, editor, *Modern Literary Criticism*, Beacon, 1958.

Hyman, Stanley Edgar, editor, *The Critical Performance*, Vintage, 1956.

Jones, Genesius, *Approach to the Purpose: A Study of the Poetry of T. S. Eliot*, Hodder & Stoughton, 1964.

Julius, Anthony, *T. S. Eliot, Anti-Semitism, and Literary Form*, Cambridge University Press, 1995.

Kim, Dal-Yong, *Puritan Sensibility in T. S. Eliot's Poetry*, P. Lang (New York City), 1994.

Lentricchia, Frank, *Modernist Quartet*, Cambridge University Press (New York City), 1994.

Lumley, Frederick, *New Trends in 20th Century Drama*, Oxford University Press, 1967.

Malamud, Randy, *Where the Words are Valid: T. S. Eliot's Communities of Drama*, Greenwood Press (Westport, CT), 1994.

Matthiessen, F. O., *The Achievement of T. S. Eliot*, revised edition, Oxford University Press, 1947.

Moody, Anthony David, editor, *The Cambridge Companion to T. S. Eliot*, Cambridge University Press (New York City), 1994.

Moody, *Thomas Stearns Eliot, Poet*, Cambridge University Press (Cambridge), 1994.

Moody, *Mapping T. S. Eliot's Peregrinations*, Cambridge University Press (New York City), 1996.

Morrison, Paul A., *The Poetics of Fascism: Ezra Pound, T. S. Eliot, Paul de Man*, Oxford University Press (New York City), 1996.

Phillips, Caroline, *The Religious Quest in the Poetry of T. S. Eliot*, Edwin Mellen Press (Lewiston), 1995.

Rexroth, Kenneth, *Assays*, New Directions, 1961.

Sharma, R. S., *Indian Response to T. S. Eliot*, Atlantic Publishers (New Delhi), 1994.

Smith, Grover Cleveland, *T. S. Eliot and the Use of Memory*, Bucknell University Press, 1996.

Southam, B. C., *A Guide to the Selected Poems of T. S. Eliot*, Harcourt Brace (San Diego), 1996.

Tate, Allen, editor, *T. S. Eliot: The Man and His Work*, Dell, 1966.

Timmerman, John H., *T. S. Eliot's Ariel Poems: The Poetics of Recovery*, Bucknell University Press (Lewisburg, PA), 1994.

Tratner, Michael, *Modernism and Mass Politics: Joyce, Woolf, Eliot, Yeats*, Stanford University Press (Stanford), 1995.

Tynan, Kenneth, *Curtains*, Atheneum, 1961.

Unger, Leonard, editor, *T. S. Eliot: A Selected Critique*, Rinehart, 1948.

Unger, Leonard, *T. S. Eliot*, University of Minnesota Press, 1961.

Untermeyer, Louis, *Lives of the Poets*, Simon & Schuster, 1959.

Weales, Gerald, *Religion in Modern English Drama*, University of Pennsylvania Press, 1961.

Wolosky, Shira, *Language Mysticism: The Negative Way of Language in Eliot, Beckett, and Celan*, Stanford University Press (Stanford), 1995.

PERIODICALS

America, September 17, 1994, p. 26.

American Literature, January, 1962.

American Quarterly, summer, 1961.
Arizona Quarterly, spring, 1966.
Atlantic Monthly, May, 1965.
Book Week, February 13, 1966.
Canadian Forum, February, 1965.
Contemporary Literature, winter, 1968.
Criticism, fall, 1966; winter, 1967.
Drama, summer, 1967.
Encounter, March, 1965; April, 1965; November, 1965.
Esquire, August, 1965.
Listener, June 25, 1967.
Nation, October 3, 1966.
New Leader, November 6, 1967.
New Republic, May 20, 1967; December 19, 1994, p. 34.
New Statesman, October 11, 1963; March 13, 1964.
New York Review of Books, March 3, 1966.
New York Times, January 5, 1965; June 14, 1965; August 22, 1989; September 23, 1996, p. B1.
New York Times Book Review, November 19, 1967; July 14, 1996, p. 30; April 26, 1998, p. 36.
New York Times Magazine, September 21, 1958.
Observer, June 11, 1967.
Partisan Review, spring, 1966.
Publishers Weekly, December 10, 1962.
Quarterly Review of Literature, numbers 1-2 (double issue), 1967.

Saturday Review, September 13, 1958; October 19, 1963; February 8,1964.
Sewanee Review, winter, 1962, spring, 1967.
Southwest Review, summer, 1965.
Times (London), September 29, 1958.
Times Educational Supplement, September 26, 1958.
Times Literary Supplement, June 1, 1967; October 2, 1992, p. 10; July 8, 1994, p. 3.
Tribune Books (Chicago), July 24, 1994, p. 5.
Virginia Quarterly Review, autumn, 1967.
Wall Street Journal, September 12, 1996, p. A12.
Washington Post Book World, May 22, 1994, p. 4.

■ Obituaries

BOOKS

Brittanica Book of the Year, 1966.
Current Biography Yearbook, 1965.

PERIODICALS

Criticism, spring, 1965.
Massachusetts Review, winter, 1965.
Newsweek, January 18, 1965.
New York Times, January 5, 1965.
Publishers Weekly, January 11, 1965.*

—Sketch by Marie J. MacNee

Philip José Farmer

■ Personal

Born January 26, 1918, in North Terre Haute, IN; son of George (a civil and electrical engineer) and Lucile Theodora (Jackson) Farmer; married Elizabeth Virginia Andre, May 10, 1941; children: Philip Laird, Kristen. *Education:* Attended University of Missouri, 1936-37, 1942; Bradley University, B.A., 1950; Arizona State University, graduate study, 1961-62.

■ Addresses

Home—5911 North Isabell Ave., Peoria, IL 61614. *Agent*—Ted Chichak, Scott Meredith Literary Agency, 845 Third Ave., New York, NY 10022.

■ Career

Writer. Worked at various jobs, 1936-56, with some periods as full-time writer; General Electric, Syracuse, NY, technical writer, 1956-58; Motorola, Scottsdale, AZ, technical writer, 1959-62; Bendix, Ann Arbor, MI, 1962; Motorola, Phoenix, AZ, 1962-65; McDonnell-Douglas, Santa Monica, CA, technical writer, 1965-69; free-lance writer, 1965-67, 1969—. *Military service:* U.S. Army Air Forces, 1942-43, aviation cadet. *Member:* Authors Guild, Authors League of America, Society of Technical Writers and Editors, Burroughs Bibliophiles, American Association for the Advancement of Science.

■ Awards, Honors

Hugo Award, World Science Fiction Convention, 1952, as the best new writer in the science fiction field, 1967, for best novella, "Riders of the Purple Wage," and 1971, for best novel, *To Your Scattered Bodies Go.*

■ Writings

The Green Odyssey, Ballantine, 1957.
Flesh (also see below), Beacon, 1960.
Strange Relations (short stories), Ballantine, 1960.
A Woman a Day, Beacon, 1960, published as *The Day of Timestop,* Lancer, 1968 (published in England as *Timestop!,* Quartet, 1973).
The Lovers, Ballantine, 1961.
The Alley God (short stories), Ballantine, 1962.
Fire and the Night, Regency, 1962.
Tongues of the Moon, Pyramid Press, 1964.
Inside Outside, Ballantine, 1964.

Cache from Outer Space, also published as *The Celestial Blueprint, and Other Stories,* Ace, 1965, revised edition, *The Cache,* Tor, 1981.

Dare, Ballantine, 1965.

The Gates of Creation, Ace, 1966, special revised edition, Phantasia Press, 1981.

The Gate of Time, Belmont, 1966, expanded edition published as *Two Hawks from Earth,* Ace, 1979.

Night of Light, Berkley, 1966.

The Image of the Beast: An Exorcism, Ritual One (also see below), Essex House, 1968.

Blown; or, Sketches among the Ruins of My Mind: An Exorcism, Ritual Two (sequel to *The Image of the Beast;* also see below), Essex House, 1968.

A Feast Unknown: Volume IX of the Memoirs of Lord Grandrith, Essex House, 1969.

Keepers of the Secrets, Sphere, 1970, Severn House, 1985.

Lord of the Trees: Volume X of the Memoirs of Lord Grandrith (also see below), Ace, 1970.

The Mad Goblin (bound with *Lord of the Trees;* also see below), Ace, 1970.

Lord Tyger (also see below), Doubleday, 1970.

Love Song: A Gothic Romance, Brandon House, 1970, limited edition, D. McMillan, 1983.

The Stone God Awakens, Ace, 1970.

Down in the Black Gang, and Other Stories, Doubleday, 1971.

The Wind Whales of Ishmael, Ace, 1971.

Tarzan Alive: A Definitive Biography of Lord Greystoke, Doubleday, 1972.

Time's Last Gift, Ballantine, 1972.

The Book of Philip José Farmer; or, The Wares of Simple Simon's Custard Pie and Space Man, DAW, 1973, revised edition, Berkley, 1982.

Doc Savage: His Apocalyptic Life, Doubleday, 1973.

The Other Log of Phileas Fogg, DAW, 1973.

Traitor to the Living, Ballantine, 1973.

Hadon of Ancient Opar, illustrations by Roy Krenkel, DAW, 1974.

(Under pseudonym Kilgore Trout) *Venus on the Half-Shell,* Dell, 1974.

Flight to Opar, DAW, 1976.

(With J. H. Rosny) *Ironcastle,* DAW, 1978.

Dark is the Sun, Ballantine, 1979.

Riverworld and Other Stories, Berkley, 1979.

Image of the Beast (contains *Image of the Beast* and *Blown*), Berkley, 1979.

Jesus on Mars (also see below), Pinnacle, 1979.

Lord of the Trees [and] *The Mad Goblin,* Ace, 1980.

Riverworld War: The Suppressed Fiction of Philip José Farmer (short stories, contains *Jesus on Mars*), Ellis, 1980.

The Unreasoning Mask, Putnam, 1981.

Flesh [and] *Lord Tyger,* New American Library, 1981.

A Barnstormer in Oz; or, A Rationalization and Extrapolation of the Split-Level Continuum, Phantasia, 1982.

Father to the Stars, Pinnacle, 1982.

Stations of the Nightmare, Tor, 1982.

River of Eternity, Phantasia, 1983.

The Grand Adventure (short stories), Berkley, 1984.

The Classic Philip José Farmer, 1952-1964, edited by Martin H. Greenberg, Crown, 1984.

The Cache, Tor, 1986.

Escape from Loki, Bantam, 1991.

Nothing Burns in Hell, Forge, 1998.

"WORLD OF TIERS" SERIES

The Maker of Universes: The Enigma of the Man-Leveled Cosmos, Ace, 1965, revised edition, Phantasia, 1980.

The Gates of Creation, Ace, 1966.

A Private Cosmos, Ace, 1968, special revised edition, Phantasia, 1981.

Behind the Walls of Terra, Ace, 1970.

The Lavalite World, Ace, 1977.

The World of Tiers, two volumes (Volume 1 contains: *The Maker of Universes* and *The Gates of Creation;* Volume 2 contains: *A Private Cosmos, Behind the Walls of Terra,* and *The Lavalite World*), Thomas Nelson-Doubleday, 1980.

Greatheart Silver, illustrations by Nick Cuti, Tor, 1982.

The Purple Book, Tor, 1982.

Red Orc's Rage, Tor, 1991.

More Than Fire: A World of Tiers Novel, Tor, 1993.

"RIVERWORLD" SERIES

To Your Scattered Bodies Go, Putnam, 1971.

The Fabulous Riverboat, Putnam, 1971.

The Dark Design, Berkley, 1977.

The Magic Labyrinth, Berkley, 1980.

Philip José Farmer: The Complete Riverworld Novels, five volumes, Berkley, 1982.

Gods of Riverworld, Phantasia, 1983.

"DAYWORLD" SERIES

Dayworld, Putnam, 1983.

Dayworld Rebel, Putnam, 1987.

Dayworld Breakup, Tor, 1990.

OTHER

The Work of Philip José Farmer (short stories), 1973.

(Compiler) *Mother Was a Lovely Beast: A Feral Man Anthology—Fiction and Fact about Humans Raised by Animals*, Chilton, 1974.

(Author, under pseudonym John H. Watson; editor, under name Philip José Farmer) *The Adventure of the Peerless Peer, by John H. Watson, M.D.*, Aspen Press, 1974.

(With Piers Anthony) *The Caterpillar's Question*, Ace, 1992.

(Editor) *Quest to Riverworld*, Warner, 1993.

Work appears in anthologies. Contributor to *Visual Encyclopedia of Science Fiction*. Contributor of short stories to *Adventure, Magazine of Fantasy and Science Fiction, Startling Stories,* and others.

■ Adaptations

The film rights to the "Riverworld" series, including *To Your Scattered Bodies Go, The Fabulous Riverboat, The Dark Design, The Magic Labyrinth,* and *Gods of Riverworld,* were sold to Walt Disney Productions in 1990.

■ Sidelights

Philip José Farmer is a prolific science fiction writer whose success is based on his deft mixture of three primary components, "religion, sex, and violence," in each of his many works, according to Franz Rottensteiner in *Science-Fiction Studies*. In addition, he is often credited with introducing the first mature depiction of human-alien sexual encounters into the genre with his 1961 book, *The Lovers*. Although Farmer is sometimes dismissed as a writer of formula fiction whose least successful works are written "hastily, sometimes downright sloppily," as reviewer Leslie A. Fiedler once charged in the *Los Angeles Times,* his admirers find Farmer's exploration of timeless themes within an action-oriented adventure plot a winning combination. Furthermore, "the number, richness, and complexity of Farmer's series," according to Thomas L. Wymer in the *Dictionary of Literary Biography,* "can lay claim to uniqueness."

Farmer's "Riverworld" series, which Roland Green of *Booklist* called "one of the largest, most ambitious, and least conventional works of modern

This first installment of the "Riverworld" series received a Hugo Award for best novel in 1971.

science fiction," may form the basis of his late-career reputation. The series is set on the planet Riverworld, where all of Earth's rivers are combined in one mammoth, serpentine river, along which live all the humans ever born, and a few of the species that preceded homo sapiens. This setting allows the author to create scenarios in which Mark Twain meets Cyrano de Bergerac, and the English King John interacts with Hitler's self-appointed successor, Hermann Goering, among others. In the first installment, *To Your Scattered Bodies Go*, Sir Richard Burton, the Victorian explorer and Renaissance man, dies in 1890 and is transported to Riverworld, where he immediately sets off to find the source of the river and of his reincarnation. "The auspicious opening [of the series] was a difficult act to follow, and many Farmerites wondered whether the Riverworld was wide enough to sustain a projected tetralogy," remarked Peter Stoler in *Time* magazine.

Farmer began the "Riverworld" series in 1952 when he entered a writing contest sponsored by two publishing companies. He won the contest with his first "Riverworld" novel but, before he could collect his $4,000 prize money, one of the publishers went bankrupt, taking his prize money with it. Worse, Farmer lost the rights to his book for many years. It wasn't until the late 1960s that the Riverworld idea was revived. He wrote a series of novelettes for magazine publication that contained "very little of the original novel, aside from the basic concept," as Farmer stated in *Dream Makers: The Uncommon People Who Write Science Fiction*. When these novelettes were published together as a novel, the result was the Hugo Award-winning *To Your Scattered Bodies Go*, and the "Riverworld" series was on its way.

If you enjoy the works of Philip Jose Farmer, you may also want to check out the following books and films:

Octavia E. Butler, *Parable of the Sower*, 1993.
John Christopher's "Tripod" trilogy, including *The White Mountains*, 1967.
Robert Silverberg, *Sailing to Byzantium*, 1985.
12 Monkeys, a film starring Bruce Willis and Brad Pitt, 1995.

As a dynamic group of Earthlings discovers the origins of Riverworld, new questions surface in this fourth "Riverworld" installment.

In *The Fabulous Riverboat*, the second novel in the "Riverworld" series, Burton teams up with Alice Liddell Hargreaves (Lewis Carroll's model for his Alice) and Samuel Langhorne Clemens (best known as Mark Twain), the latter having built a steamboat to negotiate the grand river. In addition to fighting the hostile peoples they pass on their journey toward the river's headwaters, the explorers battle each other and the mysterious creators of Riverworld, the Ethicals, who are secretly in their midst. Farmer's juxtaposition of historical figures from widely divergent periods "insinuates strands of history and myth, philosophy and ribaldry" into the multi-volume adventure story, according to Stoler.

Though the series was scheduled to end with the fourth installment, *The Magic Labyrinth*, which had followed *The Dark Design* in 1980, Farmer returned in 1983 with *Gods of Riverworld*, encouraging a reviewer for *Publishers Weekly* to remark: "The Riverworld seems to pull Farmer as the Mississippi did Twain." In this work, the humans who had learned the secret of the Ethicals' power take control of Riverworld and contend with the consequences of their newfound authority. Although critics found the work flawed, it was noted that this novel, like its precursors, contains "enough action, intrigue, and Farmer's habitual game-playing with historical characters" to satisfy fans of the series, according to *Booklist* critic Roland Green.

PHILIP JOSÉ FARMER
DAYWORLD BREAKUP

By the bestselling author of RIVERWORLD

Duncan, living in an overpopulated futuristic Earth, struggles to end the corrupt Dayworld system, whereby people are allowed to be conscious only one day per week.

The "World of Tiers"

Like the "Riverworld" series, the "World of Tiers" series relies heavily on action-packed plots. "All of [the "World of Tiers" novels] are marked by an intense sense of pulp action-adventure, with fast-paced and very physical action, battles and contests, intrigues, disguises, and surprises," remarked Wymer. "But Farmer combines this action with a fascinating sense of psychological exploration." In the first installment, *The Maker of Universes*, Robert Wolff enters the World of Tiers and leads a revolt against its Lord, an evil remnant of a technologically advanced race that rule these pocket universes for their own pleasure. Although

other writers have examined man's evolution and technological development, Farmer makes "the implication that God Himself might be just another mortal playing at scientific games," Donald A. Wollheim stated in his *The Universe Makers*.

Gates of Creation, the second work in the series, finds Wolff's own father leading an invasion of the world where Wolff now reigns. In the next three novels in the series, *A Private Cosmos, Behind the Walls of Terra,* and *The Lavalite World,* the focus shifts to Kickaha, a secondary figure in the first two books and, according to Wymer, an exemplum of Farmer's "ideal nonneurotic man, afraid only of real threats and ready to risk his life without hesitation." The series ends with *Red Orc's Rage* and *More Than Fire,* books which stage a lingering battle between good and evil, represented by Kickaha and Lord Red Orc, leader of the creators of the pocket universes.

Dayworld

Farmer turned to the Earth of the future in the "Dayworld" series, in which overpopulation—caused by the conquering of poverty, hunger, and pollution—is resolved by dividing humanity into seven categories, each allowed one day of consciousness per week then consigned to suspended animation the other six. Jeff Caird is a Daybreaker, a rebel against the system who assumes seven different personalities in his quest to remain conscious seven days a week. *Dayworld,* the first book in the series, recounts Caird's struggles to integrate his personalities and escape the grip of the Earth's corrupt leaders. This book "provides further evidence of the author's vivid imagination and ingenious storytelling skills," enthused Peter L. Robertson in *Booklist.*

The first sequel, *Dayworld Rebel,* finds Farmer's protagonist (now known as Duncan) imprisoned by the authorities, escaping, and leading a band of rebels to Los Angeles. Still running in *Dayworld Breakup,* Duncan enlists the aid of a female cop in leading a revolution to end the Dayworld system. Although some critics found that the final two novels failed to live up to the promise of the first, reviewers tended to recommend that libraries purchase the books anyway, considering Farmer's popularity. "A definite acquisition, given Farmer's vast audience," concluded Roland Green in his review of *Dayworld Breakup.*

This final novel in Farmer's popular "World of Tiers" series was published in 1993—twenty-three years after the series began.

In other books, such as *The Adventure of the Peerless Peer* and *Tarzan Alive,* Farmer plays tongue-in-cheek games using famous literary characters. In *The Peerless Peer,* he concocts a new Sherlock Holmes adventure under the pseudonym of Holmes's assistant, John H. Watson. *Tarzan Alive* is a thorough biography of the "real" Tarzan that answers questions, a reviewer for the *New York Times* maintains, that "have been plaguing practically nobody at all for many years now." Under the pseudonym Kilgore Trout, Farmer wrote *Venus on the Half-Shell,* a parody of Kurt Vonnegut. Trout, a character in several of Vonnegut's novels, is a science fiction writer who has created hundreds of books, all of them unfortunately published by pornography houses who market them under rather non-SF titles. "I did it as a tribute, the highest, to an author whom I loved and admired at that time. And I identify with Trout," Farmer explains in *Dream Makers.* Farmer's parody was so well done that several critics assumed Vonnegut had written the book. "Who is Kilgore Trout?," Walton R. Collins of the *National Observer* asked. "The odds are good that he is Vonnegut. . . . You can't read a dozen pages anywhere in *Venus* without becoming morally certain you're reading Vonnegut. The style is unmistakable."

Farmer has published several collections of his shorter pieces, including the short stories and novellas that made his early reputation. In a review of *The Classic Philip José Farmer,* the critic for *Kirkus Reviews* remarked, "Farmer . . . was instrumental in kicking science fiction out of its late-1940s puritanical rut—and these six iconoclastic, imaginative yarns aptly show how and why." *Library Journal* contributor Susan L. Nickerson recommended that readers "who know Farmer only for his more recent tepid efforts" seek out this resource for examples of his early work. *Voice of Youth Advocates* contributor Susan B. Madden found Farmer's *Purple Book,* containing "Riders of the Purple Wage," "Spiders of the Purple Mage," and others, "punny, irreverent, raunchy and bizarre." *The Grand Adventure,* which includes early pieces presaging the "Riverworld" series and what became *The Adventure of the Peerless Peer,* was also highly recommended by critics, who compared these pieces favorably to more recent efforts by the popular author. "The stories are 'classic' Farmer, well constructed, readable, and more satisfying than most of his contemporary esoteric pieces," wrote Jerry L. Parsons in the *Fantasy Review.*

From his early iconoclastic and often sexually-charged works to the late pulp-adventure multi-volume series, Farmer's vast bibliography offers something for all types of science fiction fans. Farmer's fertile imagination and swift pen have combined to make him a leading figure in genre fiction for more than three decades. While he is occasionally faulted for uneven writing, he is rarely accused of poor pacing or lack of invention. And while young fans made his "Riverworld" and "World of Tiers" series best sellers, older fans cheered the reappearance in the 1980s of many of Farmer's early short pieces in several collections. Farmer commented of his many novels in *Dream Makers:* "I can see where I could have done better. I can see innumerable cases. But it's no good to go back and re-write them, because if you did you'd lose a certain primitive vigor that they have. The thing to do is to go on and write new stuff."

■ Works Cited

Review of *The Classic Philip José Farmer, Kirkus Reviews,* December 15, 1983, pp. 1273-74.

Collins, Walton R., comments in *National Observer,* May 17, 1975.

Review of *Dayworld Rebel, Publishers Weekly,* May 15, 1987, p. 270.

Fiedler, Leslie A., "Thanks for the Feast: Notes on Philip José Farmer," *Los Angeles Times,* April 23, 1972.

Review of *Gods of Riverworld, Publishers Weekly,* August 19, 1983, p. 73.

Green, Roland, review of *The Magic Labyrinth, Booklist,* July 15, 1980, p. 1656.

Green, Roland, review of *Gods of Riverworld, Booklist,* September 15, 1983, p. 113.

Green, Roland, review of *The Grand Adventure, Booklist,* December 1, 1984, p. 482.

Green, Roland, review of *Dayworld Breakup, Booklist,* May 1, 1990, p. 1666.

Green, Roland, review of *More Than Fire, Booklist,* September 15, 1993, p. 132.

Madden, Susan B., review of *Purple Book, Voice of Youth Advocates,* February, 1983, p. 44.

Review of *More Than Fire, Publishers Weekly,* October 4, 1993, p. 68.

Nickerson, Susan L., review of *The Classic Philip José Farmer, Library Journal,* February 15, 1984, p. 390.

Parsons, Jerry L., "Farmer's Latest Is a Hit!," *Fantasy Review,* January, 1985, p. 13.

Platt, Charles, *Dream Makers: The Uncommon People Who Write Science Fiction,* Berkley Publishing, 1980.

Robertson, Peter L., review of *Dayworld, Booklist,* November 15, 1984, p. 401.

Rottensteiner, Franz, "Playing around with Creation: Philip José Farmer," *Science-Fiction Studies,* fall, 1973, pp. 94-98.

Stoler, Peter, "'Riverworld' Revisited," *Time,* July 28, 1980, pp. 68-69.

Review of *Tarzan Alive, New York Times,* April 22, 1972, p. 40.

Wollheim, Donald A., *The Universe Makers,* Harper, 1971.

Wymer, Thomas L., "Philip José Farmer," *Dictionary of Literary Biography, Volume 8: Twentieth-Century American Science-Fiction Writers,* Gale, 1981, pp. 169-82.

■ For More Information See

BOOKS

The Book of Philip José Farmer, DAW, 1973.

Brizzi, Mary, *The Reader's Guide to Philip José Farmer,* Starmont, 1980.

Clareson, Thomas D., editor, *Voices for the Future,* Volume 2, Bowling Green University Popular Press, 1979.

Contemporary Literary Criticism, Volume 19, Gale Research, 1981.

Knapp, Lawrence J., *The First Editions of Philip José Farmer, Science Fiction Bibliographies 2,* David G. Turner, 1976.

Moskowitz, Sam, *Seekers of Tomorrow: Masters of Modern Science Fiction,* Hyperion, 1974.

Walker, Paul, *Speaking of Science Fiction: The Paul Walker Interviews,* Luna, 1978.

PERIODICALS

Kirkus Reviews, February 15, 1968, p. 211; November 1, 1971, p. 1179; August 15, 1993, p. 1036.

Magazine of Fantasy and Science Fiction, July, 1980, pp. 48-49.

New York Times Book Review, April 28, 1985.

Publishers Weekly, February 19, 1968, pp. 100-1; July 9, 1979, p. 102; July 30, 1982, p. 74.

Quill and Quire, April, 1985, p. 77.

School Library Journal, November, 1977, p. 78; September, 1980, pp. 90-91; October, 1981, p. 160.

Voice of Youth Advocates, August, 1982, p. 39; December, 1990, p. 296; June, 1992, p. 93; April, 1994, p. 36.

—Sketch by Mary Gillis

Barbara Hambly

■ Personal

Born August 28, 1951, in San Diego, CA. *Education:* University of California at Riverside, M.A. in medieval history; additional studies at University of Bordeaux, France.

■ Career

Freelance writer. Has worked as a research assistant, high school teacher, and karate instructor. *Member:* Science Fiction Writers of America (president).

■ Addresses

Office—c/o Del Rey Books, 201 East 50th St., New York, NY 10022.

■ Writings

"DARWATH" SERIES

The Time of the Dark, Del Rey, 1982.
The Walls of Air, Del Rey, 1983.
The Armies of Daylight, Del Rey, 1983.

Mothers of Winter, Del Rey, 1996.
Icefalcon's Quest, Del Rey, 1998.

"SUN WOLF" SERIES

The Ladies of Mandrigyn, Del Rey, 1984.
The Witches of Wenshar, Del Rey, 1987.
The Unschooled Wizard, (includes *The Ladies of the Mandrigyn* and *The Witches of Wenshar*), Doubleday, 1987.
The Dark Hand of Magic, Del Rey, 1990.

"SUN-CROSS" SERIES

The Rainbow Abyss, Del Rey, 1991.
Magicians of the Night, Del Rey, 1992.
Sun-Cross (includes *The Rainbow Abyss* and *Magicians of the Night*), Guild America, 1992.

"THE WINDROSE CHRONICLES"

The Silent Tower, Del Rey, 1986.
The Silicon Mage, Del Rey, 1988.
Darkmage (includes *The Silent Tower* and *The Silicon Mage*) Doubleday, 1988.
Dog Wizard, Del Rey, 1993.

"STAR TREK" BOOKS

Ishmael: A Star Trek Novel, Pocket, 1985.
Ghost Walker, Pocket, 1991.
Crossroad, Pocket, 1994.

NOVELS

The Quirinal Hill Affair, St. Martin's Press, 1983, published as *Search the Seven Hills*, Ballantine, 1987.

Dragonsbane, Del Rey, 1986.

Seven Hills, Ballantine, 1987.

Search the Seven Hills, Del Rey, 1987.

Those Who Hunt the Night, Del Rey, 1988, published in England as *Immortal Blood*, Unwin, 1988.

Beauty and the Beast (novelization of television script), Avon, 1989.

Song of Orpheus (novelization of television script), Avon, 1990.

Stranger at the Wedding, Del Rey, 1994, published in England as *Sorcerer's Ward*, HarperCollins, 1994.

Bride of the Rat God, Del Rey, 1994.

Travelling with the Dead, Del Rey, 1995.

Star Wars: Children of the Jedi, Del Rey, 1995.

A Free Man of Color, Bantam, 1997.

Star Wars: Planet of Twilight, Del Rey, 1997.

Fever Season, Bantam, 1998.

Dragonshadow, Del Rey, 1999.

OTHER

(Editor) *Women of the Night*, Warner Aspect, 1994.
(Editor) *Sisters of the Night*, 1995.

Contributor of short fiction to: *Xanadu 2*, edited by Jane Yolen and Martin H. Greenberg, 1994; *South from Midnight*, Southern Fried Press, 1994; *Sandman: Book of Dreams*, 1996; and *War of Worlds: Global Dispatches*, 1996. Has also written scripts for animated cartoons.

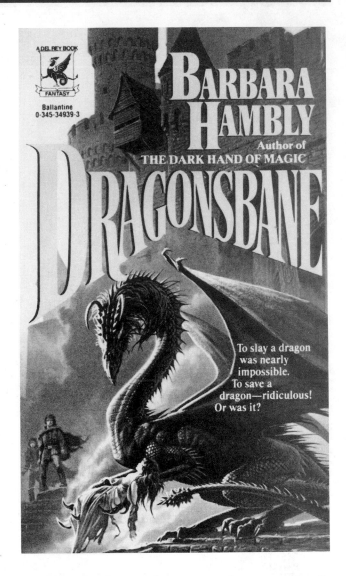

In this 1986 dragon fantasy novel, young Gareth bravely travels to the Winterlands to find dragonslayer John Aversin.

■ Work in Progress

Graveyard Dust, a "Benjamin January" mystery novel; *Fading of the Light*, a fantasy novel.

■ Sidelights

Barbara Hambly's life experiences are as varied as her fiction. The ex-model, clerk, high school teacher, black belt karate instructor, and technical writer enjoys dancing, painting, studying historical and fantasy costuming, and carpentry—and she occasionally uses these varied activities as fodder for her writing. While Hambly's novels are primarily sword-and-sorcery fantasies, she also writes in a variety of other genres—everything from vampire stories to science fiction; recently she has enjoyed success with historical mysteries such as the popular *Free Man of Color* and *Fever Season*, and she has created novelizations based on the characters in television shows like *Beauty and the Beast* and *Star Trek*.

Hambly, who has served as president of the Science Fiction Writers of America, has said that she feels the urge to write is something that's inherent. "I think a person is a writer if they HAVE to write," she said during a July 1997 online chat session with Barnes and Noble. "This is not an easy way to make a living. I think I would be doing this even if I were not making money at it. I think people who are true writers write because they have to. They can't NOT do it. They have stories in them to tell, and they have to tell them." Hambly is considered a gifted storyteller who has garnered a wide readership, and critics have praised her work. "Hambly's writing is witty and fast-paced," wrote Elizabeth Hand of the *Washington Post Book World*. David Langford, in the *St. James Guide to Fantasy Writers*, remarked that Hambly "has a special talent for reclaiming and reworking familiar themes of fantasy, making them over into a seamless gestalt which is very much her own."

Hambly was born in the Naval Hospital of San Diego, California, on August 28, 1951. She grew up in southern California, attended the University of California, Riverside, and studied for a time at the University of Bordeaux in southern France. As a girl, she was an avid reader. She fell in love with fantasy fiction after reading L. Frank Baum's classic turn-of-the-century children's tale *The Wizard of Oz*; she decided to become a writer. Hambly took a step in this direction when in 1975 she earned a master's degree in medieval history. This gave her both the research skills and the knowledge base to craft historical novels.

Hambly took her first step toward a writing career in 1978 when she penned a fantasy novel for her own enjoyment. She sold the book to a publisher on its first submission, despite the fact she did not yet have an agent. "I always wanted to be a writer but everyone kept telling me it was impossible to break into the field or make money," Hambly said in an interview with Elisabeth Sherwin in the *Davis* (CA) *Enterprise*. "I've proven them wrong on both counts."

Triumphs with "Darwath" Novels

However, it wasn't until 1982 that her writing career took off with publication of *The Time of the Dark*, the first book in the "Darwath Trilogy." The story centers on a race of creatures known as the "Dark Ones" who are eyeless, can fly, and have a taste for human flesh, and their attack on a parallel earth. Two citizens of Los Angeles, graduate student Gil Patterson and auto mechanic Rudy Solis, are drawn into the alternate world to do battle with the Dark Ones. Reviewer Michael W.

McClintock of *Science Fiction and Fantasy Book Review*, who found fault with the book, wrote that Hambly "draws Gil and Rudy effectively, and the plot shows at least the possibility of interesting development." Susan L. Nickerson in *Library Journal* described *The Time of the Dark* as "heart stopping," and noted that Hambly had written an "unusually effective" fantasy work.

The second book, *The Walls of Air*, published a year later, continues the adventure of Gil and Rudy, who have been taken to the Dark Ones' parallel world. There Rudy becomes a wizard and Gil is transformed into an elite guard. Reviews

THE NEW YORK TIMES BESTSELLER

STAR WARS

CHILDREN OF THE JEDI
BARBARA HAMBLY

Princess Leia, Han Solo, and Chewbacca search the frozen world of Belsavis for the long-lost children of the Jedi.

for this novel were mixed. Nickerson however, praised Hambly's plot for its "brisk action" and a feeling of impending menace which "keeps the reader deeply involved." The third book in the saga, *The Armies of Daylight*, gave devotees an answer to the riddle of the Dark. Roland Green of *Booklist* wrote that Hambly's work features "intelligent characterization, sound storytelling, and creative use of magic." Thirteen years after *The Armies of Daylight*, Hambly resurrected Rudy and Gil in 1996 for the novel *Mother of Winter*. Here the characters must save the earth from a glacial freeze. "The story is involving, and the narrative

intelligent," according to a *Publishers Weekly* reviewer.

If you enjoy the works of Barbara Hambly, you may also want to check out the following books and films:

P. N. Elrod, *Red Death,* 1993.
Annette Curtis Klause, *The Silver Kiss,* 1990.
Walter Mosley, *Devil in a Blue Dress,* 1990.
Interview with the Vampire, a film starring Tom Cruise and Brad Pitt, 1994.

This 1995 novel features a British espionage agent who travels on the Orient Express to save England from the notorious vampire Don Simon Ysidro.

Aside from the "Darwath" novels, the prolific Hambly has written more than two dozen other books. Among them is *Ishmael: a Star Trek Novel*, published in 1985. In Hambly's tale, one of a popular series of books based on the characters created by the late Gene Roddenberry, Spock travels back in time to visit the Earth in 1867 in an effort to thwart a Klingon plan to change human history. Roland Green of *Booklist* praised Hambly's effort, recommending it "not only for Star Trek collections but as a good novel in its own right." *Ishmael* grabs the reader's attention throughout "with humor, action and personal interplay," according to Roberta Rogow of *Voice of Youth Advocates*. Hambly added two other books to the "Star Trek" series: *Ghost Walker* in 1991 and *Crossroad* in 1994.

Hambly delved into the adventures of Princess Leia and Luke Skywalker in *Children of the Jedi* and *Planet of Twilight*, part of a series of books based on George Lucas' popular *Star Wars* films. Critics were less enthusiastic. "In her hands, the heroes of the New Republic take on a maturity and credibility that enhance their already engaging personalities," reviewer Jackie Cassada of *Library Journal* wrote of *Children of the Jedi*. Hambly's contribution rated "among the best in the series," a *Booklist* reviewer declared. The story takes Leia, Luke, Han Solo and Chewbacca on a journey to find the missing children of the Jedi. In *Planet of Twilight*, published in 1997, two factions battle for power on a planet called Nam Chorios. "Hambly is superior to most of the other SW authors at vivid word building [and] humor," wrote Roland Green of *Booklist*.

BARBARA HAMBLY
THE *NEW YORK TIMES* BESTSELLING AUTHOR
MOTHER ☾ WINTER

A deadly cold force spells doom for Darwath

Rudy and Gil attempt to save the Earth from an icy force and deadly creatures in this final book of the "Darwath" series.

Perhaps Hambly's most successful original creation is the "Sun Wolf" series, which chronicles the adventures of what Langford described as "the unbrutal mercenary Sun Wolf and his hard-bitten lady second-in-command Starhawk." *The Ladies of Mandrigyn*, the first book in the series, is a gory adventure about Sun Wolf's battle with the wizard Altiokis. It also deals with his realization of the aging process, the emergence of his own innate wizard potential, and the realization that he loves Starhawk, his longtime loyal follower. The work should "please most fantasy readers," *Library Journal* reviewer Janet Cameron predicted. Subsequent books in the "Sun Wolf" series are *The*

Witches of Wenshar and *The Dark Hand of Magic*. Hambly gave further proof of her versatility when she wrote *Dragonsbane*, a dragon fantasy novel. The book relates the adventures of a character named Prince Gareth as he deals with a demonic parent, love, rioting subjects, and a black dragon. "High school readers of both sexes will applaud with equal fervor," wrote Frank Perry of *Voice of Youth Advocates*.

Fresh Twist on Vampire Lore

In 1988 Hambly went off in another direction when she crafted a vampire story. Hambly's inventive effort had an odd twist: the vampires are the victims. *Those Who Hunt the Night* deals with a mystery being who slashes open the coffins of vampires in London and lets in lethal sunlight that allows the stalker to kill the victims as it drinks their blood. A frightened vampire enlists the help of an ex-spy to find the culprit. Susan M. Schuller, writing in *Voice of Youth Advocates*, stated that Hambly "delves into vampire lore with gusto, detailing the lust for blood and the killing urge among the undead."

While Hambly enjoyed writing her vampire book, she was so busy with other projects that a decade passed before she returned to the genre. *Traveling with the Dead* follows the adventures of James Asher, a former British espionage agent, and his wife Lydia who battle to prevent an alliance between human governments and the living dead. A *Library Journal* critic believed that *Traveling with the Dead* "captures both the subtle ambiance of turn-of-the-century political intrigue and the even more baroque pathways of the human and the inhuman heart." A reviewer in *Publishers Weekly* remarked that Hambly's "vivid portraits" of the vampires "allow them to emerge as memorable personalities distinct from the viewpoints they represent."

Mysterious New Orleans

Hambly has also ventured into the field of mystery writing. Her first novel in that genre was *A Free Man of Color*, published in 1997. Set in nineteenth-century New Orleans, the book follows the exploits of Benjamin January, a free Creole with dark brown skin. January, a trained surgeon, returns to Louisiana after living in Paris and

COME TO MARDI GRAS, 1833...
UNMASK THE SOUL OF A CITY...
AND THE TWISTED HEART OF A KILLER.

BARBARA HAMBLY

A
FREE
MAN
OF
COLOR

"MAGICALLY RICH AND POIGNANT."—*CHICAGO TRIBUNE*

Hambly received critical acclaim for this 1997 mystery novel set in nineteenth-century New Orleans.

promptly becomes a murder suspect. Hambly explained in her Barnes and Noble online interview that she did extensive research at the Historic New Orleans Collection in preparation for writing of the book. ". . . I did not think so much about writing in the voice of a black man, as writing in the voice of a historical character from another time and place," she said. Hambly's attention to detail paid off handsomely. Marilyn Stasio of the *New York Times Book Review* praised *A Free Man of Color* as a "stunning first mystery;" Dick Adler of the Chicago *Tribune Books* described it as being "magically rich and poignant." Assessing the author's work, a *Kirkus Reviews* contribu-

tor observed that Hambly has a talent for "goldstained description."

In *Fever Season*, the sequel to *A Free Man of Color*, January works at New Orlean's Charity Hospital while city is in the grip of a cholera epidemic. January also realizes that free men of color are disappearing, and his investigations into the matter lead to a horrifying conclusion. According to a *Publishers Weekly* critic, *Fever Season* is "Complex in plotting, rich in atmosphere, and written in powerful, lucid prose. . . ." A *Booklist* reviewer called the work "rich, intense, and eye-opening."

Although she juggles a seemingly unbelievable schedule, Hambly prides herself on the professionalism and thoroughness with which she practices her art. Her books go through first, second, and third drafts. Hambly begins her stories by writing a hard copy on a computer, printing it out and then going over it with a pen and rewriting, sometimes large portions, by hand. The technique has served her well. Hambly explained during the Barnes and Noble online chat that if ever she suffers from writer's block—an inability to follow through on her story—she retraces what she has written. She believes that hold-ups in her writing are likely her subconscious telling her that something is not right.

Hambly continues to maintain a hectic pace. She is working on a sequel to *Dragonsbane*, is in the process of writing *Graveyard Dust*, the third book in the Benjamin January mystery series, and she has a new fantasy novel called *Fading of the Light* in the works. Hambly, who divides her time between Los Angeles and New Orleans, shares her two homes with her author husband, George Alec Effinger, and with the couple's two Pekinese cats. Hambly has said that her greatest writing gift is always having a story to tell. As she explained in her Barnes and Noble online interview, "If everyone has one superpower, mine is—thank God and knock on wood—that so far, I seem to have a cast-iron Muse; I seem to be able to work under just about any condition."

■ Works Cited

Adler, Dick, review of *A Free Man of Color*, *Tribune Books* (Chicago), July 6, 1997, p. 2.

Cameron, Janet, review of *The Ladies of Mandrigyn*, *Library Journal*, March 15, 1985, p. 599.

Cassada, Jackie, review of *Children of the Jedi, Library Journal,* March 15, 1995, p. 101.

Review of *Children of the Jedi, Booklist,* April 1, 1995, p. 1355.

Review of *Fever Season, Booklist,* May 15, 1998.

Review of *Fever Season, Publishers Weekly,* April 27, 1998, p. 48.

Review of *A Free Man of Color, Kirkus Reviews,* May 15, 1997, p. 741.

Green, Roland, review of *The Armies of Daylight, Booklist,* September 1, 1983, p. 31.

Green, Roland, review of *Ishmael, Booklist,* July, 1985, p. 1519.

Green, Roland, review of *Planet of Twilight, Booklist,* February 1, 1997, p. 907.

Hambly, Barbara, online chat session in the barnesandnoble.com Live Events Auditorium, July 22, 1997.

Hand, Elizabeth, review of *Those Who Hunt the Night, Washington Post Book World,* January 29, 1989, p. 6.

Langford, David, "Barbara Hambly," *St. James Guide to Fantasy Writers,* Gale, 1995, pp. 261-63.

McClintock, Michael W., review of *The Time of the Dark, Science Fiction and Fantasy Book Review,* September, 1982, pp. 30-31.

Review of *Mother of Winter, Publishers Weekly,* September 16, 1996, p. 74.

Nickerson, Susan L., review of *The Time of the Dark, Library Journal,* May 15, 1982, p. 1014.

Nickerson, Susan L., review of *The Walls of Air, Library Journal,* March 15, 1983, p. 603.

Perry, Frank, review of *Dragonsbane, Voice of Youth Advocates,* August/October, 1986, p. 162.

Rogow, Roberta, review of *Ishmael, Voice of Youth Advocates,* February, 1986, pp. 393-94.

Schuller, Susan M., review of *Those Who Hunt the Night, Voice of Youth Advocates,* April, 1989, p. 42.

Sherwin, Elisabeth, interview with Barbara Hambly, *Davis (CA) Enterprise,* October 29, 1995.

Stasio, Marilyn, review of *Fever Season, New York Times Book Review,* August 2, 1998, p. 24.

Review of *Traveling with the Dead, Library Journal,* August, 1995, p. 122.

Review of *Traveling with the Dead, Publishers Weekly,* September 4, 1995.

■ **For More Information See**

PERIODICALS

Kirkus Reviews, August 1, 1996, p. 1107; November 15, 1997, p. 1678.

Library Journal, September 15, 1996, p. 101; June 1, 1997, p. 148.

New Statesman, November 28, 1986, p. 35.

Publishers Weekly, March 13, 1995, p. 63; May 5, 1997, p. 197; April 27, 1998, p. 48.

Voice of Youth Advocates, October, 1995, p. 232; August, 1998, p. 210.*

—Sketch by Diane Andreassi

Valerie Hobbs

■ Personal

Born April 18, 1941, in Metuchen, NJ; daughter of Herbert Trevor Evans and Alise (a painter; maiden name, Hansen) Minney; married Gary Johnson, 1962 (divorced, 1973); married Jack Hobbs (a teacher), June 18, 1978; children: (first marriage) Juliet. *Education:* University of California, Santa Barbara, B.A., 1968, M.A., 1978. *Politics:* Democrat. *Hobbies and other interests:* Golf, hiking, travel, poker.

■ Addresses

Home—69 Skyline Circle, Santa Barbara, CA 93109. *Office*—Writing Program, University of California, Santa Barbara, CA 93106. *Electronic mail*—hobbs@humanitas.ucsb.edu. *Agent*—Barbara Markowitz, 117 North Mansfield Ave., Los Angeles, CA 90036.

■ Career

High school English teacher on the Hawaiian island of Oahu, 1971-74; University of California, Santa Barbara, lecturer in writing, 1981—. *Mem-*

ber: PEN Center West, Society of Children's Book Writers and Illustrators, South Coast Writing Project.

■ Awards, Honors

Best Young Adult Novels citation, American Library Association, 1995, for *How Far Would You Have Gotten If I Hadn't Called You Back?*

■ Writings

FICTION FOR YOUNG ADULTS

How Far Would You Have Gotten If I Hadn't Called You Back?, Orchard Books (New York City), 1995.
Get It While It's Hot. Or Not, Orchard Books, 1996.
Carolina Crow Girl, Frances Foster Books/FSG, 1999.

OTHER

Work represented in anthologies, including *California Childhoods*, edited by Gary Soto, 1987. Contributor of stories to magazines, including *Northeast Corridor*, *Chrysalis*, *American Fiction*, *New Renaissance*, and *Kansas Quarterly*.

■ Work in Progress

Charlie's Run, a middle-grade novel about a runaway boy, for Frances Foster Books/FSG, expected 2000.

■ Sidelights

Valerie Hobbs writes about young female characters confronting a society full of difficult choices. For Hobbs, maturity is earned through the crucible of experience. Hobbs recognizes teenagers are not immune from the problems of the adult world. Suicide, alcoholism, abuse, death, and teen sex enter her narratives, grabbing the reader's attention. Loss, especially parental loss, is a theme that appears often in her books. In her debut novel *How Far Would You Have Gotten If I Hadn't Called You Back?*, Hobbs writes the story of a young woman with a love of both racing cars and the men who drive them. Hobbs's 1995 coming-of-age tale has been praised by critics for its original and sensitive portrait of a teenager struggling to find herself amid a sea of contradictory influences. Hobbs has also written *Get It While It's Hot. Or Not*, another young adult novel with a focus on friendships and teen sexual relationships.

Short stories came first for Hobbs before she attempted her first novel. "I started writing short stories because I thought they didn't seem that hard. I published about ten short stories in literary magazines and a couple of commercial women's magazines." She did not begin to write seriously until her late teens, after one of her friends met with a tragic accident. "Actually, my first novel was born when I was eighteen and wrote a truly awful short story about the death of a young man I was involved with at the time," she once told *Something about the Author (SATA)*. "Then, in 1986, I picked up the thread of that story and wrote 'Ojala 1959' for *California Childhoods,* a collection of short stories by California writers. Then I got real bold and decided there was more to tell," Hobbs added, "so I wrote a novel that ended with the same tragedy that impelled me to write the story in the first place."

Turning that story into a novel was, Hobbs acknowledged, "much harder than I expected. I then got into this place where I need to write a whole novel; I need a whole book. I can't anymore imagine writing a short story, which actually is much more difficult now that I see them both. To have everything so compact, so concisely done. A short story is very difficult. I have not written one since; I don't know if I ever will," she told *AAYA*.

In an interview with Jon Saari for *Authors and Artists for Young Adults (AAYA)*, Hobbs said ideas

This 1995 coming-of-age novel features a young girl trying to find herself in a changing era.

come to her in a variety of ways. "Some ideas just have to be written because they were a part of my life. They stayed with me from the time I was young and were always there to be written about. Other ones seem to be like magic—once in a while I get an image of something, and I suppose it is probably out of my life, too. Sometimes a character just comes: I know that sounds a little strange, but that happened with my last novel—a child just appeared to me. Ideas are gifts from the universe, it seems to me. I wish they came easily, but they don't."

First Novel a Success

Hobbs's first novel, *How Far Would You Have Gotten If I Hadn't Called You Back?,* was published in

1995. (The title comes from an expression often used by the author's father.) Sixteen-year-old Bronwyn Lewis, the book's protagonist, isn't a typical high school student. Growing up in the late 1950s, when young women her age chose role models like Doris Day and Donna Reed and looked forward to marriage and a future spending hours in the kitchen, Bronwyn would rather be behind the wheel of a dragster. Like her creator, Hobbs, the fictional Bronwyn moved from urban New Jersey to rural California at age fifteen; her interests and hobbies are different than those of the teens in her new town, and fitting in at her new high school has been almost impossible. The fact that her family is now poor and her unemployed father has attempted suicide makes Bronwyn feel even more withdrawn. Finally, friendship with Lanie, a pretty but poor young woman from the "wild side" of town allows Bronwyn a way to fit in with a peer group. She soon falls behind in school, dumps her interest in playing classical piano for rock and roll, and starts dating, drinking, and hanging out with the drag-racing crowd. A sexual fling with an older racer known as J. C. is interrupted by a budding love affair with the mature and far more suitable Will, but when Will leaves for his first year at West Point, Bronwyn returns to her old ways, with tragic consequences.

Joel Shoemaker praises *How Far Would You Have Gotten* in his review in *School Library Journal*, writing that Bronwyn's "changing self-image and relationships are beautifully detailed, as are the interesting assortment of supporting (NOT minor) characters and the physical world they inhabit." "Here's a rare commodity," writes *Booklist* reviewer Stephanie Zvirin, "a YA novel teens can really sink their teeth into. It's about love, friendship, responsibilities, rebellion, and identity. . . ." In *Voice of Youth Advocates*, reviewer C. Allen Nichols gives special praise to Hobbs's depiction of Bronwyn: "First novelist Hobbs's lyrical writing portrays Bron as a character with great depth who faces the challenges that come her way. . . . She is a talented and intelligent teen whose coming-of-age is even more painful than the average teen's." A *Publishers Weekly* reviewer also notes Bronwyn's strengths, deeming her "an unusually astute narrator" who "coolly dissects her feelings and her impressions."

How Far Would You Have Gotten wasn't written with a young adult audience in mind, although the novel was later marketed for young adult readers. Instead, Hobbs wanted to write down her personal recollections of her teen years, complete with her bout with personal tragedy and her own growing awareness of her maturing attitudes. "I think it was probably best that I didn't write [the novel] for young adults," Hobbs told Nathalie Op de Beeck in *Publishers Weekly*, "because I didn't know enough to pull punches. I just wanted to say it the way it is, the way people forget that it is. I always see those years as fraught with danger." "No matter what we think we're writing about, we're probably always writing about ourselves," Hobbs believes. "My second novel has four entirely made-up characters, but I think, at heart, they're all just different parts of who I am and have been in my life."

Today Hobbs writes for a particular audience based on what she learned in writing *How Far Could You Have Gotten*. "I think I have young adults in mind now. I did not know that market at all before I got into it, so I started to read a lot of young adult novels. I was so impressed with the quality of many of them. So many were to me honest and straightforward and cleaner than some of the novels in the adult market. I've become a real fan of young adult books," Hobbs told Saari.

There is one theme that Hobbs sees reoccurring in her books. "It seems like I am dealing with loss. I was looking at some of the funnier books that have come out lately that have some humor, like *Holes* by Louis Sachar that won the National Book Award. It is just so creative. It has humor. How wonderful would it be if I could write some humor, a different approach at looking at things. That's not where I am. I seem often to be writing about the threat of loss, of parent and children, the fear of losing a parent. I don't know exactly where that comes from, but there's a lot of that."

Hobbs's intention is to make an emotional connection with her readers where feelings are shared and insights made through the recognition of similar experiences. "I think I write to share some feelings I've had and some feelings I think a lot of people have, so when they read them there might be a moment of recognition when they say 'I'm not the only one who feels this way,' or 'I'm OK, and I can get through this.'" Hobbs added, "I remember the teenage years being very stressful and thinking I was the only one going through certain things. When I talk to teenagers now, they seem to feel that way, too. I think it gives you courage to see that somebody else went through similar situations and made it to the other side. I realize that's a part of why I write—to share common feelings," she told *AAYA.*

The Dynamics of Friendship

In her second novel, entitled *Get It While It's Hot. Or Not,* Hobbs weaves different aspects of herself into the lives of four best friends. Constant companions since the eighth grade, Megan, Mia,

Megan examines the meaning of friendship and love when one of her friends becomes pregnant.

Elaine, and Kit begin their junior year of high school in difficult circumstances. Weak-willed Kit, who lives with her alcoholic mother in a poor part of town, finds herself pregnant and bedridden, while dependable Megan, the story's narrator and moral centerpiece, risks cutting classes and lying to her parents to help Kit get through her difficult pregnancy. A boyfriend pressuring her for sex, a stint on the school newspaper during which she decides to educate her fellow students about sex issues, and serving as matchmaker for her friend Mia all keep Megan busy, but not too busy to gain an understanding of several matters of common interest to teens: birth control, AIDS, unwanted pregnancy, and dealing with parents. School newspaper censorship arises when the principal bars the publication of Megan's article on teen sex, so she finds other means to get the word out.

Hobbs's novel allows readers to "relate to Megan's struggle to define the boundaries of friendship and her responsibilities to her family and community," explains Marcia Mann in her review of *Get It While It's Hot. Or Not* in *Voice of Youth Advocates.* Janice M. Del Negro of the *Bulletin of the Center for Children's Books* adds that teen readers would likely find the "friends, group dynamics and the contemporary themes appealing." *Horn Book* reviewer Lauren Adams calls the novel "well paced and highly readable, taking on serious issues with humor and intelligence."

Hobbs has a warm regard and fine appreciation for young adults, having taught high school for three years. Her husband is a high school teacher and she is a frequent visitor to his classes—the two frequently talk about teenagers. She teaches at the University of California at Santa Barbara, saying "there's still a lot of kid in freshmen certainly. I love human beings between the ages of fifteen or sixteen and twenty-two. They don't have any guile. They are clean people," she told *AAYA.* "We haven't really wanted to think about what teenagers really know and what they really think about. It is a natural tendency to want to protect them from a lot of things, but they are adults now. Everything is so out in the open; there isn't anything that they don't know and don't talk about. To not have it in the literature seems hypocritical to say the least."

Hobbs's strongly believes that young adult book should be used in the public school curriculum.

If you enjoy the works of Valerie Hobbs, you may also want to check out the following books and films:

Judy Blume, *Tiger Eyes,* 1995.
Erika Tamar, *The Things I Did Last Summer,* 1994.
Ann B. Tracy, *What Do Cowboys Like?,* 1995.
Foxfire, a film based on the novel by Joyce Carol Oates, 1996.

"I really wish we could get more young adult literature into the hands of kids in school. I went to the local PTA and talked about this. Teachers feel they have to use only the classics, but when you look at the themes of some of the major classics they are really awful: a woman made to wear a scarlet letter on the front of her dress for the rest of her life because she had an illegitimate affair. Two fourteen-year-olds who kill themselves because their parents won't let them see each other. A man catches a fish. They aren't themes talking to students today."

Hobbs continued, "Many kids who are readers right up to middle school lose that joy in high school. I think we need to open the options to them to a wider scope of reading. Some of my favorite novels are being taught in high school to the exclusion of other kinds of literature. Not all kids can read *Tess of the D'Urbervilles* and get anything out of it. I wish there was a way to get kids more in touch with young adult literature. A lot of it is really wonderful."

On her future as a teacher, Hobbs says, "I still enjoy it, but I am ready to retire. I am ready to just write novels because I can do that everyday. It is something I want to do, and it is always there to do." She added to Saari, though, "When I am in the middle of teaching, I have to admit I enjoy it. I enjoy it because of the young people I am in contact with. Even when I retire I will probably teach one class to stay in touch."

■ Works Cited

Adams, Lauren, review of *Get It While It's Hot. Or Not, Horn Book,* December, 1996, p. 744.

Del Negro, Janice M., review of *Get It While It's Hot. Or Not, Bulletin of the Center for Children's Books,* November, 1996, p. 99.

Hobbs, Valerie, with Nathalie Op de Beeck, "Flying Starts: Three Children's Novelists Talk about Their Fall '95 Debuts," *Publishers Weekly,* December 18, 1995, pp. 28-30.

Hobbs, Valerie, comments in *Something about the Author,* Volume 93, Gale, 1997, pp. 80-83.

Hobbs, Valerie, interview with Jon Saari for *Authors and Artists for Young Adults,* December 15, 1998.

Review of *How Far Would You Have Gotten If I Hadn't Called You Back?, Publishers Weekly,* October 16, 1995, p. 63.

Mann, Marcia, review of *Get It While It's Hot. Or Not, Voice of Youth Advocates,* December, 1996.

Nichols, C. Allen, review of *How Far Would You Have Gotten If I Hadn't Called You Back?, Voice of Youth Advocates,* December, 1995, p. 302.

Shoemaker, Joel, review of *How Far Would You Have Gotten If I Hadn't Called You Back?, School Library Journal,* October, 1995, p. 155.

Zvirin, Stephanie, review of *How Far Would You Have Gotten If I Hadn't Called You Back?, Booklist,* October 1, 1995, p. 304.

■ For More Information See

PERIODICALS

Children's Bookwatch, March, 1997.
Kirkus Reviews, September 15, 1995, p. 1351; August 15, 1996.
Publishers Weekly, October 16, 1995, p. 63.

—Sketch by Jon Saari

Victor Hugo

Guernsey from 1851 to 1870. He is best known as the leader of French romanticism in literature during the 1800s and as the author of such novels *as The Hunchback of Notre-Dame* and *Les Miserables. Member:* French Academy.

■ Personal

Born February 26, 1802, in Besancon, France; died of pneumonia, May 22 (other sources cite May 23), 1885, in Paris, France; buried in the Pantheon, May 31, 1885; son of Joseph Leopold Sigisbert (an army major) and Sophie (Trebuchet) Hugo; married Adele Foucher, October 12, 1822 (died, 1868); children: Leopold II, Leopoldine, Francois-Victor, Charles, Adele. *Education:* Privately tutored, and attended schools in Spain and France, 1811-18.

■ Career

Poet, novelist, dramatist, and politician. Early in his career he founded the *magazine Le Conservateur Litteraire* in 1819, and later founded the periodicals *La Muse Francaise, L'Evenement,* and *Le Peuple Souverain.* Entering politics in 1845, he was created a peer of France by Louis-Philippe, and was subsequently elected deputy to the Constituent Assembly, deputy of Paris to the National Assembly, and senator. Due to his opposition of Louis Napoleon, he lived in exile in Brussels, Belgium, and on the British Channel Islands Jersey and

■ Awards, Honors

Honorable mention from the French Academy, about 1817, for poetry; first prize at the Floral Games at Toulouse, 1819, for the poems "Les Derniers Bardes," "Les Vierges de Verun," and "Le Retablissement de la statue de Henri IV"; created Maitre es jeuz-floraux at the Floral Games at Toulouse and recipient of a prize for the poem "Moiese sur le Nil," both 1820; royal prize from Louis XVIII, 1821 (another source cites 1822); created Chevalier of the Legion of Honor by Charles X, 1825; created officer of the Legion of Honor by Louis Philippe, 1837.

■ Writings

NOVELS

(Published anonymously) *Han d'Islande,* four volumes, [Paris], 1823, translation published as *Hans of Iceland,* [London], 1825.

Bug Jargal, 1826, adaptation published as *The Slave-King,* Carey, Lea, and Blanchard, 1833, translation published as *Bug-Jargal; or, A Tale of the Massacre in St. Domingo, 1791,* J. Mowatt, 1844.

Le Dernier Jour d'un condamne, [Paris], 1829, translation by G. W. M. Reynolds published as *The Last Day of a Condemned,* [London], 1840.

Notre-Dame de Paris, 1831, translation by Frederic Shoberl published as *The Hunchback of Notre-Dame,* two volumes, R. Bentley, 1833, Carey, Lea, and Blanchard, 1834; translation by W. Hazlitt, published as *Notre-Dame: A Tale of the Ancient Regime,* three volumes, [London], 1833; *La Esmeralda; or, The Hunchback of Notre-Dame,* [London], 1839; *Notre-Dame; or, The Bellringer of Paris,* [London], 1867; translation by Isabel F. Hapgood, published as *Notre Dame de Paris,* two volumes, T. Y. Crowell, 1888; translation by John Sturrock, *Notre-Dame of Paris,* Penguin, 1978.

Les Miserables, ten volumes, [Paris], 1862, translation by Charles E. Wilbour published as *Les Miserables,* five volumes, Carleton, 1862, new edition, AMSCO School Publications, 1970, published as *The Wretched,* 1863.

Les Travailleurs de la mer, three volumes, [Brussels], 1866, translation published as *The Toilers of the Sea,* Harper & Brothers, 1866.

L'Homme qui rit, eight volumes, Appleton, 1869, translation by William Young published as *The Man Who Laughs,* D. Appleton, 1869, published as *By Order of the King,* 1870.

Quatre-vingt treize, Librarie du Courrier des Etats-Unis (New York), 1874, translation by Frank L. Benedict published as *Ninety-Three,* Harper & Brothers, 1874.

POETRY

Odes et poesies diverses, 1822.

Odes et ballades, [Paris], 1826.

Les Orientales, C. Gosselin, (Paris), 1829, translation by J. N. Fazakerley published as *Eastern Lyrics in La Fontaine's Fables, Books I and II, and First Series of "Les Orientales," or "Eastern Lyrics" by Victor Hugo,* (French and English texts), Kerby & Endean, 1879.

Les Feuilles d'automne, 1831.

Les Chants du crepuscule, E. Renduel, 1835, partial translation by G. W. M. Reynolds published as *Songs of Twilight,* French, English & American Library (Paris), 1836.

Les Voix interieures, 1837.

Les Rayons et les ombres, 1840.

Les Chatiments, Henri Samuel (Brussels), 1853.

Les Contemplations, two volumes, Pagnerre, 1856.

La legende des siecles, five volumes, [Paris], 1859-83, translation published as *The Legend of the Centuries,* G. W. Dillingham (New York), 1894.

Les Chansons des rues et des bois, [Paris], 1865.

L'annee terrible, Michel Levy Freres (Paris), 1872.

L'Art d'etre grandpere, 1877.

Le Pape, Calmann Levy, 1878.

La Pitie supreme, [Paris], 1879.

L'Ane, 1880.

Les Quatre Vents de l'esprit, 1881.

La Fin de Satan, [Paris], 1886.

Toute la lyre, 1889-93.

Dieu, 1891.

PLAYS; ALL PRODUCED IN PARIS

Cromwell (five-act), [Paris], 1827.

Hernani; ou, L'Honneur Castillan (five-act; first produced at Comedie-Francaise, February 25, 1830), [Paris], 1830, translation by Lord F. Leveson Gower published as *Hernani,* W. Sams, 1830.

Marion de Lorme (five-act; first produced at Theatre de la Porte-Saint-Martin, August 11, 1831), 1831, adaptation by B. Fairclough published as *The King's Edict* (four-act), [London], 1872.

Le roi s'amuse (five-act; first produced at Comedie-Francaise, November 22, 1832), [Paris], 1832, translation by H. T. Haley published as *The King's Fool; or, Le roi s'amuse,* edited by William Hazlitt, the Younger, J. Clements, 1842; translation by F. L. Slous published as *Francis the First; or, the Curse of St. Vallier,* privately printed (London), 1843; translation by Edward J. Harding published as *His Kingly Pleasure,* privately printed by F. F. Bainbridge, 1902; translation by T. M. R. von Keler published as *The King Enjoys Himself,* Haldeman-Julius, 1923.

Lucrece Borgia (three-act; first produced at Theatre de la Porte-Saint-Martin, February 2, 1833), 1833, translation by W. T. Haley published as *Lucretia Borgia,* J. Clements, 1842.

Marie Tudor (three-act; first produced at Theatre de la Porte-Saint-Martin, November 6, 1833), 1833.

Angelo, Tyran de Padoue (three-act; first produced at Comedie-Francaise, April 28, 1835), Renduel, 1835, translation published as *Angelo; or, The Tyrant of Padua: A Drama of Three Days,* (parallel French and English texts), Darcie & Corbyn, 1855, adaptation by G. H. Davidson published as *Angelo, and the Actress of Padua,* G. H. Davidson, l855(?).

La Esmeralda (four-act opera; music by Louise Bertin; first produced at Academie Royale du Musique, November 14, 1836), 1836.

Ruy Blas (five-act; first produced at Theatre de la Renaissance, November, 1838), 1838, adaptation by Edmund O'Rourke, T. H. Lacy, c. 1860, translation by John Davidson published as *A Queen's Romance,* F. A. Stokes, 1904.

Also author of *Les Burgraves,* 1841, and *Napoleon le petit,* 1852.

OTHER

Litterature et philosophie melees, two volumes, J. P. Meline (Brussels), 1834.
William Shakespeare (critical essay), Librairie Internationale, 1864, translation by A. Baillot, Hurst & Blackett, 1864.
Choses vues, 1887, translation published as *Things Seen,* Harper & Brothers, 1887, another edition selected, edited and translated by David Kimber, Oxford University Press, 1964.
En voyage: Alpes et Pyrenees (description and travel), 1890, translation by Nathan H. Dole published as *Victor Hugo's Letters to His Wife and Others (The Alps and the Pyrenees),* Estes & Lauriat, 1895, another translation by John Manson published as *The Alps and Pyrenees,* Dutton, 1898.
Post-scriptum de ma vie, Calmann Levy, 1901, translation by Lorenzo O'Rourke published as *Victor Hugo's Intellectual Autobiography,* Funk & Wagnalls, 1907, new edition published as *Intellectual Autobiography,* edited by L. O'Rourke, Haskell House, 1982.

COLLECTIONS

Fairytales from the Rhine, Gallimard, 1981.

■ Adaptations

FILMS

Les Miserables, Electric Production, starring Henri Krauss, 1913, Fox Film, starring Dorothy Bernard, Jewel Carmen, William Farnum, and George Moss, 1918, Twentieth Century-Fox, starring Frederic March and Charles Laughton, 1935, Twentieth Century-Fox, starring Michael Rennie and Robert Newton, 1952, Columbia Broadcasting System, starring Richard Jordan and Anthony Perkins, 1978, TeleFrance I and Societe Francaise de Production, 1982, Warner Bros., 1995, TriStar, 1998.
The Hunchback of Notre Dame, Universal, starring Lon Chaney and Patsy Ruth Miller, 1923, RKO Radio Pictures, starring Charles Laughton,

Cedric Hardwicke, and Maureen O'Hara, 1939, National Broadcasting Co., starring Warren Clarke, Kenneth Haigh, and Michelle Newell, 1977.
The Bishop's Experiment, adapted from an incident in *Les Miserables,* Realm Television Productions, 1949.

PLAYS

Norman MacKinnel, *The Bishop's Candlesticks* (one-act; adapted from an incident in *Les Miserables*), [London], 1910.
Gilbert Hudson, *The Silver Candlesticks* (one-act; adapted from an incident in *Les Miserables*), Caxton Book Shop, 1929.
D. P. MacSheahan, *The Triumph of Love* (adaptation of *Les Miserables*), Catholic Truth Society of Ireland, 1944.
Harold H. S. Jackson, *God's Ambassador* (three-act; adapted from an incident in *Les Miserables*), Epworth Press, 1955.
Lewy Olfson, *Bishop's Candlesticks,* in *Plays,* December, 1962.
Les Miserables (musical), first stage version produced at Palais des Sports, France; first produced in London at Barbican Theatre by Royal Shakespeare Company, moved to Palace Theatre, 1985—; first U.S. production at Kennedy Center, Washington, DC, 1986, moved to Broadway, 1987.

■ Sidelights

When Victor Hugo died in 1885 at the age of eighty-three, one million mourners gathered in the streets of Paris to see his corpse borne to the Pantheon. Buried with honors usually reserved for heads of state, the author outlived neither his celebrity nor his popularity. Although often controversial and politically charged, his works were embraced by both critics and commoners. As Jean-Paul Sartre later noted, "Hugo, no doubt, had the rare good fortune to be read everywhere: he's one of our only, perhaps our only writer who has been truly popular." Sartre was not alone in expressing an ambivalent attitude toward Hugo's enduring popularity. Asked to name France's greatest poet, novelist André Gide lamented, "Victor Hugo, hélas!"

Hugo, Timothy Raser argues in *Dictionary of Literary Biography,* was a product of his time: "No century of French literature has been better represented by a single author than the nineteenth, and no writer better personifies the French nineteenth century than Victor Hugo." A potent voice in the politics of his day, Hugo was a leader of the Romantic movement in poetry, drama, and fiction. The sheer volume of his output was staggering. According to Raser: "Not simply was Hugo an observer of and participant in his times, he was also one of the most prolific writers in history, but, unlike many other prolific writers, his works are both varied and important." Not least among his achievements, his collection of poems, *Les Contemplations*, represents the acme of the genre, while the novel *Les Misérables* is widely recognized as a brilliant novel whose popularity has increased exponentially, more than one century after the author's death, with the immensely successful theatrical production of *Les Mis.*

A Military Upbringing

Born in Nancy, France, in 1773, Joseph-Léopold Sigisbert Hugo left school at the age of fifteen to enlist in the army. Soon, the son of a master carpenter found himself embroiled in the Convention, a revolutionary government. After taking part in a military action to suppress a counter-revolutionary uprising in the province of Brittany, he quickly moved up the ranks to the position of captain. On his twenty-third birthday, Hugo, who had attained the rank of Adjutant-Major, married Sophie Trébuchet, the daughter of a sea captain. Orphaned at a young age, Sophie had been reared by her aunt, who instilled in her niece a Royalist bias.

The couple already had two sons, Abel and Eugène, when their youngest child, Victor-Marie Hugo, was born on February 26, 1802, in Besançon. Named after General Victor de Lahorie—who was instrumental in furthering the senior Hugo's political aspirations and who ultimately became Sophie's paramour—Victor-Marie was a sickly infant whose prospects of surviving looked dim. Madame Dudaux described Hugo's birth in verse:

'Twas in Besançon, an old Spanish city,
A child was born, by chance,—a wind-swept grain
Whose double root was Brittany, Lorraine,—
Mute, sightless, pale was he, a thing to pity,
So faint, so frail, no baby but a ghost,
All, save his mother, gave him for lost.

His fragile neck fell sideways like a reed,
His cradle and his coffin came together:
This child whose name Life would not write or read,
This dying child that could not hope to weather
The morrow of his birth—'Tis I!

In spite of his frail condition—and contrary to the prediction of the midwife who assisted at his birth—young Victor survived.

At the age of five, Hugo left for Italy with his mother and brothers in order to rejoin his father, from whom he had been separated for three years. The elder Hugo, who held the post of Governor of Avellino, was struck by his young son's maturity. He wrote: "Victor, the youngest, shows great aptitude for his studies. He is as staid as his eldest brother, and very thoughtful. I have been more than once struck by the things he says. There is a great gentleness in the expression of his face." Hugo's stay in Italy was brief. In 1809, he returned to France to live with his mother at 12 Impasse des Feuillantines, in Paris.

Frequently separated for long periods of time, Hugo's parents were increasingly driven apart by extramarital affairs and stringent political differences. In 1811 Hugo traveled to Madrid, Spain, with his mother and brothers to rejoin Joseph Hugo. There the senior Hugo enjoyed both prestige and luxury, having been conferred the Spanish title of Count Siguenza and promoted to general in the army of King Joseph, brother of Napoleon. Living in the splendid Maserano Palace, Hugo attended the Catholic College des Nobles (in spite of his mother's adamant insistence that her son subscribed to the Protestant faith). Within three months, however, the Hugos decided to divorce, in part because Joseph refused to leave his mistress, Catherine Thomas. When Sophie Hugo returned to Paris in March of 1812, she took with her Eugène and Victor, leaving her eldest son, Abel, in the care of her ex-husband. Six months later, Lahorie, who had taken part in a conspiracy against Napoleon, was executed, having been arrested in the house of Sophie Hugo.

An Early Start

Having resettled at Les Feuillantines in Paris, Hugo began to experiment with verse writing. Although his first attempts were clumsy and inelegant, he was a gifted student and soon learned from his mistakes. In a much later biography of her husband, Adèle Foucher wrote: that the "verse he wrote at this time were very imperfect. They neither rhymed nor scanned. The child was without a master, and knew nothing of prosody. He read aloud what he had written, took notice of what was wrong, and began correcting the lines until his ear was satisfied. By a process of hit and miss, he taught himself the element of metre, caesura, rhyme, and the alternation of masculine and feminine ending. . . ." Toward the end of 1815 Hugo dedicated *Itamène,* his first tragedy in verse, to his mother, and by 1816, the young author had decided to devote himself to writing. According to Foucher's biography, he announced, "I want to be Chateaubriand or nothing" (an author who at that time enjoyed tremendous success in France), a lofty literary aspiration for a fourteen-year-old.

So young was Hugo, in fact, that the Académie Française, which had awarded one of his poems an honorable mention in the summer of 1817, expressed incredulity at his age. Hugo responded in a letter: "A slight indisposition prevents me from having the honor of going in person to express my gratitude for the favor which the French Academy has deigned to confer on me by according an honorable mention to the piece No. 15, of which I am the author. Having heard that you have raised doubts as to my age, I take the liberty of enclosing my certificate of birth. It will prove to you that the line—'I, who . . . hardly has seen the end of a mere fifteen years' is not a poetic fiction."

Together with his brother Abel, aged twenty, Hugo co-founded a literary journal, the *Conservateur Littéraire.* Published twice monthly from December 1819 until March 1821, the journal was a tribute to Chateaubriand, under whose aegis the periodical *Le Conservateur* was published. Submitted under eleven pseudonyms, Hugo's contribution to the journal was prolific, comprising more than one hundred articles on various subjects from literary to political criticism, twenty-two poems, and "Bug-Jargal," a short story published in serial form. Albeit short-lived in publication, *Conservateur Littéraire* was an important mouthpiece of the Romantics, who were at the time fomenting a literary movement. (The term *romantisme,* however, was not ascribed to the movement until 1822, having been derived from some of the writings of Mme de Staël.)

A Pensioned Poet

When Hugo's first book of poetry, *Odes et poésies diverses,* was published in June 1822, he did little to curry public favor. He wrote, "I shall send my book to the newspapers; they will notice it, if they judge proper to do so, but I will not solicit their praise as though it were an alms. I have been told as an object to this course that the newspapers have it in their power to make the success of a poor book, or to ruin that of a masterpiece. . . . Moreover, I have not, up to this time, taken a step to advance myself with a single journalist, and it is, perhaps, for this reason that the journalists accord me some measure of consideration. They respect a man who respects himself." King Louis XVIII was among those who respected Hugo's talent. Following the publication of *Odes et poésies,* the French monarch awarded Hugo a pension, granted by Royal decree, from the literary fund of the Minister of the Interior.

Hugo received a second pension for the novel *Han d'Islande,* published in 1823. Two years in the writing, the young author's first novel expressed some of the romantic tension he experienced in his own life. Hugo wrote, "I had a soul that brimmed with love and misery and youth. But to no living creature could I breathe its secrets: instead, I chose a silent confidant, a sheet of paper. . . ." Set in seventeenth-century Norway, the novel—which relates a convoluted and melodramatic account of a young man's efforts to locate documents that exonerate his lover's father—was written during Hugo's courtship of Adèle Foucher. Friends since childhood, the couple, at one time prevented from marrying, were able to wed after the publication of *Han* brought Hugo a comfortable income. On October 12, 1822, at the church of Saint Sulpice in Paris, the two were married. "What joy!," Hugo wrote to his new wife. "All this is in the past, and there is nothing but delight in our future. Nothing can separate us any longer, Adèle; nothing can now constrain our interviews, our caresses, our love! I repeat that I can hardly believe in this happiness, because it seems to me that I have, even yet, done so little to deserve so much!"

Not everyone celebrated the Hugos' marriage. Eugène Hugo, whose mental health had been deteriorating, threw a fit the evening of his brother's marriage, ruining furniture with his sword. Within a year, in June 1823, Eugène was committed to an asylum—the cost of which was borne by both Victor and Abel. That same month Hugo published a piece of criticism about Walter Scott's *Quentin Durward* in which he outlined his own vision of the novel genre. Hugo admired the drama inherent in Scott's narrative, and its ability to embrace opposing elements: "It is the novel, simultaneously drama and epic, picturesque but poetic, real but ideal, true but great, that will encompass Walter Scott in Homer." Already, Hugo was beginning to formulate his vision of literary realism.

The article was published in the *Muse Française*, a journal edited by Hugo's friend Emile Deschamps. The journal sponsored regular meetings among contributors, known as the "cénacles," which first took place at the Arsénal library, moving to

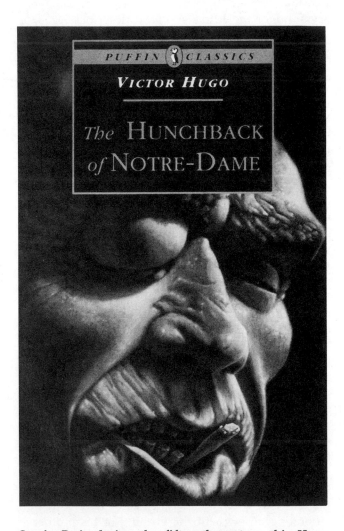

Set in Paris during the fifteenth century, this Hugo classic originally was published in 1831.

Hugo's house and then to that of the poet Charles-Augustin Sainte-Beuve. Hugo, who produced two collections of *Odes* during this time, read many of his early poems at these meetings. Also during that time Hugo's first son, Léopold II, was born, only to die three months later. Just over one year later, on August 28, 1824, his first daughter, Léopoldine, was born. Nicknamed "Didine," she was the apple of her father's eye: ". . . I stay at home, where I am happy, where I rock my baby and have an angel for a wife," Hugo wrote in a letter. "All my happiness is there; nothing reaches me from the outside. . . ."

Hugo nonetheless maintained contact with the outside. Invited to the coronation of Charles X, he published an ode, "On the Coronation of Charles X," in June 1825, the success of which greatly encouraged him. Also that year, he traveled through Switzerland and the Alps with librarian Charles Nodier, who sponsored the cénacles and eventually became a mentor to the youthful Hugo. During this time the Hugos had two sons: Charles, born November 1826, and Victor Hugo II (whose name was later changed to François-Victor), born in October 1928. Maturity and fatherhood probably played a role in Hugo's eventual rapprochement with his father, whom he grew to respect and continued to love. After his father died in January of 1928, he wrote, ". . . I have lost the man who loved me best in the world, a good and noble man, who was rather proud of me and very fond of me, a father whose interest in me never flagged."

Hugo's participation in the literary gatherings of the *Muse Française* introduced him to a figure who would play a critical role in his life. Having met Sainte-Beuve through the cénacles in 1827, Hugo soon developed a close friendship with the poet. ". . . There are only two or three things really worth having in life, and friendship is one of them," he once wrote the poet. But his friendship with Sainte-Beuve proved poisonous to his marriage: in 1831, Adèle's affair with the poet was much bruited about Paris. Hugo was devastated and found it impossible to overlook his friend's betrayal. Their attempts to continue their friendship ended in failure: Hugo wrote to his erstwhile friend, "Everything is a torture to me now. Even the obligation, imposed on me by a person whom I cannot mention here, of being always present when you are there, reminds me constantly and very painfully that we are not the friends of old

The classic 1939 film version of *The Hunchback of Notre-Dame* starred Charles Laughton as Quasimodo.

days. My poor friend, there is an element of absence in your presence which makes it even more unbearable than your real absence. . . ."

A Romantic Playwright

Already, Hugo was a prolific writer. From 1829 to 1840, he published myriad works ranging from travel literature to essays, novels, and five volumes of verse. While the publication of his novel, *Bug-Jargal*, in 1826, marked his first overt dismissal of classicism, it was the publication of *Cromwell*, in December 1827, that placed him in the vanguard of the nascent Romantic movement. A daunting and unstageable verse-drama, *Cromwell* was most noted for its preface, in which the author proposes to abandon the classical notion of drama in favor of a new set of principles. Hugo—

who as a child had seen a dismembered and crucified man, among other atrocities—insisted that drama remain faithful to the real world by portraying not just what is good and beautiful but also that which is mean, ugly, and grotesque. Wholeheartedly embraced by the country's young dramatists and poets, Hugo's preface became doctrine to the French Romantics.

Hugo's works were not always so well received. Labeled a threat to the monarchy because of its disrespectful stance toward Louis XIII, his play *Marion de Lorme* was banned by the censors in July 1829; it also prompted Hugo to sunder his friendship with Nodier, who disliked the play and failed to rally to the assistance of his onetime protégé. Hugo's iconoclastic drama *Hernani*, first staged in February 1830 at the Comédie Française, was no less provocative. A strange blend of melodrama, caricature, and fantasy, it deliberately flew in the face of the classical precepts of drama such as the unity of time, place, and action. While Romantic writers and artists flocked to the performances to demonstrate their solidarity with the author, many were openly hostile toward both the play and its author. Hugo lamented in his memoirs: "The public every night hisses all the verses. It is a rare uproar. The actors are abashed and hostile; most of them ridicule what they have to say. The press has been practically unanimous every morning in making fun of the piece and the author."

Hugo's notoriety nonetheless worked in his favor. His publisher, determined to capitalize on the public's fascination with Hugo's strange play, enticed him to produce a novel within the year. Hugo took the publisher's deadline seriously: the contract specified that the author would be fined for each week the draft was overdue. Taking up research he had begun in the late 1820s, Hugo set his new work in Paris during the Middle Ages. In her memoirs, his wife recalled, "[He] bought himself a bottle of ink and a thick, knitted shawl of grey wool in which he could wrap himself from head to heel, locked away his clothes so as to be safe from any temptation to leave the house, and walked into his novel as though it had been a prison." After six months of writing, Hugo produced *Notre Dame de Paris.*

Relentless Fatalism and *The Hunchback of Notre Dame*

Published in 1831, *Notre Dame de Paris,* translated as *The Hunchback of Notre Dame,* received some criticism for its deliberate emphasis on the grotesque. Charles de Montalembert faulted the novel for "ce melange continuel du grotesque au tragique" (this continual mixture of the grotesque and the tragic). But this mixture was exactly what Hugo admired in the works of Sir Walter Scott, who was then the most popular novelist in France; it had become, in fact, the cornerstone of his own aesthetic vision. Set in 1482—on the cusp between the Middle Ages and the Renaissance— the novel recreates in scrupulous detail the medieval city of Paris in which the Gothic cathedral of Notre Dame looms ominously in both architectural and emotional landscapes. Representing a sort of aesthetic center to both the city and to Hugo's novel, the cathedral is wrought with in- tricate detail, sometimes beautiful and sometimes grotesque, the sum total of which represents a transcendental mystery.

At the center of Hugo's story is a young Gypsy woman named Esmeralda, who is the object of the affections of three men: Claude Frollo, the deacon of the cathedral, Pierre Gringoire, an author whose talent has been overlooked, and the hunchbacked Quasimodo, who is responsible for ringing the bell at the cathedral. Esmeralda, however, loves another man—a soldier, Phoebus—who does not return her love. Equally passionate in her feelings toward Esmeralda is Paquette Chante- fleurie, an old woman whose burning hatred to- ward all Gypsies fuels her animus against the young Gypsy dancer.

First married to Esmeralda as a matter of convenience, Gringoire eventually inspires her love— only to be injured by the jealous Frollo. Although the young author survives the incident, Esmeralda is charged with his murder. Tried for both murder and witchcraft, she is tortured until she confesses; pronounced guilty at a ludicrous trial, she is rescued by Quasimodo, whose love for the Gypsy woman grew out of a simple act of kindness she showed him. Soon she encounters Paquette, who realizes that Esmeralda is, in fact, her daughter, Agnes, who had been kidnapped by Gpysies as a child. She realizes the truth too late, however, as Esmeralda is arrested and put to death. Aware that his master, Frollo, played a role in Esmeralda's fate, Quasimodo hurls the deacon to his death from atop the cathedral tower. Dejected, he makes his way to Esmeralda's grave, where he dies embracing her dead body.

At the core of Hugo's narrative is an abiding sense of fatalism. Raser noted in *Dictionary of Literary Biography,* "What becomes more apparent as one reads *Notre-Dame de Paris* is that its deep subject is decline: that of the cathedral and Paris, to be sure, but also that of the monarchy (in an often-noted scene, the king asks when his time will come), of architecture (Claude Frollo foretells the demise, with the advent of the printed book, of the cathedral as a source of knowledge), and of individual resolve (Frollo slowly gives in to his diabolical impulses)." Further, Raser notes, Hugo refers to this process as 'ANÁrKH, a Greek term for blind fate; it is this word that Frollo, driven to distraction by his preoccupation with Esmeralda, carves into a wall—a word that captures the inevitability of the tragic chain of events that his feelings for Esmeralda set in motion. Raser further noted, "However one looks at the novel—from the point of view of its description, or its characterization, or its social commentary—Hugo tells a story of relentless fatalism, of a vanishing world's resignation to its own disappearance."

Written during a period of acute political unrest, Hugo's novel received a tepid reception from French critics of the day, many of whom were offended by the author's social and political leanings. Common men and women in Hugo's novel are given political weight—an odious prospect to some who thought the author had given short shrift to the bourgeoisie. Further, the novel incensed certain other critics who objected to the novel's dearth of religious expression. The melodramatic plot, too, rife with stock figures from Romantic literature, offended critics such as John Ruskin, who dismissed Hugo's work as "disgusting." The public, however, did not find the book disgusting. In fact, it was such an immediate success that within just two years the book had already gone through several editions. It soon attracted world-wide notice and engendered scores of translations.

At The Writer's Workbench

After *Claude Gueux*, the story of a murderer who is sentenced to death, appeared in July 1834, Hugo turned his attention to drama, political statements, and poetry. A prolific and versatile poet, he is to this day known chiefly for his verse in his native France. Noted for his mastery of the language and experiments in style, he had an uncanny ability to capture a range of emotions: *Les Feuilles d'automne* (*Autumn Leaves*), published in 1831, con-

Les Miserables has been adapted to film several times, including this most recent production in 1998, starring Liam Neeson as Valjean.

veys the author's pain upon discovering his wife's love for another man; he expresses his love for his mistress, Juliette Drouet, in two collections— *Les Chants du crépuscule* (translated as *Songs of Twilight*) and *Les Rayons et les ombres* (*Sunlight and Shadows*)—while the poems of *Les Voix intérieures* (*Inner Voices*) convey the author's high regard for Napoleon.

Hugo's verse both foreshadowed and influenced later generations of poets ranging from Walt Whitman and Alfred Lord Tennyson to his compatriot, Charles Baudelaire, whose collection, *Les fleurs de mal*, is considered to be one of the most influential works in French verse. In an essay published in 1861, Baudelaire spared no praise for his predecessor, writing that "Victor Hugo was, from the onset, the man who was best endowed and most obviously chosen to express in poetry what I shall call the *mystery of life*." Beyond his ability to express universal themes, Hugo has garnered accolades for his self-appointed mission to reinvent the genre of poetry, which suffered from what critic Paul Valéry called "the decadent state of the art of verse." In his essay, "Victor Hugo, Creator through Form," published in 1958, Valéry wrote, ". . . in [Hugo] the artist is dominant. For more than sixty years he spent from five until noon each day at his poet's workbench. He spent himself in assaults on the ease and difficulties of a calling that came more and more to be his own creation. Picture this inventor at work. I mean just that: inventor; for with him the invention of form is as stimulating and urgent as the invention of images and themes."

A no less prolific playwright, Hugo enjoyed a great measure of success in the theater. His dramas focused largely on historical themes and reflected the author's abiding interest in questions concerning political power. His political critique, however, was not always well received by the censors: *Le Roi s'amuse* (translated as *The King's Fool*), for instance, was banned from the stage after its first performance in 1832 because of its critical portrayal of King François I. Hugo followed *Le Roi s'amuse* (which was the basis for the story of Verdi's opera, *Rigoletto*) with *Lucrèce Borgia*, his first prose drama. It was at rehearsals for this drama, completed and produced in 1833, that Hugo met the actress Juliette Drouet, who played the minor part of the Princesse Negroni. The two became involved in a love relationship that would span fifty years. Although the success

of his plays had provided him with financial freedom, Hugo stopped writing for the stage after his highly melodramatic *Les Burgraves*, produced in 1843, was coolly received by the theater-going public. Although he did pen one other play, *Torquemada*, written in 1869, and a number of other dramatic works, none were destined to be performed on the stage.

Politics, Exile, and *Les Misérables*

Hugo, who had been elected to the Académie Française in 1841 and elevated to the peerage in 1845, enjoyed enduring literary popularity in spite of occasional commercial and critical failures. But his political sympathies eventually made it impossible for him to remain in France. Having taken part in the revolution of 1848, he was elected to L'assemblée nationale the following year. A supporter of republicanism, he denounced Louis Napoleon's political agenda and was forced to flee the country in 1851 after the December 2 coup d'état. On December 11 he fled to Brussels, where he started to record his impressions of the coup in *Histoire d'un crime*. This and another pamphlet, disrespectfully titled *Napoléon-le-petit*, jeopardized Hugo's sanctuary in Belgium. In August of the following year he settled on the island of Jersey, moving again with his family to Guernsey in October 1855, where he would remain until his exile ended in 1870.

Exile did not silence Hugo, although he began to turn away from explicitly political works after *Les châtiments* (*The Punishments*), a collection of satirical poems denouncing Louis Napoléon and the government of the Second Empire, was published in 1853. His next publication, *Les contemplations* (1856) is widely regarded as his greatest poetic achievement. Highly personal and philosophical, the poems of *Les contemplations* address the author's grief over the death of his daughter, Léopoldine, who had been killed with her husband in a boating accident in 1843. The personal nature of Hugo's poems and the author's innovative use of metaphoric language together exerted a powerful influence over the later Symbolist poets.

Having published a number of other volumes of poetry, Hugo resumed work on "Misères," the draft of which he had composed from 1845 to 1848. Published in the spring of 1862, *Les Misérables* was a tremendous success even though

Hugo had long since lost touch with public taste. Criticized for its meandering narrative, excessive length—which spanned some fifteen hundred pages in most editions—and social criticisms, *Les Misérables* nevertheless found a wide audience from the time it was published. (It was published simultaneously in a number of countries.) The accessibility of his novel was paramount to Hugo, who insisted, in letters to his publisher, that the volumes be within the financial means of all. The culmination of Hugo's abiding interest in the plight of the underclass, *Les Misérables* is a tale of social redemption. In a letter to the poet Lamartine, Hugo explained his motives for writing this story: ". . . as far as a man can will it, I would destroy human fatality, condemn slavery, banish misery, enlighten ignorance, cure disease, illumine darkness, and detest hatred. These are my principles, and that is why I wrote *Les Misérables*." In fact, in the introduction to the novel, Hugo dedicated the book to all who endure exploitation, suffering, and ignorance. Sympathetic to the problems of the impoverished and highly critical of the legal system, the novel became a source of inspiration to social reformers in nineteenth-century France.

Les Misérables (the title of which may be rendered as both "the wretched" and "wretched") is a massive and compassionate portrait of the exploited French underclass in the early nineteenth century. Poorer than the working class, the characters who inhabit this milieu are driven to commit crimes—namely theft and prostitution—to survive. Central to the story is Jean Valjean, an ex-convict who is inspired to reform by the kindness of the Bishop Myriel. Valjean moves to the town of Montreuil sur Mer, and, under an assumed name, becomes an exemplary citizen. So successful is his transformation that he is elected mayor, and he manages to revitalize the town. In order to spare an innocent vagrant man who has been arrested for a crime he committed, Valjean is forced to reveal his own identity. Still wanted for his final crime—the theft of a coin from a young boy—he flees to Paris where he goes into hiding. He takes with him Cosette, an illegitimate girl he has saved from the mistreatment of the greedy Thénardiers, in whose care her ailing mother was forced to leave her.

Valjean raises Cosette as his daughter, and the two live together tranquilly for several years. Eventually, however, Javert, a determined policeman, dis-

---

If you enjoy the works of Victor Hugo, you may also want to check out the following books and films:

The works of Charles Dickens, including *Oliver Twist*, 1838.
Rosalind Laker, *The Sugar Pavillion*, 1994.
Judith Merkle Riley, *A Vision of Light*, 1989.
A Tale of Two Cities, a film based on Dickens's novel, 1935.

---

covers Valjean's whereabouts and sets out to arrest him. During the uprising of 1832 Valjean manages to save Marius—Cosette's love interest—and Javert. Unable to fathom Valjean's act of kindness, Javert shows no generosity when he apprehends the reformed convict, and later kills himself. Marius marries Cosette and thwarts the attempts of Thénardier to extort money from him. Also woven into the intricate plot are scores of other characters, a lengthy flashback, and numerous digressions—all of which lend an air of authenticity to Hugo's story.

Not all critics approved of Hugo's meandering narrative. Others, however, praised the author's ability to capture scene and mood in minute detail. In an 1885 essay, Scottish critic M. O. W. Oliphant noted that "Hugo has enough to spare for all subjects that occurred to him. A sunset, a landscape, a love song, alternate in his pages with a philosophical discussion or a brief and brilliant scene snatched from history, from contemporary life, from his own inner existence, all clothed in the noblest verse of which the French language is capable." Hugo's use of language, too, was a source of debate among critics. Although widely admired for his facility for expression, Hugo was criticized for the realism of some dialogues, which include accurate representations of the slang and unliterary French employed by the Parisian underclass.

The egalitarian spirit of Hugo's work also drew protest. Jules Barbey d'Aurevilly, for instance, objected to the book's "socialism." Others decried Hugo's indictment of the country's social and political machinery and feared the novel's empowerment of the exploited underclass. As Raser noted in *Dictionary of Literary Biography*, "This novel about redemption is also, necessarily, about the forces that work against happiness." Although Jean Valjean repeatedly provides evidence of his personal redemption, he encounters constant resistance from a society that refuses to acknowledge his transformation. These oppressive forces of society, Raser concluded, "are as much the subject of the novel as its nominal heroes." In a similar vein, Scottish novelist Robert Louis Stevenson wrote of the moral intention of the novel's depiction of oppressive social forces: "People are all glad to shut their eyes, and it gives them a very simple pleasure when they can forget that our laws commit a million individual injustices, to be once roughly just in the general; that the bread that we eat, and the quiet of the family, and all that embellishes life and makes it worth having, have to be purchased by death. . . . It is to something of all this that Victor Hugo wishes to open men's eyes in *Les Misérables;* and this moral lesson is worked out in masterly coincidence with the artistic effect."

"The transition was astounding. In the very heart of the city, Jean Valjean had left the city. In the blink of an eye, in the time it takes to lift a lid and let it fall, he had passed from the light of day to total darkness, from noon to midnight, noise to silence, from the thunderous commotion to the stagnation of the tomb. . . . For a few moments, he seemed to be dazed; listening, stupefied. The trap-door of salvation had suddenly opened beneath him. Divine benevolence had as it were caught him by treachery. The adorable ambushes of Providence!"
Victor Hugo, *Les Misérables*

Return from Exile

Eight years after the publication of *Les Misérables*—immediately following the defeat of Louis-Napoleon—Hugo returned to France. Crowds of people awaited his return to Paris, eager to hear the exiled author speak. "It was an indescribable welcome," Hugo wrote in his memoirs. ". . . I said to the people: 'In one hour you repay me for twenty years of exile.'" He returned, however, without his wife: on August 27, 1868, Adèle, who suffered from apoplexy, had died at the age of sixty-nine. Madame Hugo was buried in Villequier, where her daughter, Léopoldine, was interred. The Hugos' daughter, Adèle, too, was the victim of misfortune. Having fallen hopelessly in love with a soldier she had met through her father, she fol-

lowed the British lieutenant to Canada hoping to win his affection. She later wrote to her parents claiming to have been married, although no such ceremony had taken place. Returned to her father in 1872, Adèle was deemed mentally incompetent and was institutionalized until the time of her death at the age of eighty.

Hugo continued to write until he suffered a stroke in June of 1878. Convinced that the stroke was a minor setback, he did not wish to abandon his life's work. A four-month convalescence in Guernsey, however, did not restore his health. With the exception of the occasional verse, he ceased to write; he did not, however, cease to publish. A number of significant works—which, for various reasons, had never gone to press—were gradually made available to a public unaware that they had been written long before. In 1881, for instance, an old collection of poetry was published as *Les Quatre Vents de l'esprit* (*The Four Winds of the Spirit*) followed two years later by the final installment of *La Légende des siècles* (*The Legend of the Centuries*), the third in a series of poetry collections devoted to particular moments in time. The author, meanwhile, remained dear to the French, who celebrated his eightieth birthday as a national holiday. On February 26, 1881, thousands of supporters appeared in front of his home on the Avenue d'Eylau.

In spite of numerous other romantic liaisons, Hugo remained devoted to his mistress Juliette Drouet until her death. Drouet—who took on the responsibilities of a personal secretary following Hugo's stroke—died from stomach cancer on May 11, 1883. Too sick to attend the funeral, Hugo forbade anyone to mention her name in his presence. Just two years later, he succumbed to pneumonia. On the evening of May 14, 1885, Hugo took ill. Bedridden, he received friends and family during the following week; although usually lucid, he was sometimes delirious and shaken by his illness. On some occasions he uttered phrases in French, immediately translating them into Latin and then Spanish; on another he bolted from bed in the middle of the night crying, "C'est ici le combat du jour et de la nuit" (This is the struggle of day and night)—a flawless example of iambic hexameter. Finally, on Friday, May 22, having shown brief signs of recovering, he died at 1:27 in the afternoon. "I shall close my earthly eyes," Hugo had written in his will, "but my spiritual ones will remain open, wider than ever." "I decline the prayers of all Churches. I ask for a prayer from every soul." Hugo's passing was international news. His funeral on May 31 was marked by a day of mourning. A million people lined the route from the Arc de Triomphe to the Panthéon as the author's remains were transported to their final resting place in a pauper's hearse—according to the Hugo's wishes.

■ Works Cited

Baudelaire, Charles, "Victor Hugo," in *Baudelaire as a Literary Critic: Selected Essays*, translated by Lois Boe Hyslop and Francis E. Hyslop, Jr., Pennsylvania State University Press, 1964.

Dudaux, Madame, *Victor Hugo*, edited by Basil Williams, Constable & Co., 1921.

Foucher, Adèle, *Victor Hugo*, edited by Basil Williams, Constable & Co., 1921.

Maurois, Andre, *Olympio: The Life of Victor Hugo*, translated by Gerard Hopkins, Harper & Brothers, 1956.

The Love Letters of Victor Hugo 1820-1822, translated by Elizabeth W. Latimer, Harper & Brothers, 1901.

The Memoirs of Victor Hugo, translated by John W. Harding, G. W. Dillingham Co., 1899.

Meurice, Paul, editor, *The Letters of Victor Hugo*, Volume I, Houghton, 1896.

Meurice, Paul, editor, *The Letters of Victor Hugo*, Volume II, Houghton, 1898.

Oliphant, M. O. W., "Victor Hugo," in *Contemporary Review*, July, 1885, pp. 10-32.

Raser, Timothy, "Victor Hugo," *Dictionary of Literary Biography*: Volume 119, *Nineteenth-Century French Fiction Writers: Romanticism and Realism, 1800-1860*, Gale, 1992, pp. 164-92.

Stevenson, Robert Louis, "Victor Hugo's Romances," in *The Essays of Robert Louis Stevenson*, MacDonald, 1950, pp. 13-15.

Valéry, Paul, "Victor Hugo, Creator through Form," in *The Art of Poetry*, translated by Denise Folliot, Vintage Books, 1958, pp. 251-59.

■ For More Information See

BOOKS

Allen, John P., *Great Moments in the Theatre* (juvenile), Roy, 1958.

Brombert, V. H., *Victor Hugo and the Visionary Novel*, Harvard University Press, 1984.

Dewitt, William A., *Illustrated Minute Biographies* (juvenile), revised edition, Grosset, 1953.

Dictionary of Literary Biography: Volume 192, *French Dramatists, 1789-1914*, Gale, 1998.

Doyle, Ruth L., compiler, *Victor Hugo's Drama: An Annotated Bibliography, 1900 to 1980*, Greenwood Press, 1981.

Edwards, Samuel (pseudonym of Noel B. Gerson), *Victor Hugo: A Tumultuous Life*, McKay, 1971, reissued as *Victor Hugo: A Biography*, New American Library, 1975.

Foucher, Adele, *Victor Hugo raconte par un temoin de sa vie*, Lacroix & Verboeckhoven, 1863.

Grant, Elliott M., *The Career of Victor Hugo*, Harvard University Press, 1945.

Grant, Elliott M., *Victor Hugo: A Select and Critical Bibliography*, University of North Carolina Press, 1967.

Grant, Richard B., *The Perilous Quest: Image, Myth, and Prophecy in the Narratives of Victor Hugo*, Duke University Press, 1968.

Hugo, Victor, *Choses vues*, 1887, translation by David Kimber published as *Things Seen*, selected and edited by D. Kimber, introduction by Joanna Richardson, Oxford University Press, 1964.

Hugo, Victor, *Post-scriptum de ma vie*, posthumous publication, Calmann Levy, 1901, translation by Lorenzo O'Rourke published as *Victor Hugo's Intellectual Autobiography*, Funk & Wagnalls, 1907, new edition published as *Intellectual Autobiography* edited by L. O'Rourke, Haskell House Publishers, 1982.

Josephson, Matthew, *Victor Hugo: A Realistic Biography of the Great Romantic*, Doubleday, Doran, 1942, reprinted, Telegraph Books, 1982.

Laster, Arnaud, *Pleins Feux sur Victor Hugo*, Comedie-Francaise, 1981.

Latimer, Elizabeth W., translator, *The Love Letters of Victor Hugo 1820-1822*, Harper & Bros., 1901.

Lloyd, Rosemary, "The Colossus: Victor Hugo," in her *Baudelaire's Literary Criticism*, Cambridge University Press, 1981.

Meurice, Paul, *The Memoirs of Victor Hugo*, translated by John W. Harding, G. W. Dillingham Co., 1899.

Montgomery, Elizabeth Rider, *Story behind Great Books* (juvenile), McBride, 1946.

Nash, Suzanne, *"Les Contemplations" of Victor Hugo: An Allegory of the Creative Process*, Princeton University Press, 1976.

Nichol, J. Pringle, *Victor Hugo: A Sketch of His Life and Work*, Macmillan, 1893, reprinted, Richard West, 1973.

Richardson, Joanna, *Victor Hugo*, St. Martin's Press, 1976.

Swinburne, Algernon C., *A Study of Victor Hugo*, Chatto & Windus, 1886, reprinted, Folcroft, 1976.
Wack, Henry Wellington, *The Romance of Victor Hugo and Juliette Drouet*, Putnam, 1905.

PERIODICALS

Theatre Research International, spring, 1982.
Opera News, December 10, 1983.*

—Sketch by Marie J. MacNee

Paul B. Janeczko

England Association of Teachers of English, Maine Teachers of Language Arts, Maine Freeze Committee.

■ Personal

Born July 27, 1945, in Passaic, NJ; son of Frank John and Verna (Smolak) Janeczko. *Education:* St. Francis College, Biddeford, ME, A.B., 1967; John Carroll University, M.A., 1970. *Hobbies and other interests:* Swimming, cooking vegetarian meals, biking, working with wood.

■ Addresses

Home—Rural Route 1, Box 260, Marshall Pond Rd., Hebron, ME 04238.

■ Career

Poet and anthologist. High school English teacher in Parma, OH, 1968-72, and Topsfield, MA, 1972-77; Gray-New Gloucester High School, Gray, ME, teacher of language arts, 1977-1990; visiting writer, 1990—. *Member:* National Council of Teachers of English, Educators for Social Responsibility, New

■ Awards, Honors

English-Speaking Union Books-across-the-Sea Ambassador of Honor Book award, 1984, for *Poetspeak: In Their Work, about Their Work; Don't Forget to Fly: A Cycle of Modern Poems, Poetspeak, Strings: A Gathering of Family Poems,* and *Pocket Poems: Selected for a Journey* were selected by the American Library Association as Best Books of the Year.

■ Writings

Loads of Codes and Secret Ciphers (nonfiction), Simon & Schuster, 1981.
Bridges to Cross (fiction), Macmillan, 1986.
Brickyard Summer (poetry), illustrated by Ken Rush, Orchard Books, 1989.
Stardust otel (poetry), illustrated by Dorothy Leech, Orchard Books, 1993.
That Sweet Diamond: Baseball Poems, illustrated by Carole Katchen, Simon & Schuster-Atheneum, 1998.

POETRY ANTHOLOGIST

The Crystal Image, Dell, 1977.

Postcard Poems, Bradbury, 1979.

Don't Forget to Fly: A Cycle of Modern Poems, Bradbury, 1981.

Poetspeak: In Their Work, about Their Work, Bradbury, 1983.

Strings: A Gathering of Family Poems, Bradbury, 1984.

Pocket Poems: Selected for a Journey, Bradbury, 1985.

Going over to Your Place: Poems for Each Other, Bradbury, 1987.

This Delicious Day: 65 Poems, Orchard Books, 1987.

The Music of What Happens: Poems That Tell Stories, Orchard Books, 1988.

The Place My Words Are Looking For: What Poets Say about and through Their Work, Bradbury, 1990.

Preposterous: Poems of Youth, Orchard Books, 1991.

Looking for Your Name: A Collection of Contemporary Poems, Orchard Books, 1993.

Poetry from A to Z: A Guide for Young Writers, illustrated by Cathy Bobak, Simon & Schuster, 1994.

Wherever Home Begins: One Hundred Contemporary Poems, Orchard Books, 1996.

(With Naomi Shihab Nye) *I Feel a Little Jumpy around You: A Book of Her Poems and His Poems Collected in Pairs*, Simon & Schuster, 1996.

Home on the Range: Cowboy Poetry, illustrated by Bernie Fuchs, Dial, 1997.

Very Best (Almost) Friends: A Collection of Friendship Poetry, illustrated by Christine Davenier, Candlewick Press, 1998.

OTHER

Author of "Back Pages," a review column in *Leaflet*, 1973-76. Contributor of numerous articles, stories, poems (sometimes under pseudonym P. Wolny), and reviews to newspapers, professional and popular magazines, including *Armchair Detective, New Hampshire Profiles, Modern Haiku, Dragonfly, Friend, Child Life,* and *Highlights for Children.* Also contributor of articles to books, including *Censorship: A Guide for Teachers, Librarians, and Others Concerned with Intellectual Freedom,* edited by Lou Willett Stanek, Dell, 1976; *Young Adult Literature in the Seventies,* edited by Jana Varlejs, Scarecrow, 1978; and *Children's Literature Review,* Volume 3, Gale, 1978. Guest editor of *Leaflet,* spring, 1977.

■ Sidelights

"Paul Janeczko is the best collector of poems working on behalf of young adults today," according to Beth and Ben Nehms in their *English Journal* review of *Strings: A Gathering of Family Poems.* Poems from internationally known poets appear alongside those of young upstarts in the more than a dozen anthologies Janeczko has assembled. The books are distinctive because each provides multiple ways of understanding the experiences of young people through poetry while at the same time maintaining a distinct focus. Janeczko, who taught language arts for twenty-two years before becoming a full-time writer, is popular with young adults because he treats them with respect; the poems he selects are complex and challenging, and they never condescend to the reader. In his own collection of poetry, *Brickyard Summer,* Janeczko uses short, narrative poems to depict two teenage boys enjoying a summer away from school.

When Janeczko was growing up, it seemed highly unlikely that he would one day be a writer. He ranked in the middle of his class in school, but says in an interview with *Author and Artists for Young Adults (AAYA)* that he was more interested in baseball and riding bikes with his three brothers than he was in school. His mother, however, had other ideas about how he should spend his time, and in the fifth grade she made him read for twenty minutes each day. "I didn't want to read for twenty minutes," Janeczko remembers, "I had done my school work, that was reading, that was enough. I wanted to be out with my brothers, playing ball, getting into trouble." His mother prevailed, and at first Janeczko says that he started getting headaches from keeping one eye on his book and the other on the clock. Eventually, he says, "I started reading for longer and longer times, not because she was making me, but because I was finally starting to get into it. The Hardy Boys were exciting, dangerous, mysterious and funny. I didn't find out until much later that they were racist and sexist."

Janeczko attended the same schools as his older brothers, and remembers that when he was going to the Catholic High School his brother was "a thug and an outlaw and I was just this short little ninth-grader who called attention to himself by wearing a loud sweater vest." When his older brother graduated from high school his mother saw the chance to get her young son into a better school, so she transferred him to a school run by Christian brothers noted for their discipline and corporal punishment. The brothers failed to instill in him a great love for school, and his dislike is reflected in his novel, *Bridges to Cross,* which re-calls some of the difficulties of attending such a strict Catholic school.

Upon graduation from high school, Janeczko was accepted at St. Francis College, a small Catholic college in Maine. There, he explains, "I really began to change my attitude towards study, towards knowledge, towards intellectual pursuits. I saw that many of the people were just far better students than I was and realized at that point that I had wasted a lot of time. I needed to work harder just to tread water, and as I worked harder school became more interesting and satisfying." Eventually he decided to major in English. "Writing some bad poetry for the school's literary magazine," he recalls, "was almost a graduation requirement for an English major, so I did it." His English degree also taught him how to recognize and understand good poetry, though his discrimination developed slowly. Janeczko admitted in an *English Journal* essay that in high school he thought sentimental poet Rod McKuen was great: "I was touched by the Guru of Gush . . . and I hadn't been exposed to much poetry except the Greats, which to me and many of my friends meant poems difficult to read and impossible to understand. It was no surprise that I graduated from high school thinking there was an Official Approved List of Subjects You Can Write Poems About." When he graduated from St. Francis, Janeczko continues, he realized that the Official Approved List of Subjects You Can Write Poems About "was as wide as the universe. And the universe doesn't always rhyme."

Janeczko entered teaching after graduate school, he says, because "I wanted to be the teacher I never had." His enthusiasm and joy in teaching soon led him into the two activities that have dominated his professional life: writing and collecting good poems. "The late 1960s was a hell of a time to be a teacher," he remembers in his *AAYA* interview. "Paperback books were the god of the classroom, so we were reading *The Outsiders, The Pigman* and other young adult books and I read them and taught them and said 'I could do this.' As it turned out I couldn't, but I was motivated to try. The other thing that got me interested in writing was that I started writing for teaching magazines like *English Journal* and I started experiencing the narcotic of seeing my name in print in a serious way. I've never looked back since then."

Develops Interest in Poetry

Janeczko began collecting poetry as a practical response to his needs as a teacher. He recalls being encouraged to "do his own thing" in the classroom, and one of the things he wished to do was to introduce his students to poetry. He combed the huge poetry anthology that was available to him for good poems, but insists that the book "just wasn't cutting it. This was the 'Age of Aquarius' and some really challenging people were writing. Poetry was going through a period of change and I wanted the kids to experience some of that new poetry. I've always felt that any kid will read if you give him or her the right stuff, and that applies to poetry as well. I felt like if kids found contemporary poetry to their liking then somewhere down the line they may, in fact, discover and enjoy some of the classics." Janeczko was soon bringing in some of the better poems he remembered from graduate school and copying poems out of the small magazines that publish contemporary poetry. The students responded enthusiastically, hints Janeczko, partly because they liked what they were reading, and partly because they were rebels and enjoyed exploring the cutting edge of poetry.

Although Janeczko was building up quite a collection of poetry that he used in his teaching, he had no intention of doing anything with his collection—until he bumped into an editor at a teacher's convention in Las Vegas, Nevada. Soon they had agreed to publish *The Crystal Image,* Janeczko's first poetry anthology. "I had no idea then that anthologies were going to be what I would wind up doing or that poetry was going to be such an important part of my life," he tells *AAYA.* Some ten anthologies later, Janeczko has become more systematic in his compilation of poems for his anthologies. His anthologies tend to center on an idea or a theme: *Postcard Poems,* his second book, contains poems short enough to fit on a postcard sent to a friend; *Strings: A Gathering of Family Poems* collects poems about family; and *Pocket Poems: Selected for a Journey* is organized around the idea of being at home and then going out into the world and returning. Despite their thematic coherence, each of the volumes contains a wide variety of poems. In fact, Janeczko claims that the organization of any of his anthologies is more apparent to him than to anyone who might read the books. "When I put a book together it's very similar to writing a novel in the structural sense," he says. "I hope the whole book tells a story, even though nobody is going to sit down and read one of my anthologies from cover to cover like they do a novel. But if they were to do that they would begin to find a sense of continuity in the book."

One of the ways Janeczko gathers poems for his anthologies is by reading widely. "I read some poetry every day," he remarks in his *AAYA* interview, "and when I find a good poem I simply mark it off in the book, make a photocopy of it, and put it in a file that says 'New Poems.' Every so often I'll read through those and I'll say 'This is about flowers' and I'll put it in a flower folder. I don't really start thinking about a book until I say 'Boy, this flower folder or this love folder is really getting fat.'" Not all of Janeczko's groupings of poems become books, however. He remembers that at one point he had a number of wonderful poems about old age and aging, so he suggested to his editor that they do a book about this topic. The editor did not think it was a good subject for a whole book for young readers, but suggested that a book of poems about families might work. That idea was published as *Strings*. But rarely does Janeczko look for poems to fit a specific theme. "I look for poems that strike me," he says, "ones that I hope I'll be able to share with somebody someday."

Janeczko has ironed out many of the wrinkles of his selection process over the years. For instance, he learned after his second book that he did not want to write introductions to his anthologies. "What could I say in an introduction?" he asks. "I wrote one for *Postcard Poems* and it was just 'lah dee dah, lah dee dah,' here's how this idea came about, and so on. For the three pages that took I would rather have had, in retrospect, three more poems." This same principle has led him to generally exclude his own poetry as well. At first he excluded his own poetry because, when he compared his work to the other possible entries, he felt that it just was not as good. As time has gone on, however, he has made it his goal to include new poets, and that has excluded his work. "If my book has a hundred poems in it, it might have sixty poets," he remarks. "So if it comes down between putting my poems in the book or somebody else who is a new poet, I almost always go with the other person. If I write something good, I'll put it in one of my own books."

The 1993 work *Stardust otel* features fourteen-year-old Leary who composes poems about the girl he likes, his best friend, and life at his parents' weary hotel.

Janeczko has developed other methods of gathering poems, in part because he has come to know many of the poets he includes in his books. "What I've done for [several] books," he maintains, "is print out on my computer 100 postcards and send them to poets that I've used before and tell them what I'm looking for." He almost always asks for humorous poems and poems about baseball, the former because he figures that kids always need a laugh, and the latter because he is a diehard baseball fan. (Though he grew up a fan of the New York Giants and Mets, his allegiance has switched to the Boston Red Sox since he moved to New England.) He also asks his network of poets and friends to tell him about other poets he should read. Janeczko credits this network with helping him introduce new poets and new voices in his anthologies.

Janeczko's *Preposterous: Poems of Youth*, published in 1991, is primarily a book about boys, boys who are not quite men but feel the pull of manhood nonetheless. The opening poem, "Zip on 'Good Advice'" by Gary Hyland, sets the tone for the entire book by calling into question the authority of parents and their good advice. From that point on Janeczko groups his poems around such themes as anger, budding sexuality, the loss of a friend, and the delight to be found in mischief. In "Economics," a poem by Robert Wrigley, a young boy boils with rage at the man who owns everything he sees—and has a pretty daughter who seems unattainable. The boy strikes out where he can, but remains trapped in the impotence of his youth. Jim Wayne Miller's "Cheerleader" is no less striking a poem, though it deals with a very different pain of adolescence. In language reminiscent of a Catholic service, Miller condenses the sexual longing of adolescence in the image of a high school cheerleader who lives to share herself with others. She is "a halftime Eucharist" distributed to the adoring basketball fans who fill the high school gym to watch her perform. As her spin ends "The sweating crowd speaks tongues and prophecies." The poems speak to a young man's vague yearnings to have more— more knowledge, more freedom, more control— and they convey the feelings of youthful frustration.

Challenges Young Readers

Many of the poems Janeczko includes in these anthologies explore challenging and potentially controversial subject matter, and his decision to include such poems indicates his refusal to make easy distinctions between adult and young adult poetry. Janeczko insists that one of his goals is to challenge young readers, to get them to stretch their minds. At the same time, he feels that there are important differences between poetry for adults and poetry for young adults. "Young adults don't have the life experiences to understand a poem written by a man who is going through a divorce," he contends in his *AAYA* interview, "but they do understand the end of relationships, so I pick poems that deal with levels of experience that a teenager can understand." Another factor that differentiates the two types of poetry is the so-

phistication of the language, or syntax. "I would think twice," he admits, "about giving kids the poetry of Wallace Stevens [a twentieth-century poet who constructs elaborately metaphorical poems that treat language almost as a musical medium rather than a medium to convey ideas]." The poems that Janeczko selects *mean* something, though they may also be musical or metaphorical. Janeczko says that his anthologies have been successful because "they deal with themes that kids can understand, or they are told from an experience point of view, or they get readers to reach a little bit. There is something there for everyone."

In *Pocket Poems* Janeczko arranges the poems to suggest the passage of time and the passage from the security of childhood to the responsibilities of growing up. The book contains about 120 poems broken up into three sections. The first fifty poems "are about being someplace," the anthologist tells *AAYA*, and reflect the concerns of childhood and young adulthood; this first section ends with poems about going away. The middle section contains twelve seasonal poems, roughly representing the twelve months of the year, that suggest the passing of time. The final fifty poems are about being out in the world, about taking responsibility and growing up, but the section ends with poems about going back to someplace. If read continuously, the poems suggest a cyclical movement of time but, says Janeczko, "if you pick and choose your favorite poet or interesting titles you don't catch the structure. Missing the structure is not a big deal, it's just an extra thing that I do with the books." In *Don't Forget to Fly: A Cycle of Modern Poems*, however, a reviewer from *English Journal* found the book's organization to be one of its greatest strengths, commenting that "the poems are arranged like a symphony with similar subject matter grouped together."

"I put a lot of thought and effort into how the poems are arranged," claims Janeczko, "and people may not see the overall structure from beginning to end but I hope they see how poems are clustered, two or three or four together." In fact, Janeczko arranges the poems in such a way that it would be hard to read just one: the poems physically touch each other on the page. It is rare to find a poem alone on a page; instead one poem will end halfway down the page and the next will start directly below it. The reader is lured into reading that next poem and it leads to the next and so on. *Preposterous* contains a number of good examples of this type of organization. Miller's "Cheerleader" is preceded by Rodney Torreson's "Howie Kell Suspends All Lust to Contemplate the Universe," and followed by Bob Henry Baber's "Fat Girl with Baton." Torreson's poem pits Howie Kell's glib belief in creationism against the animal magnetism of Valerie Marslott, and Howie admits that his beliefs "would be shaken by [her] milky kiss." This poem is light and playful, but it also sets the stage for Miller's almost erotic consideration of a cheerleader by showing how shaken a young boy can be when he discovers physical attraction. Baber's fat girl serves as a counterpoint to these poems, for she is evidence that while some girls move in a nearly magic realm of male attention, others are destined to have their "Majorette Dreams . . . meet the ground/untouched," and for no better reason than their weight. The combination of the three poems allows a reader to consider the idea of male attraction in three very different ways, and suggests the effects that this attention has on both boys and girls. Similar groupings can be found throughout Janeczko's anthologies and they exist because, he says in his *AAYA* interview, "when people are reading the poems I want them to be thinking of things like 'Why is this poem here?,' or 'In this poem she took this point of view and I like this one better because. . . .' Although the poems speak for themselves, the alignment has something to say too."

Although each of Janeczko's anthologies has a different story to tell, the books are all similar in that they all encourage the reader to think, to play with words, and possibly to write poetry themselves. One anthology that conveys this message well is *Poetspeak: In Their Work, about Their Work*, which *English Journal* reviewer Dick Abrahamson called "a real find for teachers of poetry." In preparing this book, Janeczko asked all of his contributors to write a little note, no more than five hundred words, about one of the poems, about their writing process, or about anything else they wanted. The short essays encourage the young reader to dream, to imagine, to be a poet, for they remind the reader that poets are just people shaping their thoughts into words. Janeczko feels that this is an important message for kids to understand. He notes that the message was best expressed by Al Young's poem "Don't Forget to Fly," the last poem in the collection of the same name. "I think for some kids 'Don't Forget to Fly'

is a very important message, because they need to fly personally, creatively. As school budgets get cut and classes become more regimented it's going to be harder and harder for kids to fly. I do hope they get that message from my books, because I try to put in different ways of looking at life and I'm hoping that there are going to be poems that connect with these kids."

While the poems that Janeczko includes in his anthologies and the poems he writes are often uplifting, he feels that he can also use poetry to show young people that "life is not all glamour and glitz. There is that dark side." In "The Bridge," a poem from *Brickyard Summer*, Janeczko describes a group of boys' stoic reaction when one of their friends falls through the old railway trestle that their parents had warned them about: "The only words we said about it/were Raymond's/'We were lucky'/after we watched Marty/slide into the ambulance/wrapped in a rubber sheet." However, he recognizes that there are dangers in exploring the darker side of life. While developing another anthology, entitled *Looking for Your Name: Poems of Conflict*, he worried that the book's focus on conflict was too negative: "I'm aware that there are a lot of unhappy kids and I really don't want to add to that by giving a book that's just a real downer. My wife has been the head of a child abuse agency for the last five years, and after listening to her and just being more aware of what happens to families, I'm amazed that kids turn out as alright as they do."

Janeczko tells *AAYA*, "I don't want to be the 'Captain Bring Down' on poetry, so I try to strike a balance between the dark and the light poems, I try to write goofier ones or more 'hanging out with the guys' kind of poems. Part of what I want to do in a book is give kids some hope and some escape. If their life is a drag maybe reading one of the poems like "The Kiss" (in *Brickyard Summer*) will just give them a little spark and that's good." Many of the poems in *Brickyard Summer* explore the relationship between the narrator and his best friend, Raymond. The two boys share a deep bond, though the word "love" is never used to describe their relationship. When the glass-eyed town prophet in "Glass-Eyed Harry Coote" tells the narrator "Your gift is friendship," Raymond mutters "Should be against the law/to take money/for telling something/as plain as bark on a tree." In the course of the book the two boys share shoplifting, running from the town bullies,

If you enjoy the works of Paul Janeczko, you may also want to check out the following:

The works of Mel Glenn, including *Class Dismissed! High School Poems*, 1982, and *Who Killed Mr. Chippendale?: A Mystery in Poems*, 1996.

Anthologies by Lee Bennett Hopkins, including *Voyages: Poems by Walt Whitman*, 1988.

Ron Koertge, *Diary Cows*, 1981.

and secrets. Raymond is forgotten only at the end, when the narrator experiences his first kiss beside a moonlit pond. Though there is great excitement in the poem, there is also a melancholy sense that the friendship between the boys must change as a result of the kiss.

Janeczko quit teaching in 1990 in order to concentrate on his own writing and to spend more time visiting schools. Leaving teaching was a big step, for he had been teaching for twenty-two years. But, he declares, "It feels great! I always said that when I left teaching I wanted to leave at a time when I felt I could still do it well. I didn't want to be one of those burned out cases that just collects his pay check and counts the years to retirement. Now I can do what I want to do." His first year away from teaching was actually planned as a leave of absence, and during that year he became a father for the first time and spent a great deal of time with his new daughter, Emma. He discovered during that year how much he enjoyed writing, visiting schools, and talking to students, so he decided to make his retirement from teaching permanent. "I still get to work with kids, which is why I went into teaching in the first place," he comments, "but now I don't have to deal with the politics at the faculty meetings or correcting papers. I visit a school, I do my thing, and I leave." He misses the camaraderie of working with his friends, but says that he has made an effort to get together with those friends to watch a Boston Celtics game or a Boston Red Sox game.

Though Janeczko does not care much for the flying that being a visiting writer requires, he en-

joys the time that he spends visiting schools and talking with his young readers and their teachers and librarians. He describes what he does at the school in his *AAYA* interview: "Often I meet with a large group, like seventy kids, and I talk about the writing process, how it works for me. I show them how I get an idea and how I sometimes come up with a good poem or a funny poem. I read from *Brickyard Summer* or from whatever book I am currently working on, and then I answer questions. The other thing I'll do is hold a writing workshop with two or three classes for a period, but I've done more of the informal chatting and reading than I have the writing workshops."

Writing as a Process

One of the things that Janeczko talks to students about is the process by which he creates poems. Anyone reading Janeczko's *Brickyard Summer* would imagine that it is a collection of reminiscences about his childhood. The short poems describing the life of two boys passing the summer between eighth and ninth grade contain such clear images, such telling details, that they seem to grow out of the poet's memory. But Janeczko says that there is very little in *Brickyard Summer* that actually happened to him. "There was nothing spectacular about my childhood, but when I write I can make it funny, I can make it interesting, and I can make it exciting. I don't write the truth but I try to write what's true." Part of the difficulty in getting young people to write poems is getting them to let go of the facts of their experience when those facts do not suit the poem. "You take one little bit of your life," he advises, "and then you do something different with it, that's okay, this isn't history, this is a poem and you go with that."

Most of Janeczko's poems spring from his imagination, and begin as only an abstract idea. "Roscoe," a poem from *Brickyard Summer*, is a good example. In this poem two boys accidentally chase a neighbor's cat in front of a truck, and then hide their responsibility from the neighbor. Janeczko describes the poem's origins in his *AAYA* interview: "One of the things you grow up with when you're a Catholic is guilt. I wanted to write a poem about guilt and 'Roscoe' was my vehicle for doing that, because guilt was the experience, but I never did anything with a cat." Janeczko describes another idea he developed: "I wanted to write a poem about a dare, a group of kids saying 'I dare you to do this.' So the dare was that the narrator, much like the narrator in *Brick-yard Summer,* would go to the graveyard and kiss the tombstone of this girl who died twenty years ago at the age of sixteen, very mysteriously, no-body knows how she died or who paid for the stone angel that's above her tombstone. The dare was the idea for the poem and I tried to put clothes on it and see if it could walk around." Janeczko encourages young writers to stretch their imagination in similar ways, reminding them that they are not chained to the facts.

Another way Janeczko gets poems to work is by developing believable characters. "Sometimes I start with an idea, but a lot of times my poems are about characters. When I develop interesting characters, chances are they are going to do in-teresting things and so a lot of times I just come up with an interesting character and see what he or she does." One of the most convincing charac-ters in *Brickyard Summer* is the narrator's friend Raymond. Janeczko never had such a friend when he was young; he hung around with his broth-ers. But whenever the author visits schools stu-dents ask him if he really knew Raymond. He did not, but he enjoys the flattery.

Janeczko has promised himself a number of times that he would retire from anthologizing, not be-cause he does not like it but because he would like to spend more time on his own writing. Though he has already published a novel, *Bridges to Cross,* and a nonfiction book on secret writing, *Loads of Codes and Secret Ciphers,* his eventual goal is to write in even more areas. "If the poetry or the writing muse came in and sat in my chair—which, by the way, is an old seat from Comiskey Park in Chicago—and said 'I will grant you suc-cess in one field of writing. Which will it be?,' I would take mysteries, with poetry a close second." (His favorite mystery writers are Robert Parker and Ed McBain.) He would also like to write something about baseball, though he cannot de-cide whether it will be for kids or for adults, fic-tion or nonfiction. "Until I have the security of knowing that my writing will be my income," he tells *AAYA,* "I'll just continue doing different kinds of writing."

"The great thing about writing," Janeczko tells young people, "is that you can try different things.

W. Somerset Maugham [a noted English novelist] said there are three rules about writing a novel, and unfortunately nobody remembers what they are. I think that is also part of what I like about writing. I'm a disciplined person and I have my routine where I write, but as my wife has told me a number of times, I have this thing about authority, and I suspect that that applies to rules too. Rules? You can break the rules, and I think that is the biggest attraction about writing."

■ Works Cited

Abrahamson, Dick, Betty Carter, and Barbara Samuels, review of *Don't Forget to Fly* in "The Music of Young Adult Literature," *English Jour-nal,* September, 1982, pp. 87-88.

Abrahamson, Dick, review of *Poetspeak: In Their Work, about Their Work, English Journal,* January, 1984.

Baber, Henry, "Fat Girl with Baton," *Preposterous: Poems for Youth,* compiled by Paul B. Janeczko, Orchard Books, 1991, pp. 27-28.

Janeczko, Paul B., *Don't Forget to Fly: A Cycle of Modern Poems,* Bradbury, 1981.

Janeczko, Paul B., essay in "Facets: Successful Authors Talk about Connections between Teach-ing and Writing," *English Journal,* November, 1984, p. 24.

Janeczko, Paul B., *Brickyard Summer,* illustrations by Ken Rush, Orchard Books, 1989.

Janeczko, Paul B., *Preposterous: Poems of Youth,* Orchard Books, 1991.

Janeczko, Paul B., interview with Tom Pendergast for *Authors and Artists for Young Adults,* Gale Research, conducted February 18, 1992.

Miller, Jim Wayne, "Cheerleader," *Preposterous: Po-ems for Youth,* compiled by Paul B. Janeczko, Orchard Books, 1991, p. 27.

Nehms, Beth and Ben Nehms, "Ties That Bind: Families in YA Books," *English Journal,* Novem-ber, 1984, p. 98.

Torreson, Rodney, "Howie Kell Suspends All Lust to Contemplate the Universe," *Preposterous: Po-ems for Youth,* compiled by Paul B. Janeczko, Orchard Books, 1991, pp. 26-27.

■ For More Information See

BOOKS

Children's Books and Their Creators, edited by Anita Silvey, Houghton Mifflin, 1995.

Sixth Book of Junior Authors and Illustrators, Wilson, 1989.

Something about the Author Autobiography Series, Volume 18, Gale Research, 1994, pp. 151-64.

Twentieth-Century Young Adult Writers, St. James Press, 1994.

PERIODICALS

ALAN Review, spring, 1997, pp. 12-16.

Horn Book, March-April, 1990, p. 215; May-June, 1990, p. 343; November-December, 1998, p. 750.

Kirkus Reviews, December 1, 1998, p. 1742.

New York Times Book Review, April 27, 1980, p. 61; October 7, 1990, p. 30.

Publishers Weekly, March 16, 1998, p. 64; December 14, 1998, p. 76.

Riverbank Review, Winter, 1998/1999, p. 39.

School Library Journal, May, 1990, p. 118; March, 1991, p. 223.

—Sketch by Tom Pendergast

Paul Jennings

Personal

Born April 30, 1943, in Heston, England; immigrated to Australia in 1949; son of an engineer father and a housewife mother; married in the late 1970s, divorced about 1984; married Claire (a consultant and lecturer in language and literacy), mid-1980s; children: Gemma, Bronson, Sally, Andrew, Lind, Tracy. *Education:* Frankston Teachers College, 1963; Lincoln Institute, 1972. *Hobbies and other interests:* reading, gardening, skiing, playing the button accordion, classic English cars.

Addresses

Home—Belgrave, Victoria, Australia. *Office*—P.O. Box 189, Belgrave, Victoria 3160, Australia.

Career

Writer, speech pathologist, and special education teacher, 1963-68; speech pathologist, Ministry of Education, Australia, 1972-75; lecturer in special education, Burwood State College, 1976-78; senior lecturer, Language and Literature, Warrnambool Institute of Adult Education, 1979-88; became a full-time writer in 1989.

Awards, Honors

Young Australian Best Book awards, 1987, for *Unreal! Eight Surprising Stories*, 1988, for *Unbelievable! More Surprising Stories*, 1989, for *The Cabbage Patch Fib* and *Uncanny! Even More Surprising Stories*, 1990, for *The Paw Thing*, 1991, for *Round the Twist*, 1992, for *Quirky Tales! More Oddball Stories* and *Unmentionable! More Amazing Stories*, 1993, for *Unbearable! More Bizarre Stories*, 1994, for *Spooner or Later* and *Undone! More Mad Endings*, and 1995, for *Duck for Cover* and *The Gizmo*; Ashton Scholastic award, 1993, for *Spooner or Later* (with Ted Greenwood and Terry Denton); Australian Environment Award, 1994, for *The Fishermen and the Theefyspray* (illustrated by Jane Tanner). Jennings has also been a repeat winner of a number of other Australian child-selected awards, including Canberra's Own Outstanding List (COOL) Award, West Australian Young Readers' Book Award, Kids Own Australian Literature Award (KOALA), Kids Reading Oz Choice (KROC) Award, Books I Like Best Yearly (BILBY) Award, and South Australian CROW Award. For his body of work, Jennings has received the Gold Puffin Award, the Angus & Robertson Bookworld Award, and has been honored as an Appointed Member in the General Division of the Order of Australia.

■ **Writings**

JUVENILE

Unreal! Eight Surprising Stories, Penguin, 1985, Viking (New York City), 1991.

Unbelievable! More Surprising Stories, Penguin, 1986, Viking, 1995.

Quirky Tails! More Oddball Stories, Penguin, 1987, Puffin (New York City), 1990.

The Cabbage Patch Fib, illustrated by Craig Smith, Penguin, 1988.

Uncanny! Even More Surprising Stories, Penguin, 1988, Viking, 1991.

The Paw Thing, illustrated by Keith McEwan, Penguin, 1989.

Round the Twist, Penguin, 1990.

Unbearable! More Bizarre Stories, Penguin, 1990, Viking Penguin 1995.

The Naked Ghost, Burp! and Blue Jam, Longman Cheshire (Australia), 1991.

Unmentionable! More Amazing Stories, Penguin, 1991, Viking, 1993.

Round the Twist 1, Puffin, 1993.

Undone! More Mad Endings, Penguin, 1993, Viking, 1995.

The Gizmo, illustrated by Keith McEwan, Penguin, 1994.

The Gizmo Again, illustrated by Keith McEwan, Penguin, 1995.

Uncovered! Weird, Weird Stories, Penguin, 1995, Viking, 1996.

Come Back Gizmo, 1996.

Thirteen! Unpredictable Tales from Paul Jennings, Viking, 1996.

Sink the Gizmo, illustrated by Keith McEwan, Puffin, 1997.

Wicked, Penguin, 1998.

Singenpoo Strikes Again, Puffin, 1998.

(Contributor) *Listen Ear & Other Stories to Shock You Silly,* Puffin, 1998.

PICTURE BOOKS

Teacher Eater, illustrated by Jeannette Rowe, William Heinemann, 1991.

Grandad's Gifts, illustrated by Peter Gouldthorpe, Rigby Heinemann, 1991, Viking, 1993.

(With Ted Greenwood and Terry Denton) *Spooner or Later,* Viking, 1992.

The Fisherman and the Theefyspray, illustrated by Jane Tanner, Penguin, 1994.

(With Ted Greenwood and Terry Denton) *Duck for Cover,* Penguin, 1994.

■ **Adaptations**

Round the Twist was adapted as a television series by the Australian Children's Television Foundation, 1990.

■ **Work in Progress**

A movie script based on the author's four *Gizmo* novellas.

■ **Sidelights**

Paul Jennings is not yet the household name in North America that he is in his native Australia. However, if the reaction of reviewers and readers on this side of the globe is any indication, it seems only a matter of time until that changes. His imaginative, off-beat tales for pre-teen readers, which have been likened to the best-selling *Goosebumps* stories of R. L. Stine, are phenomenally popular Down Under. In fact, Jennings receives so much fan mail from young readers—about 5,000 letters per year—that he employs two secretaries to help him keep up with replies. Writing in a 1995 article for *Australian Way* magazine, freelance journalist Terry Lane aptly described Jennings as "a one-man industry." Indeed, he is nothing if not prolific. Jennings has written a succession of critically acclaimed bestsellers since 1989, the year that he quit his job as a special education teacher to become a full-time writer. Total sales of his books now exceed three million copies, and Jennings has won a host of awards, including the Order of Australia for his service to children's literature.

Although Jennings's stories might raise eyebrows among parents, critics have praised his efforts for getting kids to sit down and *read* in the first place. Echoing that comment, Jennings once told *Something about the Author,* "Some adults think I should write about the sorts of things that they think kids *should* read. I only want to write the sorts of things that I think kids *want* to read. Books are fantastic. That's what I want my readers to think."

Jennings lives in Australia, but he was actually born in the English town of Heston, near London, on April 30, 1943. Six years later, with the country still mired in the economic aftermath of the Second World War, Jennings's parents packed up their son Paul and his younger sister Ruth, and they emigrated to Australia. There they settled in the city of Melbourne, where Jennings's father found work as an engineer. "I had a good childhood," Jennings writes in an autobiographical sketch that appears on his Internet homepage. "I can remember all the good parts . . . very clearly. I can also remember all the fears and feelings of childhood that aren't so good. Feeling very small and powerless. The guilt and the embarrassment. The monster that I was quite sure lurked in the shadows. These are the things that I write about in my stories and which make some children ask, 'How do you know what it feels like to be me?'. It's because I haven't forgotten those feelings. . . ."

Jennings told interviewer Fay Gardiner of *Scan* magazine that his father was a man who "had very high expectations; he was a very ambitious man." On the prompting of the elder Jennings, who decided that his son should receive vocational training, Jennings quit high school in his senior year to enroll at Frankston Teachers College. "In those days, you didn't need matriculation because there was a shortage of teachers," he explained to Gardiner. After receiving his certificate, Jennings taught for the next five years in the primary school system. His work there with young people who suffered from learning disorders got him interested in this specialized area of education.

Jennings returned to college to study speech pathology—the science of speech disorders. He earned an undergraduate degree from Lincoln Institute in 1972, and then spent three years working for the Ministry of Education. In 1976, he became a lecturer in Special Education at Burwood State College, near Sydney. Then in 1979, Jennings moved on to become a senior lecturer in Language and Literature at Warrnambool Institute of Adult Education in Warrnambool, a regional city in the state of Victoria. It was during the latter part of this ten-year period that Jennings's first marriage crumbled, and he was left on his own to raise the couple's four young children. As an outlet for some of the raw emotions he was feeling, Jennings joined a creative writing class and began writing stories for young people. He recalled in an interview with Mary Jo Fresch of the Australian magazine *Dragon Lode* that he was "very interested in families with single parents to legitimize them as proper families." He was also frustrated by what he felt was a lack of good stories for young readers.

A parakeet returning from the dead and a boy with a serious fingernail problem are among the bizarre tales in this short story collection.

Jennings told Fresch that in his work he had observed that many of the books available in libraries for what he calls "reluctant readers" were either poorly written or "talked down" to children. Worst of all, they were dull. In an article in *Magpies,* Jennings defined a "reluctant reader" as being "a child for whom adults have not been able to find a good enough book." Jennings decided he would write such books for readers in the eight- to twelve-year-old age group. In preparation for doing so, he began to systematically study the structure, language, and plots of children's stories. This helped him devise a series of informal guidelines to avoid the common mistakes other authors made. The Jennings recipe for readability called for stories for young readers to be clearly and concisely written; to have predictable language patterns, short sentences, and chapters; and to include no more than two or three main characters. But above all, Jennings decided, a successful story needs a plot that is imaginative, humorous, and unpredictable. "Magic is a must," he explained in his *Magpies* article. "You can't write for children unless you can remember what it is like to be a child."

Jennings had written four brief books related to his teaching work, but he had dreamed of writing fiction for many years. In an autobiographical sketch posted on his British publisher's Internet homepage, he recalled, "One of my early

This collection of ultrastrange stories, like many of Jennings's other works, received a Young Australian Best Book Award.

attempts to get published was sending a story in to the *Women's Weekly* [magazine] when I was sixteen. They rejected the story and I was so upset by this that I didn't write again until I was thirty-nine." Encouraged by his experiences in the writing course that he was taking, Jennings submitted one of his stories to the Australian office of Penguin Publishers. As a result, he was offered an advance of $400 Australian to write some more. Jennings later told a reporter for the local newspaper, the *Warrnambool Standard,* that it took him about a year to write the seven more stories needed for the book; his efforts paid off handsomely. *Unreal! Eight Surprising Stories* was an instant bestseller. Most books for young readers available in Australian bookshops were imports written by British or American authors, and so reviewers and readers alike loved that one of their own had written a book with an Australian perspective, vernacular, and settings. But even better was the realization that the stories, full of humor, plot twists, and deliciously unexpected endings, were good enough to appeal to readers anywhere. That assessment was confirmed when *Unreal!* was subsequently reprinted in Great Britain and North America—after some of the Australianisms had been amended for the overseas markets. (This would become standard practice for all of Jennings's books.) A critic in *Publishers Weekly* praised this debut collection for being "light, fast-paced entertainment sure to satisfy appetites for the grotesque." Jeanne Marie Clancy of *School Library Journal* wrote, "Both the vocabulary and the terse, journalistic style coupled with a frequent first-person point-of-view make (*Unreal!*) a natural for reluctant readers and story-tellers."

Surprised and delighted by the success of *Unreal!,* Jennings promptly went to work on a new book, which was called *Unbelievable! More Surprising Stories.* Once again, the reception was favorable. "Stories like these can sometimes be just crazy enough to keep a child's interest going where other books fail," commented a reviewer in Jennings's hometown newspaper, the *Melbourne Herald.* "They are also shorter and less demanding than novels, which makes them an interesting alternative for reluctant or bored readers."

Writing Two Books Yearly

Having now hit his literary stride, Paul Jennings began writing feverishly. He produced a succes-

If you enjoy the works of Paul Jennings, you may also want to check out the following:

Joan Aiken, *A Whisper in the Night: Tales of Terror and Suspense,* 1988.
Chris Lynch's "He-Man Woman Haters Club" series.
The works of John Scieszka and Lane Smith, including *The Stinky Cheese Man and Other Fairly Stupid Tales,* 1992, and the "Time Warp Trio" series.

sion of best-selling books—sometimes two per year—through the late 1980s and into the 1990s. The Jennings formula clearly worked, for kids loved his stories. His books often dealt with bizarre topics; for example, there were stories about such things as a haunted outhouse, fly-killing cow "dung custard," a dead man's tattoos which come to life, and a boy's embarrassment at having to wear pink underpants with fairies on them. Predictably, some adults regard such dark humor distasteful; reviewing the 1987 short story collection *Unbelievable,* Bill Boyle of the British publication *Books For Keeps* dismissed Jennings's fiction as "definitely an acquired taste." Jennings responded to such comments by defending his work to all who would listen. "Some people feel that bleak humor is an inappropriate form to use with children. I don't agree," he explained in a 1988 speech he gave at a conference of Australian educators (a transcript of which was subsequently published in *Magpies*). "As George Bernard Shaw said, 'Life does not cease to be funny when someone dies anymore than it ceases to be serious when someone laughs.'"

With the emergence of Jennings as an important new Australian writer, people began paying more attention to what he was saying and how he was saying it. Some thoughtful reviewers pointed out that there are recurring themes in Jennings's fiction. Embarrassment is one; the vagaries of father-son relationships and the uncertainties of childhood are a couple of the others. Jennings does not deny that he tries to deal in his writing with what he feels are universal themes for young readers. "I guess basically what I do is observe very closely the world children live in now and I

put the feelings I had as a child on top of it," he told Fay Gardiner.

A "short story magician"

A great many readers around the world apparently agreed with Karen Jameyson of *Horn Book* when she hailed Jennings as a "short story magician." Jennings continued to win fans with each new book. He wrote a succession of short story collections that proved popular with readers, including *Quirky Tales: More Oddball Stories* (1987), *Uncanny! Even More Surprising Stories* (1988), *Unbearable! More Bizarre Stories* (1990), *Unmentionable!*

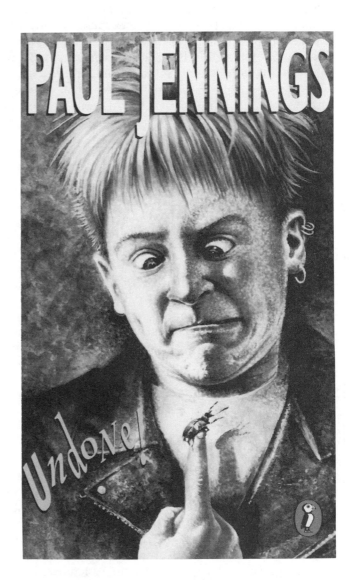

A boy develops a see-though body in this collection of eight brief but inventive stories.

More Amazing Stories (1991), and *Undone! More Mad Endings* (1993), and *Thirteen! Unpredictable Tales From Paul Jennings* (1996). Critics have also continued to praise Jennings's books, which have won him a shelf full of literary awards, including Young Australian Best Book awards each year from 1987 to 1995.

Despite his phenomenal success, Jennings has refused to rest on his laurels. He has tried his hand at longer fiction; he wrote two books about a clever cat: *Paws* and a sequel called *Singenpoo Strikes Again*. And Jennings created a four-part series that began with a 1994 novella called *The Gizmo*, which recounts the strange adventures of a boy who on a dare steals a mysterious electronic gizmo from a market stall. The unlucky thief discovers that the device sticks to anyone who touches it and that it exchanges the unlucky person's clothes for those of any passersby. Ann Darnton of *School Library Journal* praised *The Gizmo* as "an amusing and well-written book," while George Hunt of *Books for Keeps* described it as "a lurid and slightly risqué story [that] . . . might well appeal to older readers who are more at home with comic books." Jennings related the further adventures of the Gizmo in three other books: *The Gizmo Again*, *Come Back Gizmo*, and *Sink the Gizmo*.

Jennings moved in another new direction when he collaborated with fellow children's author Morris Gleitzman to write a six-part "serial story" called *Wicked*. According to reviewer Elaine McQuade of *School Librarian*, *Wicked* "is a wild, fantastic, roller-coaster of an adventure, full of 'slobberers' and evil rates and other gross creatures. But underlying the gripping story is a sensitive examination of the death of a parent, of the effects of divorce, and of the difficulties of living within a step family."

Picture Books Have Purpose

In recent years, Jennings has also worked successfully with various illustrators to create picture storybooks. Sometimes the themes have been serious; that was the case when Jennings wrote the text for *The Fisherman and the Theefyspray*, an impassioned book about animal conservation and endangered species that won an Australian Environment Award. At times, Jennings's themes have been light-hearted, as was the case in *The Cab-* *bage Patch Fib*, a hilarious lesson in the "facts-of-life." And at other times, Jennings's themes have been educational as well as fun, as was the case in *Spooner or Later,* a game book where silly illustrations are accompanied by "spoonerisms"— wordplay in which the beginnings of the words in a phrase are reversed, so "read the book" becomes the nonsensical "bead the rook." Jennings delights in this kind of humor, but he notes it also has a more serious purpose. Picture books are a publishing genre which he feels have been neglected as a potential tool to grab reluctant young readers. "Picture books are capable of giving enormous pleasure," Jennings explained in an essay *Magpies*. "It is only the stigma of being seen with them that confines picture books to the lower grades."

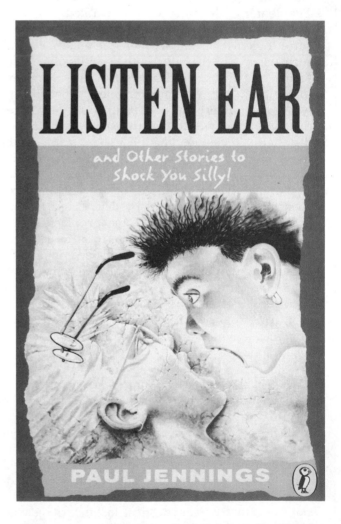

A youngster who tells a lie is chased by his own face in this collection of funny, gross, scary, weird, and shocking tales.

Given the popularity and the strong visual component of Jennings's storytelling, it was almost inevitable that film producers would come knocking on his door. Sure enough, in 1990 he was enlisted to begin writing scripts based on his stories for a weekly Australian television series called *Round the Twist*. Then, in an unabashed marketing ploy, Jennings joined forces with illustrators Glenn Lumsden and David de Vries to start recycling the scripts into a series of comic books. Reviewing their first effort, *Round the Twist 1*, Kevin Steinberger of *Magpies* noted that while the publication had "great visual appeal," it—and others pending in the series—would be "less imaginative reads than the original short stories which have already proved their appeal convincingly."

Regardless of what television critics or book reviewers have said, the *Round the Twist* television series was a hit. In response, Jennings has now written television scripts for more than two dozen of his short stories, and he has decided to try his hand at writing for the movies. According to information that Jennings posted on his Internet Web site in the fall of 1998, he was hard at work on a script for a feature film. "This is all highly secret but I can tell you that [it] is based on my four Gizmo books," he teased. Based on his track record so far, Jennings's foray into movies is sure to be a success.

■ Works Cited

Boyle, Bill, review of *Unbelievable!*, *Books for Keeps*, September, 1987.

Clancy, Jeanne Marie, review of *Unreal!*, *School Library Journal*, December, 1991, p. 117.

Darnton, Ann, review of *The Gizmo*, *School Library Journal*, November, 1995, p. 152.

Fresch, Mary Jo, "Unreal! Unbelievable! Meet Australian Author Paul Jennings," *Dragon Lode*, November, 1994.

Gardiner, Fay, "Real! Bearable! And Believable!," *Scan*, May, 1991.

Hunt, George, review of *The Gizmo*, *Books For Keeps*, November, 1995, p. 12.

Jameyson, Karen, "News from Down Under," *Horn Book*, July-August, 1992, p. 499.

Jennings, Paul, "Unreal . . . That's for certain," first published in *Warrnambool Standard*, November 16, 1985, found on Paul Jennings' Internet homepage at http://people.enternet.com/~jennings/educ/wrtt.htm.

Jennings, Paul, "The Man on the Stairs," *Magpies*, September, 1988, pp. 9-12.

Jennings, Paul, "Keeping the Magic Going," *Magpies*, March, 1990, pp. 5-9.

Jennings, Paul, comments in *Something About the Author*, Volume 88, Gale, 1996, pp. 114-17.

Jennings, Paul, autobiographical sketch on the author's Internet homepage, found at http://people.enternet.com/~jennings/educ/wrtt.htm.

Jennings, Paul, autobiographical sketch on the Puffin (UK) Internet homepage, found at http:/www.puffin.co.uk/living/aut_25.htm.

Lane, Terry, "Unbeatable!", *Australian Way*, December, 1995.

McQuade, Elaine, "Finding the Right Book for the Right Child," *School Librarian*, Summer, 1998.

Steinberger, Kevin, review of *Round the Twist 1*, *Magpies*, November, 1993, pp. 33-34.

Review of *Unbelievable! More Surprising Stories*, *Melbourne Herald*, October 30, 1986.

Review of *Unreal! Eight Surprising Stories* and *Uncanny! Even More Surprising Stories*, *Publishers Weekly*, October 11, 1991, pp. 63-64.

■ For More Information See

BOOKS

Children's Literature Review, Volume 40, Gale, 1996, pp. 117-28.

ON-LINE

Penguin Books Web site located at http://www.penguinputnam.com.

PERIODICALS

Booklist, October 15, 1988, p. 423; March 15, 1990, pp. 1467, 1471; August, 1991, p 2147; March 15, 1993, p. 1314; January 1, 1995, p. 816.

Books For Keeps, July, 1986, p. 17; July, 1989, p. 10; July, 1991, p. 12; September, 1993, p. 13; September, 1996, p. 16.

Bulletin of the Center for Children's Books, September, 1991, p. 43.

Carousel, Winter, 1996, p. 23.

Children's Book Review Service, December, 1991.

Five Owls, May/June, 1996, p. 104.

Horn Book, July/August, 1992, pp. 497-500.

Junior Bookshelf, April, 1996, p. 78.

Kirkus Reviews, October 15, 1991, p. 1344; January 1, 1993, p. 62.

Magpies, September, 1988; September, 1990; September, 1993, p. 39; July, 1998.

New Advocate, Fall, 1996, pp. 327-28.

Publishers Weekly, October 11, 1991, p. 63; December 11, 1995, p. 71; August 31, 1998, p. 21.

Puffin Post, Spring, 1996.

Reading Time, Volume 42, number 2, p. 17.

School Librarian, November, 1993, p. 156.

School Library Journal, January, 1992, p. 113; January, 1995, p. 108.

Tribune Books (Chicago), February 12, 1995, p. 6.

Voice of Youth Advocates, October, 1995, p. 234.

—Sketch by Ken Cuthbertson

Sebastian Junger

■ Personal

Born in 1962, in Massachusetts; son of Miguel (a physicist) and Ellen (an artist) Junger. *Education:* Graduated from Wesleyan University, 1984.

■ Addresses

Home—Manhattan, NY. *Office*—c/o W. W. Norton, 500 Fifth Ave., New York, NY 10110. *E-mail*—sjunger@literati.net.

■ Career

Writer and freelance journalist. *City Paper*, Washington, DC, journalist. Has also worked as a high-climber for tree-cutting services.

■ Awards, Honors

"International Books of the Year" list, *Times Literary Supplement*, 1997, for *The Perfect Storm*.

■ Writings

The Perfect Storm: A True Story of Men Against the Sea, Norton, 1997.

Junger's work has appeared in *Men's Journal, Outside, American Heritage, New York Times, New York Times Magazine, This Old House,* and *Michigan Quarterly Review.* Contributor of short story "How Do You Like the South?" to the anthology *American Fiction,* edited by Wallace Stegner.

■ Adaptations

The Perfect Storm was optioned for a film by Warner Brothers and has been adapted for audio cassette by Random House AudioBooks, 1997.

■ Sidelights

Sebastian Junger's 1997 book, *The Perfect Storm*, catapulted the first-time author to the sort of celebrity for which most writers hunger their entire lives. His book about a sea tragedy rode the waves of the *New York Times* bestseller list for months. The paperback rights fetched a sum in the seven figures. In addition, Junger's agent sold the film rights, and Junger's dust-jacket photo adorned articles in magazines and newspapers from the august to the fluffy—from *Times Literary Supplement* to *People*; the latter even included him in their "Sexiest Man" issue. "It's totally bewildering," Junger told an on-line interviewer for Amazon.com, referring to his overnight success. "I mean, a couple of years ago I couldn't even make a living as a freelance journalist. There was no transition from no living to way-too-much living. No transition at all."

The story of six fishermen who went down with their ship, the *Andrea Gail*, in the waters off Nova Scotia in a 1991 storm, *The Perfect Storm* caught the imagination of the reading public not only in the United States, but also in England. Yet it was a most unlikely success. "In a way, there's no story," Junger told Sam Jemielity in a *NewCity* on-line interview. "There's a big hole in the middle of the story, because no one can ever know what happened to that boat. As soon as they leave [port], there's almost no storyline. There's no dialogue, there's no thoughts; it's all conjecture." Resisting temptations to fictionalize his account, Junger stuck to the facts, as understated as they might be, and to information gleaned from interviews with the survivors of other fishing boats that weathered the largest waves ever recorded in the Atlantic.

Junger saw his book initially as something that would appeal to a small audience, perhaps only a local one at that, for it was largely set in the fishing town of Gloucester, Massachusetts. "It didn't have 'bestseller' written on it," Junger explained to Ellen Barry in an interview for the *Providence Phoenix*. "I didn't want to invent dialogue or fictionalize or any of the stuff that readers love. I was sure I was condemned to write a journalistically interesting book that wouldn't fly. It would be too heavy. The topic is too weird and idiosyncratic. It's all the things that kill books."

But *The Perfect Storm* was, as it proved, unsinkable, selling over half a million copies in hardcover. "I think people are fascinated by danger and risk and these crushingly powerful forces of nature," Junger told Amazon.com. "And they should be. I mean if a volcano erupting or a storm at sea or someone being killed in a war isn't compelling, what is? I think there's a normal human fascination with things that can annihilate us." Junger's fascination with those things that can "annihilate us" started with his own youth.

Suburban Youth—On the Edge

Junger's own childhood showed glimmerings of the chance-taking that would that would later turn him into a journalist who would cover subjects of extreme danger. The son of an Austrian-born father and a mother of English-Irish-Scottish ancestry, Junger was a child not only of blended cultures, but also of eclectic interests. His physicist father and artist mother taught him early on to value his "creative qualities as a human being," as Junger told Jemielity in *NewCity*. He grew up in suburban Belmont, Massachusetts, a "shy, alienated little kid," as he described himself to Laurel Touby in a *New York* profile. Given his family background, he felt a bit of an outsider among the other kids at school and in the neighborhood. An early incident concerning baseball cards brought this home to him. Junger, wanting to be part of a crowd who traded baseball cards, tried to bring his meager supply to the exchange table only to be told by the leader of the group that he did not belong there. "And I'm like . . . that's exactly what I'm thinking," Junger related to Jemielity. "My father is European. He never played baseball with me. . . . But I think that feeling of not quite being included contributed to me as a writer."

A voracious reader of books about Native Americans, Junger was impressed by their manhood rituals. He devised his own coming-of-age rites and survival games, such as swimming in Cape Cod in the middle of winter or jumping onto a moving train. "I wasn't violent," Junger told Touby. "It was a question of daring." Surfing introduced him to the sea and its varied moods, but he lived a mostly suburban childhood, later attending Wesleyan University where he played on the soccer team and earned a degree in cultural anthropology—as good a preparation as any for an aspiring writer. "I grew up in the suburbs, I went to private school," Junger told Barry in the *Providence Phoenix*. "You feel emasculated by that kind of background when you look at a man who has been in 50-foot seas and come back with a weird look in his eyes."

An Intellectual Hobo

Junger decided to put the sheltered past behind him upon graduation. He began his writing career as a journalist for the *City Paper*, a free alternative weekly in Washington, D.C., where one of his stories dealt with favoritism in the award of cable franchises. Restless, he set out to travel around the country, working at odd jobs and assigning himself stories that interested him. Touby in *New York* characterized Junger as "An intellectual hobo" during these years, writing on subjects from the smallest border town in Texas to tugboats in Boston harbor. He kept telling himself that as long as he wrote about things that he really liked, then it would show in the writing, and sales would take care of themselves.

One such self-assigned story, on the blues singer Robert Johnson, earned him a mere $50 from the *Michigan Quarterly Review*. During these years he also experimented with fiction, publishing a short story in a collection edited by Wallace Stegner, but he finally decided to concentrate on nonfiction. "I felt that either I was going to have to compromise my interests or the publishing world was going to have to change—which is not going to happen, obviously," Junger told the Amazon.com interviewer. "I was on the verge of giving up on trying to make a living writing about what I wanted to write about."

Some early sales encouraged him, including a piece for the *New York Times Magazine;* "Hitting the Wall" was a somewhat tongue-in-cheek look at how males deal—or don't deal—with anger. In the article, Junger tells his own story of how he broke the fifth metacarpal in his hand in that age-old male ritual of hitting the wall to demonstrate anger. "I did it after a monthlong difference of opinion with my girlfriend," Junger wrote in "Hitting the Wall." "Things finally boiled over. I picked a soft spot on the wall and hit it with all my might." That soft spot turned out to have a stud hidden beneath it, necessitating a trip to the emergency room. The article is part re-creation of this visit, part rumination on the male need to show temper, and part humorous advice column on how to hit the wall without causing injury. Already evident in this early piece is Junger's understated, distanced tone—he may be writing about violence, but does it in a matter-of-fact manner. Touby quoted one of Junger's editors, Hampton Sides from *Outside* magazine, commenting on this aspect of Junger's writing: "He approaches those stories gently, almost as a scholar or a naturalist would. He's old school—his interest is almost Victorian, like Herman Melville or Joseph Conrad." In his article, Junger pulls back

from the pain of the incident to report anatomy: "The fifth metacarpal goes from the wrist to the knuckles of the little finger. If it's broken near the knuckle (a so-called boxer's break), it can tolerate a fair amount of angulation. . . ." This fascination with how things work, this cool journalistic distancing is a technique that would serve him well in the writing of *The Perfect Storm.*

Meanwhile, Junger was also putting bread on the table with manual labor—working as a tree cutter and trimmer. A chainsaw, body harness, and ropes are all part of the paraphernalia that he donned for his work as a high-climber, the most dangerous of jobs on the tree-cutting crew. "Tree work grounds me," Junger told Touby in *New York* magazine. "It's who you are now and how you master each moment that counts." It was his own dangerous job that first got him interested in other such risky work. A gash in the leg laid him up for a time, and it was then he took a hard look at the possibilities of writing an entire book about dangerous occupations. He spent two months in Idaho with smoke jumpers, an experience which became a chapter of his planned book.

Subsequently he sold a condensed version of this chapter to *Men's Journal,* and then began work on another chapter for the book, this one about six men who died on a swordfish boat off the Grand Banks in the storm of 1991. Junger himself had been living in Massachusetts at the time of this storm, and it seemed a likely candidate for a chapter of his book. However, at his agent's suggestion, he wrote a book proposal about this sea story, a long shot in Junger's mind. After leaving the treatment with his agent, Junger set off for the war zone in Bosnia to gather information on other people with dangerous occupations—war correspondents. While there, he got a call from his agent: the book proposal had been sold for $35,000. Junger was on the next flight out.

The Perfect Storm

Junger's work had just begun; now he had to turn this sample chapter into a real book. "My agent sold the book, but even then I thought, 'No one wants to read about the history of Gloucester. No one wants to read about a storm,'" Junger told Amazon.com. "I had some definite concerns because, well, all that happens is a boat disappears. No one knows exactly what happened to it." So

Junger had to fill in his story with what happens to the other people on shore, with information both esoteric and commonplace about fishing, weather patterns, the history of Gloucester, Massachusetts, where the hapless crew set out from, and even a close taxonomy of the swordfish. "I didn't want to fictionalize at all," Junger told Amazon.com. "I'm not a fiction writer. I have been, and it was very depressing, so I got clear of that."

In early drafts he did attempt some fictional recreation of the last minutes of the *Andrea Gail*, the swordfish boat that was lost in the storm, but he quickly gave this approach up. "Recreating the last days of six men who disappeared at sea presented some obvious problems for me," Junger wrote in the "Foreword" to *The Perfect Storm*. "On the one had, I wanted to write a completely factual book that would stand on its own as a piece of journalism. On the other hand, I didn't want the narrative to asphyxiate under a mass of technical detail and conjecture." Junger skirted the fine line between each extreme in his telling of the events leading up to the storm of the century in late October 1991 off the Northeast coast of the United States, and of the loss of life aboard one swordfish boat caught in it.

Junger's cast of characters include crew members from the *Andrea Gail:* its captain, Billy Tyne, and crew members Alfred Pierre, David Sullivan, Bugsy Moran, Dale Murphy, and Bobby Shatford. He also tells the stories of those left on shore: wives, girlfriends, and mothers. Early chapters of the book take the reader into the lives of those who fish for a living—of the boom-or-bust nature of it all, and the economic pressures that drive young men and women to take on one of the most dangerous jobs around. As Junger noted in the book, "More people are killed on fishing boats, per capita, than in any other job in the United States." The town of Gloucester itself loses a chunk of its population every year to the sea. "Since 1650," Junger wrote, "an estimated ten thousand Gloucestermen have died at sea, far more Gloucestermen than died in all the country's wars."

Junger also tells the story of this sea tragedy from the point of view of the members of other fishing boats, ones that survived the storm. Prominent among these is Linda Greenlaw, a college-educated skipper of the *Hannah Boden*, who as

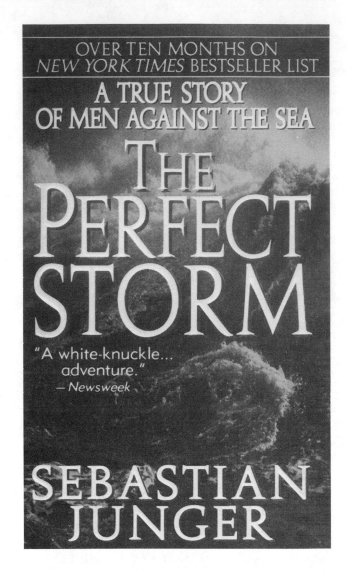

Junger relates the ill-fated voyage of the *Andrea Gail*, a six-man crew ship that sank off the coast of Nova Scotia during a 1991 storm.

Junger described her, is not only one of the few women in the industry, "she's one of the best captains, period, on the entire coast." Since publication of *The Perfect Storm*, Greenlaw has become a mini-celebrity, with a book contract of her own.

But it is not only the human drama that made Junger's book such a quirky winner; he also manages to blend whole cargo ships full of information regarding the history of the swordfish industry, the setting of fish lines at night, the placement of fuel tanks for proper balance—all sorts of technical details that he found while researching the subject. One chapter even details the

If you enjoy the works of Sebastian Junger, you may also want to check out the following books and films:

John Krakauer, *Into the Wild*, 1996, and *Into Thin Air*, 1997.
Gary Paulsen, *Hatchet*, 1987.
Das Boot, a film about life on a German U-boat, 1981.

anatomy of death, giving a close physiological description of death by drowning. Added to this mix is a fine eye for detail, as in this description of one early evening aboard the *Andrea Gail*: "The boat rolls along atop an old decayed swell, and the crew catch up on their sleep and take turns at the helm. A new moon rises behind them on October 7th, and they follow its pale suggestions all through the day until late in the afternoon. The sunset is a bloody rust-red on a sharp autumn horizon, and the night comes in fast with a northwest wind and a sky rivetted with stars. There's no sound but the smack of water on steel and the heavy gargle of the diesel engine."

From late September to mid-October the fishing is poor, but by the third week of October the luck changes for the men aboard the *Andrea Gail*. Their twenty-hour days are paying off, and by October 25, the boat has taken 40,000 pounds of swordfish and tuna, valued at about $160,000. Tyne sets a course for home, hoping to beat the other boats in the fleet and capture the highest prices for his catch. Halfway home on October 28, the *Andrea Gail* is south of Nova Scotia when nature meets her head on. A strong nor'easter out of Canada merges forces with the tail end of Hurricane Grace and is subsequently pushed back to the New England coast by a high pressure region. It's a once-in-a century occurrence—a "perfect" storm in meteorological parlance.

When the storm hits, 100-foot waves and 120-mile-per-hour winds sweep across the Atlantic. The last radio message from the *Andrea Gail*—"She's comin' on boys, and she's comin' on strong."—was sent at 6 p.m. on October 28. All that was left of the fishing boat afterward were fuel drums found far to the west of its last location. Not a romantic ending to a story, but then Junger had not set out to romanticize the lives of fishermen. "These

port towns and fishing communities either get romanticized in literature or not written about at all," Junger told Amazon.com in his interview. Junger pulled no punches about the lives of people in Gloucester, Massachusetts, many who had taken him into their confidence, had re-opened healing emotional wounds to talk about lost loved ones. "Ultimately they liked the book," Junger went on. "They felt it gave them voice."

The Critical Response

The citizens of Gloucester were not the only appreciative audience. The critical response was immediate and laudatory. A critic in *Kirkus Reviews* noted that the "experience of being caught at sea in the maw of a 'perfect' storm . . . is spell-bindingly captured by Junger. . . . [His] fine dramatic style is complemented by a wealth of details that flesh out the story. . . . Reading this gripping book is likely to make the would-be sailor feel both awed and a little frightened by nature's remorseless power." A *School Library Journal* reviewer called the book "True adventure at it's best," while *Time*'s John Skow noted that Junger was "grimly precise about the mechanics of drowning" and presented a "fine, boozy picture of the fishermen's bars of Gloucester, Mass., the *Andrea Gail*'s home port." Tom De Haven, writing in *Entertainment Weekly*, echoed Junger's own early doubts about the book, asking "Who'd have figured that bad weather—really bad weather—would enthrall beach readers this summer?" De Haven remarked that *The Perfect Storm* was "Ferociously dramatic and vividly written," and concluded that it "is not just the best book of the summer. It's an incredible experience."

Concluding an extensive review of *The Perfect Storm* in the *New York Times Book Review*, Anthony Bailey declared that Junger's work was "thrilling—a boatride into and (for us) out of a watery hell." A similar response came from Richard Ellis, writing in the *Los Angeles Times Book Review*: "*The Perfect Storm* is a wild ride that brilliantly captures the awesome power of the raging sea and the often futile attempts of humans to withstand it." A critic in *Publishers Weekly* summed up its review by noting that the book "is a thrilling read and seems a natural for filming." The reception to the book across the Atlantic was equally positive. Writing in the *Times Literary Supplement*, John Sutherland called Junger's book "terse" and "extraordinarily readable," concluding that "This is a fine and moving book which deserves to succeed." Robert Stone included *The Perfect Storm* among his picks for "International Books of the Year" in *Times Literary Supplement*, dubbing it a "nonfiction book of great power."

A patch of rough water hit with publication of a New York *Observer* article claiming that Junger had played hard and fast with the facts, bringing into question once again the entire genre of so-called "literary journalism" and faction, a trend in books started by Truman Capote with his *In Cold Blood* of 1966. However, as one fisherman whom Junger had interviewed subsequently told Ellen Barry in the *Boston Phoenix*, "The true test is probably the fishermen and their reactions. [Junger] put it so that even if you were a pig farmer from Ohio, you could understand."

This mini-tempest did not command Junger's attention for long; he was too busy getting on to other projects. In March 1998, he was one of the first journalists on the scene in Kosovo to verify the Serb atrocities in the town of Prekaz. He got into Kosovo, supposedly off-limits to journalists, by driving over the mountains of Montenegro. It is not so much an attraction to danger that drives Junger, but a quiet respect for those who undergo the challenge of danger on a daily basis. Said Junger to Jemielity, "I'm always going to write about people on the edge of something."

■ Works Cited

Bailey, Anthony, "The Tempest," *New York Times Book Review*, June 22, 1997, p. 8.

Barry, Ellen, "In Gloucester, a Local Storm Made Good," *Boston Phoenix*, August 21-28, 1997.

Barry, Ellen, "Backwash: Is This Boat Taking on Water?", *Providence Phoenix*, August 28-September 4, 1997.

De Haven, Tom, review of *The Perfect Storm*, *Entertainment Weekly*, August 1, 1997, p. 66.

Ellis, Richard, "Sturm und Drang," *Los Angeles Times Book Review*, May 25, 1997, p. 8.

Jemielity, Sam, "Storm Trooper," *NewCity*, www.opus1.com/~tw/WW/02-02-98/chicago_bookfeat.html.

Junger, Sebastian, "Hitting the Wall," *New York Times Magazine*, August 16, 1992, p. 14.

Junger, Sebastian, *The Perfect Storm*, Norton, 1997.

Junger, Sebastian, on-line interview with Amazon.com at www. amazon.com/exec/obidos/...sebastian.html/002-9657243-8324223.

Review of *The Perfect Storm*, *Kirkus Reviews*, March 15, 1997, p. 440.

Review of *The Perfect Storm*, *Publishers Weekly*, April 7, 1997, p. 83.

Review of *The Perfect Storm*, *School Library Journal*, November, 1997, p. 149.

Skow, John, "Cast Up on the Sea," *Time*, June 23, 1997, p. 80.

Stone, Robert, et al, "International Books of the Year," *Times Literary Supplement*, December 5, 1997, p. 12.

Sutherland, John, "The Same Cruel Life," *Times Literary Supplement*, July 18, 1997, p. 8.

Touby, Laurel, "Hot Type," *New York*, May 19, 1997, p. 40.

■ For More Information See

PERIODICALS

Booklist, March 15, 1998, p. 1210.

Entertainment Weekly, September 5, 1997, p. 68.

Library Journal, May 14, 1997, p. 90.

London Review of Books, November 27, 1997, p. 34.

Newsweek, June 16, 1997, p. 55.

Observer, August 10, 1997, p. 14.

Publishers Weekly, December 16, 1996, p. 25; July 28, 1997, p. 21; March 2, 1998, p. 9.

School Library Journal, December, 1997, pp. 29, 38.*

—Sketch by J. Sydney Jones

Jackie French Koller

■ Personal

Born March 8, 1948, in Derby, CT; daughter of Ernest James (an electrical engineer) and Margaret (a homemaker; maiden name, Hayes) French; married George J. Koller (president of a hospital) July 11, 1970; children: Kerri, Ryan, Devin. *Education:* University of Connecticut, B.A., 1970.

■ Addresses

Home—Westfield, MA.

■ Career

Author. *Member:* Society of Children's Book Writers and Illustrators and former SCBWI regional advisor.

■ Awards, Honors

Koller has received a number of awards, including American Library Association Best Books for Young Adults, American Library Association Notables, International Reading Association Teacher's Choice, International Reading Association Young Adult's Choice, American Bookseller's Association Pick of the Lists, New York Public Library Reluctant Reader Recommended List, Bulletin for the Center for Children's Books Blue Ribbon, Bank Street College Annual Book Award, Honor Book and Junior Library Guild.

■ Writings

FOR CHILDREN

Impy for Always, Little, Brown, 1989.
The Dragonling, Little, Brown, 1990.
Mole and Shrew, Atheneum, 1991.
Fish Fry Tonight!, Crown, 1992.
Mole and Shrew Step Out, Atheneum, 1992.
The Dragonling, Archway Minstrel, 1996.
A Dragon in the Family, Archway Minstrel, 1996.
No Such Thing, Boyds Mills Press, 1997.
Dragon Quest, Archway Minstrel, 1997.
Mole and Shrew, All Year Through, Random House, 1997.
Dragons of Krad, Archway Minstrel, 1997.
Dragon Trouble, Archway Minstrel, 1997.
Dragons and Kings, Archway Minstrel, 1998.

FOR YOUNG ADULTS

Nothing to Fear, Harcourt, 1991.
If I Had One Wish. . ., Little, Brown, 1991.

The Last Voyage of the Misty Day, Atheneum, 1992.
The Primrose Way, Harcourt, 1992.
A Place to Call Home, Atheneum, 1995.
The Falcon, Atheneum, 1998.

OTHER

Also contributor of the long poem *What If?*, to *Cobblestone*; "Home Early," published in *Spider*, 1994; ""Oink!" Said the Cat," published in *Ladybug*, 1996.

■ Work in Progress

The Promise, for Knopf, 1999; *One Monkey Too Many*, for Harcourt, 1999; *Bouncing on the Bed*, for Orchard, 1999; *Nickommoh! A Thanksgiving Celebration*, 1999. A short story, "Brother, Can You Spare a Dream?," will appear in *Time Capsule Anthology*, edited by Don Gallo, for Bantam, 2000.

■ Sidelights

Jackie French Koller has spent her life immersed in stories, listening as her mother read to her when she was a baby; conjuring up make-believe adventures to entertain herself; and developing a lifetime habit of avid reading. As a young mother, Koller found herself steeped in books again, this time for her infant daughter, Kerri. Like giving birth over and over again, the stories that Koller had inside her began emerging. "At first I wrote them for Kerri and the two little brothers who followed her, but gradually I began to share them with others, and people began to encourage me to try publication," Koller said in an interview with Diane Andreassi for *Authors and Artists for Young Adults*. Then after her youngest child was out of diapers Koller began attending writers' conferences where she learned her trade. Six years and hundreds of rejection slips later she began her journey as a professional writer. Koller sold *Impy for Always*, a chapter book, and just a couple of weeks later sold a novel, *Nothing to Fear*. Her writing has been praised by reviewers like Esther Sinofsky of *Voice of Youth Advocates*, who applauded Koller's second historical fiction novel, *The Primrose Way*. Sinofsky felt the book would be good for teachers of history, women's studies, and multiculturalism. "Recommend this book to young adults who enjoy good historical fiction," the critic remarked.

Koller's life and at least two books were inspired by her parents, who met at the end of World War II, married soon after, and moved to Connecticut. Koller's mother, Margaret, was one of nine children who grew up in poverty in New York City during the Great Depression. Margaret's father was an abusive alcoholic who rarely worked, and her mother supported their family by working as the janitor of their building. But Margaret's family was often hungry and poorly clothed, so as a sophomore in high school Koller's mother dropped out of school to work full-time so she could help support her brothers and sisters. Koller's mother's childhood struggles inspired *Nothing to Fear*. Koller's father's life was equally difficult and was the backdrop for her short story "Brother, Can You Spare a Dream?" Koller's paternal grandfather was also an alcoholic. Koller's father, Ernest, was a teen when his father went to jail for killing a woman in a hit-and-run accident. Meanwhile Koller's grandmother took up with a hobo.

After Koller's grandfather was released from jail, her grandparents went through a number of separations and reconciliations until they finally divorced. Determined to make a better life for himself, Ernest graduated from high school and put himself through engineering school by working four jobs. World War II began and Koller's father joined the Navy as an officer. He met Margaret and they were married. "Needless to say, my parents didn't have the best role models in the marriage or parenting department, and they hit many snags along the way, but they tried hard to give us children the best life they possibly could, and my memories of early childhood are good ones," Koller said in the *AAYA* interview.

As a youngster, Koller developed the ability to entertain and amuse herself. "I didn't have any imaginary friends per se, but I developed a vivid imagination and was forever pretending," she said in the *AAYA* interview. "I would dream up great adventures for my siblings and friends to act out, and I, of course, was always the star, the hero, or, one might say, the main character, for as I look back now I can see that those early games of pretend were my first attempts at creating stories." A tomboy who was quite bossy around children her age, Koller described herself as "the one who came up with the ideas for what we should do and how we should do it." Koller was very quiet, however, around adults because she was raised with the philosophy that children should be seen and not heard: "I was a great listener, though, and loved to creep to the top of the stairs and eavesdrop when my parents were having guests or parties."

As soon as Koller could read to herself, it became a constant pastime. She loved to curl up in a cozy corner or in the crook of a tree and read for hours. Her favorites, books that her mother gave her and had been her best loved novels, were *Black Beauty, Heidi, Little Women* and fairy tales. "I could never get enough fairy tales," Koller ex-

"Compelling."—*Booklist*
"Highly satisfying."—*School Library Journal*

THE
PRIMROSE
WAY

GREAT
EPISODES

JACKIE FRENCH KOLLER

After sixteen-year-old Rebekah Hall befriends members of the Pawtucket tribe, she begins to question her Puritan heritage in Koller's 1992 historical novel.

plained in the *AAYA* interview. As a youngster, school work came easily to her, and she was a straight A student. As she grew bored and disenchanted with the work, her grades dropped; however, she rarely got less than a B. "These days I would have been put in accelerated classes and challenged, and I would probably have had a much better school experience, but in the post war years there were thirty-five kids in a class and little time or money for special programs," Koller explained in the *AAYA* interview.

Growing Pains

As an adolescent Koller was tall, bright, and tomboyish; this did not put her on the "most popular list" in school. By the time she entered sixth grade, she had sprouted to five foot eight inches tall, which made her the tallest student in the class. "To make matters worse, I got 103 on my first science test and word spread that not only was I a giant, I was a brain, too—the kiss of death for a girl back then," Koller told *AAYA*. She had a hard time making friends and finally connected with other misfits who were also struggling. In high school, Koller remembers, she was often the last to be chosen by team captains, sat out dance after dance at school events, and never was asked for a date. Adding to that turmoil, her parents were having troubles and home was not a refuge. She took solace in books and nature. Living near woods, beautiful ponds, and streams, Koller went hiking alone after school and found herself daydreaming at length, making up stories in which she was beautiful, popular, glamorous, famous, mysterious—whatever she felt like that day. She would return home, dive into a book, and lose herself in the story and characters, leaving all the pain of the real world behind.

During this time, Koller never dreamed of being a writer. "I didn't think it was something an ordinary person could do, and no one ever told me otherwise," Koller told *AAYA*. While she always wrote well, no teacher ever encouraged her to pursue it as a career. In fact, it was her art work that drew the most attention and initially she thought she might be an animator. Then she considered art school, until her father convinced her it was a risky business. Instead, Koller enrolled at the University of Connecticut and studied interior design, but it never really excited her. Her social life, however, took off. She was no longer the tallest woman in class, and she finally fit in because being smart was admired in college. "I had friends and dates and was courted by the most prestigious sororities on campus, and had to pinch myself sometimes to see if I was still really me underneath," Koller told *AAYA*. She met George J. Koller her junior year, and they were married in 1970. Her husband went on to graduate school, and she supported them by working in the insurance industry. With the birth of her first child, Kerri, also came the beginning of her new career as a writer. As Koller read to her infant child, her own imagination became rekindled and her daydreams became reality in print. At first she wrote her stories solely for Kerri (and later Kerri's two younger brothers), and gradually Koller began to share them with others who encouraged her to get them published.

Koller's first young adult work, *Nothing to Fear*, is about an Irish immigrant family living in poverty in New York City during the Depression. The only family income is what Danny can make shining shoes and what his mother earns doing laundry. His father leaves town to seek work and Danny becomes the man of the house. Pregnant and weary, his mother loses her laundry work and Danny begins begging for food. The family finally finds relief, ironically, by helping a sick and hungry stranger who appears at their doorstep. Rosemary Moran of *Voice of Youth Advocates* described the story as "in turn depressing and enriching." Ann Welton of *School Library Journal* stated that the work had a strong "plot line and numerous interesting supporting characters will hold readers' attention." Zena Sutherland, in a review for *Bulletin of the Center for Children's Books*, was less impressed when she wrote: "Believable but banal." She believed the novel doesn't offer "fresh twists" to already published fiction about the Depression. However, a critic in *Kirkus Reviews* remarked that *Nothing to Fear* is an "involving account of the Great Depression . . . conjuring an entire era from the heartaches and troubles of one struggling family."

In 1992 came *The Last Voyage of the Misty Day*, which Koller described as being inspired by her father's lifelong love of the sea and fascination with boats of all kinds. The story concerns Denny who moves with her mother from New York City to the coast of Maine after her father's death. Struggling with a new climate and isolation, Denny meets her odd neighbor, Mr. Jones, who

---

If you enjoy the works of Jackie French Koller, you may also want to check out the following books and films:

Jennifer Armstrong, *Bridie of the Wild Rose*, 1994.
Patricia Calvert, *Yesterday's Daughter*, 1986.
Jean Thesman, *When the Road Ends*, 1992.
This Boy's Life, a film starring Leonardo DiCaprio, 1993.

---

works endlessly repairing the wrecked boat that he has made his home. She ultimately learns that people aren't always what they seem. Susan Knorr of *School Library Journal* described the work on the boat as "nicely integrated" into the plot, but she also felt that Denny's "overblown emotional shifts, along with occasional trite dialogue" may put readers off. Zena Sutherland in *Bulletin of the Center for Children's Books*, however, stated that the book's conclusion as rewarding, saying it "moves to a dramatic ending."

By this time, Koller had begun to hone her own writing style and was building a tunnel to the publishing world. Another 1992 novel, *The Primrose Way* is about a sixteen-year-old girl, Rebekah Hall, who comes to live with her Puritan father in seventeenth-century Massachusetts. Pretending that she is converting the local Native Americans, Rebekah befriends Qunnequawese, the chief's niece. This awakens a cultural understanding between the two. Rebekah's interest in the Native American way of life makes her question the Puritan salvation. Her problems worsen as she falls in love with the tribe's holy man, Mishannock. Getting inside the psyche of her characters meant learning the history of the time and cultural mores. "I try to find as much original source material as possible—diaries, journals, letters—and then I also read extensively, including ethno-historical studies on the people and times," Koller told *AAYA*. While some reviewers found flaws, like Ilene Cooper in *Booklist* who wrote, "Koller has a few awkward moments at first," most gave the work high praise. Sinofsky wrote in *Voice of Youth Advocates* that Koller has written a "beautiful story" of Rebekah searching for her identity, with "carefully researched" scenes depicting early Massachusetts. A contributor in *Kirkus*

Reviews proclaimed that Koller creates a vivid landscape that "successfully de-romanticizes the early settlers' struggles and avoids the absolutes (us-good, them bad)." Barbara Chatton in *School Library Journal* was equally impressed, remarking: "Koller's carefully researched book incorporates authentic language in a readable text."

Earns Reviewers Praises

Koller did extensive research about the foster care system, interviewing a social worker, before she introduced her readers to Anna O'Dell in *A Place*

ifteen-year-old Anna O'Dell struggles alone to care for her two younger siblings after her alcoholic mother commits suicide.

to Call Home. One day the fifteen-year-old Anna returns home from school and finds her infant brother, Casey, screaming. Anna instantly knows that her alcoholic mother has left them for good. This time, however, her mother is found drowned in a lake, having committed suicide. Anna is determined to keep her five-year-old sister, Mandy, and Casey together with her. Anna, who is biracial, shows her intelligence, strength, and determination to fight for "the greater good for her family," according to Hazel Moore in a review for *Voice of Youth Advocates.* Carolyn Noah of *School Library Journal* called this novel an "eloquent depiction of impoverishment and courage." She went on to say that the novel is "fast paced" and "compelling," with "satisfying social values." Merri Monks of *Booklist* stated that *A Place to Call Home* is a "finely written novel that shows the tragic" outcome of sexual abuse and family rejection. In fact, these issues are Koller's main concern with society today. "We pay a lot of lip service to the importance of "family values and education, but very little ever changes," Koller told *AAYA.* "Children should be our number one national priority—their health, their well being, their education. Children's caregivers should be among the most highly respected and highly paid professions we have."

In *The Falcon,* published in 1998, Koller uses a journal format to bring out a secret about Luke, the work's protagonist. Luke's self-destructive behavior lands him in a psychiatric hospital, and he must heal a deep emotional scar on his way to recovery. "Luke's strong voice comes through quite believably throughout," according to Roger Leslie in *Booklist.* Paula Rohrlick of *Kliatt* called the novel an "involving and often suspenseful tale."

Koller, whose hobbies include making ginger bread houses, lives and writes at home, on ten acres on a mountaintop in Western Massachusetts with her husband, her youngest son, and two Labrador retrievers. She writes at least seven hours a day, four times a week. "I talk to myself a lot," Koller told *AAYA.* "That's the only way I can describe it. I get an idea for a story and I decide on the main character and then I walk around having conversations with that character until I know him or her well enough to start putting his/her story down on paper." Koller said that she always keeps her audience in mind while she is writing and that she often stops and asks herself if the story is going to hold the interest of a reader, and whether or not it is a subject to which a young reader can relate. "Sometimes I start out thinking I'm writing a picture book and then realize that it's getting too involved and sophisticated, so I'll start over with an older audience in mind and write the story as a chapter book or novel," Koller told *AAYA*. "I hope young readers will see themselves or others that they know in my books and that my books will encourage a love of reading."

■ **Works Cited**

Chatton, Barbara, review of *The Primrose Way, School Library Journal*, September, 1992, p. 278.

Cooper, Ilene, review of *The Primrose Way, Booklist*, October 15, 1992, p. 418.

Knorr, Susan, review of *The Last Voyage of the Misty Day, School Library Journal*, June, 1992, p. 116.

Koller, Jackie French, interview with Diane Andreassi for *Authors and Artists for Young Adults*, fall, 1998.

Leslie, Roger, review of *The Falcon, Booklist*, April 15, 1998, p. 1436.

Monks, Merri, review of *A Place to Call Home, Booklist*, October 15, 1995, p. 396.

Moore, Hazel, review of *A Place to Call Home, Voice of Youth Advocates*, February, 1996, p. 373.

Moran, Rosemary, review of *Nothing to Fear, Voice of Youth Advocates*, October, 1991, p. 228.

Noah, Carolyn, review of *A Place to Call Home, School Library Journal*, October, 1995, p. 155.

Review of *Nothing to Fear, Kirkus Reviews*, March 1, 1991.

Review of *The Primrose Way, Kirkus Reviews*, September 15, 1992, p. 1189.

Rohrlick, Paula, review of *The Falcon, Kliatt*, July, 1998.

Sinofsky, Esther, review of *The Primrose Way, Voice of Youth Advocates*, December, 1992, p. 280.

Sutherland, Zena, review of *Nothing to Fear, Bulletin of the Center for Children's Books*, March, 1991, p. 168.

Sutherland, Zena, review of *The Last Voyage of the Misty Day, Bulletin of the Center for Children's Books*, April, 1992, p. 211.

Welton, Ann, review of *Nothing to Fear, School Library Journal*, May, 1991, p. 93.

■ **For More Information See**

PERIODICALS

Bulletin of the Center for Children's Books, January, 1993.

Horn Book Guide, December, 1995.

Voice of Youth Advocates, June, 1992.

—Sketch by Diane Andreassi

Nancy Kress

■ Personal

Born January 20, 1948, in Buffalo, NY; daughter of Henry Francis (a purchasing agent) and Angelina (a homemaker; maiden name, Canale) Koningisor; married Michael J. Kress, 1973 (divorced, 1984); married Charles Sheffield (an author), January, 1998; children: (first marriage) Kevin Michael, Brian Stephen; (stepchildren) Rose, Toria. *Education:* State University of New York at Plattsburgh, B.S. (summa cum laude), 1969; State University of New York at Brockport, M.S. (education), 1978, M.A. (English), 1979. *Politics:* Independent. *Religion:* None.

■ Addresses

Home—Silver Spring, MD. *Electronic mail*—nankress @aol.com; http://www.sff.net/people/nankress. *Agent*—Ralph Vicinanza, 111 Eighth Ave., Suite 1501, New York, NY 10011.

■ Career

Writer, 1981—. Fourth-grade teacher, Penn Yan, NY, 1970-73; State University of New York, Brockport, college instructor (intermittent), beginning 1980; Stanton & Hucko (advertising agency), Rochester, NY, copywriter, 1984-89. Teacher of writing at various places, including Bethesda Writing Center, Bethesda, MD, Clarion Writers' Conference, and Cleveland State Imagination Workshop. Member, Literacy Volunteers. *Member:* Science Fiction Writers of America.

■ Awards, Honors

Nebula Awards, Science Fiction Writers of America, 1985, for story "Out of All Them Bright Stars," 1991, for novella "Beggars in Spain," and 1997, for novelette "The Flowers of Aulit Prison"; Hugo Award, Science Fiction World Convention, 1992, for novella "Beggars in Spain."

■ Writings

"BEGGARS" SCIENCE FICTION SERIES

Beggars in Spain (novella), Axolotl, 1991.
Beggars in Spain (novel; expanded from her novella), Avon, 1993.
Beggars and Choosers, Tor, 1994.
Beggars Ride, Tor, 1996.

SCIENCE FICTION AND FANTASY

The Prince of Morning Bells, Pocket Books, 1981.
The Golden Grove, Bluejay Books, 1984.
The White Pipes, Bluejay Books, 1985.

Trinity and Other Stories Bluejay Books, 1985.
An Alien Light, Arbor House, 1988.
Brain Rose, Morrow, 1990.
The Aliens of Earth (short stories), Arkham House, 1993.
Beaker's Dozen (short stories; includes "The Flowers of Aulit Prison"), Tor, 1998.
Maximum Light, Tor, 1998.

Contributor of short stories to science fiction and fantasy magazines, including *Analog, Galaxy, Isaac Asimov's Science Fiction Magazine, Omni, Twilight Zone,* and *Universe.* Contributor to anthologies, including *Killing Me Softly,* edited by Gardner Dozois, HarperPrism, 1995; *Cat Tails,* edited by Ellen Datlow, Avon, 1996; *Intersections,* edited by John Kessel, Tor, 1996; *Black Swan, White Raven,* edited by Ellen Datlow, Avon, 1997; *Future Histories,* edited by Stephen McClelland, Horizon House, 1997, and various *Year's Best Science Fiction* and *Year's Best Fantasy* anthologies.

OTHER

Beginnings, Middles, and Ends (nonfiction), Writer's Digest Books, 1993.
Oaths and Miracles (fiction), Forge, 1996.
Dynamic Characters (nonfiction), Writer's Digest Books, 1998.
Stinger (sequel to *Oaths and Miracles*), Forge, 1998.

Kress's work has been translated into Swedish, French, Italian, German, Spanish, Polish, Croatian, Lithuanian, Romanian, Japanese, and Russian. Author of monthly column, "Fiction," *Writer's Digest.*

■ **Work in Progress**

Another science fiction novel.

■ **Adaptations**

The short story "Touchdown" has been adapted for a star show at Strasenburgh Planetarium in Rochester, NY.

■ **Sidelights**

"All forms of biological manipulation will be *it* for the twenty-first century," predicted award-win-

ning science fiction writer Nancy Kress in an interview with *Authors and Artists for Young Adults.* "We're on the verge of a biotech explosion. And all these techniques, not just the ones that alter germ-line DNA, will pose ethical questions: tissue engineering, genome recording, patenting discoveries, medical cures. It's fascinating." Kress skillfully conveys that fascination with scientific possibilities and human potential in her work, which includes fantasy, science fiction, and contemporary thrillers. She is perhaps best-known for her "Beggars" trilogy, which examines the various social and political complications that arise when a group of humans are genetically engineered to no longer need sleep. In addition to exploring the various ways in which technology could change what we consider "human," the author has considered such subjects as past-life experiences, reincarnation, and human-alien relations. Her work is not limited to novels, however; as Don D'Ammassa observed in *St. James Guide to Science Fiction Writers,* "Kress is one of those rare writers who seems equally at ease writing novels and short stories," and she has won three Nebulas and one Hugo for her shorter fiction.

Kress was born in Buffalo, New York, and was raised in nearby East Aurora, a quiet town which featured farmlands, orchards, and forests. She had no early desire to become a writer, but spent most of her childhood using her imagination, either reading or playing in the nearby woods. "We played a lot of imaginative games," Kress noted in her *AAYA* interview. "The players were usually me, my best friend Peggy, and our two little sisters, six years younger. We were pioneers making a homestead; we were princesses in an enchanted forest; we were survivors fleeing a flood or earthquake (much tree-climbing). Sometimes our dolls got involved in these games, too. They ended up very battered after a few years. So did we—I spent most of my childhood with skinned knees, bramble cuts, and mosquito bites."

Reading was a favorite activity as well, and "I read everything, with a total lack of discrimination," the author noted. "Children's books, adult books, cereal boxes, my mother's forbidden confession magazines. In the second grade, my favorite book was *The Boxcar Children.* I, too, wanted a life without adult supervision! By sixth grade, I liked Nancy Drew and Zane Grey; in eighth grade, *Gone with the Wind.*" Despite her voracious appetite for books, Kress didn't discover science fiction until she was fourteen. "The first SF book I read was Arthur C. Clarke's *Childhood's End,* and I fell in love," she recalled. Her enthusiasm for reading translated into success at school; "I liked school and did well in it, especially English," she remarked. Nevertheless, she had no ambitions to become a writer herself. Instead, after graduating from high school, she attended a small teacher's college in upstate New York.

Although Kress came of age during the turbulent era of the 1960s, her college experiences were rela-

First awarded a Nebula Award for best novella in 1991, this work about genetically modified humans who don't require sleep also received a Hugo Award in 1992.

tively "staid," as she described them to *AAYA.* "My college was in a small, conservative town, and it was filled with basically conservative people. We had a few sit-ins against the war, most noticeably when a Marine recruiter was on campus. And integration was proceeding, a new experience for most of us. I'm sure there were drugs around, although I was not a user. But for the sixties, it was pretty tame." Despite the relative lack of excitement, Kress found her years at college very rewarding. "I liked college, much better than I'd liked high school. I liked the classes, the freedom, the socializing. I had a wonderful time, and still was able to graduate summa cum laude. But, again, it was not a very difficult school. I wish now I'd been more ambitious in my choice of a college, but in my second-generation Italian-American family, it was considered radical to send a girl to college at all. Boys got educated; girls got married."

After receiving her diploma in elementary education, Kress took a job teaching the fourth grade in the Finger Lakes region of New York. In her interview, Kress recalled her teaching years fondly: "I liked planning social study projects and carrying them out with the kids. Salt-flour maps, plays about American history, comic books of the Civil War—it was my favorite subject to teach. I liked the nine and ten year olds, the last age before the rocky shores of adolescence. They're curious, open, increasing their autonomy. They're also funny!" Her career did have a couple of drawbacks, however: "My least favorite part of teaching was what is euphemistically called 'classroom management,'" the author recalled. "I'm a lousy disciplinarian, alas." After four years teaching, Kress left her job to marry Michael Kress in 1973.

Launches Literary Career

The couple had two children, Kevin and Brian, and it was after the birth of her younger son that Kress began to write. Though she hadn't read much science fiction while in school—"partly because I was reading required books, partly from a misplaced literary snobbism (I was an English major)"—she picked up on the genre again as an adult. "At that time I discovered Ursula Le Guin, both *The Left Hand of Darkness* and *The Dispossessed,*" the author remarked in her interview. "She blew me away. She still does." When Kress began writing her own stories, "from the very start, what I wrote came out as SF. I really don't know why." The author continued, "I'd always read SF, but I'd also always read mainstream, too." In 1976, her first story appeared in *Galaxy*, and sales followed to *Isaac Asimov's Science Fiction Magazine* and *Omni*.

In 1981, Kress published her first novel, the fantasy *The Prince of Morning Bells*. This "witty, slyly humorous story," as Don D'Ammassa described it, relates the adventures of a young girl and her magical pet as they journey through strange lands, each of which tends to exaggerate certain human traits. Kress's second novel, *The Golden Grove*, is a darker fantasy, centered on a mysterious island where women devote themselves to weaving marvelous tapestries from spider silk. 1985's *The White Pipes* was Kress's third fantasy, this time taking place in a medieval world where "Storygivers" can illustrate their tales with magical images. Fia is one such Storygiver, and her troubles begin when she enters the Kingdom of Veliano. Fia's son is stolen by her ex-lover, and she must enter a competition to earn the "White Pipes" of the title, a magical instrument that gives the player enhanced mental powers that can control people who hear them. *Analog* reviewer Tom Easton noted that Kress's "latest excellent fantasy" is "concerned with the nature of love and its reconciliation with submission." While noting that Kress "does well in her depiction of the insular life of a castle," a *Publishers Weekly* critic found Fia's story somewhat "farfetched and contrived." *Booklist* contributor Peter L. Robertson, however, concluded that *The White Pipes* is a "superior novel."

While Kress's first novels were fantasies, with her next work the author returned to science fiction. "I started with SF short stories, moved to fantasy novels (my first three) and then to SF novels," the author noted in her interview. "I don't know what dictated any of these choices—they were just what I wanted to write at the time." Kress's first science-fiction novel was 1988's *An Alien Light*, "superficially an old story retold," as Don D'Ammassa described it. The novel is set on the colony of Qom, where an alien race called the Ged has placed two warring communities of humans in order to study them. After members of the Jelite and Delysian societies discover the purpose of the aliens' research, they realize they must work together to save their peoples. While recognizing that the idea of aliens observing humans in action is "a perennial chestnut," a *Publishers Weekly* critic praised the novel's background as "well drawn," and added that "the conceptual breakthroughs are nicely handled." Gerald Jonas of the *New York Times Book Review* similarly found the alien society convincingly portrayed, but faulted the novel as "repetitive," with characters "more like bundles of attributes than people." *Analog*'s Easton, however, praised Kress for her "emphasis on the characters" and noted that with this SF debut novel "Kress makes a strong bid for [a future] Grandmaster Nebula."

In her next novel, *Brain Rose*, Kress explores some of the issues of ecology, society, and human nature that have come to characterize much of her work. This 1990 novel takes place in Earth's near

This second novel in the "Beggars" series continues the story of the Sleepless in an America on the verge of collapse.

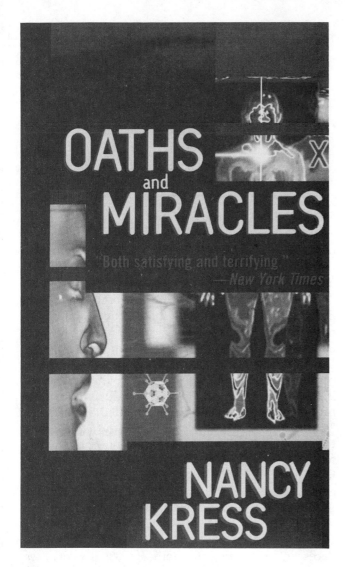

OATHS and MIRACLES

"Both satisfying and terrifying."
— New York Times

NANCY KRESS

An FBI agent and the widow of a murdered scientist investigate the scientist's death in this 1995 sci-fi thriller.

future, where AIDS has been conquered—only to give way to a plague that hinders its victims' memory. America seems to have recovered from near-environmental disaster, riots, and a repressive government. The scientific development that shapes the novel is an operation that allows people to access memories of their past lives. Three individuals—a politician, a famous actor's daughter, and a jewel thief—undergo the operation, and their attempts to integrate their new memories reveal some startling truths about the Memory Plague that could save humanity. *Locus* reviewer Carolyn Cushman noted that if the reader can accept the concept of the Past Life

Access Operation, "*Brain Rose* is a fun and exciting thriller, at its strongest when conveying a sense of tragedy and futility." Comparing it to the work of Robert Silverberg, *Washington Post Book World* contributor Paul Di Filippo hailed the novel for its "fully fleshed and feathered characters, energetic language and . . . conceptual daring." *Brain Rose*, the critic concluded, "represents a new peak for this writer."

Kress's success with the science fiction novel was no surprise to anyone who had been keeping up with her short fiction. The author continued to write short stories at the same time she produced longer works; in 1985, she won her first Nebula for the story "Out of All Them Bright Stars." A frequent contributor to science fiction anthologies, Kress has also released several of her own story collections. Her first, *Trinity and Other Stories*, contains stories such as "Trinity," in which three clones attempt to prove the existence of God, and "With the Original Cast," in which an actress playing Joan of Arc discovers she is the reincarnation of the martyred saint. The collection displays a "depth of imagination unusual even among SF writers," according to *Analog*'s Easton, who also hailed its "distinct warmth of human perception." The 1993 compilation *The Aliens of Earth* shows a similarly broad range of tales, including the time-travel story "The Price of Oranges"; "People Like Us," which includes a tennis-playing alien; and "The Battle of Long Island," which examines how alternate pasts bring different meanings to one woman's life. "The generating force in these stories is less in the fantastic events than in the emotional conditions or moral situations for which they are correlatives," Russell Letson observed in *Locus*, adding that Kress is "both a craftsman and a moralist." The 1998 collection *Beaker's Dozen* likewise demonstrates how Kress's work "never [contains] the crude infodumps or token, thin characters endemic to much of the genre," as a *Publishers Weekly* reviewer commented. The compilation includes "Dancing on Air," a novella about stage mothers and their illegally enhanced daughters; "Summer Wind," a tale of time and aging; and "Always True to Thee, in My Fashion," a parody involving mood-altering designer drugs. Although faulting some of the stories for a "crowding of thematic metaphors," the critic hailed the author's ability to create "compelling human beings (or other sentients) entangled with one another in ways that are psychologically real."

Engineering Human Evolution

One of Kress's most acclaimed works of short fiction is the Hugo and Nebula-winning novella "Beggars in Spain," which the author later developed into the first of a trilogy of novels. As the novel opens in the year 2008, scientists have learned to manipulate DNA enough for people to order genetically modified children. While previous modifications have involved appearance and intelligence, a new modification allows the creation of a person who has no need of sleep. Leisha Camden is one such person, and as she matures it is discovered that not only do the "Sleepless" have the advantage of eight extra hours a day, they have the physical advantage of avoiding the effects of aging. Rather than appreciate the superior gifts of the Sleepless, society comes to fear them, and the Sleepless encounter prejudice and hatred.

Over the next eighty-five years, most Sleepless withdraw into a super-secure space station called Sanctuary, where they develop an economic empire based on their breakthroughs in technology. Leisha Camden is one of the few Sleepless left on Earth, where she tries to bridge the growing gap between the social classes: the Livers, an uneducated leisure class who are supported by the government in exchange for their votes; the "donkeys," genetically modified Sleepers who run the government; and the Sleepless. The essential problem facing the Sleepless is summed up in a parable: while one person can help a single beggar, one cannot provide for all the beggars in Spain. So what happens, asks one of Leisha's fellow Sleepless, "if you walk down that street in Spain and a hundred beggars each want a dollar and you say no . . . but they're so rotten with anger about what you have that they knock you down and grab it and then beat you out of sheer envy and despair?"

The Sleepless of Sanctuary take steps to avoid being overwhelmed by "beggars," including the creation of a new generation of "Superbright" Sleepless. Their plans go awry, however, after the Superbrights are unexpectedly changed by the art of a Liver. This leads Leisha to conclude that "there are no permanent beggars in Spain. . . . The beggar you give a dollar to today might change the world tomorrow." *Beggars in Spain* "is a thoughtful, carefully constructed exploration of various ethical questions, particularly about the

If you enjoy the works of Nancy Kress, you may also want to check out the following books and films:

Dean Koontz, *Watchers*, 1987.
Lois Lowry, *The Giver*, 1993.
Connie Willis, *Impossible Things*, 1994.
The Boys from Brazil, a film starring Laurence Olivier and Gregory Peck, 1978.

obligations of being among the well-off, whether through one's own efforts or the luck of the draw," Russell Letson summarized in *Locus*. "Kress' masterful plotting nearly compensates for the literary drawbacks of the sf thought experiment," Faren Miller noted in another *Locus* review, adding that while "the portrait of an evolving future society lacks the texture, the fully messy contrariness of real life," the "presentation of ideas in action is fascinating." While Gerald Jonas of the *New York Times Book Review* faulted the novel for "an excess of ambition," *School Library Journal* contributor Cathy Chauvette recommended the novel for all readers, noting that "the always-exhilarating Kress will challenge YA's most outrageous expectations . . . with [her] brisk prose, stimulating ideas, and a variety of challenging characters."

Beggars and Choosers "is as intriguing as its predecessor," according to Beth Karpas in *Voice of Youth Advocates*. This 1994 sequel takes up approximately twenty years after *Beggars in Spain* left off. Although the Supers prevented Sanctuary's revolutionary attack against the United States, they are still looked upon with prejudice and have created an island enclave where they work in isolation. The country has enjoyed the benefits of virtually unlimited, cheap energy for many years now, but the political contract between donkeys and Livers is starting to break down as the machines that serve them begin to malfunction. The scientific breakthrough key to this novel is the development of nanotechnology: machines so small they can work on the cells of the human body. Nevertheless, "Kress's work remains strongly character driven," Roland Green of *Booklist* stated, this time focusing on Livers and donkeys instead of Sleepless. "Her latest novel isn't merely an excellent and thoughtful work of science fiction but is also an important commentary of some of the key issues we'll be facing in the next century," a *Publishers Weekly* critic asserted. As Frank McConnell similarly concluded in *Commonweal*, *Beggars and Choosers* "reminds me of what s-f at its best—as in H. G. Wells—can be."

The 1996 novel *Beggars Ride* concludes the series, "an exploration of human evolution that deserves to be ranked with Frank Herbert's Dune books and Orson Scott Card's Ender tetralogy," Roland Green stated in *Booklist*. In this novel, nano-technology created by the Supers has modified humanity to allow their bodies to overcome disease and hunger. Livers no longer need government aid for food or medicine, so their donkey government is of little use any more. When a plague arrives that begins to affect its sufferers with severe phobias, it is an un-Changed donkey woman who holds out hope for humanity's salvation. "The scale of Kress's vision is large as she lays out a drama that—convincingly if unsurprisingly—argues that moral quandaries can't be addressed by technology," a *Publishers Weekly* critic remarked. The novel demonstrates the author's "strengths of world-building and character development," Beth Karpas noted in *Voice of Youth Advocates*, concluding that *Beggars Ride* is "a powerful conclusion to a trilogy that has set a new archetype for genetic science fiction."

Issues of biology and genetic engineering also play a role in Kress's 1997 novel *Maximum Light*. America in the year 2034 is a country where chemical pollution and a declining birthrate have made children a valuable commodity. Genetic research is illegal, so black markets deal in fertile reproductive organs, as well as the "vivifacture" of child-substitutes, created by attaching cloned human faces and hands onto the bodies of living chimpanzees. The story is narrated by three characters: Shana Walders, an aspiring young soldier who discovers some of these illegal substitutes; Cameron Atuli, a gay dancer who has lost his memory; and Nick Clementi, a terminally ill doctor who hopes to solve the puzzle of humanity's infertility crisis. A *Publishers Weekly* critic noted that while the novel's positive conclusion "seems forced," the author's "plot moves briskly and her premise grips." "Science fiction fans will enjoy this creative, original glimpse into Earth's future," Meg Wilson remarked in *Voice of Youth Advocates*, adding that the stories of the three protagonists "intertwine in a complex, intriguing mystery which Kress brings to a satisfying conclusion."

The Thrill of Technology

Though she has received acclaim for her science fiction, Kress has also ventured into the genre of the technothriller. As she described them in her *AAYA* interview, "thrillers are intended for people who don't read much SF, and they take place in the very near future, usually. So more time is spent explaining the science, and much less time world-building. You can't go as 'far out' as you can in SF. These aren't limitations to me—just differences." The 1996 novel *Oaths and Miracles* introduces freelance journalist Judy O'Brien Kozinski, whose geneticist husband has just been murdered. With the assistance of FBI agent Robert Cavanaugh, Judy discovers a plot involving organized crime, a customized killer virus, and an apocalyptic religious cult. "The plot is ultimately far-fetched," stated a *Publishers Weekly* critic, "but Kress, a witty and engaging writer, is in lucid command of key principle of, and advances in, molecular biology." Gerald Jonas, on the other hand, found Judy's "role in unraveling the mystery behind her husband's death . . . as credible as it is surprising," and added in his *New York Times Book Review* assessment that the novel's conclusion "is both satisfying and terrifying." Agent Cavanaugh returns in the 1998 sequel *Stinger*, in which he works with an African American epidemiologist to solve the riddle of an outbreak of malaria which kills people with the sickle-cell anemia gene.

Kress is able to write convincingly about science and technology despite having no educational background in those fields. "I wish I did have a science background," she said in her interview. "Since I don't, I read *Scientific American* and *Nature* and *Science*, and bother people who are knowledgeable to help me out. Recently I married a scientist, so now I mostly bother him about physics, and other people about biology." Science alone doesn't determine what she will write, however, as character plays a great part in each work. She begins with one or two characters and creates a problem for them to face. "I plunge in happily with my character and situation and write until I run out of steam," she explained to *AAYA*. "Then I analyze what I've written for story— where does this seem to be going? Who wants what? Why can't they get it? What could go wrong? This process usually yields another burst of writing. I proceed this way until, about two-thirds of the way to the end, the piece crystallizes for me. If it doesn't, I'm in trouble. If it does, there's still much rewriting, because I've changed course so many times in the process of composition. My first drafts are a mess," she admitted. "Surprisingly, most pieces actually do get completed in this haphazard way. . . . Although there *is* one novel I abandoned four hundred pages in. It just wasn't adding up to anything."

Discovering what her characters can do and what worlds they will encounter, however, is part of the adventure of writing for Kress. "I think I have the best job in the world," she proclaimed in her interview. "I envision going on doing it, writing novels and stories. What will they be about, what direction will they go? I have no idea. That's a large part of the enjoyment."

■ Works Cited

Review of *An Alien Light, Publishers Weekly*, December 25, 1987, p. 64.

Review of *Beaker's Dozen, Publishers Weekly*, July 13, 1998, p. 66.

Review of *Beggars and Choosers, Publishers Weekly*, October 3, 1994, p. 53.

Review of *Beggars Ride, Publishers Weekly*, October 28, 1996, p. 62.

Chauvette, Cathy, review of *Beggars in Spain, School Library Journal*, September, 1993, pp. 260-61.

Cushman, Carolyn, review of *Brain Rose, Locus*, November, 1989, pp. 21, 23.

D'Ammassa, Don, "Nancy Kress," in *St. James Guide to Science Fiction Writers*, 4th edition, St. James Press, 1996, pp. 532-34.

Di Filippo, Paul, review of *Brain Rose, Washington Post Book World*, January 28, 1990, p. 8.

Easton, Tom, review of *The White Pipes, Analog Science Fiction/Science Fact*, September, 1985, p. 184.

Easton, Tom, review of *Trinity and Other Stories, Analog Science Fiction/Science Fact*, May, 1986, pp. 186-87.

Easton, Tom, review of *An Alien Light, Analog Science Fiction/Science Fact*, May, 1988, pp. 181-82.

Green, Roland, review of *Beggars and Choosers, Booklist*, October 1, 1994, p. 245.

Green, Roland, review of *Beggars Ride, Booklist*, November 15, 1996, p. 576.

Jonas, Gerald, review of *An Alien Light, New York Times Book Review*, April 24, 1988, p. 28.

Jonas, Gerald, review of *Beggars in Spain, New York Times Book Review,* June 13, 1993, p. 22.

Jonas, Gerald, review of *Oaths and Miracles, New York Times Book Review*, March 10, 1996, p. 19.

Karpas, Beth, review of *Beggars and Choosers, Voice of Youth Advocates*, April, 1995, p. 34.

Karpas, Beth, review of *Beggars Ride, Voice of Youth Advocates*, June, 1997, p. 118.

Kress, Nancy, in an e-mail interview with Diane Telgen for *Authors and Artists for Young Adults*, September-October, 1998.

Letson, Russell, review of *Beggars in Spain, Locus*, February, 1993, pp. 29-30.

Letson, Russell, review of *The Aliens of Earth, Locus*, January, 1994, p. 27.

Review of *Maximum Light, Publishers Weekly*, December 8, 1997, p. 60.

McConnell, Frank, review of *Beggars and Choosers, Commonweal*, December 2, 1994, p. 27.

Miller, Faren, review of *Beggars in Spain, Locus*, February, 1993, p. 19.

Review of *Oaths and Miracles, Publishers Weekly*, November 20, 1995, p. 68.

Robertson, Peter L., review of *The White Pipes, Booklist*, April 1, 1985, pp. 1101-2.

Review of *The White Pipes, Publishers Weekly*, December 7, 1984, p. 65.

Wilson, Meg, review of *Maximum Light, Voice of Youth Advocates*, August, 1998, p. 211.

■ For More Information See

PERIODICALS

Analog Science Fiction/Science Fact, May, 1994, pp. 154-65; March, 1995, pp. 162-63.

Booklist, December 15, 1987, p. 678; April 1, 1993, p. 1416.

Fantasy Review, April, 1985, pp. 24-25.

Kirkus Reviews, December 1, 1989, p. 1713; September 1, 1994, p. 1173; November 15, 1997, p. 1678; September 15, 1998, p. 1315.

Library Journal, December, 1987, p. 130; September 15, 1994, p. 94.

New York Times Book Review, August 18, 1996, p. 10.

Publishers Weekly, September 21, 1998, p. 76.

Tribune Books (Chicago), January 28, 1990, p. 7.

Voice of Youth Advocates, February, 1986, p. 394.

Washington Post Book World, October 31, 1993, p. 8.

—Sketch by Diane Telgen

Jonathan Larson

New York Drama Critics Circle and Outer Critics Circle Awards for Best Musical, Drama Desk Awards for Best Musical, Best Book of a Musical, Best Music, and Best Lyrics, and Obie Award for Outstanding Book, Music, and Lyrics, all for *Rent*.

■ Personal

Born February 4, 1960, in White Plains, NY; died of an aortic aneurysm, January 25, 1996, in New York, NY; son of Allan (a retired business executive) and Nanette Larson. *Education:* Attended Adelphi University.

■ Career

Playwright, composer, and lyricist. Songwriter for television shows, including "Sesame Street" on PBS. Worked as a waiter at the Moondance Diner, New York City, for ten years.

■ Awards, Honors

Richard Rodgers Development Grant and Stephen Sondheim Award, both for *Superbia*; Richard Rodgers Studio Production Award, American Academy of Arts and Letters, 1994, for the workshop version of *Rent*; Antoinette Perry (Tony) Awards for Best Musical, Best Book of a Musical, and Best Score of a Musical, Pulitzer Prize, 1996,

■ Writings

THEATER

Rent (musical), produced off-Broadway at the New York Theater Workshop, then at the Nederlander Theater, 1996.

Also wrote the musicals *J. P. Morgan Saves the Nation* and *Superbia*; and the rock monologue *Tick, Tick . . . Boom!*, produced off-Broadway at the New York Theater Workshop.

■ Sidelights

When Roger, a character in the hit musical *Rent*, sings "One song/Glory/One song/Before I go/Glory/One song to leave behind . . ./Find/Glory/In a song that rings true/Truth like a blazing fire/An eternal flame," his is a passionate urgency. He is a punk rocker who has AIDS, and he wants to write one good song before he dies. *Rent*'s young composer and lyricist Jonathan Larson was looking for glory, too. Driven by a lifelong passion for American musical theater, he wanted to suffuse it with the energy of contemporary storytelling and popular music. In doing so, he hoped to change it so that it might ring true for more diverse—and younger—audiences. "Those are not our people uptown; those are not our stories uptown; that's not our music," Larson once told a friend, according to Paula Span in the *Washington Post.* "He wanted to be the pied piper, leading his generation and the one behind him back to Broadway, back to musical theater," Larson's father Allan told Span.

And so Larson set out to write *Rent,* his "rock opera for the '90s," as it was billed, a show that celebrates the lives and loves of a group of disaffected young artists who are struggling songfully with drug addiction, AIDS and poverty in New York City's eclectic East Village. "Jonathan listened to what he heard around him—the need for community, the paralyzing fear of AIDS—and he created *Rent* out of that," his friend Molly Ringwald, the actress, wrote in an article in *Interview* magazine.

With an inexperienced cast of young unknowns and a small production budget of $200,000, *Rent* was staged in a 150-seat, off-Broadway theater. It opened in February 1996 to rave reviews, won the Pulitzer Prize for drama—only the seventh musical to win the prize and the first to do so before opening on Broadway—and immediately became the hottest ticket in town. After just two months, the downtown show went uptown, moving to the Nederlander Theater on Broadway. There it won four Tony Awards, including one for best new musical. Bloomingdale's opened a boutique selling *Rent*-inspired street grunge clothing; producers began vying for movie and recording rights; and, a touring production of *Rent* went on the road. Richard Zoglin of *Time* hailed *Rent* as "Broadway's dream come true: an audacious, really new musical with crossover appeal and a half a dozen star-making roles. . . . All that's missing is its creator to take a bow—and promise us more."

That's because Larson's dream of glory came true without him. Just hours after the final dress rehearsal on the night before *Rent* was to open, a roommate found Larson on the floor of their apartment, dead from an aortic aneurysm (a break in the artery that carries blood from the heart). He was just thirty-five. "His simultaneous death and triumph is a metaphor for the heartbreak and hope, the paradox of the American Dream," concluded Jack Kroll in *Newsweek.*

Years in the Making

Larson's was a decidedly "downtown" lifestyle, lived on waiter's wages in a Greenwich Village loft which he shared with a changing cast of roommates. Writing in *Newsweek,* Gregory Beals quoted one of those former roommates as saying that Larson "spent the last weeks of his life overstressed by the demands of his work, and poor as the characters in his show." Larson was in poor health, and he sold some of his book collection only days before his death so that he could buy a movie ticket. But poverty was the price he willingly paid in his pursuit of creative success. Larson grew up in White Plains, New York, a middle-class suburb. "He was lousy at sports," his sister Julie Larson McCollum recalled in an *Entertainment Weekly* article by Kipp Cheng. "So there was nothing else for him to do. . . . Early on we were given a sense of social awareness and a love for theater. I think Jonathan tried to combine the two," she said.

Larson wrote songs and performed in his student years at Adelphi University on Long Island, where he majored in drama. He then moved to New York City, intent on making it in the theater. He took whatever songwriting work he could, which included composing songs for television and for book cassette adaptations of the animated children's movies *An American Tale* and *The Land before Time,* but he mainly supported himself by working as a waiter in the Moondance Diner in SoHo. Two of his musicals were produced in New York workshops: *Superbia*—winner of a Richard Rodgers Development Grant and a Stephen Sondheim Award—and *J. P. Morgan Saves the Nation,* as was his rock monologue *Tick, Tick . . . Boom!*

Then came *Rent.* It was an "overnight success," that was at least seven years in the making. Larson had already been working on it for several years when in 1992 he showed a draft to James Nicola, the artistic director of the New York Workshop Theater. The downtown theater, which was being renovated at the time, had a shabby appeal that Larson thought was perfect for *Rent,* whose stage directions call for what "seems more like a pile of junk than a set." Although he was

The cast of the award-winning Broadway musical *Rent* performing in June, 1996.

impressed with Larson's songwriting skills, Nicola saw room for improvement in the show's dramatization. He worked with Larson over the next couple of years, and Larson's theater idol, Stephen Sondheim, who had critiqued some of Larson's earlier work, gave advice, too. When Larson won the prestigious Richard Rodgers Studio Production Award, the $50,000 that came with it meant that in 1994 he had the money to bring *Rent* to life—for seven performances under the direction of Michael Greif. Two producers were wowed by the show and put up the money for a six-week run, which included a salary for Larson. This finally allowed him to quit his diner job.

The final weeks of revisions and production work were both strenuous and stressful, and so no one was too surprised when Larson got sick. During the last week of rehearsals, chest pains sent him to hospital emergency rooms on two occasions. Tests and x-rays were read as normal both times. On the first visit, he was told he had food poisoning and his stomach was pumped; on the second, he was diagnosed with a virus. On his last

evening of life, Larson attended his show's final dress rehearsal and gave an interview to a *New York Times* reporter, telling him, "I think I may have a life as a composer." He died at home hours later. (An investigation by the New York State Health Commissioner resulted in the involved hospitals being fined for procedural errors, and Larson's family later filed a malpractice suit. Any awards from the lawsuit were to go to establish a foundation in Larson's name.)

La Vie Bohème

Beals wrote that Larson "was fiercely engaged with the multiracial, multisexual world downtown, determined to bring it to the stage with sensitivity and affection." Larson had seen a children's version of Giacomo Puccini's classic opera *La Bohème* when he was a child. *Rent* is Larson's contemporary reimagining of the opera, a period piece (produced exactly 100 years before *Rent* in 1896, and set some sixty years earlier) about a band of poor Italian-speaking bohemians living in

Paris's Left Bank. Larson's bohemia is New York's East Village, where eight life stories—with several non-traditional love dramas among them—play out against the backdrop of a Christmastime rent strike against a young landlord, Ben. He wants to see the neighborhood go upscale and overlooks the plight of its resident poor and homeless. Roger, the rock songwriter, falls in love with Mimi, a heroin-addicted stripper. Puccini's Mimi dies of tuberculosis; Larson's Mimi nearly succumbs to AIDS-related illness, but makes a dramatic recovery. Instead, the AIDS plague claims Angel, a transvestite street drummer, mourned by his lover Tom Collins, a computer science teacher who philosophizes about technology's effects on society. Maureen is a performance artist involved in a tumultuous lesbian relationship with a lawyer, Joanne. Mark, Maureen's ex-boyfriend, is a filmmaker and the show's narrator. He tries to interpret the lives and times in which he and his friends find themselves. *Rent* is about loss and grief. But it is also about love and grace and joy, too. Marginalized as they are, Larson's characters "revel in their joy, their capacity for love—and most important—in their tenacity, all in a ceaseless outpouring of melody," Frank Rich wrote in a *New York Times* review.

In melding opera with pop culture, Larson created a show that was both something old and something new. "That's why I got so excited about *Rent*," director Michael Greif told Patrick Pacheco in the *Los Angeles Times*. "Here was an opportunity to express things you generally don't find expressed in musical theater, yet it was a wonderful hybrid of some very operatic impulses, some very conventional musical theater impulses, and some not very conventional musical theater impulses, such as collage and nonrealistic storytelling. As I read on and listened, the doors of possibility opened," Greif said of his introduction to *Rent* in its early days of production development.

The final product looked young and hip and decidedly different from usual Broadway fare. The fresh-faced cast of unknowns wore head mikes to amplify their slang-talk and their singing, and they were costumed in what another *New York Times* reviewer described as "grunge-meets-salsa-meets-B-Boy-meets-Riot-Grrrl-clothes: plaid pants, plastic pants, print pantyhose, jeans, layered tops, slip dresses, ankle-high, knee-high and thigh-high boots, and caps of various kinds." In many ways, *Rent* sounded different, too. A small onstage en-

---

If you enjoy the works of Jonathan Larson, you may also want to check out the following:

The Puccini opera *La Bohème*, on which *Rent* was based.
The Broadway musicals *Hair, Jesus Christ Superstar, and A Chorus Line*, and *Bring in da Noise, Bring in da Funk*.

---

semble of black-clad musicians replaced the traditional pit orchestra. "Larson's score is the post-Sondheim musical's most successful attempt yet to fuse the eclectic energies of contemporary pop music with the needs of the theater. His versions of gospel, rock, reggae, even a tango, add up to a brilliant portrait of the crazy cubistic face of today's pop," wrote Kroll in *Newsweek*. Upon the release of the original Broadway cast recording of *Rent*, a *Rolling Stone* reviewer noted that Larson "was a gifted melodicist with a special knack for exuberant choral interplay and for dosing racy showpieces with beguiling, melancholy interludes."

Notable among *Rent*'s more than thirty songs are its full-cast anthems. The first act's finale, "La Vie Bohème," is a rhyme-streamed tribute to the characters' way of life that is as confrontational as it is tongue in cheek: "To riding your bike, midday past the three-piece suits/To fruits, to no absolutes/To Absolute, to choice, to the *Village Voice*, to any passing fad/To being an us, for once/Instead of a them/La Vie Bohème . . . To sodomy/It's between God and me/To S & M/La Vie Bohème."

Act II opens with a moving gospel song "Seasons of Love," which asks, "Five hundred twenty-five thousand/Six hundred minutes/How do you measure—measure a year?/In daylights—in sunsets/In midnights—in cups of coffee/In inches—in miles/In laughter—in strife . . ./How do you measure/A year in the life?" and suggests that life ought to be measured in love. Though it is these big songs that are most memorable, Donald Lyons, writing in the *Wall Street Journal*, found that *Rent* "is indeed stronger in emotion than narrative" and that it is in "the intimate but charged personal songs that *Rent* excels, as when Mark and Joanne share the pains of loving an egoist in 'Tango

Maureen' or when Roger paints his musical vision in 'Glory' or Roger and Mimi exchange 'Light My Candle' and 'I Should Tell You.' What Mr. Larson knew so well . . . is that each song must contain and enact a conflict."

Yet for all its novelty and Generation X appeal, Larson's understanding of and reverence for musical theater's traditions show forth in *Rent*. "Larson was a protege of Stephen Sondheim, the bringer of psychological complexity and literate doubt to the form, and that's the tradition it works in—and surpasses. It's the best new musical since the 1950s, the time of Leonard Bernstein's *Candide* and John Latouche's *The Golden Apple*," wrote Lyons. According to Rich in the *New York Times*, Sondheim himself called Larson's work "generous music" that "lovingly merges the musical theater traditions of past generations, including Mr. Sondheim's own, with rock."

Unfinished Glory

Larson's fusion musical did not translate into a transformed theater experience for some critics. The *National Review*'s James Gardner stated that "despite its studied hipness and its aspirations to be the voice of the Nineties, *Rent* . . . is pretty much the same old showbiz fare." Ed Siegel of the *Boston Globe* commented on "the emptiness of its bohemianism." Wrote Siegel, "When nothing is shocking anymore what is there to be bohemian about? The freedom to wear tight pants? In terms of content, *Rent* is little more than a fashion statement." Some critics cited specific structural flaws: too many songs and subplots resulting in an overweight story line and superficial character treatment. "It is good-natured, fully energized, theatrically knowing and occasionally witty. It is also badly manufactured, vaguely manipulative, drenched in self-pity and sentimental in a way that make Puccini and his librettists (Illica and Giacosa) look like cynics," observed Robert Brustein in the *New Republic*, adding that "Larson was a sophisticated librettist, if a somewhat sloppy architect."

In the end, Larson's was an unfinished glory. "This is doubly sad when you consider that the gifted young man was groping his way to a unified personal style that this uneven, scattershot show does not yet achieve," wrote John Simon in *New York*. Yet even some of *Rent*'s detractors concluded that what Larson accomplished through *Rent* mattered more than the show's flaws. As Bernard Holland remarked in the *New York Times*, "Whether or not *Rent* succeeds as an opera, a musical or anything else is beside the point for present purposes. The effort behind it and the sense of adventure it represents say something serious about a sophisticated culture trying painfully to create a more inclusive art." If *Rent* is drenched in urgency and sentiment, so too were the myth-making circumstances of its creator's biography, which, some argue, was a catalyst for *Rent*'s spontaneous success. With the experiences of Larson's own life inextricably wound into the story of *Rent*, it becomes hard to discern whether Larson's art was imitating his short life and untimely death or the other way around. Wrote John Lahr in the *New Yorker*, "His songs have urgency—a sense of mourning and mystery which insists on seizing the moment. 'No day but today' is the show's last sung line—at once a plea and a philosophy." As for his aim to make the musical relevant again, Lahr surmised, "Larson is certainly not the first composer to take aim at that elusive target, but he may be the first to have hit it."

■ Works Cited

Beals, Gregory, "The World of 'Rent'," *Newsweek*, May 13, 1996, pp. 58-59.

Brustein, Robert, "The New Bohemians," *New Republic*, April 22, 1996, pp. 29-31.

Cheng, Kipp, "Jonathan Larson: The Late Composer's Rock Opera 'Rent' Gave Musical Theater a New Lease on Life," *Entertainment Weekly*, December 27, 1996, p. 34.

Gardner, James, "Lowering the Rent," *National Review*, June 3, 1996, pp. 56-57.

Holland, Bernard, "Flaws Aside, *Rent* Lives and Breathes," *New York Times*, March 17, 1996, p. B-31.

Kroll, Jack, "A Downtown 'La Bohème'," *Newsweek*, February 26, 1996, p. 67.

Lahr, John, "Hello and Goodbye," *New Yorker*, February 19, 1996, pp. 94-96.

Lyons, Donald, "*Rent*, New Musical is Deserved Hit," *Wall Street Journal*, March 6, 1996, p. A-18.

Pacheco, Patrick, "Life, Death and *Rent*," *Los Angeles Times*, April 14, 1996, p. 4.

"*Rent* is Brilliant and Messy All at Once," *New York Times*, February 25, 1996, pp. B-5, 22.

Rich, Frank, "East Village Story," *New York Times*, March 2, 1996, p. A-19.

Ringwald, Molly, "Jonathan Larson," *Interview*, June, 1996, p. 104.

Rolling Stone, December 26, 1996-January 9, 1997, pp. 192, 194.

Siegel, Ed, "Rent Has a Lease on Energy," *Boston Globe*, November 19, 1996, p. D-1.

Simon, John, "All in the Family," *New York*, March 4, 1996, p. 65.

Span, Paula, "The Show Goes On," *Washington Post*, April 18, 1996, p. C-1.

Zoglin, Richard, "Lower East Side Story," *Time*, March 4, 1996, p. 71.

■ **For More Information See**

PERIODICALS

Atlantic Monthly, September, 1996.
Entertainment Weekly, May 10, 1996; June 14, 1996.
Los Angeles Times, April 30, 1996, p. F-1.
New Leader, June 3-17, 1996, pp. 22-23.
Newsweek, May 13, 1996, pp. 54-57.
New York Times, February 26, 1996, pp. C-9, C-11.
People, February 24, 1997, p. 93.
Rolling Stone, May 16, 1996; June 27, 1996, p. 59.*

—Sketch by Tracy J. Sukraw

Madeleine L'Engle

■ Personal

Surname pronounced "leng-*el*"; given name, Madeleine L'Engle Camp; born November 29, 1918, in New York, NY; daughter of Charles Wadsworth (a foreign correspondent and author) and Madeleine (a pianist; maiden name, Barnett) Camp; married Hugh Franklin (an actor), January 26, 1946 (died September, 1986); children: Josephine (Mrs. Alan W. Jones), Maria (Mrs. John Rooney), Bion. *Education:* Smith College, A.B. (with honors), 1941; attended New School for Social Research, 1941-42; Columbia University, graduate study, 1960-61. *Politics:* "New England." *Religion:* Anglican.

■ Addresses

Home—924 West End Ave., New York, NY 10025; Crosswicks, Goshen, CT 06756. *Agent*—Robert Lescher, 67 Irving Place, New York, NY 10003.

■ Career

Active career in theatre, 1941-47; teacher with Committee for Refugee Education during World War II; St. Hilda's and St. Hugh's School, Morningside Heights, NY, teacher, 1960-66; Cathedral of St. John the Divine, New York City, librarian, 1966—. University of Indiana, Bloomington, member of faculty, summers, 1965-66 and 1971; writer-in-residence, Ohio State University, Columbus, 1970, and University of Rochester, New York, 1972. Lecturer. *Member:* Authors Guild (president), Authors League of America, PEN.

■ Awards, Honors

And Both Were Young was named one of the Ten Best Books of the Year, *New York Times*, 1949; Newbery Medal from the American Library Association, 1963, Hans Christian Andersen Award runner-up, 1964, and Sequoyah Children's Book Award from the Oklahoma State Department of Education, and Lewis Carroll Shelf Award, both 1965, all for *A Wrinkle in Time; Book World*'s Spring Book Festival Honor Book, and one of *School Library Journal*'s Best Books of the Year, both 1968, both for *The Young Unicorns;* Austrian State Literary Prize, 1969, for *The Moon by Night;* University of Southern Mississippi Silver Medallion, 1978, for "an outstanding contribution to the field of children's literature"; American Book Award for paperback fiction, 1980, for *A Swiftly Tilting Planet;* Smith Medal, 1980; Newbery Honor Book, 1981, for *A Ring of Endless Light;* Books for the Teen Age selections, New York Public Library, 1981, for *A Ring of Endless Light,* and 1982, for *Camilla;* Sophie Award, 1984; Regina Medal, Catholic Library Association, 1984; *A House Like a Lotus* was exhibited at the Bologna International Children's Book Fair, 1985; Adolescent Literature Assembly Award for Outstanding Contribution to Adolescent Literature, National Council of Teachers of English, 1986.

■ Writings

PICTURE BOOKS

Dance in the Desert, illustrated by Symeon Shimin, Farrar, Straus, 1969.
Everyday Prayers, illustrated by Lucille Butel, Morehouse, 1974.
Prayers for Sunday, illustrated by Lizzie Napoli, Morehouse, 1974.
Ladder of Angels: Scenes from the Bible Illustrated by the Children of the World, Seabury, 1979.
The Glorious Impossible, illustrated by Giotto, Simon & Schuster, 1990.

JUVENILE FICTION

And Both Were Young, Lothrop, 1949, reprinted, Delacorte, 1983.
Camilla, Crowell, 1965, reprinted, Delacorte, 1981.
Intergalactic P.S.3, Children's Book Council, 1970.
The Sphinx at Dawn: Two Stories, illustrated by Vivian Berger, Harper, 1982.

"AUSTIN FAMILY" SERIES

Meet the Austins, illustrated by Gillian Willett, Vanguard, 1960.
The Moon by Night, Farrar, Straus, 1963.
The Twenty-Four Days before Christmas: An Austin Family Story, illustrated by Inga, Farrar, Straus, 1964, new edition, illustrated by Joe De Velasco, Shaw, 1984.
A Ring of Endless Light, Farrar, Straus, 1980.
The Anti-Muffins, illustrated by Gloria Ortiz, Pilgrim, 1981.

"TIME FANTASY" SERIES

A Wrinkle in Time, Farrar, Straus, 1962.
A Wind in the Door, Farrar, Straus, 1973.
A Swiftly Tilting Planet, Farrar, Straus, 1978.
A House Like a Lotus, Farrar, Straus, 1984.
Many Waters, Farrar, Straus, 1986.
Madeleine L'Engle's Time Quartet, Dell, 1987.
An Acceptable Time, Farrar, Straus, 1989.

"CANNON TALLIS MYSTERY" SERIES

The Arm of the Starfish, Farrar, Straus, 1965.
The Young Unicorns, Farrar, Straus, 1968.
Dragons in the Waters, Farrar, Straus, 1976.

FICTION FOR ADULTS

The Small Rain: A Novel, Vanguard, 1945, published as *Prelude*, 1968, new edition under original title, Farrar, Straus, 1984.
Ilsa, Vanguard, 1946.
Camilla Dickinson, Simon & Schuster, 1951, also published for young adults as *Camilla*.
A Winter's Love, Lippincott, 1957, reprinted, Ballantine, 1983.
The Love Letters, Farrar, Straus, 1966.
The Other Side of the Sun, Farrar, Straus, 1971.
A Severed Wasp (sequel to *The Small Rain*), Farrar, Straus, 1982.
Certain Women, Farrar, Strauss, 1992.
A Live Coal in the Sea, Farrar, Strauss, 1996.
The Other Side of the Sun, Shaw, 1996.
(Editor with Luci Shaw) *Winter Song*, Shaw, 1996.
Miracle on 10th Street and Other Christmas Writings, Shaw, 1998.

NONFICTION

(Editor with William B. Green) *Spirit and Light: Essays in Historical Theology*, Seabury, 1976.
And It Was Good: Reflections on Beginnings, Shaw, 1983.
Dare to Be Creative, Library of Congress, 1984.
(With Avery Brooke) *Trailing Clouds of Glory: Spiritual Values in Children's Books*, Westminster, 1985.
A Stone for a Pillow: Journeys with Jacob, Shaw, 1986.
Sold into Egypt: Joseph's Journey into Human Being, Shaw, 1989.
The Rock That Is Higher: Story as Truth, Shaw, 1993.
Penguins and Golden Calves, Shaw, 1996.
Mothers and Daughters, with photographs by Maria Rooney, Shaw, 1997.
Bright Evening Star: Mysteries of the Incarnation, Shaw, 1997.
(With Luci Shaw) *Friends for the Journey*, Shaw, 1997.
My Own Small Place: Madeleine L'Engle's Thoughts on Developing the Writing Life, compiled by Lil Copan, Shaw, 1999.

"CROSSWICKS JOURNALS" AUTOBIOGRAPHIES

A Circle of Quiet, Farrar, Straus, 1972.

The Summer of the Great-Grandmother, Farrar, Straus, 1974.

The Irrational Season, Seabury, 1977.

Two Part Invention: The Story of a Marriage, Farrar, Straus, 1988.

POETRY

Lines Scribbled on an Envelope and Other Poems, Farrar, Straus, 1969.

The Weather of the Heart, Shaw, 1978.

Walking on Water: Reflections on Faith and Art, Shaw, 1980.

A Cry Like a Bell, Shaw, 1987.

PLAYS

18 Washington Square, South: A Comedy in One Act (first produced in Northampton, MA, 1940), Baker, 1944.

(With Robert Hartung) *How Now Brown Cow*, first produced in New York, 1949.

The Journey with Jonah, illustrated by Leonard Everett Fisher (one-act; first produced in New York City, 1970), Farrar, Straus, 1967.

OTHER

Contributor of articles, stories, and poems to periodicals, including *McCall's*, *Christian Century*, *Commonweal*, *Christianity Today*, and *Mademoiselle*. Collections of L'Engle's manuscripts are housed at Wheaton College, at the Kerlan Collection of the University of Minnesota, Minneapolis, and at the de Grummond Collection of the University of Southern Mississippi.

■ Adaptations

A Wrinkle in Time was recorded by Newbery Award Records, 1972, and adapted as a filmstrip with cassette by Miller-Brody, 1974; *A Wind in the Door* was recorded and adapted as a filmstrip with cassette by Miller-Brody; *Camilla* was recorded as a cassette by Listening Library; *A Ring of Endless Light* was recorded and adapted as a filmstrip with cassette by Random House. *And Both Were Young*, *The Arm of the Starfish*, *Meet the Austins*, *The Moon by Night*, *A Wrinkle in Time*, and *The Young Unicorns* have been adapted into braille; *The Arm of the Starfish*, *Camilla*, *Dragons in the Waters*, *A Wind in the Door*, and *A Wrinkle in Time* have been adapted as talking books; *The Summer of the Great-Grandmother* is also available on cassette.

■ Sidelights

Madeleine L'Engle is a writer who resists easy classification. She has successfully published plays, poems, essays, autobiographies, and novels for both children and adults. She is probably best known for her "Time Fantasy" series of children's books, including *A Wrinkle in Time*, *A Wind in the Door*, and *A Swiftly Tilting Planet*. These novels combine elements of science fiction and fantasy with L'Engle's constant themes of family love and moral responsibility.

As the daughter of a respected journalist and a gifted pianist, L'Engle was surrounded by creative people from birth. She wrote her first stories at the age of five. She was an only child; in her autobiographies she writes of how much she enjoyed her solitude and of the rich fantasy life she created for herself.

Speaking of her childhood, L'Engle explains in *The Summer of the Great-Grandmother*: "[My mother] was almost forty when I was born. . . . Once she and Father had had their long-awaited baby, I became a bone of contention between them. They disagreed completely on how I ought to be brought up. Father wanted a strict English childhood for me, and this is more or less what I got—nanny, governesses, supper on a tray in the nursery, dancing lessons, music lessons, skating lessons, art lessons."

Her father's failing health sent her parents to Switzerland and young Madeleine to a series of boarding schools, where she found herself very unpopular because of her shy, introspective ways. "I learned," L'Engle recounts in *The Summer of the Great-Grandmother*, "to put on protective coloring in order to survive in an atmosphere which was alien; and I learned to concentrate. Because I was never alone . . . I learned to shut out the sound of the school and listen to the story or poem I was writing when I should have been doing schoolwork. The result of this early lesson in concentration is that I can write anywhere."

L'Engle became involved in theatre at Smith College, acting as well as writing plays. Soon after graduation, she was made an understudy for a

Broadway production. Later she was given a few small roles and the position of assistant stage manager for Anton Chekhov's *Cherry Orchard*. The play ran for two years, and one of the performers, Hugh Franklin, eventually became L'Engle's husband. Throughout her career in the theatre, the author's writing continued, and both her theatre and boarding school experiences are evident in her first published novel. *The Small Rain* features Katherine Forrester, the daughter of a concert pianist. As a young child, Katherine plays a small role in a Broadway production, and the actors, stage hands, and dressing rooms become her world. Later, as a boarding school student, she

finds solace in her music and becomes increasingly dedicated to it. *The Small Rain* thus illustrates "one of L'Engle's predominant themes: that an artist must constantly discipline herself; otherwise her talent will become dissipated and she will never achieve her greatest potential," commented Marygail G. Parker in the *Dictionary of Literary Biography*.

After publishing several books in the late 1940s, L'Engle's career as a writer was postponed in favor of raising her own family. During the 1950s, she and her husband operated a general store in rural Connecticut. L'Engle still wrote stories in her spare time, but these were invariably rejected by magazines. As she recounts in *A Circle of Quiet*: "During the long drag of years before our youngest child went to school, my love for my family and my need to write were in acute conflict. The problem was really that I put two things first. My husband and children came first. So did my writing." On her fortieth birthday, in 1958, discouraged by several years of rejections, she renounced writing completely, but found that she was unable to stop. She explains, "I had to write. I had no choice in the matter. It was not up to me to say I would stop, because I could not. It didn't matter how small or inadequate [was] my talent. If I never had another book published, and it was very clear to me that this was a real possibility, I still had to go on writing." Soon thereafter, things began to change for the author, and her writing began to sell again.

Award-winning Novel Initially Rejected by Publishers

Selling *A Wrinkle in Time*, however, proved a challenge. The juvenile novel was rejected by twenty-six publishers in two years. Reasons given vary. The book was neither science fiction nor fantasy, impossible to pigeon hole. "Most objections," L'Engle recalled in an interview with *Children's Literature in Education*, "were that it would not be able to find an audience, that it was too difficult for children." Speaking to Michael J. Farrell in the *National Catholic Reporter*, L'Engle commented that *A Wrinkle in Time* "was written in the terms of a modern world in which children know about brainwashing and the corruption of evil. It's based on Einstein's theory of relativity and Planck's quantum theory. It's good, solid science, but also

L'Engle received the Newbery Award among other accolades for this 1962 time fantasy.

MADELEINE L'ENGLE

THE SUMMER
of the
GREAT-GRANDMOTHER

The Crosswicks Journal · Book Two

Themes of living and dying are discussed in the second book of the autobiographical "Crosswicks Journals," published in 1974.

it's good, solid theology. My rebuttal to the German theologians [who] attack God with their intellect on the assumption that the finite can comprehend the infinite, and I don't think that's possible."

The book was finally accepted by an editor at Farrar, Straus. "He had read my first book, *The Small Rain,* liked it, and asked if I had any other manuscripts," L'Engle recalled for *More Books by More People.* "I gave him *Wrinkle* and told him, 'Here's a book nobody likes.' He read it and two weeks later I signed the contract. The editors told me not to be disappointed if it doesn't do well and that they were publishing it because they loved it." The public loved the book too. *A Wrinkle in Time* won the Newbery Medal in 1963,

the Lewis Carroll Shelf Award in 1965, and was a runner-up for the Hans Christian Andersen Award in 1964.

Speaking with Roy Newquist in his *Conversations,* L'Engle recalled winning the Newbery Medal: "The telephone rang. It was long distance, and an impossible connection. I couldn't hear anything. The operator told me to hang up and she'd try again. The long-distance phone ringing unexpectedly always makes me nervous: is something wrong with one of the grandparents? The phone rang again, and still the connection was full of static and roaring, so the operator told me to hang up and she'd try once more. This time I could barely hear a voice: 'This is Ruth Gagliardo, of the Newbery Caldecott committee.' There was a pause, and she asked, 'Can you hear me?' 'Yes, I can hear you.' Then she told me that *Wrinkle* had won the medal. My response was an inarticulate squawk; Ruth told me later that it was a special pleasure to her to have me *that* excited."

In *A Wrinkle in Time,* young Meg Murry, with the help of her friend Calvin O'Keefe, must use time travel and extrasensory perception to rescue her father, a gifted scientist, from the evil forces that hold him prisoner on another planet. To release him, Meg must learn the power of love. In *A Critical History of Children's Literature,* Ruth Hill Viguers calls *A Wrinkle in Time* a "book that combines devices of fairy tales, overtones of fantasy, the philosophy of great lives, the visions of science, and the warmth of a good family story. . . . It is an exuberant book, original, vital, exciting. Funny ideas, fearful images, amazing characters, and beautiful concepts sweep through it. And it is full of truth."

According to L'Engle, writing *A Wrinkle in Time* was a mysterious process. "A writer of fantasy, fairy tale, or myth," she explained in *Horn Book,* "must inevitably discover that he is not writing out of his own knowledge or experience, but out of something both deeper and wider. I think that fantasy must possess the author and simply use him. I know that this is true of *A Wrinkle in Time.* I can't possibly tell you how I came to write it. It was simply a book I had to write. I had no choice. And it was only *after* it was written that I realized what some of it meant."

In his book *A Sense of Story: Essays on Contemporary Writers for Children,* John Rowe Townsend examines the themes in L'Engle's work: "L'Engle's main themes are the clash of good and evil, the difficulty and necessity of deciding which is which and of committing oneself, the search for fulfillment and self-knowledge. These themes are determined by what the author *is;* and she is a practising and active Christian. Many writers' religious beliefs appear immaterial to their work; Miss L'Engle's are crucial." Townsend sees a mystical dimension to *A Wrinkle in Time.* In that book, he writes, "the clash of good and evil is at a cosmic level. Much of the action is concerned with the rescue by the heroine Meg and her friend Calvin O'Keefe of Meg's father and brother, prisoners of a great brain called IT which controls the lives of a zombie population on a planet called Camazotz. Here evil is obviously the reduction of people to a mindless mass, while good is individuality, art and love. It is the sheer power of love which enables Meg to triumph over IT, for love is the force that she has and IT has not."

L'Engle went on to write *A Wind in the Door* and *A Swiftly Tilting Planet,* which feature the characters introduced in *A Wrinkle in Time* and further develop the theme of love as a weapon against darkness. By the third book in the series, Meg and Calvin have become husband and wife and are expecting their first child, Polly. Polly has adventures of her own in novels such as *A House Like A Lotus* and *An Acceptable Time.* Although the series has been criticized as too convoluted for young readers, and some reviewers find the Murry family a trifle unbelievable and elitist, most critics praise the series for its willingness to take risks. Michele Murray, writing of *A Wind in the Door* in the *New York Times Book Review,* claimed that "L'Engle mixes classical theology, contemporary family life, and futuristic science fiction to make a completely convincing tale." Speaking of this work, *School Library Journal* contributor Margaret A. Dorsey asserted: "Complex and rich in mystical religious insights, this is breathtaking entertainment."

"Austin Family" Books Explore Complex Issues

L'Engle has also created a second family, the Austins, in *Meet the Austins, The Moon by Night, A Ring of Endless Light,* and other works. These characters, like those in the "Time Fantasy" series, explore philosophical and spiritual issues as they negotiate their relationships and the chal-

---

If you enjoy the works of Madeleine L'Engle, you may also want to check out the following books and films:

Chester Aaron, *Out of Sight, Out of Mind,* 1984.
John Peel, *Uptime, Downtime,* 1992.
Ouida Sebestyen, *Far From Home,* 1980.
Time after Time, a film starring Malcolm McDowell, 1979.

---

lenges that growing up entails. But the Austins' journeys—unlike Meg and Calvin's voyages across galaxies and time—involve more familiar settings and events.

In *Meet the Austins,* L'Engle's 1960 novel, the four children—John, Vicky, Suzy, and Rob—face the prospect of adopting Maggy, a spoiled and unruly foster child who initially turns their household upside-down, but slowly adjusts to her new home and becomes a member of the family. A *Times Literary Supplement* contributor noted that although the family is "much too good to be real," Maggy's "gradual improvement and acceptance by the others are the best part of the book." *The Moon by Night,* published in 1963, takes place throughout the family's cross-country camping trip. Fourteen-year-old Vicky, who narrates the story, meets Zachary Gray at a camping ground. A complex, older boy whose ideas bear little resemblance to those of Vicky's small-town family and friends, Zachary both frightens and fascinates her. The Austins continue to encounter Zachary along the way, and later Vicky meets Andy, a sunny, down-to-earth boy who competes with Zachary for her affections. In the course of their travels, Vicky learns that the world is far more complicated than she had imagined.

A Ring of Endless Light, which was named a Newbery Honor Book in 1981, finds the Austins spending the summer caring for their dying grandfather at his home near the ocean. It is sixteen-year-old Vicky's first experience with death, and the concept raises new and difficult questions. Then Commander Rodney, a Coast Guard officer and cherished family friend, is killed rescuing a drowning young man. Vicky learns that the young man was Zachary Gray, who is once again trailing Vicky, and that his near-drowning was a suicide attempt. At the funeral, Vicky meets Adam Eddington, who works with Vicky's older brother John at the marine biology station. As the summer progresses, Vicky finds four men dependent on her in different ways. She reads to her grandfather, a wise minister who, in his coherent moments, helps her sort out her confusion. Troubled Zachary takes Vicky for exciting but dangerous adventures and leans on her emotionally. Vicky also befriends Commander Rodney's grieving son Leo, who seeks more than friendship, and assists

In this fourth book of the "Austin Family" series, sixteen-year-old Vicki searches for answers about death and love while she helps care for her dying grandfather.

Adam with his project at the marine biology station. Although Adam thinks of Vicky as John's younger sister, thwarting her hopes for a romantic relationship, it is their work with dolphins that reveals Vicky's gift for telepathic communication and helps her find a new understanding of life and death. Carol Van Strum, writing in the *Washington Post Book World*, commented, "The cosmic battle between light and darkness, good and evil, love and indifference, personified in the mythic fantasies of the *Wrinkle in Time* series, here is waged compellingly in its rightful place: within ourselves."

L'Engle's practice of reviving characters from earlier novels makes all her works for young people—whether realistic or fantasy—part of an intricately connected whole. The Murry, O'Keefe, and Austin characters become increasingly real as they age and progress through their life-cycles. Similarly, new facets of Zachary Gray and Adam Eddington emerge when they are placed in diverse situations. Originally associated with Vicky Austin, Zachary meets Polly O'Keefe in Greece in *A House Like a Lotus*. In *An Acceptable Time*, Zachary visits Polly at her grandparents' house, and the two travel three thousand years into the past, to the same community that Polly's uncle, Charles Wallace, visits as a teenager in *A Swiftly Tilting Planet*. Before he meets the Austins, Adam Eddington is featured in a dangerous escapade involving Dr. Calvin O'Keefe's biological research and his twelve-year-old daughter Polly in *The Arm of the Starfish*.

Explaining her storytelling method in *Something about the Author Autobiography Series*, L'Engle stated, "I start with what I know with all five senses, what I have experienced, and then the imagination takes over and says, 'But what if—' and the story is on." The author's ability to entertain is evident in her popularity with readers. A *Publishers Weekly* survey of the nation's booksellers ranked her in the top six best-selling children's authors, while in an overview of children's book publishing, *American Bookseller* ranked L'Engle among the ten most popular children's authors in the country. But the writing process also fulfills an essential need for the author. As she stated in *Something about the Author Autobiography Series*, "Often I am asked, 'Are you writing anything now?' Of course I'm writing something now. I'm not nice when I'm not writing."

■ Works Cited

Dorsey, Margaret A., review of *A Wind in the Door*, *School Library Journal*, May, 1973, p. 81.

Farrell, Michael J., "Madeleine L'Engle: In Search of Where Lion and Lamb Abide," *National Catholic Reporter*, June 20, 1986.

Hopkins, Lee Bennett, *More Books by More People*, Citation, 1974.

L'Engle, Madeleine, "The Expanding Universe," *Horn Book*, August, 1963.

L'Engle, Madeleine, *A Circle of Quiet*, Farrar, Straus, 1972.

L'Engle, Madeleine, *The Summer of the Great-Grandmother*, Farrar, Straus, 1974.

L'Engle, Madeleine, *Something about the Author Autobiography Series*, Gale, Volume 15, 1993, pp. 187-99.

Review of *Meet the Austins*, *Times Literary Supplement*, May 19, 1966, p. 433.

Murray, Michele, review of *A Wind in the Door*, *New York Times Book Review*, July 8, 1973, p. 8.

Newquist, Roy, *Conversations*, Rand McNally, 1967.

Parker, Marygail G., "Madeleine L'Engle," *Dictionary of Literary Biography*, Volume 52: *American Writers for Children since 1960: Fiction*, Gale, 1986.

Rausen, Ruth, "An Interview with Madeleine L'Engle," *Children's Literature in Education*, Number 19, winter, 1975.

Townsend, John Rowe, "Madeleine L'Engle," *A Sense of Story: Essays on Contemporary Writers for Children*, Lippincott, 1971, pp. 120-29.

Van Strum, Carol, "Glimpses of the Grand Design," *Washington Post Book World*, May 11, 1980, pp. 15-16.

Viguers, Ruth Hill, "Golden Years and Time of Tumult, 1920-1967: Worlds without Boundaries and Experiences to Share," *A Critical History of Children's Literature*, edited by Cornelia Meigs, Macmillan, revised edition, 1969, p. 481.

■ For More Information See

BOOKS

Chase, Carole F., *Suncatcher: A Study of Madeleine L'Engle and Her Writing*, Innisfree Press, 1998.

Children's Literature Review, Gale, Volume 1, 1976, Volume 14, 1988.

Contemporary Literary Criticism, Volume 12, Gale, 1980.

Huck, Charlotte S., *Children's Literature in the Elementary School*, 3rd edition, Holt, 1976, pp. 246-303.

Nodelman, Perry, editor, *Touchstones: Reflections on the Best in Children's Literature*, Volume 1, Children's Library Association, 1985, pp. 123-31.

Norton, Donna E., *Through the Eyes of a Child: An Introduction to Children's Literature*, 2nd edition, Merrill Publishing, 1987, pp. 294-95.

Shaw, Luci, editor, *The Swiftly Tilting Worlds of Madeleine L'Engle*, Shaw, 1998.

Viguers, Ruth Hill, *Margin for Surprise: About Books, Children, and Librarians*, Little, Brown, 1964, pp. 3-34.

PERIODICALS

Children's Literature in Education, summer, 1976, pp. 96-102; winter, 1983, pp. 195-203; spring, 1987, pp. 34-44.

Christian Century, April 6, 1977, p. 321; November 20, 1985, p. 1067.

Christianity Today, June 8, 1979.

Language Arts, October, 1977, pp. 812-16.

Lion and the Unicorn, fall, 1977, pp. 25-39.

New York Times Book Review, January 11, 1981, p. 29.

Publishers Weekly, June 20, 1980, p. 67.

Washington Post Book World, April 12, 1981, p. 12; September 13, 1981, p. 12.

Richard Linklater

■ Personal

Born c. 1962; children: Lorelei. *Education:* Attended the University of Texas.

■ Addresses

Agent—c/o Writers Guild of America, 8955 Beverly Blvd., West Hollywood, CA 90048.

■ Career

Screenwriter and director of motion pictures, including *Slacker*, 1991, *Dazed and Confused*, 1993, *Before Sunrise*, 1995, *subUrbia*, 1997, and *The Newton Boys*, 1998. Previous jobs include working on an offshore oil rig.

■ Awards, Honors

Silver Bear for Best Director, Berlin International Film Festival, 1995, for *Before Sunrise*.

■ Writings

SCREENPLAYS

It's Impossible to Learn to Plow by Reading Books, 1988.
Slacker, Orion Classics, 1991.
Dazed and Confused, MCA/Universal, 1993.
(With Kim Krizan) *Before Sunrise,* Columbia, 1995.
The Newton Boys, 20th Century Fox, 1998.

Linklater has also appeared as an actor in *Beavis and Butt-head Do America* and *Underneath.*

■ Adaptations

The screenplay for *Dazed and Confused* was adapted for a novel of the same name, St. Martin's Press, 1993.

■ Sidelights

In less than a decade, Richard Linklater has gone from making movies for $23,000 to making them for $27 million. His first nationally distributed feature, *Slacker,* featured a cast of some 100 unknown actors who worked for nothing; his 1998 feature, *The Newton Boys,* featured some of the hottest beefcake in Hollywood. *Slacker* was a storyless sortie into the world of disaffected youth; *The Newton Boys* was more like "the *Butch Cassidy* of the Nineties," according to Neva Chonin of

Rolling Stone. In between these extremes, Linklater took a look at high school antics in *Dazed and Confused,* at romance and the art of conversation in *Before Sunrise,* and at alienated suburban youth in *subUrbia,* adapted from the play by Eric Bogosian. Whether contemporary or historical, "Linklater's films have all successfully captured youth just being themselves," according to Chris Gore in *Film Threat.*

Known for his deadpan humor and stream-of-consciousness treatments, Linklater is a specialist in compressed time. His movies often take place within one day, something of a Joycean tour-de-force. And like Joyce, there is joy in word play and sometimes obscure references. A self-taught filmmaker, Linklater writes most of his own screenplays. After the quirky success of *Slacker,* Hollywood sought him out, making the question of financing easier, but in the main not hampering his indie approach to filmmaking. As Gore noted in *Film Threat,* the characters in Linklater's films "avoid . . . cliches and seem to be more well-rounded 'real' people. They act and react in ways that perhaps a real person would."

Growing Up Absurd in Texas

Linklater grew up in Texas, the youngest child in the family. "My parents divorced when I was seven," Linklater told *Rolling Stone's* Chonin. "I lived with my mother in Huntsville, population 18,000. It's where the state prison is. The only big excitement comes when they execute people." A good student until he hit high school, the teenage Linklater liked cars, stereos, and sports, in about that order. Later film was added to that list. "I spent all my time either in a movie theater or reading about film," Linklater told Gore. "I had grown up in Texas, so [film] was not really an option as a career choice." But he always felt that he wanted to be a writer of some sort, and this desire was mixed with a fascination for things

Linklater, a high school student himself in the mid-1970s, examines the 1970s high school experience in 1993's *Dazed and Confused.*

technical and mechanical. Once he reached his twenties, Linklater finally saw how the two could work together.

After high school, Linklater attended the University of Texas for a couple of years, working summers on an oil rig. But college did not provide what he wanted. He studied theater there, however, which let him know that in spite of being shy, he enjoyed the collaborative effort of the artistic ensemble. "My whole life for two years was working, reading and watching movies," Linklater recalled in *Rolling Stone.* From 1982 to 1984 his life revolved around someone else's celluloid world. Then in 1984 he bought his first camera and began to teach himself how to shoot film, learning in the process that he had always had this in the back of his head. All the stories he wanted to tell were ones that could be filmed. Here was the blend of writing and technical tinkering he had always enjoyed.

"I was just amazed at how patient and systematic I was," Linklater told Tim Rhys in *Movie-Maker.* "I mean, I was 22, and [the technical exercises] involved touching the camera for the first time. I had shot some stuff when I was in junior high and stuff, but I was like, 'Okay I'm gonna learn how to do this.'" Linklater thought vaguely about attending film school, but decided to follow his own path, learning by himself at his own pace and from his own mistakes. In 1986, after over two years of exercises, Linklater began shooting his first film, "an official prequel to *Slacker,*" as Linklater told Gore in *Film Threat.* Shot for less than $3,000 on a Super-8 camera, "it would have been my graduate thesis," he told Gore, if he had gone to film school.

The eighty-eight-minute film was two years in the making and features Linklater traveling around the country by train. Shooting the film on his own, he also became the nameless figure in all the shots. He would set up the camera on its tripod, push the button and do the scene, mostly just walking or sitting. Linklater noted that there was more dialogue in the first five minutes of *Slacker* than in the entire hour and a half of *It's Impossible to Learn How to Plow by Reading Books,* or simply *Plow* as the film is usually referred to. In this first film, Linklater explored what have become his trademark themes: alienation and the difficulties of communicating. "I think it's a good 20's angst movie and the formal design of it is

to make you alienated as a viewer," Linklater told Gore, "so you can guess it's not for everyone." After the success of later Linklater films, *Plow* played some theaters in 1997 and was released on video.

Slacker

With *Plow* behind him, Linklater was ready to take on a more ambitious project, one that had already been floating around in his head and for which he had begun to take copious notes. Little did he know he was about to add a new word to the media dictionary with which to describe the twenty-something generation. "I wanted to capture the way you walk around for a day and have these brief encounters with people you kind of know," Linklater explained to Dana Thomas of the *Washington Post.* "I wanted it to be like you're going home alone after a full day of activity and you're like piecing it all together . . . trying to make sense of it."

A movie without narrative, *Slacker* features one hundred characters, half of whom Linklater selected from the Austin rock scene, and none of them professional actors. Yet the movie is not a night of improvisation: the cast worked from a tightly scripted text based on overheard conversations that Linklater had recorded over the years. As Linklater told Rhys in his *MovieMaker* interview, a script "has to be tight before it can be loose." Improvisation does not mean turning on a camera and seeing what will happen. "It's too expensive," Linklater explained. "I think that falls into laziness." Instead, Linklater's casts rehearse scenes rigorously to get the feel of dialogue or monologue. The improvisation happens at rehearsals; the tiny tweaking of script that later appear on film.

Linklater has commented that *Slacker* was actually seven years in the making, including the years of research. Shot in the summer of 1989, locations for the film included the streets of Austin—where he had gone to school—and Linklater's own home. He became writer, director, and producer of this stream-of-consciousness movie which owes a tip of the hat to *La Ronde* by the Viennese playwright, Arthur Schnitzler. As in the Schnitzler play, Linklater's movie characters hand off the baton to an ever-increasing ensemble of players; one scene bumps against the next, like a dramatic tag-team match. The tone for this elaborate dance is set with the first scene, in which Linklater himself plays the character of someone arriving in Austin by bus. Taking a taxi, this nameless character proceeds to bend the oblivious driver's ear with a nonstop take on the road-not-taken and the possibility that separate realities are established by each choice we make. Linklater, in the course of his film, seems to be attempting to leave no road untaken.

Most of the characters in the movie have managed to keep the 'real' world at bay; they are students or recent graduates, and there are some older characters as well, including an ex-con and an aging radical who lies about service in the Spanish Civil War. Most seem to be getting by, cultivating their minds with Kennedy conspiracies or trying to make a dime hawking a Madonna Pap smear. As a contributor in *Rolling Stone* noted in its review of the movie, "Though the film includes a fight, a burglary and a hit-and-run matricide, it is crowded with talk, not incident." Such talk includes memorable lines that give *Slacker* its alienated tone: "I may live badly," says a hitchhiker, "but at least I don't have to work to do it." Perhaps the emblematic quote of the entire film comes when one character chooses a card from an Oblique Strategies deck—something of an I Ching for modern youth. The card tells it all: "Withdrawing in disgust is not the same as apathy."

Linklater's film spent a year making the rounds of the festivals and then was picked up by Orion Classics for national distribution. Mainstream recognition followed. Writing in the *Washington Post*, Hal Hinson remarked that the movie "is a work of divine flakiness," and the "heart and soul of this small-budget gem . . . are devoutly given over to that deep, rich vein of crackpot Americana." Hinson concluded that Linklater, in celebrating the marginality of these disaffected characters, produced "a work of scatterbrained originality, funny, unexpected, and ceaselessly engaging." Roger Ebert noted in the Chicago *Sun-Times* that *Slacker* "is a movie with an appeal almost impossible to describe, although the method of the director . . . is clear as day. . . . Linklater has invented his whole style in order to listen to these people. He doesn't want to go anywhere with them. He doesn't need a car chase to wrap things up. He is simply amused." A reviewer in *Time* called the film a "loping, loopy, sidewise, delightful comedy,"

in which Linklater turned his Austin into a contemporary Haight-Ashbury.

In a review of independent releases, *Premiere*'s J. Hoberman commented that *Slacker* "is the ultimate college-town comedy and takes it title from the new subculture of deadbeat youth it purports to portray." Hoberman concluded that "*Slacker*'s generous panoply of magical thinking and cracked metaphysics . . . suggests a grass-roots answer to David Byrne's *True Stories*." It was clear that Linklater had arrived when *Variety*, the industry publication, praised his film. A reviewer for the magazine remarked that "one of the picture's strengths is its humor, which arrives unpredictably," and went on to commend Linklater for "his fluid, on-the-move style that easily picks up new characters when the previous one is dropped."

Dazed and Confused

Linklater's success with *Slacker* raised heads in Hollywood and brought him $6 million for his next movie, a story about the final day of class at one high school in 1976. Harking back to his own high school days—he was a freshman in 1976—Linklater built his script around a core of stock high school characters from the star quarterback who is beginning to question authority, to the older grad who still hangs out with the younger crowd. The story once again takes place in compressed time—about eighteen hours, from the final bell of classes to dawn. Again, Linklater's camera follows the cast of characters as they cruise, get wasted at a beer blast, or just hang out at the local pool hall. *Dazed and Confused* takes its name from a Led Zeppelin song, and music of the 1970s figures prominently in the picture—the music budget consumed over ten per cent of the total budget.

Unlike *Slacker,* this Hollywood-financed second feature had more of a narrative line, following Randy "Pink" Floyd as he struggles with his conscience about whether or not to sign a morality pledge for the football coach—no drinking and no drugs. But those are two things all the characters partake of hugely in this film that *Entertainment Weekly*'s Owen Gleiberman called perhaps "the most slyly funny and dead-on portrait of American teenage life ever made." The storyline also follows the fortunes of a group of junior high students—boys and girls—who will be freshmen

Jessie, played by Ethan Hawke, and Celine, played by Julie Delpy, meet on a train headed for Vienna the night before Jessie must return to the United States in *Before Sunrise*, released in 1995.

next year and are thus the victims of senior hazing, including rather rigorous paddling. Casting for *Dazed and Confused*, as many reviewers noted, once again showed Linklater at his best. Ben Affleck as the sadistic O'Bannion and Matthew McConaughey as Wooderson, the graduate who never leaves town, were among several young actors to get a boost in their career with this movie.

Dazed and Confused became an instant success with the younger generation who identified with the aimlessness of the film's characters. A box-office success, Linklater's second feature film was also praised by critics. "Once every decade or so, a movie captures the hormone-drenched, fashion crazed, pop-song driven rituals of American youth culture with such loving authenticity that it comes

to seem a kind of anthem," Gleiberman wrote in *Entertainment Weekly*, comparing *Dazed and Confused* to George Lucas's *American Graffiti*. Desson Howe declared in the *Washington Post* that the film "ought to be in a prominent place at the Library of Congress" alongside "other quintessentially American works" because it "reflects American culture so well." Howe concluded that there "is a knowing, sympathetic and witty spirit about the exercise that makes you laugh as you wince. . . ." *Newsweek*'s Jeff Giles dubbed the film a "crushingly funny and knowing ode to misspent youth," while *Rolling Stone*'s Chris Mundy called it "hysterical" and a movie to be seen "at all costs."

One fallout of the movie was criticism of the emphasis on drugs and beer drinking by teenagers. But Linklater has noted that he was recording the way things are in his film, not propagandizing. "I smoked a little pot in high school," Linklater told Gore in *Film Threat*. "If I was in prison, I would stay high, probably . . . but if you want to get much done, I wouldn't suggest drugs or television."

Human Behavior Versus Movie Behavior

Linklater has been praised for his ability to make his characters come across as real on camera, for the way he works in production with efficient rehearsals, and for shooting that gets the job done and allows the real voice of real people to come through. As Linklater explained to Gore, it's a matter of "human behavior versus movie behavior." This trait can be clearly seen in Linklater's 1995 film *Before Sunrise* in which two characters talking through the night in Vienna comprise the entire film. Ethan Hawke plays the young American, Jessie, who is traveling by train from Budapest to Vienna to catch a morning plane. On the train, he meets a young French student, Celine, played by Julie Delpy, and he convinces her to get off in Vienna with him. Twelve hours later, they are still talking, having crammed a good six month's worth of such dialogue into their night-time roaming in the Austrian capital.

Partly financed by Vienna's Film Financing Fund, *Before Sunrise* was co-written with Kim Krizan, and like Linklater's earlier movies, this one takes place in a matter of hours filled with the two character's discussions about life and love. One of the takes in the movie lasts six minutes, a technique Linklater uses to make his characters seem real, vulnerable, human. *New Yorker*'s Anthony Lane felt that the film "disobeys all kinds of rules; it consists mostly of two people wandering around getting to know each other, which sounds very close to boring; and the other figures who turn up—geeky actors, a poet, a belly dancer, even a fortune-teller—are borderline bohemian, which sounds very close to embarrassing. . . . You pre-

subUrbia was Linklater's 1997 film about a group of small-town slackers.

pare to wince, but the essential good humor of the movie gets there just in time." Writing in *Rolling Stone*, Peter Travers called *Before Sunrise* "a sharp, sexy funny romance with a radical core of intelligence that catches the fever and fleetingness of love." Brian D. Johnson called it "a delicious new film" in *Maclean's*, and David Denby, reviewing the picture in *New York*, dubbed *Before Sunrise* a "lovely romantic comedy." Denby also noted that "a willfully vulnerable movie like *Before Sunrise* enters our derisive culture like a dolphin plunging into a tank of sharks. Linklater won a Silver Bear award at the Berlin Film Festival for his directing of this third feature film.

Linklater's next movie, *subUrbia*, was the first he directed from someone else's screenplay, adapted from Eric Bogosian's 1994 play. Once again, however, Linklater explores the borderline of alienated youth in America. The action this time takes place primarily in the parking lot of a convenience store where a cast of slackers hangs out and talks. As Jack Kroll noted in *Newsweek*, "Their talk is the lingua franca of the grunge mind as it oozes into the millennium in America." This cast of beautiful losers have their lives turned upside down one night with the return of an old buddy, Pony, who has become a minor rock star. Mike D'Angelo called the movie "a slacker version of *Waiting for Godot*," in *Entertainment Weekly*, while Stuart Klawans remarked in the *Nation* that *subUrbia* was a "surprisingly quiet, meditative picture" which "takes its rigor from Linklater's style but its energy from the actors."

Beyond Alienation

With *The Newton Boys*, Linklater made a break with the types of non-narrative movies for which he has become known. This 1998 release was the result of three years of research into the lives and misadventures of a quartet of bank-robbing brothers in Texas of the 1920s. The four brothers, actual historical characters, were dirt-poor farm boys who advanced to fancy suits and fancy women as the result of over eighty successful bank robberies from 1919 to 1924. The Texas connection interested Linklater, as did the fact that the four got away with their crimes largely without violence: they never killed anyone. Unlike the later Bonnie and Clyde, these four brothers lived to a ripe old age, one of them even appearing on television in the 1980s.

If you enjoy the works of Richard Linklater, you may also want to check out the following films:

Chasing Amy, starring Ben Affleck and Joey Lauren Adams, 1997.
Fast Times at Ridgemont High, starring Sean Penn, 1982.
Singles, starring Matt Dillon and Bridget Fonda, 1992.

Linklater told Chonin in *Rolling Stone* that Willis Newton was his first active hero, "someone who plotted his course and imposed his will on the world." He added that the characters in his other films were inert. "People thought I was some anti-story guy, which wasn't the case," he told Chonin. Featuring Matthew McConaughey as Willis Newton and Ethan Hawke as Jess, the film brought together actors Linklater had earlier directed in other films, and Linklater's script followed closely the historical course of the brothers' adventures in Texas and further afield. Reviews for this more traditional movie were mixed. *Time*'s Richard Schickel felt that Linklater had made "an agreeable movie," but one that lacked "the edge and intensity" of his earlier films. Travers noted in *Rolling Stone* that "At its best, the film has an easygoing charm that befits a story without much violence," while a reviewer in *People* noted that Linklater "shows considerable appreciation for both period details and his Texas locale. . . ."

As several critics have noted, Linklater, of all the crop of talented young directors to appear in the 1990s, may be the one to last. His blend of quirky viewpoint with his proven production abilities have endeared him to Hollywood. Despite his success, Linklater maintains something of a slacker image, more comfortable in jeans, tennis shoes, and a t-shirt than in Armani suits. But his ambition is anything but slacker-like. He has established an Austin-based production company for his films, Detour Productions, and has also instituted a film festival in his adopted city. His life still revolves around making movies that he loves. As he told Gore in *Film Threat*, "I get up almost every day thinking '. . . You know, I'm really lucky to be able to do this right now. It might not always be this good.'"

■ Works Cited

Chonin, Neva, "Richard Linklater," *Rolling Stone*, April 2, 1998, p. 34.

D'Angelo, Mike, review of *subUrbia*, *Entertainment Weekly*, August 22, 1997, p. 139.

Denby, David, "A Foreign Affair," *New York*, February 6, 1995, pp. 58-59.

Ebert, Roger, review of *Slacker*, *Sun-Times* (Chicago), August 23, 1991.

Giles, Jeff, "Rock 'n' Roll High School," *Newsweek*, October 4, 1993, p. 88.

Gleiberman, Owen, review of *Dazed and Confused*, *Entertainment Weekly*, September 24, 1993, p. 68.

Gore, Chris, "Richard Linklater," *Film Threat*, Number 1, 1996, pp. 6-11.

Hinson, Hal, review of *Slacker*, *Washington Post*, August 23, 1991, p. C2.

Hoberman, J., "Two Wild and Crazy Films," *Premiere*, June, 1991, pp. 27, 29.

Howe, Desson, review of *Dazed and Confused*, *Washington Post*, October 22, 1993.

Johnson, Brian D., "Seducing Strangers," *Maclean's*, February 6, 1995, p. 72.

Klawans, Stuart, review of *subUrbia*, *Nation*, March 3, 1997, pp. 35-36.

Kroll, Jack, review of *subUrbia*, *Newsweek*, February 17, 1997, p. 66.

Lane, Anthony, review of *Before Sunrise*, *New Yorker*, January 30, 1995, pp. 93-95.

Linklater, Richard, *Slacker*, Orion Classics, 1991.

Mundy, Chris, review of *Dazed and Confused*, *Rolling Stone*, September 11, 1993, p. 17.

Review of *The Newton Boys*, *People*, April, 6, 1998, p. 19.

Rhys, Tim, interview with Richard Linklater, *MovieMaker*, http://www.indienews.com/moviemaker/features/linklater.html.

Schickel, Richard, "Our Gang," *Time*, April 6, 1998, p. 70.

Review of *Slacker*, *Rolling Stone*, July 11, 1991, p. 115.

Review of *Slacker*, *Time*, July 29, 1991, p. 63.

Review of *Slacker*, *Variety*, January 28, 1991, p. 71.

Thomas, Dana, review of *Slacker*, *Washington Post*, August 23, 1991, p. C2.

Travers, Peter, review of *Before Sunrise*, *Rolling Stone*, February 23, 1995, p. 79.

Travers, Peter, review of *The Newton Boys*, *Rolling Stone*, April 16, 1998, pp. 88-89.

■ For More Information See

BOOKS

Contemporary Authors, Volume 152, Gale, 1996, pp. 279-80.

ON-LINE

Salon, http://www.salonmagazine.com/feb97/suburbia970207.html.

PERIODICALS

Austin Chronicle, September 24, 1993.

Entertainment Weekly, June 26, 1992, p. 118; October 8, 1993, p. 26; July 21, 1995, pp. 70-71.

Metro Times (Detroit), April 1-7, 1998, p. 18.

National Review, March 6, 1995, pp. 69-70.

New Republic, July 8, 1991, p. 26.

New Statesman & Society, December 4, 1992, p. 33.

New York, July 22, 1991, p. 43.

New Yorker, October 4, 1993, pp. 214-16.

People, February 6, 1995, p. 16.

Rolling Stone, February 13, 1993, p. 82.

Time, October 11, 1993, p. 83.*

—Sketch by J. Sydney Jones

Han Nolan

Miracle; New York Public Library Best Books for the Teen Age list, 1994, for *If I Should Die Before I Wake,* 1996, for *Send Me Down a Miracle,* and 1997, for *Dancing on the Edge;* American Library Association Best Books citation and National Book Award, both 1997, both for *Dancing on the Edge.*

■ Personal

Born August 25, 1956, in Birmingham, AL; married September 12, 1981. *Education:* University of North Carolina at Greensboro, B.S. in dance, 1979; Ohio State University, master's degree in dance, 1981. *Hobbies and other interests:* Reading, hiking, running, swimming.

■ Addresses

Office—c/o Harcourt Brace & Company, 525 B St., Suite 1900, San Diego, CA 92101-4495.

■ Career

Writer. Teacher of dance, 1981-84. *Member:* Society of Children's Book Writers and Illustrators, PEN.

■ Awards, Honors

People's Choice Award and National Book Award nominee, both 1996, both for *Send Me Down a*

■ Writings

If I Should Die Before I Wake, Harcourt, 1994.
Send Me Down a Miracle, Harcourt, 1996.
Dancing on the Edge, Harcourt, 1997.

■ Work in Progress

A Face in Every Window, a young adult novel, for Harcourt.

■ Sidelights

The 1997 winner of the National Book Award for her young adult novel, *Dancing on the Edge,* Han Nolan speaks directly to teenage readers in a voice at once empathic and down-home humorous. The author of three published novels, Nolan has already captured a wide and loyal readership with her themes of tolerance and understanding, and with her youthful protagonists who discover—in the course of her books—who they are and what they want. "Thoughtful is how I would describe my books," Nolan told *Authors and Artists for Young Adults* (*AAYA*) in an interview. "I put a lot of thought into my novels and I hope they are also thought-provoking, but I guess that is for someone else besides me to judge."

Unlike many young adult authors, with Nolan there was no serendipity in the audience for whom she chose to write. From the beginning of her career she set out to write novels for young readers. "I really love the YA readership, teens. I like how their minds work. They're just coming into their own; it's an exciting, new, and scary time for them. They are learning how the world works. It's feverish and passionate. Also, I liked my own teen years. It's a time for us to wake up. We're no longer blind children led by our parents." Nolan hopes her books provide a chance for teens "to enter a private world and stop and think about their lives," as she told *AAYA*. "They need this chance to go somewhere private and think about things that they might not be able to talk about with their friends."

Nolan's books have dealt with neo-Nazis, religious zealotry, and the lies a family promulgates to supposedly protect its children. Her characters—Hilary, Charity, Miracle—are young women on the cusp, emerging into an uncertain adulthood from shaky adolescence. They are young women who must learn to stand up for themselves—to throw off the influences of adults and peers and find their own center in a turbulent universe. Hilary in *If I Should Die Before I Wake* becomes a time-traveler to learn a lesson of tolerance, literally trading places with the Jews who she professes to hate. Her own experience of the dark night of the Holocaust changes her profoundly and allows her to become her own person. Likewise, Charity in *Send Me Down a Miracle* learns—in a less dramatic manner perhaps—to stand up for herself and thus be able to deal with her dominating father. And Miracle, the protagonist of *Dancing on the Edge*, must pass through the private hell of psychosis before she puts to rest the secrets that have riven her family. "Thoughtful" is indeed the word that comes to mind when reviewing Han Nolan's work.

A Child of Two Worlds

Born in the South, Nolan was raised in the North, specifically the northeast urban sectors around New York City. As a result, she has something of a dual citizenship to regional America: roots in the Southern sensibility of languorous tales after dinner, and feet firmly planted in the go-ahead urban ethic. The next to youngest of five children, Nolan and the rest of her family "moved around a lot," as she told *AAYA*, "something that teaches you how to make new friends quickly." Friends and neighborhoods changed, but a constant in the family was a love of books and the arts. "We were big time readers in my family. I remember my father used to bring three books home every night for my mother, and she would finish them by the next morning."

Like the rest of her family, Nolan loved books and reading from an early age. "As a young child, the book that really influenced me to become a writer was *Harriet the Spy*. After reading that, I of course wanted to be a spy not a writer, but I did begin keeping journals of my observations like Harriet. It's the journal-keeping that was so influential, that helped turn me into a writer. I still keep journals." Later favorite authors were Charles Dickens and John Steinbeck. "I also loved to write stories, and began putting them down on paper as soon as I learned how to write."

School was another matter, however. "Elementary school was very difficult for me," Nolan related to *AAYA*. "I was a hyperactive kid as a result of food allergies that I've only recently discovered. So it was hard for me to pay attention." Junior high was a more positive experience, and when she was thirteen, Nolan began dancing, an activity that enabled her to focus: "As a result, I'd say I had very happy teen years." Added to this life in New York were summers Nolan and her family spent in the South, in Dothan, Alabama, where many of her relations lived on one street. There she got into touch with another part of her heritage, listening to a favorite aunt stretch out the evening with her long tales. "My Southern relatives loved to sit and listen to these stories. Everything is a story, a blend of wit, humor, and intelligence. They had the ability to laugh at everything, including themselves. There was seriousness in these long tales, and tragedy, too. But they were always leavened with humor. When I was a child I would sit and listen for hours."

Upon graduation from high school, Nolan decided to go south for college. "I chose the University of North Carolina at Greensboro because of the

Sixteen-year-old Hilary Burke—a present day neo-Nazi—learns what it's like to be hated when she time-travels to a Polish ghetto during the Holocaust as a Jewish girl in Nolan's 1994 novel.

dance major they offered. The program turned out to be incredibly well-rounded, requiring courses in the sciences, physical education, and education, and in addition there were all the English courses I naturally gravitated to. So I had a full education." Graduating in 1979, she went on to a master's program in dance at Ohio State where she met her future husband, who was working on his doctorate in Classics. In 1981 she graduated, married, and began teaching dance. When the couple decided on adopting children several years later, Nolan also opted for a career change. "I wanted to be home with my kids," she noted

in her *AAYA* interview, "so I thought about work I could do at home. I always loved to write and took some creative writing classes, but it was not something you could actually do for a living. I fancied being able to write and living on Cape Cod, but those were fantasies, not reality. I just always figured I would do something more practical." Then discussing it with her husband one afternoon, he helped make the decision for her. "Suddenly he just took off, saying he'd be back in a bit. When he finally came back he had one of these writers' market guides for me, and that just started me writing."

A Ten-Year Apprenticeship

Thus began Nolan's writing career. She studied not only markets, but every book on writing technique that she could get her hands on. She wrote stories and sent some out with no success. Then she tackled lengthier projects, writing a mystery that won some attention with a publisher but was not purchased. Nonetheless, there was encouragement in the fact that an editor had taken interest in her work. She joined or formed writers' groups where she happened to be living—in Pennsylvania and Connecticut. All the while there were children to raise in addition to learning how to become a writer. She began another mystery, but one of the characters was stubbornly going off on her own, dreaming about the Holocaust.

"This kept coming into the story and getting bigger and bigger," Nolan recalled. In addition to Nolan's subconscious at work, there were also contemporary events impinging. "Here I was in Connecticut, and I discovered that there was a KKK group in town. Hate crimes were being reported, and I was appalled by this whole neo-Nazi fascination. As a young teenager I came across Viktor Frankl's *Man's Search for Meaning* in my parents' bookshelves, and reading that I remember how shocked I was to read about the Holocaust. First, that this should have been allowed to happen, and second, that I had not known about it before—that it was not being taught to us as students. There was a kind of horror I internalized then that finally found a way to come out in my writing. A sense of horror that was recharged by events around me."

Nolan recast the character from her mystery into Hilary Burke, a young neo-Nazi who is lying in a coma in a Jewish hospital, for her 1994 novel, *If I Should Die Before I Wake*. Hilary has history: her father died years before, his death caused (so Hilary believes) by a Jew, and her Bible-thumping mother temporarily abandoned her. She has found a home with a group of neo-Nazis; her boyfriend is the leader of the group. Hilary now lies in a hospital as a result of a motorcycle accident. In her coma, she sees another patient, an elderly Jewish woman named Chana in her room. Chana is a Holocaust survivor, but to Hilary she is sarcastically labeled "Grandmaw." Suddenly

Hilary spins back in time, trading places with Chana, becoming herself the persecuted young girl in Poland. She experiences firsthand the horrors of the Holocaust: her father is shot; she lives in the ghetto for a time; she escapes with her grandmother from the ghetto only to be captured, tortured, and sent to Auschwitz-Birkenau. Hilary constantly drifts back to herself in the hospital. Meanwhile, her mother, a born-again Christian, and her boyfriend visit. By the end, "Hilary has come back from her own near-death experience as well as Chana's to be a more understanding, tolerant person," Susan Levine wrote in *Voice of Youth Advocates*.

"I wanted to say to neo-Nazis 'How would you like this to happen to you?'," Nolan told *AAYA*. "I wanted to put them into the same situations the Jews suffered. The writing of the book was very difficult. Working on the historical parts, I felt that I was actually there. I was afraid to write the book. I didn't think that I had enough talent to tackle the subject. And I'm not Jewish. But it was a story I had to tell. I was so compelled, and I wanted to write the book not so much for Jewish readers—they know their history—but for non-Jewish teenagers. To let them know, to make sure that we can't let this happen again. Just can't. I knew I was going to take some flack for the book and I did."

The first review Nolan read—or actually had read to her by her husband over the phone while attending a writer's conference—questioned the taste of the book. This was shattering enough for Nolan to later warn off a would-be purchaser of her first novel at the conference. "I told this person, 'Oh no, you don't want to read that. It got a bad review.' What did I know? I was just starting." Most reviewers, however, responded positively to this first effort. Levine went on in her *Voice of Youth Advocates* review to note that the novel is a history and ethics lesson enveloped in a riveting plot. Levine concluded that Nolan had written "an interesting and moving story." Roger Sutton, writing in the *Bulletin of the Center for Children's Books*, commented that Nolan is forthright in dealing with her material, "and her graphic descriptions of camp life have a morbid interest that teeters on exploitation but comes down on the side of the truth." *Booklist*'s Mary Harris Veeder stated that Nolan's "first novel has great strengths and weaknesses." Among the latter, Veeder felt, were the time travel episodes and certain contemporary

Charity, the fourteen-year-old daughter of a preacher, questions her strict religious upbringing after a girl from her small southern town claims to have seen Jesus Christ.

H A N   N O L A N

Dancing on the Edge

Raised by her grandmother, a young girl searches for her true identity in this 1997 novel, winner of the National Book Award.

characterizations. "Chana's story, however, is brilliantly rendered," Veeder noted, and "carries memorable emotional impact." A contributor in *Kirkus Reviews* remarked that "Nolan's first novel is ambitious indeed," and concluded that "the book as a whole is deeply felt and often compelling."

Hitting Her Stride

Nolan was already 100 pages into her next novel by the time of publication of *If I Should Die Before I Wake.* "My next book was lighter," Nolan told *AAYA.* "It was a fun book to write, because I used material from my own summers in the South. I needed something lighter after writing

about the Holocaust. We were still living in Connecticut, and I was now taking my own children down to Dothan for the summers. It brought back all those old memories for me." Soon these memories were added to by the fact that Nolan and her family moved to the South, to Birmingham, Alabama.

Nolan began to find her own writing method also. Starting with a character or situation or location rather than a plot outline, she writes long enough to get to know her characters and where they want to take things. This can take up to sixty pages of manuscript, much of which gets tossed with revisions and tightening of story. "My characters are made up as I go along," Nolan explained to *AAYA.* "They're all parts of me, composites. It's sort of like Michelangelo's theory of sculpture. The figure is already there under the stone; it's the artist's job to release it by chipping away. The first sixty pages are me chipping away at the stone.

"And there's a vagueness to the whole process. You have something you want to say in the first place. That's why you sit down to write. But it's elusive, and I tend to write around what the thing is I really want to say. Sometimes it's difficult for me to confront it, to come face to face with what it is I truly want to say. It's like I'm looking through a tiny pinhole at first, and sometimes this broadens to a window, but mostly it's a very narrow view I'm allowed through my characters and story. Much of the time I am writing in the dark. I'm seeing it all in my mind."

With *Send Me Down a Miracle,* Nolan follows the fortunes of fourteen-year-old Charity Pittman as she battles for a sense of self in her hometown of Casper—a locale inspired by the Dothan of Nolan's childhood. Charity feels trapped at home with her younger sister Grace and preacher father now that her mother has left them. The father's stern interpretation of Christianity has chased away Charity's mother, but soon Charity is attracted to the cosmopolitan Adrienne Dabney, returned from New York to her family home where she sets about trying a deprivation experiment. For three weeks Adrienne locks herself away in her inherited home, without visitors, light, or food. Emerging from the experiment, she says that Jesus has visited her, sitting in the chair in her living room. This proclamation splits the small town asunder: Charity and many others believe in the chair and its miraculous powers; Charity's father calls it all blasphemy, warning that Adrienne is evil incarnate. Caught between the prickly father whom she loves and Adrienne, who has taken her on as a friend and fellow artist, Charity must finally learn to make up her own mind. When her father comes to destroy the chair, Charity is there to stand up to him finally.

"The dichotomy of professing one's faith and actually living it is interestingly portrayed throughout this novel," commented Jana R. Fine in a *School Library Journal* review of *Send Me Down a Miracle.* Fine also noted that readers were brought into the "heart of a young girl" who learns to meld her religious background with compassion and forgiveness. A critic in *Kirkus Reviews* called *Send Me Down a Miracle* a "busy, hilarious, tragic story," and concluded that "readers will be dizzied by the multiple subplots and roller-coaster highs and lows" in this story of a small town. A *Horn Book Guide* contributor noted that this "offbeat coming-of-age novel is peopled with a host of peculiar, yet intriguing, characters," and *Booklist*'s Ilene Cooper remarked that Nolan's "plot is intricate, sharp, and invigorating." Award committees agreed with the reviewers: *Send Me Down a Miracle* was nominated for the National Book Award in 1996.

Dancing on the Edge

Nolan's next book, *Dancing in the Edge,* three years in the writing, was inspired by her own adopted children. "I wanted to somehow deal with the theme of adoption, the difficulty such children have in finding their own identity not knowing their birth parents. This search for identity is so vital to all of us, and some children without families have to borrow an identity to be able to find their own. I once knew a person who'd been adopted. This person used to go to the drawer where her birth certificate was kept just to make sure she really existed. So in part this novel is for those kids in search of an identity, and also it's a novel about secrets, about the damage secrets can do in a family. Children can read adults; they know when we're lying. The truth may be hard, but it's better than lies. The truth can cure."

Miracle McCloy, the young protagonist of *Dancing on the Edge*, is so named because she was delivered after her mother was killed in an acci-

---

If you enjoy the works of Han Nolan, you may also want to check out the following books and films:

Bruce Brooks, *Asylum for Nightface*, 1996.
Sharon Creech, *Walk Two Moons*, 1994.
Jane Yolen, *The Devil's Arithmetic*, 1988.
I Never Promised You a Rose Garden, a film based on the novel by Joanne Greenberg, 1977.

---

dent. Her spiritualist grandmother Gigi calls it "the greatest miracle to ever come down the pike," but Miracle is not convinced. She feels a misfit, hardly special at all. She is ten at the beginning of the novel, living in Alabama with her father, Dane, a one-time child prodigy who now sits around in his bathrobe in the basement all day, and with Dane's mother, Gigi, who spends her time with matters of the occult. Dane suddenly disappears one day, and Gigi tells Miracle that her father has "melted." Gigi and Miracle then go to live with Opal, Gigi's ex-husband. Here Miracle finds some stability in the form of her gruff grandfather who buys her a bicycle and starts her in dancing lessons. Dance proves to be a momentary salvation for Miracle, something that actually makes her feel as special as everyone is always saying she is. But when she starts imitating her grandmother's occult fancies, casting spells and making love potions for her classmates, troubles arise. Accused of being a phony by another student, Miracle sets herself on fire.

Fourteen at the time of this attempted suicide, Miracle is put into a mental hospital and it is here that her Aunt Casey and a kindly doctor help her to come to terms with the secrets in her life. This second part of the novel details Miracle's therapy and recovery as she slowly uncovers the truths that have eluded her all these years. She discovers that her mother, a ballerina, was committing suicide when struck by a speeding ambulance and that she has been abandoned by her father. "Nolan skillfully discloses" the nature of her cast of offbeat characters, a *Kirkus Reviews* critic noted, calling the novel "intense" and "exceptionally well-written." Miriam Lang Budin, writing in *School Library Journal,* dubbed *Dancing on the Edge* an "extraordinary novel," and concluded that

"Nolan does a masterful job of drawing readers into the girl's mind and making them care deeply about her chances for the future." Again award committees agreed. *Dancing on the Edge* was nominated for a National Book Award, the first time an author has been nominated for that prestigious award two years in a row. And 1997 proved to be Nolan's lucky year. Her novel won the National Book Award, commended by the panel of judges as "a tale of chilling reality."

Nolan was already deep into her next novel by the time of the awards ceremony, but found taking time out from her writing and going to New York to be "great, pure fun," as she told *AAYA*. Awards are one form of feedback for Nolan, who does not pay much attention to reviews any longer. Another form of response to her work comes in letters from fans. These letters, interestingly enough, come not just from young readers. "Adults seem to enjoy reading my books, as well as teens," Nolan told *AAYA*. "I try to write on many different levels and add layers of understanding to my novels. So it is heartening to know that the books speak across the generations. But in the end I think sometimes adults underestimate teenagers. If the letters I receive from young readers is any indication, we need to write to them, not write down to them. They are out there and they are hungry for good literature. Don't underestimate them."

■ Works Cited

Budin, Miriam Lang, review of *Dancing on the Edge*, *School Library Journal*, September, 1997.

Cooper, Ilene, review of *Send Me Down a Miracle*, *Booklist*, March 15, 1996, p. 1263.

Review of *Dancing on the Edge, Kirkus Reviews*, August 1, 1997, p. 1227.

Fine, Jana R., review of *Send Me Down a Miracle*, *School Library Journal*, April, 1996, p. 157.

Review of *If I Should Die Before I Wake, Kirkus Reviews*, March 1, 1994, p. 308.

Levine, Susan, review of *If I Should Die Before I Wake, Voice of Youth Advocates*, June, 1994, p. 88.

Nolan, Han, *Dancing on the Edge*, Harcourt, 1997.

Nolan, Han, interview with J. Sydney Jones for *Authors and Artists for Young Adults*, conducted October 13, 1998.

"Nolan Wins 1997 National Book Award," *School Library Journal*, January, 1998, p. 22.

Review of *Send Me Down a Miracle, Horn Book Guide*, Fall, 1996, p. 304.

Review of *Send Me Down a Miracle, Kirkus Reviews*, March 15, 1996, p. 451.

Sutton, Roger, review of *If I Should Die Before I Wake, Bulletin of the Center for Children's Books*, April, 1994, pp. 267-68.

Veeder, Mary Harris, review of *If I Should Die Before I Wake, Booklist*, April 1, 1994, p. 1436.

■ For More Information See

PERIODICALS

ALAN Review, Winter, 1998.

Bulletin of the Center for Children's Books, July, 1996, p. 382; December, 1997, pp. 135-36.

Horn Book Guide, Fall, 1994, p. 322.

Kliatt, July, 1996, p. 15.

Publishers Weekly, January 31, 1994, p. 90; August 18, 1997, p. 94; November 24, 1997, p. 14.

School Library Journal, April, 1994, pp. 152-53.

Voice of Youth Advocates, June, 1996, p. 99; June, 1997, p. 86.

—Sketch by J. Sydney Jones

Robert B. Parker

■ Personal

Born September 17, 1932, in Springfield, MA; son of Carroll Snow (a telephone company executive) and Mary Pauline (maiden name, Murphy) Parker; married Joan Hall (an education specialist), August 26, 1956; children: David F., Daniel T. *Education:* Colby College, Maine, B.A., 1954; Boston University, M.A., 1957, Ph.D., 1970.

■ Addresses

Agent—Helen Brann Agency, 94 Curtis Rd., Bridgewater, CT 06752.

■ Career

Curtiss-Wright Co., Woodridge, NJ, management trainee, 1957; Raytheon, Co., Andover, MA, technical writer, 1957-59; Prudential Insurance Co., Boston, MA, advertising writer, 1959-62; Parker-Farman Co.(advertising agency), Boston, partner, 1960-62; Film consultant to Arthur D. Little, 1962-64. Boston University, Boston, lecturer in English, 1962-64; Massachusetts State College at Lowell (now University of Lowell), instructor in English, 1964-66; Lecturer, Suffolk University, 1965-66. Massachusetts State College at Bridgewater, instructor in English, 1966-68; Northeastern University, Boston, assistant professor, 1968-74, associate professor, 1974-76, professor of English, 1976-79; novelist, 1979—. *Military service:* U.S. Army, 1954-56. *Member:* Writers Guild.

■ Awards, Honors

Edgar Allan Poe Award, Mystery Writers of America, 1976, for *Promised Land.*

■ Writings

(With others) *The Personal Response to Literature,* Houghton (Boston), 1970.
(With Peter L. Sandberg) *Order and Diversity: The Craft of Prose,* Wiley (New York City), 1973.
(With John R. Marsh) *Sports Illustrated Weight Training: The Athlete's Free-Weight Guide,* Lippincott (Philadelphia), 1974.
(With Joan Parker) *Three Weeks in Spring* (nonfiction), Houghton, 1978.
Wilderness (novel), Delacorte (New York City), 1979.
Love and Glory (novel), Delacorte, 1983.
The Private Eye in Hammett and Chandler, Lord John (Northridge, CA), 1984.
Parker on Writing, Lord John, 1985.

(With Raymond Chandler) *Poodle Springs*, Putnam, 1989.

(With Joan Parker; photographs by William Strode) *A Year at the Races*, Viking (New York City), 1990.

Perchance to Dream: Robert B. Parker's Sequel to Raymond Chandler's "The Big Sleep" (novel), Putnam, 1991.

All Our Yesterdays (novel), Delacorte, 1994.

(With photographs by Kasho Kumagai) *Spenser's Boston*, Otto Penzler, 1994.

(Editor) *The Best American Mysteries 97*, Houghton, 1997.

Night Passage, Putnam, 1997.

Trouble in Paradise, Putnam, 1998.

Boston Tapestry (travel), Towery Publishing, 1999.

"SPENSER" DETECTIVE SERIES

The Godwulf Manuscript, Houghton, 1974.
God Save the Child, Houghton, 1974.
Mortal Stakes, Houghton, 1975.
Promised Land, Houghton, 1976.
The Judas Goat, Houghton, 1978.
Looking for Rachel Wallace, Delacorte, 1980.
Early Autumn, Delacorte, 1981.
A Savage Place, Delacorte, 1981.
Surrogate: A Spenser Short Story, Lord John, 1982.
Ceremony, Delacorte, 1982.
The Widening Gyre, Delacorte, 1983.
Valediction, Delacorte, 1984.
A Catskill Eagle, Delacorte, 1985.
Taming a Sea-Horse, Delacorte, 1986.
Pale Kings and Princes, Delacorte, 1987.
Crimson Joy, Delacorte, 1988.
Playmates, Putnam, 1989.
The Early Spenser: Three Complete Novels (contains *The Godwulf Manuscript*, *God Save the Child*, and *Mortal Stakes*), Delacorte, 1989.
Stardust, Putnam, 1990.
Pastime, Putnam, 1991.
Double Deuce, Putnam, 1992.
Paper Doll, Putnam, 1993.
Walking Shadow, Putnam, 1994.
Thin Air, Putnam, 1995.
Chance, Putnam, 1996.
Small Vices, Putnam, 1997.
Sudden Mischief, Putnam, 1998.

Also author with wife, Joan Parker, of several television scripts for series *Spenser: For Hire*, two *B. L. Stryker* television movies for Burt Reynolds, and four television movies based on the "Spenser" television series. Contributor to *Lock Haven Review* and *Revue des langues vivantes*. Contributor of restaurant reviews to *Boston Magazine*, 1976.

■ Adaptations

The *Spenser: For Hire* television series, American Broadcasting Corp. (ABC), 1985-88, was based in part on Parker's works; film rights have been sold to many of the Spenser novels.

■ Sidelights

"Machismo got a bad name starting with the feminist movement, where it was used to label male behavior that women found offensive," the novelist Robert B. Parker once told Amanda Smith in a *Publisher's Weekly* interview. "But if you called it a commitment to honorable behavior, it wouldn't sound half so bad. . . . To act courageously and to refuse to be dishonored isn't a bad code." Parker's stand-up fictional protagonist, Spenser—he goes tersely by his last name in the books—is machismo with a Parker twist. He's a gumshoe, a PI, the inheritor of a long line of tradition from fellow traveler's in the hard-boiled school of detective fiction, all the way from Dashiell Hammett's Sam Spade and Raymond Chandler's Philip Marlowe to Ross Macdonald's Lew Archer. Like those earlier doyens of the genre, Spenser is flip and fast-talking, as quick with his fists as he is with his mouth. But unlike them, he is not an existential loner. An outsider, perhaps, but definitely linked to the world through his psychotherapist girlfriend, Susan Silverman, and sometimes sidekick, Hawk.

Unmarried, still Spenser is attached. And the relationship between him and Susan, developing slowly over the years, has in part kept readers coming back for more throughout the two dozen plus novels in the Spenser series. Newgate Callendar itemized the ingredients for the success of the Spenser books in a *New York Times Book Review* critique of Parker's eleventh title in the series, *The Widening Gyre*. Callendar describes him as a man's man, a former professional fighter who will not back down to any opposition. Yet, he is honest and sensitive. "Spenser may be something of a smart aleck but only when he is faced with pomposity and pretension," Callendar said. "Then he reacts, sometimes violently." While Spenser is educated and well read, he does not flaunt his knowledge. Moreover, his girlfriend is the perfect foil and as smart as he. "Pushed as he is by his social conscience, he is sometimes dogged enough to seem quixotic," Callendar added.

Though the adjusted nose angle and scar tissue around the eyes attest to his former career as a boxer, Spenser is no mere quasi-legal hired thug: he likes the finer things, noting with intense detail his dining habits—usually gourmet—and dress—casual but not sloppy. Spenser is literate—his musing allusions range from Greek tragedy to pop music—but such knowledge does not prevent him from taking the law into his own hands if need be. Indeed, Spenser often places himself above the law, devising his own chivalric code of honor. This private code of honor is a persistent Parker/Spenser theme, creating a sense of Hemingway, and this was noted by David Geherin in his *Sons of Sam Spade, The Private-Eye Novel in the 70s.* "The pervasive influence of Hemingway can be seen in all of Parker's writing," Geherin remarked. More to the point, Parker himself, through the character of Susan, is aware of this debt. At one point in the third book in the series, *Mortal Stakes*, Susan tells Spenser that he ought to lose all this "Hemingwayesque nonsense."

A reviewer in *Time*, critiquing *Taming a Sea-Horse*, remarked that while the hero of the traditional hard-boiled detective novel got the girls, the villains, and the money, "Robert B. Parker, the genre's leading writer, resurrects a more chivalric code for his beefy detective Spenser." *Chivalric* is the operative word here, for Parker's hero consciously re-creates a knight's code of honor, albeit a very contemporary code for a late twentieth-century knight. "Part of Robert Parker's charm lies in the Romantic vision that he describes in his Spenser novels," wrote D. M. Bakker in an extended *Armchair Detective* review of Parker's *Pale Kings and Princes*. "The title character, Spenser, embodies all that we have come to expect of the 'guys in the white hats': he has the strength of ten, and he always wins because he is pure of heart. The conflicts in which Parker involves his character are worthy of so gallant a knight because they are for mortal stakes." Spenser is a "romantic diddle," as Susan calls him in the 1989 *Playmates* over a dinner of roast pheasant and Peking Duck, preceded by sweet and sour Thai soup and black bean cake. The novelist Frederick

Busch noted in a Chicago *Tribunes Book* review of *Pale Kings and Princes* that "Spenser is our representative, carrying what light is left to us and standing up against what organized crime has most to do with: self-indulgent bullies."

Romantic, heroic, or just plain smash-mouth, Spenser has found a legion of loyal fans across a wide spectrum of readers, not the least of them teens. For this last group Parker's snappy dialogue provides speed-of-light readability, and his emphasis on themes from child pornography and kidnaping to college athletics, as well as his use of many younger secondary characters, draw the young adult audience and adults. *Armchair Detective* reviewer Anne Ponder called Parker's Spenser books "the best American hard boiled detective fiction since Ross Macdonald and Raymond Chandler," and reader affection for the novels spawned a television series adapted from the Spenser books.

The Artist as Professor

Parker is, as Smith pointed out in *Publishers Weekly*, "primarily a Massachusetts product." He was born in Springfield and raised there and in New Bedford. When it came time for college, he stayed in New England, attending Colby College in Maine. After college, he served two years in the army in Korea, then returned to Massachusetts where he earned a master's in English at Boston University. Parker married in 1956 and began a family, ultimately consisting of two sons. Writing, an early ambition, was put on hold while he earned a living. He took jobs as a technical and advertising copy writer for six years until he became a lecturer in English at Boston University in 1962. "I had to support everybody and I didn't have the time to write," Parker noted in an interview with *Contemporary Authors* (*CA*). "But I had always wanted to, and I manipulated myself (and Joan [his wife] helped me considerably in that) into a position of being a college professor so that I would have time to write, which I then did."

Parker's academic career took him to a half dozen small colleges in and around Boston as he progressed from instructor to assistant professor to associate and full professor of English. He earned a doctorate in English from Boston University with his thesis on detective novelists, comparing Chandler, Hammett, and Macdonald. Smith noted in *Publishers Weekly* that the writing of his thesis took

Parker only two weeks. The doctorate earned Parker a full professorship at Boston's Northeastern University, and also educated him in the ways of genre writing.

When he began his first book, it was little wonder that it turned out to be a detective novel, or that it owed a great deal to Chandler. Parker has noted that he set out consciously to imitate Chandler in his early books. "Originally, Spenser came out to be the second coming of Philip Marlowe," Parker told Joseph A. Cincotti in a review of *Pastime* in the *New York Times Book Review*. He went on to tell Cincotti that in the early books "I made every effort to write just like Raymond Chandler. The degree to which those early books are different is the degree to which I failed in my attempt." The very name of Parker's hero echoes Chandler's. The latter named his protagonist after the Elizabethan dramatist and author of *Dr. Faustus*; Parker's Spenser is named after the Elizabethan poet and author of *The Fairie Queene*. Increasingly however, as the Spenser series gained in popularity, Parker went his own way with the conventions of the private-eye form. As Geherin noted, "Parker is . . . attempting to extend the dimensions of the detective novel." Geherin went on to explain that Parker was pushing the envelope of the genre by "combining elements of the hard-boiled novel with his own interest in the psychology of his characters and their relationships, and with a critical attitude toward contemporary America and American values. . . ."

Parker's first novel, *The Godwulf Manuscript*, written in his spare time over the course of several years, was sold within three weeks of completion. In it, much of Parker's fictional world is established: the Boston locale, Spenser the romantic hero battling the wrongs of society, and the snappy dialogue about which reviewers continually rave. Spenser is called in to investigate the disappearance of a fourteenth-century illuminated manuscript from a college library. As Callendar put it in the *New York Times Book Review* of the novel, "Along the way he runs into student activists, the Mob, drugs, sex and the usual package." Callendar also noted that in this first novel, Parker had created the "very exemplar" of the private eye species: "a tough, wise-cracking, unafraid, lonely, unexpectedly literate type."

Over the next five years, Parker wrote four more Spenser novels, each one gaining the series more

readers. Finally in 1979, Parker was able to quit teaching and devote himself full time to his first love, writing. As Parker noted in his *CA* interview, teaching "was not a labor of love." Rather, he went into it looking for a way to have more time to devote to writing. "I'm not terribly happy with the academic world," Parker said in *CA*, but he puts it much more strongly in the words of a character in *Playmates*. Discovering that one of her students, a star college basketball player, cannot read, a young assistant professor explains how this could happen: "It happens because nobody gives a goddamn. Me included. The students are the necessary evil in the teaching profession. Other-

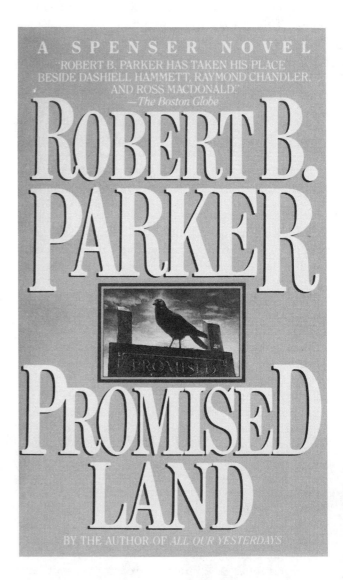

This fourth novel from the "Spenser" series garnered an Edgar Alan Poe Award in 1976.

wise it's a pretty good deal. You don't work hard, you have a lot of time off. The pay's not much, but nobody hassles you. You can read and write and publish, pretty well unimpeded except for the students. Most of us don't like them much."

Parker, however, is not totally negative about his years of education and teaching. He took from his study of English and American literature "a kind of allusiveness," as he told *CA.* "I think whatever resonance I may be able to achieve is in part simply from the amount of reading and learning that I acquired along the way. So [the Ph.D.] probably helped. I don't think that I would be writing differently if I didn't have it, in terms of style, but I think there's a dimension to my work that I wouldn't have if I'd had much less education."

The Spenser Novels

The second Spenser novel, *God Save the Child*, introduced his future paramour, Susan Silverman, a novelistic device that initiated the social network that Spenser develops over the course of the books. The fourth in the series, the award-winning *Promised Land*, brings Hawk on board, Spenser's black alter ego. Hawk, a mob enforcer, often teams up with Spenser to don the white hat. Several books later, Paul Giacomin, who plays the role of surrogate son to the childless Spenser, makes his entrance. Featured in *Early Autumn*, he makes return performances in *The Widening Gyre* and *Pastime*. In addition to these usual suspects, Parker also hosts a band of other secondary bad guys, cops, and enforcers who appear and re-appear throughout the series.

Early books in the series, are, as Parker admits, conscious pastiches of Chandler, though even by the second in the series, *God Save the Child*, in which Spenser is hired to find a fifteen-year-old boy, the author has begun to find his own voice. Callendar, in the *New York Times Book Review*, noted that it "is more deft, smoother and sharper in characterization," and "has a great deal more personality and character" than the first. By his third book, *Mortal Stakes*, with its baseball setting, Parker seemed to have hit his stride. Reviewing the book in the London *Times*, mystery writer H. R. F. Keating noted that a "literary strain has been present more or less in all [Parker's] novels. . . . There is a concern with human beings that rises at times to compassion. . . ." Keating went on to

point out that this seriousness "is always well compensated for by Parker's dialogue." The wise-cracking Spenser carries the story along with his wit and observations of the American scene.

Parker's fourth Spenser novel, *Promised Land*, won him an Edgar Allan Poe Award. In this tale, Spenser is hired to locate a runaway wife, and when he does Spenser soon finds that the woman has problems with the mob, problems that are ultimately sorted out with the help of Hawk. In a review of *Promised Land*, a *Publishers Weekly* contributor stated that "Robert Parker energizes this gritty, professionally honed yarn with flashes of comic dialogue. . . ." Callendar, however, writing in the *New York Times Book Review*, felt that Spenser's philosophizing might have gotten out of hand: "There is more navel-watching here than at a convention of gurus." In his fifth novel, *The Judas Goat*, Spenser, hired by a millionaire, goes to London and Europe to track down the right-wing terrorists who killed the man's wife and daughters and left him, the millionaire, crippled. Not much navel watching here; the book is filled with action and adventure.

Throughout the novels appearing in the 1980s, Spenser continued to build his code of honor, taking on cases from protecting a lesbian writer in *Looking for Rachel Wallace*, to dealing with the sexual exploitation of children in *Ceremony* and *Taming a Sea-Horse*, to investigating drug smuggling in *Pale Kings and Princes* and *Pastime*. Spenser even becomes involved in the cut-throat world of politics in *The Widening Gyre* and takes part in a medieval quest in *A Catskill Eagle*. In the latter title, Spenser must save Susan from a rival suitor. Along the way he gets help from a lesbian journalist and an older psychotherapist as well as some secretive U.S. agencies. While some reviewers found a weakening of the series during these years, others found the character of wise-cracking Spenser a welcome relief. Of *Ceremony*, Robin W. Winks remarked in the *New Republic*, that "Parker hasn't been this good since *Promised Land*, though even when he is bad he is good." While Paul Stuewe, writing in *Quill and Quire*, felt the series had "hit the bottom" with *A Catskill Eagle* and that Spenser "no longer seems to inspire his creator," a critic in *Time* called that same book Parker's "best mystery novel," and concluded that Parker "brings off the baroque and potentially murky tale with characteristic clarity, humor and excitement." If the reviewers could not

The 1980s television series *Spenser: For Hire* featured Avery Brooks (left) as Hawk and Robert Urich as Spenser.

agree among themselves, the reading public could: each successive Spenser title was bound for the bestseller lists.

For his part, Parker does not read the reviews. "I don't read anything about myself," Parker told *CA*. "Criticism and reviews are not useful to writers, they're useful to other people. I have not read any of it in years." Parker does what a writer should do—he writes. "When I finish one book, I have some TV and movie stuff that I fiddle around with. And after a couple of months, I sit down and think up the next book. It takes a few months, probably, or a few weeks; or sometimes, if I'm lucky, about five days. I make a two- or three-page treatment of the basic story, develop that into a chapter outline, and then I write the book. I write five pages a day each weekday. I don't revise in any significant degree. When it's done, I send it in and they print it and publish it."

Never a great note taker, Parker does little research for his books. "What I do is write about places I can write about without having to leave my desk, so I don't have to do research," Parker told *CA*. Parker's plots come out of his own interests—in sports, in psychology, and in what makes people tick. "I don't know any crooks or wiseguys" Parker told Cincotti in the *New York Times Book Review*. "I don't know anything about fingerprinting or ballistics or any of that stuff, and if you're good you can fake most of that. I don't do research." However, Parker did admit to Cincotti one small bit of research—the purchase of a Browning 9-millimeter pistol, the type that Spenser carries.

Many reviewers noted an uplift in the series with the 1991 *Pastime*, which once again featured Paul Giacomin, introduced as a fifteen-year-old in *Early Autumn*. In that book, Spenser saves the boy from his divorced parents; in *Pastime* Spenser helps Paul find his missing mother in a novel that Bruce Cook, writing in the *Chicago Tribune,* called "the best Spenser novel in years, possibly the best ever." Catherine Foster remarked in the *Christian Science Monitor* that Parker "manages to combine a delicately nuanced psychological study of family relationships with a hard-boiled mystery" in this eighteenth Spenser novel. Writing in the *New York Times Book Review,* Michael Anderson presented a state-of-the-series declaration in his review of *Pastime:* "Spenser's sagas are less tales of ratiocination than fables of exemplary conduct. . . . Throughout the 18 novels, Mr. Parker has provided a continuing narrative on the refinement of a moral sensibility. . . . Spenser's endeavors to act honestly and honorably."

Reviewing Parker's 1989 *Playmates,* R. W. B. Lewis provided a similar summation of the series in the *New York Times Book Review.* Lewis noted that by about the sixth Spenser title "it was clear that we were witnessing one of the great series in the history of the American detective story." Lewis also felt that the series let down with some books in the 1980s, resorting to the "chase-and-rescue" format in stories with "double-digit" body counts. However, Lewis concluded that with *Playmates,* the series had revived itself and provided a cause for "wonder and rejoicing." The popularity of the Spenser books inspired a television series, *Spenser: For Hire,* based on the famous shamus, which lasted two seasons.

Further novels of the 1990s include, among others, *Double Deuce,* set in a Boston housing project and dealing with the drive-by shooting of a teenage mother; *Walking Shadow,* wherein Spenser must solve a murder in the artistic world of experimental theater; *Thin Air,* set in a depressed Massachusetts factory town and dealing with the kidnaping of a cop's wife; and *Small Vices,* in which Spenser is nearly killed. Reviews of these ran the familiar gamut between complaints about a tired series and enthusiastic praise announcing a rebound. Almost all reviewers, however, agreed on the reliability of Parker's dialogue to deliver. Writing in the *New York Times Book Review,* Loren D. Estleman noted of *Double Deuce* that it "is a lean welterweight of a book" and that its "prose is taut, the language spare and to the point." Estleman concluded that "As a writer perfects his craft his books should get shorter, not longer. In the age of bloated best sellers, Robert B. Parker upholds that rule virtually single-handedly."

If you enjoy the works of Robert B. Parker, you may also want to check out the following books and films:

Raymond Chandler, *The Big Sleep,* 1939.
Loren D. Estleman, *Sugartown,* 1984.
Ross Macdonald, *The Drowning Pool,* 1950.
The Maltese Falcon, a classic private eye film starring Humphrey Bogart, 1941.

Throughout the series, the relationship between Susan and Spenser also grows, so that by *Walking Shadow,* the twenty-first Spenser novel, the two have purchased an old farmhouse near Concord together. Can wedding bells be far distant? For Geherin, writing in *The Sons of Sam Spade, The Private-Eye Novel in the 70s,* this romantic alliance is one of the features of Parker's books that sets them apart from the rest. "Parker's handling of Spenser's relationship with Susan effectively disproves [Raymond] Chandler's assertion that the love story and the detective novel cannot exist in the same book," Geherin wrote. "Not only do they coexist in Parker's novels, the love story adds an element of tension by serving as a poignant reminder of the vast differences that separates the mean streets from the quiet ones."

Other Mean Streets

Though best known for his Spenser series, Parker has also written several non-series novels: *Wilderness, Love and Glory,* and *All Our Yesterdays.* These range in storyline from the tale of a man who must take the law into his own hands to protect his wife from a psychopathic gangster in *Wilderness,* to the Boston-Irish family drama of *All Our Yesterdays.* While reviewers were not as kind to these mainstream novels as with Parker's Spenser books, they mostly agreed with *New York Times Book Review* critic Walter Walker, writing of *All Our Yesterdays* that bottom line Parker provides "a most satisfying reading experience."

Parker proved himself the heir to the Raymond Chandler legacy when that writer's estate approached him to complete an unfinished Chandler novel, *Poodle Springs.* One-upping that accomplishment, Parker also went on to write a sequel to Chandler's classic *The Big Sleep* with his *Perchance to Dream.* More interesting for Parker's series fans is the new set of tales he is building around Jesse Stones, a former Los Angeles cop with a heavy drinking problem. With the 1997 series premiere, *Night Passage*, Stones is hired as police chief of Paradise, Massachusetts, brought on board because the city fathers think they can control him. Reviewing that book in *Entertainment Weekly*, Gene Lyons noted that Parker "has rarely composed a bad sentence or an inert paragraph," and that he was "the reigning champion of the American toughguy detective novel." The second book in the series, *Trouble in Paradise*, features Stones battling a ruthless gang of thieves as he fights his personal demons, according to a *Publishers Weekly* critic who concluded that "Parker fans and all who love muscular crime will appreciate this tale."

Meanwhile, Parker is also continuing the Spenser series, for which he may always be best known. In the final analysis it is the brawny ex-boxer with a taste for fine food and punchy one-liners who is Parker's bread and butter. As Parnell Hall remarked in a 1994 *New York Times Book Review* critique of *Walking Shadow*, "Spenser is aging gracefully, and if he has lost a step along the way, he is still the cockiest and wittiest P.I. on the block. He is also a hero, . . . a knight in shining armor born 500 years too late, a champion of the underdog. In an age of cynicism, he is someone you can still identify with, care about and root for."

■ Works Cited

Anderson, Michael, "In Pursuit of an Oily Chipmunk," *New York Times Book Review*, July 28, 1991, p. 10.

Bakker, D. M., "In Thrall to 'La Bell Dame Sans Merci'," *Armchair Detective*, Summer, 1992, pp. 296-300.

Busch, Frederick, "Against the Odds," *Tribune Books* (Chicago), June 28, 1987, p. 3.

Callendar, Newgate, review of *The Godwulf Manuscript*, *New York Times Book Review*, January 13, 1974, p. 12.

Callendar, Newgate, review of *God Save the Child*, *New York Times Book Review*, December 15, 1974, p. 10.

Callendar, Newgate, review of *Promised Land*, *New York Times Book Review*, October 31, 1976, p. 40.

Callendar, Newgate, review of *The Widening Gyre*, *New York Times Book Review*, May 1, 1983, p. 27.

Review of *A Catskill Eagle*, *Time*, July 1, 1985, p. 59.

Cincotti, Joseph A., "The Author Packs a Rod," *New York Times Book Review*, July 28, 1991, p. 10.

Cook, Bruce, review of *Pastime*, *Chicago Tribune*, July 28, 1991, p. 6.

Estleman, Loren D., "Spenser among the Gangs," *New York Times Book Review*, May 31, 1992, p. 34.

Foster, Catherine, "Of Mobsters, Murder, and Caring," *Christian Science Monitor*, September 3, 1991, p. 13.

Geherin, David, "Robert B. Parker," *Sons of Sam Spade, The Private-Eye Novel in the 70s: Robert B. Parker, Roger L. Simon, Andrew Bergman*, Frederick Ungar Publishing Co., 1980, pp. 5-82.

Hall, Parnell, "Foul Play," *New York Times Book Review*, June 5, 1994, p. 50.

Keating, H. R. F., "The Classic Private Eye," *Times* (London), November 4, 1978, p. 9.

Lewis, R. W. B., "Spenser on the Rebound," *New York Times Book Review*, April 23, 1989, p. 13.

Lyons, Gene, review of *Night Passage*, *Entertainment Weekly*, October 10, 1997, p. 87.

Parker, Robert B., *Mortal Stakes*, Houghton, 1975.

Parker, Robert B. *Playmates*, Putnam, 1989.

Parker, Robert B., interview in *Contemporary Authors*, *New Revision Series*, Volume 26, Gale, 1990, pp. 312-16.

Ponder, Anne, *Armchair Detective*, Fall, 1984.

Review of *Promised Land*, *Publishers Weekly*, July 26, 1976, p. 70.

Smith, Amanda, "Robert B. Parker," *Publishers Weekly*, July 8, 1988, pp. 36-37.

Stuewe, Paul, review of *A Catskill Eagle*, *Quill and Quire*, August, 1985, p. 49.

Review of *Taming a Sea-Horse*, *Time*, July 7, 1986, p. 61.

Review of *Trouble in Paradise*, *Publishers Weekly*, July 27, 1998, p. 52.

Walker, Walter, "War and Angst," *New York Times Book Review*, February 12, 1995, p. 32.

Winks, Robin W., review of *Ceremony*, *New Republic*, June 13, 1983, p. 36.

■ For More Information See

BOOKS

Carr, John C., *Craft of Crime*, Houghton, 1983.

Contemporary Literary Criticism, Volume 27, Gale, 1984.

St. James Guide to Crime and Mystery Writers, 4th edition, Gale, 1996, pp. 818-20.

PERIODICALS

Armchair Detective, Winter, 1991, p. 113; Winter, 1993, p. 112.
Booklist, January, 1997, p. 779.
Boston Globe, May 20, 1994.
Chicago Tribune, September 20, 1985; May 29, 1994.
Clues: A Journal of Detection, Fall/Winter, 1980; Spring/Summer, 1984.
Critique, Fall, 1984.
Globe and Mail (Toronto), May 12, 1984; June 6, 1984; June 15, 1985; June 21, 1986.
Kirkus Reviews, January 15, 1997, p. 90; July, 1997, p. 987.
Kliatt, January, 1997, p. 38.
Library Journal, April 1, 1992; October 1, 1994.
Los Angeles Times, January 26, 1981; March 20, 1981; June 21, 1982; January 17, 1984; February 16, 1986; July 3, 1994, p. 10; October 9, 1994, p. 15.
Los Angeles Times Book Review, July 6, 1986; May 10, 1987.
New Republic, March 19, 1977; November 4, 1978.
New Statesman and Society, April 19, 1991, p. 37.
Newsweek, June 7, 1982; June 17, 1985; July 7, 1986.
New Yorker, July 13, 1987.
New York Times, January 21, 1981; September 20, 1985; July 2, 1987; June 4, 1992; May 11, 1995; August 15, 1996, p. B5.
New York Times Book Review, January 13, 1974; December 15, 1974; November 11, 1979; August 2, 1981; May 1, 1983; May 20, 1984; June 30, 1985; June 22, 1986; May 31, 1987; October 15, 1989; January 27, 1991; May 12, 1991, p. 34; May 21, 1995; May 19, 1996, p. 21; September 27, 1998.
Observer (London), March 31, 1991, p. 54; May 19, 1991, p. 59; January 12, 1992, p. 7.
People, May 7, 1984.
Publishers Weekly, May 4, 1990; November 23, 1990; April 4, 1994; March 20, 1995; January 27, 1997.
Southwest Review, Autumn, 1974.
Time, July 27, 1987.
Times (London), May 4, 1987.
Times Literary Supplement, November 30, 1990, p. 1287; November 25, 1994, p. 21.
USA Today, March 20, 1987.
Washington Post, May 17, 1983; March 7, 1984; June 19, 1992; December 20, 1994.
Washington Post Book World, April 15, 1984; June 15, 1986; June 21, 1987; May 24, 1992, p. 6.*

—Sketch by J. Sydney Jones

Elizabeth Ann Scarborough

Hospital, Kansas City, MO; former medical/surgical nurse at St. David's Hospital, Austin, TX. Freelance writer, 1979—. *Military service:* U.S. Army, Nurse Corps; served in Vietnam; became captain. *Member:* Science Fiction Writers of America, Society for Creative Anachronism.

■ Personal

Born March 23, 1947, in Kansas City, MO; daughter of Donald Dean (a telephone installer) and Betty Lou (a registered nurse) Scarborough; married Richard G. Kacsur, June 15, 1975 (divorced January 1, 1982). *Education:* Bethany Hospital School of Nursing (Kansas City, MO), R.N., 1968; University of Alaska, Fairbanks, B.A., 1968. *Politics:* "Pragmatic humanist." *Religion:* "Disorganized Christian universalist."

■ Addresses

Home and office—Port Townsend, WA. *Agent*—Merrilee Heifetz, 21 West 26th St., New York, NY 10010.

■ Career

Author and journalist. Formerly associated with Gallup Indian Medical Center and with Bethany

■ Awards, Honors

Nebula Award, Science Fiction Writers of America, 1989, for *The Healer's War.*

■ Writings

FANTASY NOVELS

The Harem of Aman Akbar; or, The Djinn Decanted, Bantam, 1984.
The Drastic Dragon of Draco, Texas, Bantam, 1986.
The Goldcamp Vampire; or, The Sanguinary Sourdough, Bantam, 1987.
The Healer's War, Doubleday, 1989.
Nothing Sacred, Doubleday, 1991.
Last Refuge, Bantam, 1992.
The Godmother, Ace Books, 1994.
The Godmother's Apprentice, Ace Books, 1995.
Carol for Another Christmas, Ace Books, 1996.
The Godmother's Web, Ace Books, 1998.
The Lady in the Loch, Ace Books, 1998.

"ARGONIA" SERIES

Songs of Sorcery, Bantam, 1982.
The Unicorn Creed, Bantam, 1983.
Bronwyn's Bane, Bantam, 1983.
The Christening Quest, Bantam, 1985.
Songs from the Seashell Archives (contains *Song of Sorcery, The Unicorn Creed, Bronwyn's Bane*, and *The Christening Quest*), two volumes, Bantam, 1987-88.

"SONGKILLER" SERIES

Phantom Banjo, Bantam, 1991.
Picking the Ballad's Bones, Bantam, 1991.
Strum Again?, Bantam, 1992.

"POWER" SERIES; WITH ANNE MCCAFFREY

Powers that Be, Del Rey Books (New York City), 1993.
Power Lines, Del Rey Books, 1994.
Power Play, Del Rey Books, 1995.

OTHER

An Interview with a Vietnam Nurse, Bantam, 1989.
(Editor with Anne McCaffrey) *Space Opera*, DAW, 1996.
(Editor with Martin H. Greenberg) *Warrior Princesses*, DAW, 1998.

Contributor to magazines and newspapers, including *Alaskafest* and *Alaska Today*.

■ Sidelights

Recognized as a popular and influential author of comic fantasy for adults, Elizabeth Ann Scarborough is also the creator of realistic fiction for middle graders—published under the name Elizabeth Scarboro—that is praised for its well-developed characterizations and authentic depiction of children's feelings. As Elizabeth Ann Scarborough, she has written works that characteristically blend humor and fantasy to describe earthy protagonists, chiefly female, and charming animals who embark on exciting quests; Scarborough has also collaborated with fantasist Anne McCaffrey on a series

of science fiction novels. Published for adults but appreciated by young people, her books are acknowledged for their originality, intelligence, and unconventionality as well as for their wit, fast pace, and light-hearted approach. In the fantasy genre, Scarborough is perhaps best known as the creator of the "Argonia" and "Songkiller" series; in the former, the author describes the adventures of a cheerful young witch, Maggie Brown, and her mother Bronwyn in the secondary world Argonia, while the latter describes how a group of courageous figures restore folk music to the world after it has been eliminated by demons. Scarborough is also well regarded for writing *The Healer's War*, a semi-autobiographical novel set during the Vietnam War that combines fantasy and mysticism with stark reality. Winner of the Nebula Award in 1989, the story focuses on an army nurse who is given special healing powers by a magic amulet. Writing in the *St. James Guide to Fantasy Writers*, Cosette Kies comments, "Scarborough's output to date gives proof of her importance in the contemporary fantasy-genre scene. It is probable that she has influenced some newer writers, who also create humorous fantasy with down-to-earth heroines and delightful animal companions. Scarborough's own development as a writer appears to be leading her into a spare and lean phase with more emphasis on stories of the future rather than on the alternative worlds of high fantasy."

Born in Kansas City, Missouri, Scarborough was educated as a nurse and served in the U.S. Army Nurse Corps both in the United States and in Vietnam before becoming a full-time writer in 1979; she also received a degree in history from the University of Alaska at Fairbanks in 1987. "I started out," she said in the *St. James Guide to Fantasy Writers*, "writing humorous fantasy—at first traditional and then historical western and Arabian Nights, which interested me after I studied Middle Eastern dance." Scarborough's first books are contributions to the "Argonia" series, fantasies that include archetypal characters from folk and fairy tales such as witches, dragons, magicians, and unicorns and center on quests by what Cosette Kies calls "very human protagonists," adding: "There is playfulness and cheerfulness throughout the stories, with puns and comic situations to create humor as fast-paced as the action."

Scarborough's first departure from "Argonia" was *The Harem of Aman Akbar*, a comic novel set in

"I chose to write the book as fiction because, as somebody is frequently misquoted as saying, fiction is supposed to make sense out of real life. And if there was ever an episode in my life that needed sense made out of it, it was Vietnam."

—Elizabeth Ann Scarborough, discussing her work *The Healer's War*

the Middle East about how a young bride reverses a spell placed on her unfaithful husband by a genie. *Los Angeles Times Book Review* critic Kristiana Gregory claims that Scarborough's story "is fun, a wild fantasy . . . pulsing with color and noise like a marketplace at noon," while *Booklist* reviewer Roland Green says, "This excellent piece of humorous fantasy is witty, fast-paced, intelligent, and features excellent characterization." With *The Christening Quest*, Scarborough returns to Argonia; in this novel, according to Margaret Miles in *Voice of Youth Advocates*, the author "uses her accustomed blend of fairy tale, gypsies, and Arabian Nights to produce another chuckle-filled light fantasy adventure." The novel describes the rescue of Princess Romany, the first-born daughter of Princess Bronwyn, who has been kidnapped by money-hungry magicians; the baby is rescued by Bronwyn's brother and cousin in an adventure, according to Roland Green of *Booklist*, "as filled with action and humor as any of the preceding books." Writing in *Fantasy Review*, Douglas Barbour says that *The Christening Quest* is "light entertainment and . . . enjoyable because it does try in its small way to undercut some of the sexist conventions of the genre, unlike most of what passes for writing . . . these days." *Songs from the Seashell Archives* is a two-volume omnibus containing the four volumes of the "Argonia" quartet.

Scarborough's next two novels, *The Drastic Dragon of Draco, Texas* and *The Goldcamp Vampire*, are fantasies with historical settings that feature author/journalist Pelagia Harper as their protagonist; in *The Drastic Dragon*, Pelagia is captured by Indians and meets a fire-breathing dragon in her attempt to write about the romance of the Wild West, while in *The Goldcamp Vampire* Pelagia encounters the son of Count Dracula, who is masquerading as the potential buyer of an Alaskan saloon during the Gold Rush. Writing in *Library*

Journal, Jackie Cassada calls *The Drastic Dragon* a "superbly told tale that may even attract some Western fans," while *Voice of Youth Advocates* reviewer Pat Pearl calls *The Goldcamp Vampire* a "cheerfully macabre, amusingly told story with a frostily vivid Klondike-of-the-Gold Rush background." Cosette Kies says of *The Goldcamp Vampire* that "Scarborough's originality is evident in the fact that she sets her vampire story in a land where night goes on for months, wonderful for recruiting vampires but not so great for unwilling recruits," and notes of the two novels that the settings "of the frontier, both in Texas plains and the Yukon goldfields, provide the journalist heroine . . . with colorful milieus in which to pursue mystery, magic and the supernatural."

Nebula Winner

The publication of *The Healer's War* marked a departure in Scarborough's literary style: the author moved from her characteristic humorous fantasy to creating a strongly realistic antiwar novel about a young woman's coming of age that contains fewer fantastic elements than her other books. In the words of *Booklist* reviewer Mary Banas, Scarborough "expertly blends suspense, dark humor, and realism into a powerful, soul-stirring mix that, for the first time, shows the Vietnam War from a woman's perspective." Cosette Kies concurs, acknowledging that the novel, the author's first to be published in hard cover, is "in amazing contrast" to Scarborough's earlier fantasies. *The Healer's War* focuses on twenty-one-year-old Kathleen (Kitty) McCully, a character that the author based largely on herself. A nurse from Kansas who is stationed in a Vietnam hospital, Kitty is given an amulet by an old Vietnamese mystic just before he dies. The amulet allows Kitty to sense the aura of each person she meets and to learn their true motives; in addition, she receives the power to heal. Kitty experiences the horrors of war but also goes on a spiritual journey, coming to realize the special qualities of Vietnam and its people. While trying to save the life of a young amputee, Kitty is captured by the Viet Cong but uses her skills as a healer to survive. After being rescued by American troops and sent back to America, Kitty tries to adjust to Stateside life and to find purpose in her new existence.

Writing in *Voice of Youth Advocates*, Syrul Lurie says that Scarborough's "depiction of a time and place in American history [is one] which every young adult should internalize and never forget," while *Kirkus Reviews* notes that the author "writes powerfully and convincingly of the war itself." Sybil Steinberg of *Publishers Weekly* states, "Although the moralizing invites comparison with TV's *M*A*S*H* and *Twilight Zone,* Scarborough's light, fluid storytelling and the authentic, pungent background keep this novel interesting." In her author's note in the paperback edition of *The Healer's War,* Scarborough says, "I chose to write the book as fiction because, as somebody is frequently misquoted as saying, fiction is supposed to make sense out of real life. And if there was ever an episode in my life that needed sense made out of it, it was Vietnam. In a nonfiction account, I could talk only about myself, what I saw and felt. I wasn't very clear about that when I started writing." In 1988, Scarborough published a second book about her Vietnam experience, *An Interview with a Vietnam Nurse.*

With *The Secret Language of the SB,* Scarborough—as Elizabeth Scarboro—makes her first contribution to the genre of realistic fiction for children. Directed to middle graders and told in a series of connected vignettes, the story describes how eleven-year-old Adam becomes friends with Susan, a Taiwanese orphan who comes to live with him and his family until her adoptive parents are ready to take her. Although both of the children face difficulty adjusting to the new situation, they become close friends, developing a secret language (SB stands for "something big," the feeling that Adam gets before important things happen) and helping each other; for example, Adam teaches Susan to read while she teaches him about sharing. At the end of the book, Adam accepts the pain of separating from Susan when she goes to live with her new family and becomes, in the words of *School Library Journal* reviewer Sylvia S. Marantz, "a wiser and enriched person." *Publishers Weekly* claims that this "skillfully written debut novel shows a clear understanding of a fourth-grader's interests and fears," while a reviewer in *Bulletin of the Center for Children's Books* calls *Secret Language* a "promising first effort."

The author's next book for children, *Phoenix, Upside Down,* is another story for middle graders written as Elizabeth Scarboro; in this work, fourth-grader Jamie and her family move from Boulder, Colorado, to Phoenix, Arizona, where her father has taken a new job. Jamie gradually learns to accept her new setting with the help of two sympathetic adults, a neighbor and a teacher. "Although Jamie's young age may deter some potential readers, and Scarboro leaves several story threads unresolved," concludes *Booklist* reviewer Kay Weisman, "this will be welcomed by middle-graders dealing with similar problems."

With her "Songkiller" saga, Scarborough created a comic fantasy series that is considered a thinly veiled and incisive depiction of the censorship of contemporary music. She bases the series on the premise that a cabal of devils, who realize that music—especially folk music—is one of the few things that truly edifies the human race, attempts to wipe out the art form off the face of the earth. In the first volume, *Phantom Banjo,* the devils kill folk musicians and destroy the folk music archives at the Library of Congress, among other unsavory activities; as each artist dies and each medium preserving the music is ruined, human beings find that they have lost their familiarity with popular songs. In addition, little music is allowed on the airwaves; the radio, for example, broadcasts mostly news. Before his death, legendary folk artist Sam Hawthorne wills his banjo to Mark Mosby, a singer and fan. Before he dies in a car accident, Mosby goes to see Willie MacKai, a Texas resident and retired singer, and gives the banjo—named Lazarus—to him. This act begins a journey that takes Willie and Lazarus, a remarkable instrument that plays music with or without human hands, on a quest to save the music. "Good fun," writes *Voice of Youth Advocates* contributor Penny Blubaugh, "and very close to the bone." Writing in *Booklist,* Roland Green concludes that *Phantom Banjo* has "just about every virtue one can reasonably expect in a contemporary fantasy tale."

In the second volume of the series, *Picking the Ballad's Bones,* Willie and other keepers of the flame go to England, meet the ghost of Sir Walter Scott, and agree, as part of a deal, to spend seven years living out the stories told by the old ballads so that they might be retrieved for humanity; the deal is arranged by the former Faerie Queen, who is also known as Lady Luck, and, in recent years, has gone by the name of Torchy. "The second part [of the saga]," writes Tom Whitmore in *Locus,* "is a good continuation of the first. . . . It's light, amusing, and quick; once again, the very real background to this story . . . sits in the background and is not obviously real.

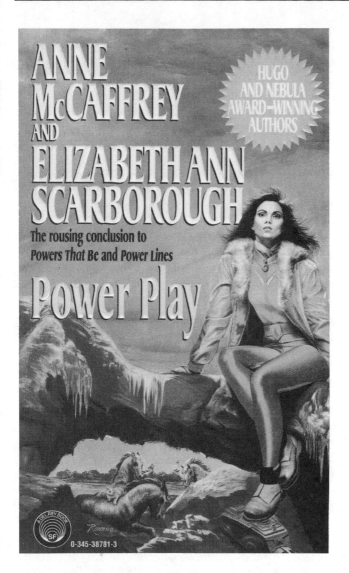

In the final novel of the "Power" series, Yanaba Maddock is taken hostage in an attempt to destroy the planet Petaybee.

It doesn't take demons to keep the music out of our ears, unfortunately." *Booklist* reviewer Roland Green concurs, saying that this volume of the "superior black comedy fantasy trilogy . . . is contemporary fantasy of a very high order." In the conclusion to the series, *Strum Again?*, the questers return to the United States and—with Torchy's assistance—reintroduce folk songs into the national consciousness while fighting opposition from public and private institutions which, it turns out, are controlled from Hell. Green calls the book an "absorbing, tension-filled story that demands a good deal of erudition of its readers but repays their efforts."

Success with Science Fiction

In addition to her other works, Scarborough has made several well-received contributions to the science fiction genre. *Nothing Sacred* is a novel based on a vivid dream had by the author while completing *The Healer's War.* In the words of Gerald Jonas in the *New York Times Book Review,* Scarborough "heralds a new subgenre that might be called New World Order Science Fiction." Set in the year 2069 and written in the form of a prison journal, the book describes a post-holocaust world where the Pentagon has become part of the North American Continental Allied Forces (NACAF), a group that supplies professional soldiers to international warmakers. NACAF allies are involved in a conflict with Russia, China, and India. After a forty-two-year-old warrant officer, Vivika Jeng Vanachek, is shot down during an aerial mapping mission in the mountains of Tibet, she is captured by local guerrillas, who imprison, torture, and brainwash her. As the novel progresses, it becomes clear that Viv is in Shambala, an enchanted paradise reminiscent of Shangri-La that is the last safe spot in a decimated world. While she helps organize an old library, Viv eventually becomes reconciled to her new situation. Jonas writes that Viv "is an engaging sort once she gets her wits about her. . . . [Her] irrepressible flippancy nicely undercuts the creeping pietism that seems to be an occupational hazard of Tibetan sagas."

Scarborough notes in the *St. James Guide to Fantasy Writers* that she introduces *Nothing Sacred* at author readings with the comment, "There's good news and bad news. The bad news is, I end the world. The good news is, there's a sequel." *Last Refuge* is that sequel: set twenty years after the conclusion of *Nothing Sacred,* the novel features the granddaughter of Viv Vanachek, Chime Cincinnati, who is Shambala's emissary to the outside world. Accompanied by her father Mike, Viv's son, Chime goes on a quest to discover what is causing Shambala's babies to be born without souls. After Chime and Mike find another enchanted valley, ruled by the evil Master Meru, the pair outwit Meru and guide the living and the dead, whose souls will be used to infuse the children of Shambala, to safety. A critic in *Kirkus Reviews* notes, "Any exoticism the Buddhist background might have added is lost in Scarborough's paradoxically rationalistic explanation of the supernatural. . . . The novelties that made the first book

If you enjoy the works of Elizabeth Ann Scarborough, you may also want to check out the following books and films:

Robert Levy, *The Misfit Apprentice*, 1995.
Caroline Stevermer, *A College of Magics*, 1994.
Megan Whalen Turner, *Instead of Three Wishes*, 1995.
Starship Troopers, a film based on the novel by Robert A. Heinlein, 1997.

interesting cannot rescue this one." *Booklist*'s Roland Green disagrees, noting that "a vivid and powerful yarn awaits the many fans who have made Scarborough so popular."

Powers that Be, Scarborough's first collaboration with Anne McCaffrey, is set in a future with a definite militaristic bent. When Major Yanaba Maddock, a female soldier, is sent to the frontier planet Petaybee as a spy, she discovers a rebel plot to destroy the corporation that controls the planet. After becoming sympathetic to the settlers, who are environmentally conscious and humane, as opposed to the coldly bureaucratic corporation, Yanaba decides to become a rebel. The sequels, *Power Lines* and *Power Play*, describe the conflict between the settlers and the corporation.

Scarborough is also the author of the "Godmother" books, stories that center on a fairy godmother named Felicity Fortune who assists those in need. Felicity belongs to the Godmothers' Union and is hampered by strict union regulations as well as budget cutbacks. In *The Godmother*, which is set in Seattle, she manages to help an overwrought social worker with her caseload of destitute clients. Writing in *Voice of Youth Advocates*, Denise M. Thornhill calls *The Godmother* "not just a fantasy novel—it is also a problem novel." *The Godmother's Apprentice* finds Felicity in Ireland with her new apprentice, fifteen-year-old Sno Quantrill. Drawing on folklore, fairy tales, and mythology, Scarborough tells a complex tale involving an Irish terrorist, house spirits, and a talking toad; *Voice of Youth Advocates* critic Donna L. Scanlon notes that the author draws "the various threads . . . together into a well-woven, compelling plot with a satisfactory ending."

Scarborough comments, "After fifteen years of nursing, an important job for which I was not temperamentally suited, I'm finally doing what I always wanted to do. I am getting paid for my ridiculous ideas and off-the- wall jokes, the same sort that always got me into trouble in other lines of work. (I was lucky they didn't court martial me before I got out of the Army Nurse Corps!)" Commenting in the *St. James Guide to Fantasy Writers*, she adds, "Lately, I've been trying to blend some serious content with humor in *The Godmother* and to some extent in the books I've been writing in Ireland with Anne McCaffrey set in our new world. My experience living in Fairbanks, Alaska, for 15 years, and in the military, helped me to make my contributions to Petaybee, the world Anne and I created together. My many friendships with concerned and caring social workers and other non-cynical types inspired [my "Godmother" books]."

■ Works Cited

Banas, Mary, review of *The Healer's War*, *Booklist*, November 1, 1988, p. 450.

Barbour, Douglas, "Too Nice a Quest," *Fantasy Review*, October, 1985, p. 20.

Blubaugh, Penny, review of *Phantom Banjo*, *Voice of Youth Advocates*, December, 1991, p. 326.

Cassada, Jackie, review of *The Drastic Dragon of Draco, Texas*, *Library Journal*, May 15, 1986, p. 81.

Green, Roland, review of *The Harem of Aman Akbar*, *Booklist*, December 15, 1984, p. 561.

Green, Roland, review of *The Christening Quest*, *Booklist*, October 1, 1985, pp. 195-96.

Green, Roland, review of *Phantom Banjo*, *Booklist*, June 15, 1991, p. 1937.

Green, Roland, review of *Picking the Ballad's Bones*, *Booklist*, December 1, 1991, p. 684.

Green, Roland, review of *Strum Again?*, *Booklist*, April 15, 1992, p. 1509.

Green, Roland, review of *Last Refuge*, *Booklist*, June 15, 1992, p. 1787.

Gregory, Kristiana, review of *The Harem of Aman Akbar*, *Los Angeles Times Book Review*, December 9, 1984, p. 14.

Review of *The Healer's War*, *Kirkus Reviews*, September 15, 1988, p. 1366.

Jonas, Gerald, review of *Nothing Sacred*, *New York Times Book Review*, April 21, 1994, p. 24.

Kies, Cosette, essay in *St. James Guide to Fantasy Writers*, St. James Press, 1996, pp. 514-16.

Review of *Last Refuge, Kirkus Reviews,* June 15, 1992, p. 754.

Lurie, Syrul, review of *The Healer's War, Voice of Youth Advocates,* June, 1989, p. 118.

Marantz, Sylvia S., review of *The Secret Language of the SB, School Library Journal,* June, 1990, p. 126.

Miles, Margaret, review of *The Christening Quest, Voice of Youth Advocates,* February, 1986, p. 397.

Pearl, Pat, review of *The Goldcamp Vampire, Voice of Youth Advocates,* June, 1988, p. 97.

Scanlon, Donna L., review of *The Godmother's Apprentice, Voice of Youth Advocates,* June, 1996, p. 110.

Scarborough, Elizabeth Ann, *The Healer's War,* Doubleday, 1989.

Scarborough, Elizabeth Ann, commentary in *St. James Guide to Fantasy Writers,* St. James Press, 1996, pp. 514-16.

Review of *The Secret Language of the SB, Bulletin of the Center for Children's Books,* May, 1990, p. 226.

Review of *The Secret Language of the SB, Publishers Weekly,* May 18, 1990, p. 85.

Steinberg, Sybil, review of *The Healer's War, Publishers Weekly,* September 16, 1988, p. 63.

Thornhill, Denise M., review of *The Godmother, Voice of Youth Advocates,* December, 1994, p. 290.

Weisman, Kay, review of *Phoenix, Upside Down, Booklist,* June 1, 1996, p. 1724.

Whitmore, Tom, review of *Picking the Ballad's Bones, Locus,* October, 1991, p. 56.

■ **For More Information See**

PERIODICALS

Analog, February, 1995, p. 159; May, 1996, p. 144.

Booklist, September 1, 1994, p. 28; December 15, 1995, p. 689.

Kirkus Reviews, July 1, 1994, p. 892; October 15, 1995, p. 1462; November 1, 1998, p. 1561.

Kliatt, March, 1996, p. 20.

Library Journal, November 15, 1995, p. 103.

Locus, August, 1994, p. 62.

Magazine of Fantasy and Science Fiction, March, 1996, p. 56.

Publishers Weekly, August 29, 1994, p. 64; November 27, 1995, p. 56; November 23, 1998, pp. 63-64.

School Library Journal, June, 1996, p. 124.*

—Sketch by Gerard J. Senick

Paul Theroux

■ Personal

Surname rhymes with "skiddoo"; born April 10, 1941, in Medford, MA; son of Albert Eugene (a salesman) and Anne (maiden name, Dittami) Theroux; married Anne Castle (a broadcaster), December 4, 1967 (divorced 1993); children: Marcel Raymond, Louis Sebastian. *Education:* Attended University of Maine, 1959-60; University of Massachusetts, B.A., 1963; Syracuse University, further study, 1963.

■ Addresses

Home—East Sandwich, MA 02537.

Career

Soche Hill College, Limbe, Malawi, lecturer in English, 1963-65; Makerere University, Kampala, Uganda, lecturer in English, 1965-68; University of Singapore, Singapore, lecturer in English, 1968-71; professional writer, 1971—. Visiting lecturer, University of Virginia, 1972-73. Has given numerous lectures on literature in the United States and abroad. *Member:* American Academy and Institute of Arts and Letters.

■ Awards, Honors

Robert Hamlet one-act play award, 1960; Playboy Editorial Award, 1971, 1976; *New York Times Book Review* "Editors' Choice" citation, 1975, for *The Great Railway Bazaar: By Train through Asia;* American Academy and Institute of Arts and Letters award for literature, 1977; Whitbread Prize, 1979, for *Picture Palace;* American Book Award nominations, 1981, for *The Old Patagonian Express: By Train through the Americas,* and 1983, for *The Mosquito Coast;* James Tait Black Memorial Prize, 1982, for *The Mosquito Coast;* Thomas Cook Travel Book Prize, 1989, for *Riding the Iron Rooster: By Train through China.* Honorary degrees from Trinity College and Tufts University, both in 1980, and the University of Massachusetts—Amherst, 1988.

■ Writings

NOVELS

Waldo, Houghton (Boston), 1967.
Fong and the Indians, Houghton, 1968.
Girls at Play, Houghton, 1969.
Murder in Mount Holly, Alan Ross, 1969.
Jungle Lovers, Houghton, 1971.

Saint Jack (also see below), Houghton, 1973.
The Black House, Houghton, 1974.
The Family Arsenal, Houghton, 1976.
Picture Palace, Houghton, 1978.
The Mosquito Coast, with woodcuts by David Frampton, Houghton, 1982.
Doctor Slaughter (also see below), Hamish Hamilton, 1984.
Half Moon Street: Two Short Novels (contains *Doctor Slaughter* and *Doctor DeMarr*), Houghton, 1984.
O-Zone, Putnam, 1986.
My Secret History, Putnam, 1989.
Chicago Loop, Random House, 1991.
Millroy the Magician, Random House, 1994.
My Other Life, Houghton, 1996.
On the Edge of the Great Rift: Three Novels of Africa, Penguin, 1996.
Kowloon Tong, Houghton, 1997.

SHORT STORIES

Sinning with Annie and Other Stories, Houghton, 1972.
The Consul's File, Houghton, 1977.
World's End and Other Stories, Houghton, 1980.
The London Embassy, Houghton, 1982.
The Collected Stories, Viking, 1997.

NONFICTION

V. S. Naipaul: An Introduction to His Works, Africana Publishing, 1972.
The Great Railway Bazaar: By Train through Asia, Houghton, 1975.
The Old Patagonian Express: By Train through the Americas, Houghton, 1979.
Sailing through China, illustrated by Patrick Procktor, Houghton, 1984.
The Kingdom by the Sea: A Journey around Great Britain, Houghton, 1985.
(With Steve McCurry) *The Imperial Way: By Rail from Peshawar to Chittagong*, Houghton, 1985.
Sunrise with Seamonsters: Travels and Discoveries 1964-1984, Houghton, 1985.
(With Bruce Chatwin) *Patagonia Revisited*, Houghton, 1986.
Riding the Iron Rooster: By Train through China, Ivy, 1989.
Travelling the World, Random House, 1990.
The Happy Isles of Oceania: Paddling the Pacific, Fawcett, 1992.

(Author of introduction) Gerard D'Aboville, *Alone: The Man Who Braved the Vast Pacific & Won*, translated by Richard Seaver, Arcade Publishing, 1994.
The Pillars of Hercules: A Grand Tour of the Mediterranean, Putnam, 1995.
Sir Vidia's Shadow: A Friendship Across Five Continents, Houghton, 1998.

Also author of the play, *White Man's Burden*, 1987, and of the television play *The London Embassy* (adaptation of Theroux's short story collection of the same title), 1987.

JUVENILES

A Christmas Card, illustrated by John Lawrence, Houghton, 1978.
London Snow: A Christmas Story, illustrated by Lawrence, Houghton, 1979.
The Shortest Day of the Year: A Christmas Fantasy, Sixth Chamber Press, 1986.

OTHER

Education by Radio: An Experiment in Rural Group Listening for Adults in Uganda, Adult Studies Center, Makerere University College, 1966.
(With Peter Bogdanovich and Howard Sackler) *Saint Jack* (screenplay; based on Theroux's novel of the same title), produced by New World/ Shoals Creek/Playboy/Copa de Oro, 1979.
(Author of introduction) V. S. Pritchett, *Dead Man Leading*, Oxford University Press, 1984.
(Author of introduction) Thomsen Moritz, *The Saddest Pleasure: A Journey on Two Rivers*, Graywolf Press, 1990.
(Author of introduction) *Red Express: A Rail Journey from the Berlin Wall to the Great Wall*, edited by Michael Cordell, Prentice Hall, 1991.
(Author of foreword) Jocelyn Fujii, *Under the Hula Moon: Living in Hawaii*, Crown, 1992.
(Translator) Abdelrahman Munif, *Variations on Night and Day*, Pantheon, 1993.

Contributor of fiction and nonfiction to *Encounter, Atlantic Monthly, Commentary, Granta, National Geographic, Playboy, Harper's Bazaar,* and other periodicals; contributor of numerous reviews and essays to *New York Times, New York Times Book Review, New Statesman, Times* (London), and other periodicals in the United States and England.

■ Adaptations

Saint Jack was adapted for a motion picture, 1979; *The Mosquito Coast* was adapted as a motion picture, 1986; *Doctor Slaughter* was adapted as the motion picture, *Half Moon Street*, 1986.

■ Sidelights

The author of over three dozen books, Paul Theroux has earned a reputation as travel writer par excellence and as a novelist whose works speak of colonialism and of the expatriate experience. For many years a resident of England, Theroux, born in Massachusetts, returned to his native country in the mid-1990s and has also become a chronicler of late twentieth-century America. Theroux sets his novels in Africa, the Far East, England, and the U.S.—all places where he has resided. He has chronicled picaresque rogues and serial killers with his fiction, winning awards for *Picture Palace* and his Swiss Family Robinson epic, *The Mosquito Coast,* and he has seen three of his works adapted for film: his Singapore novel, *Saint Jack,* and his London novel, *Half Moon Street,* and *The Mosquito Coast.* As a novelist, Theroux has been compared to Graham Greene, Joseph Conrad, and V. S. Naipaul, writers who have explored the clash between Westerners and the developing world. Many of Theroux's protagonists are outsiders who can only discover themselves in foreign terrain.

Novels such as *The Mosquito Coast, O-Zone,* and *Millroy the Magician,* while furthering many of the writer's themes and motifs, also appeal to readers across the generations because of their youthful protagonists or narrators. Theroux's travel books, including *The Great Railway Bazaar, The Old Patagonia Express,* and *Riding the Iron Rooster* also appeal to readers of all ages who yearn for adventure and travel by rail. In his travel writing, Theroux has been compared to Mark Twain, one of the few other writers to publish bestsellers in the travel genre. As a short story writer, Theroux has also made his mark, and additionally, he has written several Christmas novellas with younger readers in mind. In a word, Theroux is prolific.

As the writer Jonathan Raban, an Englishman living in the United States, put it in a *Saturday Review* analysis of *The Mosquito Coast,* "One needs energy to keep up with the extraordinary, produc-tive restlessness of Paul Theroux . . . the most gifted, most prodigal writer of his generation." And in a review of Theroux's collection of essays, *Sunrise with Seamonsters,* Michiko Kakutani noted in the *New York Times* that "Mr. Theroux always has a distinct point of view." Kakutani concluded that Theroux was a "gutsy, personal and astonishing writer."

From Massachusetts to Africa

Theroux was the third of seven children born to Albert Eugene and Anne Dittami Theroux, a shoe-leather salesman and a former school teacher, and grew up in Medford, Massachusetts, a Boston suburb. As Theroux put it in his 1985 collection of essays, *Sunrise with Seamonsters,* "It was part of my luck to have been born in a populous family of nine unexampled wits." His parents were also of "populous" families: "together they have produced the equivalent of a multi-national (French-Canadian-American-Italian) corporation of people." The family was not only populous, but talented and ambitious. Theroux's own branch of this extended family produced several writers—Paul, his novelist older brother Alexander, and younger brother Peter, a travel writer—as well as another brother who became an expert in trade with China.

"'Find your nitch,' my father used to say," Theroux wrote in *Sunrise with Seamonsters.* "The idea was that there would be a painter, a priest, a doctor, a nun, a teacher, and so forth." Theroux, intended for a career in medicine, abandoned that plan when faced with the obstacle of organic chemistry. Theroux also recalled a childhood of freedom but little privacy, and one informed with a deep sense of being protected. "For the first fourteen years of my life, or more, all my needs were met, all the society I required was available to me; practically and intellectually I was provided for within the family: books, clothes, conversation, jobs, medical care, spiritual comfort, even a girl-friend. . . ."

Theroux is a well-known inventor of his own history. Two later novels, *My Secret History* and *My Other Life,* are witness to his flexible autobiographical skills. Theroux gives varying accounts of his intellectual development as a child. To Joseph Barbato, writing in *Express,* Theroux maintained that he was an early and avid reader. "You can't hide very easily in a large family, but there was always privacy in reading. The earliest books I read as a child were about travel. Books about fur trapping in Hudson Bay, about catching animals in Africa, being a doctor up the Amazon—that kind of book. . . . Reading ought to be a pleasure. It ought to take you away." Yet in an essay in *Sunrise with Seamonsters* recounting his visit to the twentieth reunion of his class at Medford High, Theroux saw it differently. "For twenty years, until the reunion, these high school days had receded and become distorted in a haze that made retrospection bearable. I saw myself as bespectacled and bookish, a bit of a shut-in, boning up for the Science Fair."

This "intellectual preparation for becoming a writer" was not the whole truth, however. "I read [S. J.] Perelman and J. D. Salinger for laughs, John O'Hara for sex, and pored much more seriously over the L.L Bean catalog. . . ." He played no sports; instead he and his friends caught frogs for dissection, were fascinated by guns, and made miniature bombs. They traded comic books, went ice-fishing in winter and skinny-dipping in the summer. In high school he tried not to be bored by teachers who he characterized as "peevishly elderly" and who "kept discipline but imparted little wisdom."

After graduating from high school, Theroux spent a year at the University of Maine, but transferred the following year to the University of Massachusetts where he became involved in the nascent anti-war movement, refusing to join the normally mandatory ROTC program. He was also arrested for leading a student anti-war demonstration. Graduating from college in 1963, he attended graduate studies briefly at Syracuse University, then taught in Italy for a short time. Thereafter he joined the Peace Corps and was sent to Limbe, Malawi, in south central Africa where he taught English. He also began his writing career while a young volunteer in this obscure country. He wrote articles for African papers as well as the *Christian Science Monitor*, and created his own English teaching text. In 1965, Theroux was deported from Malawi, a result of articles he had written for a German publication which in fact turned out to be a cover for a German intelligence agency, and because of associations with leaders who fell from favor with the regime of the then ruler, Hastings Banda. A further result was his expulsion from the Peace Corps.

The Early Novels

Theroux's time in Africa was not yet over, however. He next moved to Uganda where he lectured at Makerere University in Kampala. It was there he met his wife, Anne, a fellow teacher and later a broadcaster. They were married in 1967, the same year his first novel, *Waldo*, was published. In this debut novel, an important theme that runs throughout much of Theroux's work is announced: the attempt of man to put some order and meaning to his life. Opening with a pie being flung in the face of the eponymous hero, the novel proceeds to follow the fortunes of Waldo from a school for delinquent boys to his fame as a cabaret entertainer where he writes inside a bubble in the middle of the dance floor.

Reviewing the book in *Harper's*, Roderick Cook noted that this first novel had "a lot of wit and laughter," and that the author had "a wild flair for dialogue and the vivid scene." Told in an episodic narrative, *Waldo* is very much a first novel. *Fong and the Indians*, set in Kenya, followed in 1968. The story of Sam Fong, a Chinese Catholic living in Africa, this second novel looks at the plight of the expatriate. Fong, a carpenter by trade, is forced to be a grocer and is constantly under threat of deportation. Outsiders are also the theme of his next novel, *Girls at Play*, the story of five schoolteachers who are thrown together in the Kenyan bush where they teach at a school for African girls. Laurence Lafore, writing in the *New York Times Book Review*, called the book "a novel of interlocking horrors: of lonely women exiled from society by their own peculiarities." Lafore concluded that this book which ends in tragedy "is very convincing." Reviewing the same novel in the *Chicago Tribune Book World*, Shane Stevens first compared Theroux to Joseph Conrad, concluding that "*Girls at Play* has the right feel to it. Yes, Conrad was right and nothing has really changed. Africa does have an imbalance lurking in the bush that is deadly to the Western psyche, and that will corrupt and destroy it."

While he was busy with this novel, Theroux and his pregnant wife were attacked by a mob protesting the policies of the all-white government of Rhodesia. "Many of the Africans who had set upon us were my students—so they said on Monday morning," Theroux recalled in another essay in *Sunrise with Seamonsters*. "They were not apologetic. They simply said that Africans were being

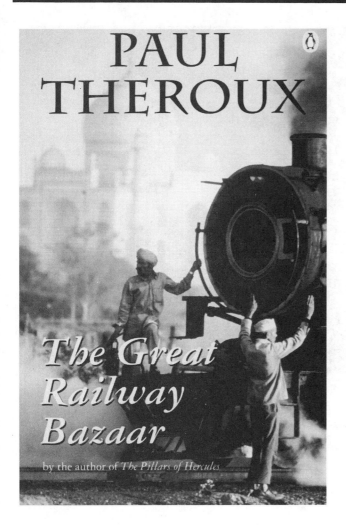

PAUL THEROUX

The Great Railway Bazaar

by the author of *The Pillars of Hercules*

Theroux writes about his four-month journey crossing Asia by way of railroad in this 1975 bestseller.

persecuted in Rhodesia, and that whites. . . . And here I stopped their explanation. Was I a white man to them, just a color, nothing more. . . . I remember thinking: *I have no business to be here.*" However, Africa had been a sort of school for him, and importantly it was in Uganda where he met the writer V. S. Naipaul, who became a mentor and friend for the next thirty years.

In 1968, Theroux got a job teaching English at the University of Singapore. He published a further African title, *Jungle Lovers*, while in Singapore. This novel was set in Malawi, and in it, as some reviewers have mentioned, Theroux attempted to tell the other half of *Heart of Darkness*—what it was in Africa that could drive Conrad's mysterious protagonist, Kurtz, mad. Calvin Mullet must leave

his native Massachusetts to make a living selling insurance in Malawi where he meets up with an American of a very different stripe, Marais, there to foment revolution. Though both want to change the lives of the Africans, they are equally unsuccessful in this novel which Susan Hill characterized as "fine" and "rich" in the *New Statesman*, and which a *Times Literary Supplement* reviewer called "comic and disturbing." L. J. Davis, in his lengthy review of the novel in the *Chicago Tribune Book World*, focused on the comparison to Conrad's *Heart of Darkness*, noting that Theroux's novel "is a first-rate performance—informative, colorful, and insightful."

An English Householder

In 1971, with five novels under his belt, Theroux decided to leave teaching, and Singapore, and turn professional writer in England. His wife was English, so it seemed the logical thing to settle in that country, living in the London suburbs and writing novels, essays, and book reviews. While in Singapore he had agreed not to write about the island, but once in England he was free to work on his Singapore novel, *Saint Jack*. Once again the narrator and principal protagonist, Jack Flowers, is an exile, but this time a middle-aged American expatriate pimp and hustler always eager to make deals and try to beat the system. Jack daydreams of making it big and being saved from his life on the edge, but is doomed to an unchanging existence as he gets older. A critic in the *Virginia Quarterly Review* called Jack "an irresistible rogue," and writing in the *Washington Post Book World*, Jonathan Yardley concluded that "Jack Flowers is funny, endearing, outrageous, poignant, noble—and utterly believable. . . . He is Paul Theroux's finest accomplishment."

Taking something of a critical drubbing with his next novel, *The Black House*, Theroux turned his hand to travel writing, boarding a train at London's Victoria Station to begin a four-month journey through Asia. His intention was to do the entire trip by rail, and during the course of his travels he compiled four thick notebooks of impressions and vignettes which he later edited. The result, *The Great Railway Bazaar: By Train through Asia*, put Theroux's name on the bestseller maps. "I have seldom heard a train go by and not wished I was on it," Theroux wrote in the introduction to his travel book. "Those whistles sing

Harrison Ford plays the eccentric Allie Fox in this 1986 film adaptation of *The Mosquito Coast.*

bewitchment: railways are irresistible bazaars, snaking along perfectly level no matter what the landscape, improving your mood with speed, and never upsetting your drink."

Theroux's odyssey through Asia, the Far East, and the then Soviet Union was related with humor and a keen eye for detail. Robert Towers, writing in the *New York Times Book Review,* noted that though *The Great Railway Bazaar* was "a travel book and not a novel, it incorporates many of the qualities of Theroux's fiction: it is funny, sardonic, wonderfully sensuous and evocative in its descriptions, casually horrifying in its impact." Towers drew special attention to Theroux's "comic celebration of seediness," an element in the work that the reviewer found more British than American, and an indication of the effects Theroux's own expatriate status had on his writing. Towers concluded that Theroux's travel narrative "is the most consistently entertaining and the least boring book I have encountered in a long time." Other review-

ers agreed, including the British short story writer and novelist V. S. Pritchett, who remarked in the *New Statesman* that Theroux "has Dickens's gift for getting the character of a man or woman in a flash." Pritchett went on to give Theroux's travel narrative high praise: "The whole book is more than a rich and original entertainment. His people, places and asides will stay a long time jostling in the mind of the reader." Reviewing the travel book in the *Washington Post Book World*, David Roberts stated that Theroux's account "represents travel writing at its very best—almost the best, one is tempted to say, that it can attain."

Somewhat ironically, this travel book attained for Theroux what his carefully wrought novel writing had been, to that point, unable to do: bring him not only a degree of fame but also financial independence. Theroux has written several other travel accounts since 1975. Two others are descriptions of rail travel, one through South America, *The Old Patagonian Express,* and another an account of his travels in China, *Riding the Iron Rooster*. Additionally there are explorations of the Pacific Islands in *The Happy Isles of Oceania*, rambles around the coast of his adopted homeland in *The Kingdom By the Sea*, and a tour of the Mediterranean in his 1995 *Pillars of Hercules*. Though none of these received the same resoundingly positive critical reception as *The Great Railway Bazaar*, most reviewers found things to like about each book, and they consolidated Theroux's position as a travel writer of note.

In an interview with Robert J. Guttman of *Europe* magazine, Theroux expanded on this dual role as a writer. Responding to Guttman's question whether he was a "novelist that travels or a traveler who's a novelist," Theroux replied: "I'm a writer who, when he doesn't have a fictional idea, takes a trip. I'm glad that I discovered that you can make a living—or that you can sing for your supper because travel's expensive. . . . It would be pretty miserable not having a book to write, a short story or a novel or something, and then having to do something like play golf. . . . The novelists that I've known, when they're not writing, they're going crazy."

The Mosquito Coast

Theroux's panacea against such craziness led to a roll call of other novels written concurrently with his travel books: a London novel about terrorism and economic malaise, *The Family Arsenal*, a novel about the roots of ambition in the art world, *Picture Palace*, and the two short novels included in *Half Moon Street*, also set in London, along with several short story collections. One of Theroux's most popular novels was *The Mosquito Coast*, a story told from the point of view of the thirteen-year-old son of a manic and eccentric American, Allie Fox, who takes his family into exile from modernity to the jungles of Honduras. Made into a movie starring Harrison Ford, *The Mosquito Coast* established Theroux's name as a novelist with the general public—and especially the American public—just as *The Great Railway Bazaar* did for him as a travel writer.

"In Allie Fox, Theroux has created his first epic hero," noted Raban in a *Saturday Review* critique of the book. Fleeing what he believes to be a doomed America, Fox takes his family from Massachusetts to set up a new life in Central America,

founding a new country of their own. Allie tells his family of disciples, "It's the empty spaces that will save us. No funny bunnies, no cops, no crooks, no muggers, no glue sniffers, no aerosol bombs." But Allie takes Yankee ingenuity along with him, the continual tinkering mind of the North American. In Honduras he plans to bring ice to the ice-less, a scheme like most of his which is bound for failure if not tragedy. Allie's thirteen year-old son narrates all this, and in ways "*The Mosquito Coast* is a seemingly straightforward adventure story which ends with a splotch of *Lord of the Flies*-like horror and which trails clouds of dark parable behind it," as Jack Beatty noted in his review of the novel in the *New Republic*. Commenting that the book could be read on several levels and therefore enjoyed by young readers as well as adults, Beatty concluded that "this modern *Swiss Family Robinson* is a displaced dream of parricide. The kids should love it."

Like all good novels, *The Mosquito Coast* elicits a variety of reactions and interpretations. The American writer Frederick Busch saw Theroux's work as a gothic novel, a sort of comeuppance for the technological age, and a blending of Dr. Faustus and Frankenstein. "Surrounding this abstraction are some first-rate writing," Busch noted in *Washington Post Book World*, "a true professional's ability to move an entire family from New England to Honduran jungles convincingly, and marvelous descriptions of the people and conditions with which the Fox family meets." The critic Robert Towers decided in the *New York Review of Books* that Theroux's novel was "a brilliant display-piece, the latest and most spectacular of Theroux's performances. Perhaps we should think of him as the Paganini of contemporary novelists and stop worrying about the coherence of his authorial identity."

American Themes

If *The Mosquito Coast* was a parable of contemporary America, Theroux's next novel, *O-Zone*, was a projection of that condition fifty years into the future. A major departure for Theroux, *O-Zone* follows many of the conventions of science fiction to tell its story. The O-Zone of the title is the American heartland, or at least an enormous chunk of it, left supposedly devastated by a nuclear accident. To the residents of crushingly over-populated areas of urban America such as

New York City, the O-Zone symbolizes both terror and possible escape. The world has become divided into the haves or "owners," and the have-nots, the suffering poor or "aliens." Owners live protected lives, sealed in hermetic suits as they travel about the contaminated wastelands. The book relates the adventures of eight urbanites, ultimately led by fifteen-year-old computer genius Fizzy, who take off for O-Zone and are surprised to find more of a paradise than a hell.

Here the visitors regain some of their lost humanity. The area is far from unpopulated; as with Australia in a distant century, O-Zone has become the dumping ground for criminals and undesirables, but they and the region have "mutated into a peculiar version of paradise—a cross between the Garden of Eden and Love Canal," according to Susan Fromberg Schaeffer, writing in the *New York Times Book Review*. "In the end, *O-Zone* is a kind of neo-Thoreauvian, Rousseauean work, a *Lord of the Flies* in reverse," Schaeffer noted. Jon Clute, writing in *New Statesman*, felt that though the science fiction aspects of the novel took too long to develop, the character of Fizzy Fisher was "an inspired creation," and through the course of the novel "Theroux finally makes one able to believe in the seamy, fractured nightmare of his fascist America; he grasps the nettle of his vision." Clute concluded that "Those who put up with the earlier ramblings will feel rewarded for their persistence." John Sutherland in the *London Review of Books* echoed this sentiment, remarking that while the literary territory of O-Zone "may be a new world for Theroux . . . it's been mapped out by any number of SF writers." However, Sutherland also found that the "conventions of dystopia give some fresh scope to the author's fixed ideas about civilization and barbarism," and that "the evolution of the odious Fizzy from nerd to manhood is gripping."

In 1989, Theroux published the first of his notional autobiographies, *My Secret History*, followed the next year by *Chicago Loop*, a story of a serial killer who ultimately turns against himself. Divorced in 1993, Theroux returned to live in the United States after nearly thirty years living abroad. He lived eighteen of those in London, where his sons were raised. Both sons were also educated in England, one at Cambridge and the other at Oxford. Theroux's London experience was far from that of the visitor: he bought and sold several houses, drove a car, did the shopping, and worked daily.

But at the end of his marriage he returned to the United States to the home he had earlier purchased on Cape Cod. He also spends part of the year in Hawaii where he raises bees.

Homes changed, but not Theroux's prodigious output. In 1994, he published *Millroy the Magician*, another book told from a youthful perspective. Jilly Farina, fourteen going on fifteen, is the narrator of this "comic version of the second coming," as Charles Johnson described the novel in the *New York Times Book Review*. Jilly, visiting the Barnstable County Fair, is awed by the feats of the magician named Millroy—so awed that she decides to join up with him, running away from her abusive, drunken father. Dressed as a boy, Jilly

A NEW YORK TIMES NOTABLE BOOK

PAUL THEROUX

MILLROY THE MAGICIAN

"BRILLIANT...WONDERFUL...
MILLROY'S MAGIC POPS OUT AT
THE READER FROM THE FIRST PAGE."
—JOHN UPDIKE
THE NEW YORKER

Fourteen-year-old Jilly Farina disguises herself as a boy to become Millroy the Magician's assistant in this 1994 tale.

becomes Millroy's assistant on stage, but soon she discovers that he is far more than a country-fair prestidigitator. He has in fact travelled the world and is an adept of yoga. A once immensely fat person, Millroy has had a conversion to eating health food, his own personal salvation and the message he wants to spread to a hamburger-gulping world. He takes this message first to a kiddy show in Boston, where he becomes host for a time, and then to a diner he opens once he is fired from television. Millroy has received his nutritional message from the Bible, concocting a diet of lentils, figs, barley, honeycombs, melons, and bread which he says will keep the world regular and long-lived.

Soon Millroy's one diner becomes a chain of Bible-food diners, though in the end, as with most saviors, Millroy too "falls victim to celebrity and gossip," according to R. Z. Sheppard in *Time* magazine. Sheppard noted that Millroy "would alone make this a novel to conjure with," but that Theroux "adds another delight, Jilly Farina, a plucky adolescent with an artless narrative voice." Sheppard, among other critics, also drew attention to the parallels with Mark Twain's Huckleberry Finn: the flight from a drunken parent and the cross-dressing to hide identity on the road. In the end, the pair light out for Hawaii, as Huck did for the territories. Sheppard concluded that Millroy and Jilly are "the most enchanting characters Theroux has ever pulled out of his hat." *Booklist*'s Donna Seaman concluded that Theroux's ingredients cooked up "an irresistible, adroit, often hilarious, and strangely romantic tale about the fate of a genuine prophet in the age of fast-food cynicism and the enduring mystery and power of love." Johnson commented in the *New York Times Book Review* that "those who reach the end of Mr. Theroux's three-ring circus of a novel see its final act as worth the price of admission." In a lengthy *New Yorker* review of the book, novelist John Updike commented that "a tenderness exists in this novel, and a jubilation, not hitherto conspicuous among this earnest and prolific author's qualities."

Prolific is a word often used to describe Theroux, who generally turns out a book a year. Curmudgeonly is another, though Theroux tends to dismiss such criticism as mistaking misanthropy for irony. He is the master of the marginal man, whether his protagonists be foreigners in a distant land or natives, they are all in a sense strangers in a strange land seeking self-knowledge. From Allie in Honduras to Fizzy in O-Zone and Millroy in America, they are a band of misfits and outsiders who beguile readers with their oft-mentioned Dickensian dimensions. For Theroux they are all part of the territory of the work he has taken on, that peculiar form of therapy known as writing.

"Writing made me a free man," Theroux told Anthony Weller in a *GEO* magazine interview. "No other profession could have done that. When you think that writing is something you do by yourself, that you're making something out of nothing, it's like a conjuring trick in one sense—there *is* nothing like it. Except, I suppose, painting, composing music, the other creative professions. All of those make you free."

If you enjoy the works of Paul Theroux, you may also want to check out the following books:

Emma Bull, *Bone Dance,* 1991.
Clyde Edgerton, *Killer Diller,* 1991.
Frances Temple, *Grab Hands and Run,* 1993.

■ Works Cited

Barbato, Joseph, "Books Should Take You Away," *Express,* June, 1982.

Beatty, Jack, review of *The Mosquito Coast, New Republic,* February 24, 1982, p. 40.

Busch, Frederick, "Dr. Faustus in the Jungle," *Washington Post Book World,* February 14, 1982, pp. 1-2.

Clute, Jon, "Off Limits," *New Statesman,* October 17, 1986, pp. 29-30.

Cook, Roderick, review of *Waldo, Harper's,* May, 1967, pp. 17-18.

Davis, L. J., review of *Jungle Lovers, Chicago Tribune Book World,* August 8, 1971, p. 8.

Guttman, Robert J., "Paul Theroux's Mediterranean Odyssey," *Europe,* February, 1996, pp. 26-32.

Hill, Susan, "Jungle Book," *New Statesman,* June 11, 1971, p. 815.

Johnson, Charles, "Salvation through Weight Control," *New York Times Book Review,* March 6, 1994, p. 9.

Review of *Jungle Lovers, Times Literary Supplement,* June 25, 1971, p. 725.

Kakutani, Michiko, review of *Sunrise with Seamonsters, New York Times,* June 5, 1985, p. C24.

Lafore, Laurence, review of *Girls at Play, New York Times Book Review,* September 28, 1969, p. 5.

Pritchett, V. S., review of *The Great Railway Bazaar, New Statesman,* October 17, 1975, pp. 474-76.

Raban, Jonathan, "Theroux's Wonderful, Bottomless Novel," *Saturday Review,* February, 1982, pp. 55-56.

Roberts, David, review of *The Great Railway Bazaar, Washington Post Book World,* September 7, 1975, p. 1.

Review of *Saint Jack, Virginia Quarterly Review,* Winter, 1974.

Schaeffer, Susan Fromberg, "Nerd of Paradise," *New York Times Book Review,* September 14, 1986, pp. 12-13.

Seaman, Donna, review of *Millroy the Magician, Booklist,* October 15, 1993, p. 395.

Sheppard, R. Z., "High-Fiber Moralist," *Time,* March 7, 1994, pp. 69-70.

Stevens, Shane, "Strangers in Africa," *Chicago Tribune Book World,* February 8, 1970, p. 13.

Sutherland, John, "Fiction and the Poverty of Theory," *London Review of Books,* November 29, 1986, pp. 14-15.

Theroux, Paul, *The Great Railway Bazaar,* Houghton, 1975.

Theroux, Paul, *The Mosquito Coast,* Houghton, 1982.

Theroux, Paul, *Sunrise with Seamonsters,* Houghton, 1985.

Towers, Robert, review of *The Great Railway Bazaar, New York Times Book Review,* August 24, 1975, p. 1.

Towers, Robert, "Moby-Dad," *New York Review of Books,* April 15, 1982, p. 37.

Updike, John, "The Good Book as Cook Book," *New Yorker,* March 14, 1994, pp. 92-94.

Weller, Anthony, "Paul Theroux," *GEO,* November, 1983.

Yardley, Jonathan, review of *Saint Jack, Washington Post Book World,* September 14, 1973.

■ **For More Information See**

BOOKS

Contemporary Authors New Revision Series, Volume 45, Gale, 1995, pp. 425-33.

Contemporary Literary Criticism, Gale, Volume 5, 1976, Volume 8, 1978, Volume 11, 1979, Volume 15, 1980, Volume 28, 1984, Volume 46, 1988.

Dictionary of Literary Biography, Volume 2: *American Novelists Since World War II,* Gale, 1978, pp. 478-83.

PERIODICALS

Antioch Review, winter, 1977.

Atlantic, October, 1973; April, 1976; October, 1983.

Booklist, May 15, 1997, p. 1542.

Books Abroad, summer, 1969; winter, 1971.

Book World, February 8, 1970, August 8, 1971.

Chicago Tribune Book World, September 16, 1979; February 21, 1982; August 15, 1982; March 27, 1983; November 13, 1983; June 30, 1985; February 9, 1986.

Choice, July, 1973.

Christian Science Monitor, September 5, 1968.

Commentary, June, 1967.

Commonweal, May 29, 1994.

Critique, March, 1981.

Detroit News, June 4, 1978; September 9, 1979; November 13, 1983; February 16, 1986.

Economist, July 23, 1988, p. 77; October 24, 1992, p. 102; November 20, 1993, p. 111.

Encounter, July, 1973.

Entertainment Weekly, December 1, 1995, p. 69; July 11, 1997, p. 63.

Esquire, December, 1971; April, 1983; September, 1996, pp. 182, 184.

Globe and Mail (Toronto), October 19, 1985.

Harper's, March, 1976; September, 1977; April, 1982.

Hudson Review, Winter, 1974-75; Autumn, 1978.

Kenyon Review, September, 1967.

Library Journal, March 1, 1994, p. 138; March 15, 1995, p. 102; April 1, 1995, p. 142; September 15, 1995, p. 85; February 1, 1996, p. 90; August, 1996, p. 115.

Life, May 21, 1971.

London Magazine, January, 1970.

London Review of Books, February 8, 1996, p. 18.

Los Angeles Times, November 13, 1983; October 25, 1984; September 26, 1986.

Los Angeles Times Book Review, October 7, 1979; September 21, 1980; April 18, 1982; March 13, 1983; September 21, 1986.

Maclean's, August 15, 1988, p. 50; August 14, 1989, p. 55.

National Observer, October 6, 1969.

National Review, June 29, 1971; November 10, 1972; June 2, 1989, p. 58.

New Republic, November 29, 1969; September 25, 1976; November 27, 1976; September 22, 1979; April 11, 1983; July 17, 1989, p. 40; March 2, 1992, p. 29.

New Statesman, October 4, 1974; March 26, 1976; September 1, 1978; October 24, 1980; June 20, 1997.

New Statesman & Society, September 16, 1988, p. 40; June 30, 1989, p. 33; April 6, 1990, p. 38; November 6, 1992, p. 49; October 8, 1993, p. 38.

Newsweek, September 24, 1973; November 11, 1974; September 8, 1975; June 19, 1976; August 15, 1977; September 10, 1979; March 1, 1982; April 25, 1983; October 24, 1983; October 22, 1984; August 12, 1985.

New York, February 28, 1994, p. 127.

New Yorker, November 11, 1967; November 8, 1969; December 29, 1975; January 7, 1985; February 16, 1987, p. 108; August 10, 1992, p. 80; June 26, 1995, p. 144.

New York Review of Books, September 23, 1971; September 30, 1976; November 10, 1977; August 17, 1978; June 2, 1983.

New York Times, May 29, 1971; July 22, 1976; August 23, 1977; April 30, 1978; May 31, 1978; April 27, 1979; August 28, 1979; February 11, 1982; February 28, 1983; October 13, 1983; October 1, 1984; September 23, 1996, p. B2.

New York Times Book Review, November 3, 1968; August 8, 1971; November 5, 1972; September 9, 1973; September 8, 1974; December 28, 1975; July 11, 1976; August 21, 1977; June 18, 1978; July 22, 1979; August 26, 1979; August 24, 1980; February 14, 1982; March 20, 1983; October 23, 1983; April 22, 1984; October 28, 1984; June 2, 1985; November 10, 1985; May 10, 1987, p. 34; July 19, 1988, p. 17; June 4, 1989, p. 1; March 17, 1991, p. 7; December 1, 1991, p. 20; June 14, 1992, p. 7; December 6, 1992, p. 52; November 5, 1995, p. 11; September 27, 1998; November 1, 1998, p. 39.

North American Review, winter, 1972.

Observer, June 30, 1996, p. 15.

Ontario Review, fall, 1974; fall-winter, 1976-77.

Playboy, January, 1973; February, 1987, p. 22; July, 1988, p. 32; July, 1989, p. 26; April, 1991, p. 30; July, 1992, p. 25; April, 1994, p. 32.

Publishers Weekly, July 26, 1976; March 7, 1994, p. 48; June 24, 1996, p. 43; June 9, 1997, p. 39; August 31, 1998, p. 54.

Punch, December 10, 1969; October 13, 1982.

Saturday Night, April, 1989, p. 61.

Saturday Review, September 28, 1968; July 24, 1976; September 3, 1977; July 8, 1978; October 27, 1979; November-December, 1983.

School Library Journal, October, 1994, p. 158.

Spectator, June 12, 1971; October 12, 1974; March 15, 1975; October 18, 1975; March 27, 1976; June 4, 1977; September 16, 1978; October 17, 1981; June 30, 1984; June 29, 1985; July 6, 1996, p. 32.

Time, August 23, 1968; August 25, 1975; August 2, 1976; September 5, 1977; June 5, 1978; February 22, 1982; October 31, 1983; July 1, 1985; May 16, 1988, p. 95; May 22, 1989, p. 112; March 25, 1991, p. 71; June 15, 1992, p. 73; November 6, 1995, p. 83; June 2, 1997.

Times (London), October 6, 1983; June 6, 1985; September 1, 1986; October 11, 1986; October 16, 1986.

Times Literary Supplement, April 11, 1968; June 12, 1969; November 17, 1972; April 27, 1973; October 4, 1974; March 14, 1975; March 26, 1976; June 3, 1977; October 31, 1980; November 21, 1980; October 16, 1981; October 8, 1982; October 28, 1983; June 8, 1984; August 2, 1985; October 31, 1986; July 5, 1996.

Tribune (London), October 5, 1979.

Tribune Books (Chicago), March 27, 1994, p. 4.

U.S. News and World Report, December 17, 1979.

Village Voice, November 15, 1983; July 30, 1985.

Virginia Quarterly Review, Winter, 1969; Winter, 1970.

Voice Literary Supplement, March, 1982.

Wall Street Journal, September 13, 1996, p. A10.

Washington Post, September 20, 1979; November 23, 1985.

Washington Post Book World, September 15, 1974; May 30, 1976; July 11, 1976; August 21, 1977; June 25, 1978; September 2, 1979; August 17, 1980; March 6, 1983; October 16, 1983; December 9, 1984; July 7, 1985; February 27, 1994, p. 2; October 8, 1995, p. 5.

Yale Review, Spring, 1979.*

—Sketch by J. Sydney Jones

Sue Townsend

■ Personal

Born April 2, 1946, in Leicester, Leicestershire, England; married (marriage dissolved); three children. *Education:* Attended English secondary school. *Politics:* Socialist. *Religion:* Atheist. *Hobbies and other interests:* Walking, reading, eating, drinking, canoeing, traveling alone.

■ Addresses

Home—Leicester, Leicestershire, England. *Agent*—Giles Gordon, 43 Doughty Street, London, WC1N 2LF, England.

■ Career

Writer. Has also worked in various capacities, including garage attendant, hot dog saleswoman, dress shop worker, factory worker, and trained community worker.

■ Awards, Honors

Thames Television Bursary, 1979, for *Womberang;* West Australian Young Readers Book Award, Sec-

ondary (ages 13-15) category, Australian Library and Information Association, 1985, for *The Secret Diary of Adrian Mole, Aged 13 3/4,* and Overseas Secondary category, 1986, for *The Growing Pains of Adrian Mole;* Best Books for Young Adults, American Library Association, 1986, for *The Adrian Mole Diaries;* Books I Love Best Yearly (BILBY) Award, Read Alone Secondary category, 1990, for *The Secret Diary of Adrian Mole, Aged 13 3/4.*

■ Writings

NOVELS

The Secret Diary of Adrian Mole, Aged 13 3/4, illustrated by Caroline Holden, Methuen, 1982, Avon, 1984 (also see below).

The Growing Pains of Adrian Mole, Methuen, 1984, Grove, 1986 (also see below).

The Adrian Mole Diaries: A Novel (contains *The Secret Diary of Adrian Mole, Aged 13 3/4* and *The Growing Pains of Adrian Mole*), Methuen, 1985, Grove, 1986.

The Secret Diary of Adrian Mole, Aged 13 3/4 Song Book, Methuen, 1985.

Rebuilding Coventry: A Tale of Two Cities (novel), Methuen, 1988, Grove Weidenfeld, 1990.

Mr. Bevan's Dream, Chatto & Windus, 1989, Trafalgar Square, 1990.

(With Margaret Hilda Roberts) *True Confessions of Adrian Albert Mole,* Teen (London), 1991 (also see below).

Adrian Mole from Minor to Major: The Mole Diaries, The First Ten Years (contains *The Secret Diary of*

Adrian Mole, Aged 13 3/4, The Growing Pains of Adrian Mole, True Confessions of Adrian Albert Mole, and *Adrian Mole and the Small Amphibians*), Methuen, 1991.

The Queen and I, Methuen, 1992, Soho, 1993.
Adrian Mole: The Wilderness Years, Methuen, 1993.
Adrian Mole: The Lost Years, Soho, 1994.
Ghost Children, Methuen, 1997.

PLAYS

Womberang (one-act play), first produced in Leicester, England, at the Leicester Haymarket Theatre, 1979; produced on the West End at the Soho Poly, 1980 (also see below).
The Ghost of Daniel Lambert, first produced at Phoenix Arts Centre and Leicester Haymarket Theatre, Leicester, England, 1981.
Dayroom, first produced at Croydon Warehouse Theatre, Croydon, England, 1981.
Bazaar and Rummage, first produced at Royal Court Theatre Upstairs, 1982.
Captain Christmas and the Evil Adults, first produced at Phoenix Arts Centre, Leicester, 1982.
Are You Sitting Comfortably, first produced at Croydon Warehouse Theatre, Croydon, 1983.
Groping for Words (two-act play), first produced in London at the Croydon Warehouse, 1983 (also see below).
The Great Celestial Cow, first produced in Leicester, at the Leicester Haymarket Theatre, October, 1984; produced on the West End at the Royal Court Theatre, 1984.
Bazaar and Rummage, Groping for Words, Womberang: Three Plays (play collection), Methuen, 1984.
The Secret Diary of Adrian Mole, Aged 13 3/4: The Play (two-act play; first produced in Leicester at the Phoenix Theatre, September, 1984; produced on the West End at Wyndham's Theatre, December 12, 1984), with songs by Ken Howard and Alan Blaikley, Methuen, 1985.
Ten Tiny Fingers, Nine Tiny Toes, Heinemann, 1991.
The Queen and I, with songs by Ian Dury and Mickey Gallagher, Methuen Drama in association with the Royal Court Theatre, 1994, revised version, Samuel French, 1996.

■ Adaptations

The Secret Diary of Adrian Mole, Aged 13 3/4 (seven-part radio series), British Broadcasting Corporation Radio 4, first broadcast as *Nigel Mole's Diary,* in January, 1982.

Bazaar and Rummage (teleplay), British Broadcasting Corporation, 1983 (also see below).
The Growing Pains of Adrian Mole (five-part radio series), BBC-Radio 4, 1984, (cassette), EMI Records/Listen for Pleasure, 1985.
The Secret Diary of Adrian Mole, Aged 13 3/4 (computer game), Mosaic, 1985.
The Secret Diary of Adrian Mole, Aged 13 3/4 (six-part television series), Thames Television, September, 1986.
The Growing Pains of Adrian Mole (television series), Thames Television, 1987.
The Growing Pains of Adrian Mole (computer game), Mosaic, 1987.

Contributor to BBC-TV series *Revolting Women,* 1981; author with Carole Hayman of a comedy series, *The Refuge,* BBC-Radio 4, 1987. Contributor to periodicals, including the *London Times, New Statesman, Airport, Guardian, Observer,* and *Marxism Today;* regular column appeared in *Woman's Realm,* 1983-85. The Adrian Mole books have been translated into twenty-two languages.

■ Sidelights

Sue Townsend, who got her start as a writer for the theater, penned a series of fictional diaries of a self-obsessed teenager that critics deemed one of the literary phenomena of the 1980s. A runaway bestseller in Great Britain, *The Secret Diary of Adrian Mole, Aged 13 3/4* led not only to additional diaries but to a television program and a musical play as well as a computer game and other consumer items. In the United States, where the books first appeared as *The Adrian Mole Diaries,* reviewers wondered whether American youth would follow Adrian's use of British slang, and whether American readers would be as intensely moved as the British public by the books' detailed satire of the decay of living standards under Prime Minister Margaret Thatcher. The nearly invariable conclusion was that Townsend's "funny, poignant, sardonic but also compassionate" fictional diaries, in the words of *New York Times Book Review* critic Norma Klein, "deserve at least some portion of the attention they received in their native country."

Townsend began her writing career as a playwright, after spending many years in menial jobs to support herself and her four children. Critics note that her feisty, at times embittered female

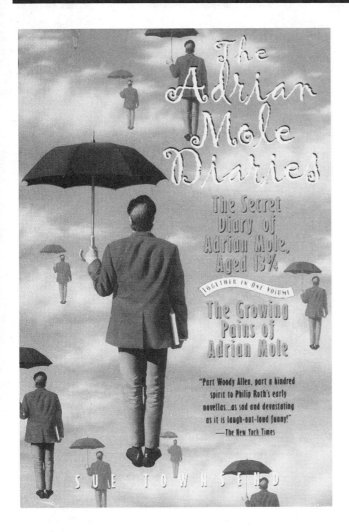

Published together, Townsend's first two works from the "Adrian Mole" series feature the personal accounts of a self-obsessed British teen.

rummage sale by their manipulative social worker. "By dramatising fear, Townsend encourages people to see problems not as personal failures but as part of a larger social pattern," noted John Lahr in *New Society*. Thus, in another early play, *Groping for Words*, Townsend casts the British education system as an instrument of class control through her portrayal of characters who go through elaborate ruses in order to hide their illiteracy from society at large. Townsend's "characters are affectionately drawn" in these short pieces, according to Diana Devlin, who critiqued the published collection of these plays in *Drama*, and "her situations capture the bizarre aspects of what passes for 'normal' life."

Townsend's sharply humorous plays and stories demonstrate that she is "a satirist of the first or-

Now in his twenties, Adrian Mole writes about his attempts to establish himself as a writer in this 1994 work.

characters, as well as the often weak-willed and morally spineless male characters in her works, may well be a product of the author's own unhappy experiences with the opposite sex, particularly with the husband who abandoned her and their children when she was in her early twenties. "That the mass of women lead lives of quiet desperation is one of Sue Townsend's recurrent themes, and their liberation from boring or violent men one of her favourite fantasies," observed Shena Mackay in the *Times Literary Supplement*. Townsend's first play, *Womberang*, features Rita Onions, a woman who rallies and cajoles the other patients in a gynecological waiting room into discarding their fear of authority and standing up for themselves. In the farcical *Bazaar and Rummage*, a group of agoraphobics is bullied into hosting a

der," according to Emily Melton in a *Booklist* review of *Adrian Mole: The Lost Years*. Melton added: "Without ever being maudlin, cruel, silly, or sentimental, [Townsend] provokes sidesplitting laughter, a few tears, and a wonderfully warm feeling that there is indeed hope for the planet." In *The Secret Diary of Adrian Mole, Aged 13 3/4* and its several sequels, the objects of Townsend's satire include the feckless sixties generation as adults and the quality of British life under Prime Minister Margaret Thatcher. Townsend's title protagonist is sanctimonious, snobbish, gloomy, and whiny all at the same time. During the year chronicled by the first diary, Adrian recounts the ongoing battles between his parents, culminating in his mother running off with the next-door neighbor; the loss of his father's job; being bullied at school; his unrequited love for Pandora, a classmate of higher social status; his worries over pimples and the size of his penis; and the time he spends with a cranky retiree as part of a Good Samaritans project. *The Growing Pains of Adrian Mole*, the second volume of the diary, documents ages fifteen to sixteen, including the birth of Adrian's baby sister, a blind date, the continued extra-marital affairs of both of his parents, and running away from home—even though no one takes much notice.

If you enjoy the works of Sue Townsend, you may also want to check out the following books and films:

Judith Clarke, *The Heroic Life of Al Capsella*, 1990.
Paul Zindel, *The Amazing and Death-Defying Diary of Eugene Dingman*, 1987.
What's Eating Gilbert Grape, a film starring Johnny Deppt, 1993.

Townsend pokes fun at the royal family in this 1993 work, which was also produced as a play in 1994.

The first two volumes of the diary were published in the United States under one cover with the title *The Adrian Mole Diaries*, along with the addition of a glossary of British terms, which appears in the form of a letter from Adrian to Hamish Mancini, who has asked him to explain certain things. For readers in the United States, this was followed by *Adrian Mole: The Lost Years*, in which Adrian's diaries track his angst-ridden progress into his early twenties. The main action of this latter story concerns the fate of young writer Adrian's first novel, which at seven hundred pages contains no vowels, and of his love life. When Adrian's novel, "Lo! The Flat Hills of My Homeland," is rejected by several publishers, he determines to add vowels and more sex to spice up his story. *School Library Journal* contributor Grace Baun dubbed *Adrian Mole: The Lost Years* "very funny and entertaining," and while many reviewers continued to remark on the success of the ongoing diaries' humorous depiction of young manhood, it was also frequently noted that Mole's observations of his world simultaneously paint a fairly grim picture of life among the British lower-

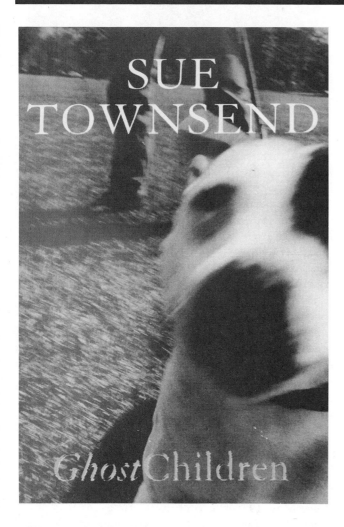

Suspense abounds in this dark love story, published in 1998.

middle classes during Margaret Thatcher's tenure as prime minister. Indeed, it is this element that distinguishes the *Adrian Mole Diaries* from mere "harmless fun," according to William Grimes of the *Village Voice.* "What makes the diaries something more is their sharply observed social realism, which gives, in quick takes, a picture of shabby lower-middle-class life in the English Midlands. It succeeds brilliantly in conveying the texture of life among Britain's 'nouveau poor' (as Adrian's mother refers to the Mole family)."

Indeed, partly because of this issue, there was some question among critics whether the Mole books should truly, or solely, be considered young adult fare. Several commentators pointed out that despite his centrality to the novels, "the subject matter is not Adrian Mole's growing pains," as

Nigel Andrew asserted in the *Listener,* "but the pains and idiosyncrasies of the various adult characters, comically refracted in Mole's dawning consciousness." Other critics questioned the suitability of the language for this age group, first because the use of British slang and brand names might cause some readers difficulty, and second because of the use of obscene language. "My fear for Adrian Mole in America," asserted *New York Times Book Review* contributor Norma Klein, "is that . . . he will be perceived as falling between two stools: too radical and shocking for teen-agers, at least as they are seen by the library establishment, but uninteresting to adults by virtue of being under college age. Yet it is hard to conceive of anyone of either age group with even a passing interest in the best contemporary fiction who will not find the diaries a delight."

"Children take to the books partly, I gather, because the disgusting details of Adrian's spots, the mention of his wet dreams and of his regular measuring of his 'thing', break taboos," observed Peter Campbell in the *London Review of Books.* "But more because—despite his hypochondria, his naff intellectual ambitions, his deeply untrendy tastes— he is a hero who suffers as they suffer." Townsend herself speculated in a 1987 interview with *Contemporary Authors* on the source of Mole's popularity with readers worldwide: "Adolescence is such a strong experience, and the emotions bound up in it are so common to all of us, that everybody recognizes those feelings. And I think to a certain extent everybody sees himself as this brave little soldier plodding through life, misunderstood by the rest of the world."

"Dear Mole. He is, for me, one of the key literary characters of our time," sighed a reviewer for the *Times Educational Supplement.* However, few American critics responded this extravagantly to Adrian Mole, the character on whom Townsend's reputation is substantially based, though several compared him to J. D. Salinger's central protagonist in his classic novel of youthful angst, *Catcher in the Rye.* Some reviewers in the United States expressed a doubt whether young adult readers would be able to make sense of Adrian's British slang, and others claimed that young readers, failing to grasp the social and political satire of the books, would merely be pleasantly scandalized by Adrian's wry observations. Others have maintained that Adrian's humorous experiences and the motions that they engender are universal.

■ Works Cited

Andrew, Nigel, "Diary Makes Dead Good Social History!!!" *Listener*, October 3, 1985, pp. 117-18.

Baun, Grace, review of *Adrian Mole: The Lost Years*, *School Library Journal*, January, 1995, p. 146.

Campbell, Peter, "Adrian," *London Review of Books*, December 5, 1985, p. 18.

Devlin, Diana, review of *Bazaar and Rummage*, *Groping for Words*, and *Womberang*, in *Drama*, winter, 1984, p. 49.

Grimes, William, "Drear Diary," *Village Voice*, June 3, 1986, p. 45.

Klein, Norma, "I Was a Teen-Age Intellectual," *New York Times Book Review*, May 25, 1986, p. 9.

Lahr, John, "A Female Trickster," *New Society*, March 24, 1983, pp. 274-75.

Mackay, Shena, "Lady into Tramp," *Times Literary Supplement*, September 16, 1988, p. 1012.

Melton, Emily, review of *Adrian Mole: The Lost Years*, *Booklist*, August, 1994, p. 1993.

"Still Muddling On," *Times Educational Supplement*, September 29, 1989, p. 32.

Townsend, Sue, interview with Jean W. Ross in *Contemporary Authors*, Volume 127, Gale, 1989, pp. 456-60.

■ For More Information See

BOOKS

Contemporary Literary Criticism, Volume 61, Gale, 1990, pp. 406-21.

Twentieth-Century Young Adult Writers, St. James Press, 1994, pp. 650-51.

PERIODICALS

Booklist, May 1, 1986, p. 1284; May 15, 1986, p. 1412; March 1, 1990, p. 1266; February 1, 1991, p. 1123; January 15, 1992, p. 933.

Books, September, 1988, p. 15; October, 1989, p. 27; July, 1991, p. 11; September, 1991, p. 22; November, 1992, p. 10; September, 1993, p. 22; July, 1994, p. 8.

Kirkus Reviews, April 1, 1986, p. 504; January 1, 1990, p. 15; July 1, 1993, p. 814.

Library Journal, February 15, 1990, p. 214; January 1, 1994, p. 165.

New Statesman & Society, September 10, 1993, p. 41; September 12, 1993, p. 37.

Newsweek, May 5, 1986, p. 76.

New York, May 19, 1986, p. 120.

New Yorker, May, 1986, p. 120.

New York Times Book Review, April 22, 1990, p. 24; September 12, 1993, p. 13; December 5, 1993, p. 64; September 25, 1994, p. 40; February 26, 1995.

Publishers Weekly, August 23, 1985; March 21, 1986, p. 76; January 12, 1990, p. 48; June 28, 1993, p. 58; August 29, 1994, p. 63.

School Librarian, December, 1983, p. 383; December, 1984, p. 382.

School Library Journal, September, 1984, p. 134; February, 1987, pp. 34-35.

Spectator, December 16, 1989, p. 32; November 21, 1992, p. 39; September 4, 1993, p. 29.

Time, May 19, 1986, p. 100.

Times Educational Supplement, November 4, 1988, p. 25; September 29, 1989, p. 32; December 11, 1992, p. 34.

Voice of Youth Advocates, December, 1986, p. 222.

Washington Post Book World, May 13, 1984, p. 18; November 1, 1992, p. 15; August 29, 1993.*

—Sketch by Mary Gillis

Michael Whelan

■ Personal

Born June 29, 1950, in Culver City, CA; son of William R. (an aerospace engineer) and Nancy (Sloet) Whelan; married Audrey Price (a mail order business publisher), December 34, 1978; children: Adrian, Alexa. *Education:* San Jose State University, B.A. (art), 1973; attended Art Center College of Design, Los Angeles (now Pasadena), 1974. *Avocational interests:* Martial arts, digital art, music.

■ Addresses

Home—Danbury, CT. *Office*—Glass Onion, P.O. Box 88, Brookfield, CT 06804. *Electronic mail*—whelanart@aol.com.

■ Career

Freelance artist. Co-owner, with wife, Audrey, of Glass Onion (a gallery and mail order business), Brookfield, CT. *Exhibitions:* Whelan has had one-man shows at Brigham Young University, the Franklin Mint Museum, the Butler Museum of Art (Youngstown, OH), and numerous colleges, universities, and science centers across the United States; he has participated in group exhibitions at the New Britain Museum of Art, the Canton Museum of Art, two shows at the Delaware Museum of Art, and the Bronx Museum of Art.

■ Awards, Honors

First place for professional science fiction art, World Science Fiction Convention, 1974, for painting *Outbound;* Hugo Awards for Best Professional Artist, 1980, 1981, 1982, 1983, 1984, 1985, 1986, 1988, 1989, 1991, and 1992; World Fantasy Award (Howard Award) for Best Artist, 1981, 1982, and 1983; Hugo Award for Best Non-Fiction Book, 1988, for *Michael Whelan's Worlds of Wonder;* Hugo Award for Best Original Artwork, 1992, for *Summer Queen;* SuperHugo for Best Artist of the Last 50 Years; Society of Illustrators Gold Medal; Communications Arts Award for Excellence; Grumbacher Gold Medal; Whelan has also won Nebula and Locus Awards, as well as "best of show" at numerous art exhibitions.

■ Writings

Wonderworks: Science Fiction and Fantasy Art, Donning (Norfolk, VA), 1979.
Michael Whelan's Worlds of Wonder, foreword by Isaac Asimov, Del Rey, 1987.

The Art of Michael Whelan, Bantam, 1993.
Something in My Eye, Mark V. Ziesing, 1996.

Contributor of illustrations to children's book *The Adventure of Little Fuzzy*. Whelan's artwork has appeared on the covers of numerous novels, and in calendars, magazines, album and CD covers, and advertisements.

■ Sidelights

For a science fiction or fantasy novelist to have a book published with cover art by Michael Whelan could mean one of two things: either the book has been judged by the publisher to rank among such greats as Isaac Asimov and Anne McCaffrey, or the book is a miserable failure. What could explain this odd dichotomy? Whelan explained the phenomenon by quoting publisher George T. Delacorte, Jr., in the interview compendium *The Sound of Wonder: Interviews from "The Science Fiction Radio Show."* As Delacorte said, "What you do when you have a good painter, a good cover artist, is use him for your best books or your worst books. That way you cover all of your bases." In other words, excellent cover art accentuates a brilliant novel, but it can also save a publisher from losing too much money on a poor one. It is true, after all, that an eye-catching cover illustration can sell a book, and Michael Whelan is the acknowledged master artist of the science fiction and fantasy book jacket. He is also, however, an all-around accomplished painter who has done much to help sci-fi and fantasy art gain acceptance in the art world.

Whelan is in such demand by publishers that his services are typically booked two years in advance. His original paintings command high price tags, as well. He has won more Hugo Awards for best professional artist than any other painter, as well as winning numerous other prizes. In fact, Whelan has earned so many Hugos—seven in a row from 1980 to 1986 alone—that he removed himself from competition in 1987 so that someone else could get the prize. His achievements were typified when he was given the SuperHugo for Best Artist of the Last 50 Years. There are some who might argue that Whelan isn't a "real artist" because his subject matter is almost always anchored in the realms of science fiction and fantasy, and because, somewhat ironically, he paints in a highly realistic style that is not generally considered "state of the art." Whelan's work, it's true, is not abstract or experimental, but his technical achievements can't be denied.

Whelan's Early Influences

Whelan was born in 1950 in Culver City, California. His father worked in the aerospace industry, and this had some influence on Whelan's early interest in science fiction. "Because my father worked in the space industry," the artist told *Authors and Artists for Young Adults (AAYA)* in an interview, "I experienced a number of things while growing up which made me think the Bonestell vision of the future [Chesley Bonestell (1888-1986) is famous for his space art] would be my reality as an adult. For example, when my father worked at White Sands Proving ground, I was allowed to hang around at the Navy air base. They were testing parachute recovery systems. They sent recovery teams out to find the missile after it came down, and I still remember sitting in the back of one of the jeeps as we raced across the desert to the crash site. It was very exciting.

"We often lived near missile bases, where the roar of rockets blasting off was almost a commonplace experience in the 1960s. Whenever a big one took off from Vandenberg (this was when I was in eighth grade) our teacher would let us go outside to watch it go up and out. Sometimes they'd go astray and have to be blown up. What a thrill that was. Of course—being too young to realize the millions of dollars of taxpayers' money being lost each time it happened—we'd all cheer. We just wanted to see the fireworks! Anyway, the effect of events such as these was to cause me to grow up thinking of SF as a view to our probable future. If you had asked me whether we would have colonies on the Moon and Mars by the year 2000, I would have said, 'Of course!' Even as late as 1970, who could have known that we'd get only as far as the Moon and then lose interest in further manned exploration?"

Always the artist, the young Whelan liked to spend time making his own drawings based on books he had read or movies he had watched. "The biggest influences on me when I was young were the movies and book covers I saw. Then, when I began to read more, it was the stories themselves. As I grew older, I went through succeeding phases of being attracted to different au-

L'Echelle, a 1984 work, was originally commissioned for Waldenbooks.

thors and artists. In my early teens, I was fond of Frank Frazetta and St. John and Roy Krenkel, as well as some comic book artists. In high school I also discovered Michelangelo and the Renaissance artists. In college, I became interested in Maxfield Parrish, N. C. Wyeth, and the Golden Age illustrators, as well as contemporary artists of the visionary school." Whelan also found an influence in his father. "My father was an amateur cartoonist, and I remember seeing the cartoons he drew on the envelopes of his letters he sent to my mom when he was in the war. He had some talent, but never developed it, which I thought was a shame. Though I felt they didn't want me to consider it as anything other than a hobby, my parents did encourage my art interests."

Financial Success and the Struggle for Critical Acceptance

Despite his early love of art, when it came time for college Whelan felt, largely because of his parents' urgings, that he should pursue a more practical career. He decided he would study to be a doctor and attended pre-med classes at San Jose State University. "I had been told," he said in his interview, "that the arts were too competitive and financially unreliable to make it worth pursuing." But his love of art could not be denied, and he eventually switched his major to painting, graduating as a President's Scholar in 1973 with a degree in art but also just a few credits short of a biology degree. Whelan lacked the self-confidence to set out on his own immediately, however, and so he entered the Los Angeles Art Center College of Design. Nine months later, after concluding that his instructors weren't teaching him anything he didn't already know, Whelan quit school to pursue his painting career.

Success was immediate. In the fall of 1974, Whelan won his first of what was to be many awards: first place at the World Science Fiction Convention for his painting *Outbound*. The achievement was astounding for an artist who had not even had his first commissioned painting yet. Encouraged, Whelan began submitting his art to publishers, and he was soon hired by Ace, DAW, and others to create cover art for their books. In *The Sound of Wonder*, Whelan described how he sold his first work. Leaving his home in California, he drove his Volkswagen to the east coast,

"and for 2 weeks I just sat down and painted. I had 7 pieces at the end of that time. So I had a portfolio of pieces and I went around first to Marvel Comics—you know, starting low, at least in my opinion at this point. And I showed it to Roy Thomas, who was the editor-in-chief at that time, and he bought three pieces out of the portfolio. So my first cover assignments weren't really commissioned from me; they were bought from me because they were already done."

Whelan paints in a highly realistic manner, though his subjects range from humans to dragons and dwarfs. Although the artist has no objection to abstract or impressionistic styles, he holds strong

This 1986 work appears on the cover of C. J. Cherryh's *Chanur's Homecoming.*

beliefs in what a painter should know before proceeding on to these types of art. And one of the most important disciplines an artist should have, he believes, is a thorough knowledge of anatomy, which he was fortunate enough to acquire while in school. One of the satisfactions of his art, Whelan told *AAYA*, is "the challenge of making it look as though imaginary creatures could exist. That's the real fun part of what I do: making up something that has never been. Of course, having a knowledge of anatomy is part of the game, extrapolating how a particular fanciful beast would have to be constructed to enable it to do the things it does."

In Whelan's mind, one of the main things wrong with training in current art schools is the disregard for the basics. "I have art students corresponding with me, art students that come to conventions to see me and talk to me," Whelan related in *The Sound of Wonder*. "'Where can I go to find out how to draw a person? Where can I go to find out how to render something the way it looks in real life?' Because all they are getting are classes in abstract painting, how to express your feelings. You can't express your feelings unless you have a vocabulary and you've got to learn the vocabulary, the fundamentals, first. If you decide to cast those aside, fine. But first you've got to have a grounding in the academic training."

Along with too much emphasis on abstract painting, the other problem Whelan faces in the artistic world is its lack of respect for fantasy and sci-fi painters. Whelan has had his art displayed in a number of exhibitions, but these have usually been at science and fantasy conventions, or similar gatherings. "It is nearly impossible for anyone who does the kind of work I do to get into galleries," he said in *The Sound of Wonder* back in 1985, "to get any kind of critical recognition at all. It is only in the last few years that it is starting to show much hope. The art schools, as usual, are often years behind the real world." When asked by *AAYA* whether this situation has improved in recent years, the artist replied, "Yes, I'm seeing some change of attitude in some of the art schools. Fewer students seem to be having the intense resistance I (and many of my peers) experienced when we were studying. The change is slow to come, and I still hear quite a few complaints nevertheless. As for the art world, the answer is yes and no. While artists who paint SF

and fantasy are able to make very good incomes, critical acceptance seems hard as ever to get. This may be starting to change, however. There was recently a very favorable review of SF art in a prestigious New York-based art publication, which, hopefully, will herald a time of appreciation and favorable critical appraisal of our art."

About High-Tech Art and Artistic Discipline

One of the new influences in the world of art has been the integration of illustration and technology in the form of computer graphics. Whelan offered his insights about this to *AAYA:* "Digital art offers the artist the one thing not available ever before in history: the chance to create art with an unlimited ability to make nondestructive edits. This is good and bad. It can liberate one from the fear of making mistakes. But it can also lead to endless tinkering and tweaking, and foster the inability to develop the image in one's head first and quickly carry the work to its completion. The best way to create a montage-style illustration is via the computer, and there have arisen a number of first-class artists who do excellent work that way, which is great because I can't stand doing them myself!

"I've been seduced by the digital siren call myself, and in fact the first Gold Medal ever awarded at the Society of Illustrators for a digital artwork was for a piece I did a couple of years ago titled *Crux Humanus*. It was done for a CD cover, but another approach was selected in the end for the cover, so it was never used.

"I've found the computer to be more useful in the early stages of an illustration, especially if one is dealing with a wishy-washy client who can't make a decision without seeing all the possible permutations of an image. It is so much easier to generate alternate versions of a piece digitally because one can grab, copy, and rearrange so handily. Now that I'm doing very little illustration, I find myself not using the computer very much.

"The art schools are falling all over themselves in their haste to offer digital art instruction to prospective students. To be honest, though, I suspect many would-be artists are attracted to the digital medium because they think they can thus create art without having to learn how to draw. In fan-

Whelan, winner of the SuperHugo for Best Artist of the Last 50 Years, completed *Passage: Verge* **in 1984.**

tasy art, though, you have this problem: where are you going to get a photo of a dragon to scan and drop into a digital book cover assignment?"

So Whelan still advocates that all artists learn the basics. Whelan himself knows his anatomy so well that he rarely uses live models to pose for his paintings, going mostly by his own knowledge of biology. Oddly enough, he has said that he often forgets how he does his own paintings, blaming a terrible memory. "That is why a lot of my art work looks different from one piece to another," he said in *The Sound of Wonder*. "I think that from one painting to another I forget how to do a painting, rather than that I deliberately try to vary it. There are artists like Norman Rockwell who develop a technique for doing a painting back when they were 18 or something and never vary from that for their entire lifetime. . . . But I never have a set procedure. The way I did this painting is totally different from the way I did this [other] one. . . . I think I have it down to about 8 different approaches now, probably, but it doesn't make it easier."

Of Book Jackets, CDs, and Symbolism

One complaint Whelan has always had about his own painting is that it takes him far too long for his tastes to get one completed. That is one reason why he uses acrylic paints rather than oils: acrylic paint dries quicker, allowing him to keep painting up to the last few minutes before a deadline. Booked years in advance, he has drawers full of concepts and ideas that he wants to get to but never has the time. Nevertheless, Whelan would like to make more time for personal paintings, and for these he sometimes chooses oils or something besides acrylics for his medium. Personal pursuits allow him more freedom in his format, since painting book covers and other commissioned pieces has its limitations. "[Most] of my personal work is quite a bit larger than my illustration: some of the paintings are four or five feet on a side," Whelan said in an interview for Walden Books' *Hailing Frequencies*. "I paint them for myself and put them up on the walls, and that's pretty much the end of their travels."

He also related that his personal paintings have less detail in them, more space, fewer figures. They are a reaction against the constraints of book jacket art, in which there is little space to work with, and what space there is has to convey something about the book's story. Although he has tried to achieve a balance between his personal and commissioned art, so far this hasn't worked out. "I've tried for years to make it happen, without success," he told *AAYA*. "I finally threw in the towel and stopped taking illustration commissions so I can concentrate solely on my gallery work for the next several years. Whenever I try to do both, I always fill up my schedule with the illustration assignments and leave myself no time to get my other work done!"

When doing a book jacket illustration, Whelan would always read the manuscript, not just once, but at least twice. The second time through, the artist would make notes about scenes, what the characters look like, and so forth. After that, a number of sketches would follow. Sometimes coming up with a cover concept was a very laborious process, while at other times a certain image would come to mind immediately, and the cover would be easier to do. When Whelan was having a particularly rough time with an illustration, he would run several ideas past the editor for some input. The artist also got feedback from the authors. This was especially helpful when the author wasn't specific about certain details. "I talked to Anne McCaffrey at length about the actual details of the dragons [in her *The White Dragon*]," he said in *The Sound of Wonder*, "as she saw the dragons in her book. Whether they had forked tails or tails that ended in a point or whatever, or a barb."

In addition to book jackets, Whelan has also done many illustrations for record and music CD covers. The artist told *AAYA* about the difference between doing a book versus a CD illustration: "Obviously, the first difference is that there is no story to read. Second, there are some record companies which insist on keeping the artwork—something I refuse to include with the deal. Then there are the different ways the recording artist gets involved with the assignment. This can be a rewarding collaboration or a hellish trial, depending on the ego and lack of visual sense of the recording artist. I've experienced both, but I ain't naming names! The final difference between the publishing and the recording industries is that I've found the former to be generally professional and fair, while the latter is rife with liars, cheats, and thieves. Thank goodness I'm not a musician."

Whelan has never liked letting go of his original art. He related why in discussing one of his favorite works with his *AAYA* interviewer: "If I imagine myself on a desert island and I could only have one painting to take with me, I think it would be *Passage: The Avatar*. It is my favorite for a number of reasons. It's in blue, my favorite color. It works very well as a focus point for meditation, which is one of the reasons I painted it. Looking at it gives me a sense of peace and tranquility, something I can always use more of. It is large (compared to my other works: 4' x 4'). The process of creating it was unusual and enjoyable, and seeing the painting recalls the good feeling I had at the time I painted it. Unfortunately, I sold it quite some time ago! I've decided to paint some more in that series next year—and I'll keep one for myself!"

The haunting 1990 painting *Armenia* showcases Whelan's considerable talents.

Whether doing a commissioned illustration or his own art, much of Whelan's work contains symbolic imagery. "I'm of two minds when it comes to the use of symbolism in art in general," he told *AAYA*. "Symbolism is an important part of communication in any artistic form, and can convey certain themes and emotional states more accurately than a purely narrative or descriptive approach. However, it sometimes happens that an artist gets so lost in his own world of symbolic representation that the message gets obscured entirely. The audience is left scratching its head, or worse, ignoring the artwork because they realize they haven't a hope of puzzling out the meaning inside. My use of symbolism comes from several different complimentary approaches. I have employed it as a way to encourage new pictorial images, as a way to communicate difficult ideas, and as a way to convey multiple meanings in the same picture. Because of the universality of many key symbols in human life . . ., using symbols carefully can give one's artwork an emotional resonance that transcends cultural and societal boundaries, giving it a sense of meaning which can reach a very wide audience."

Whelan Branches Out

Whelan does like to reach as wide an audience as possible. Toward this end, he cofounded Glass Onion, a studio and mail-order business he runs with his wife, Audrey, to make his art available to those on a limited budget. Whelan once commented that even Stephen King—at a time when the now-famous horror writer was just coming into prominence—was not able to buy one of his original paintings. In order to make Whelan's work affordable, Glass Onion sells prints that anyone can easily purchase. Much of his artwork

Whelan's *Weyrworld* graces the cover of Anne McCaffrey's 1991 novel *All the Weyrs of Pern*, part of her acclaimed series following the adventures of the dragonriders of Pern.

oeuvre can also be enjoyed in his published collections, including *Wonderworks, Michael Whelan's Worlds of Wonder, The Art of Michael Whelan,* and *Something in My Eye,* the lattermost of which is a collection of Whelan's horror paintings. Although horror art has always been a part of his work, the artist told *AAYA,* "I'm not sure that there is a good reason for horror art to exist, and that ambivalence is reflected in my introduction to *Something in My Eye.* At the moment, I don't feel an artist should devote his talent to adding to the ugliness of the world . . . but I may change my mind tomorrow!"

In addition to his studio, Whelan has in the past tried branching out into other areas, including illustrating a children's book and working with Hollywood, but none of them ever worked out. "The children's book was an adaptation of the first Fuzzy novel by H. Beam Piper," Whelan told *AAYA.* "The book was called *The Adventure of Little Fuzzy.* When the time came to do the painting for it, I decided I had too little time to do the whole thing, so I asked my friend David Wenzel to help me out with it. David is wonderfully skilled with pencil and watercolor rendering, and we work well together. So the project turned out to be an enjoyable and successful enterprise. Unfortunately, the book is now out of print. My paintings *Peekaboo Fuzzies* and *Adventure of Little Fuzzy* were painted for that book.

"I've worked on several movie projects," Whelan continued, "usually at the front end, when the producers are trying to sell the idea to studios or money interests, and almost all the work I did has been lost or acquired and stored someplace. None of my work has ever made it to the screen, unless the preliminary studies of the creature I did for *Predator* were used at all. I don't remember at all what I painted for the screenplay, because it was such a rush job. I literally painted the scenes overnight and sent them out the following morning. I never made any copies of the work, and I don't recall whether what I did resembled anything that made it to the screen.

"My greatest involvement was for a film project derived from the 'Hoka' books by Poul Anderson and Gordon Dickson. [The "Hoka" stories are about a race of teddy-bear-like creatures with overly developed imaginations who take on the personalities of famous literary characters from Earth.] We got as far as defining characters and

If you enjoy the works of Michael Whelan, you may also want to check out the following:

The fantasy art of Frank Frazetta, including *The Fantastic Art of Frank Frazetta,* 1975.
The work of fantasy artists Greg and Tim Hildebrandt, including *The Art of the Brothers Hildebrandt,* 1979.

Rick Baker making a full-sized talking Hoka in his workshop! But, like most film efforts I've been involved in, the project died while still in the development stage. My paintings *Napoleon Hoka, Sherlock Hoka,* and *Moriarty Hoka,* among others, were originally for that movie. . . . David Wenzel was in on that project as well. He did some hilarious sketches and drawings for that script. Too bad it never happened.

"I'm not interested in movie work anymore. It's simply not rewarding enough emotionally. It's always rush, rush, rush, and then ninety percent of the time your work is cut and never makes it to the screen, or the project dies and all the effort is wasted. Often, the movie people insist on keeping the original artwork, too. In general, I hate collaborative efforts, and art direction by committee, for which movie productions are notorious. And again, it is devoting my valuable time to someone else's vision, not my own. That is my chief concern at this stage of my life. I have been approached on three occasions by production companies desiring to base elements of their films on works I've done. That's a different thing, something I don't have any problem with, as long as the plot isn't about something I have a moral objection to. Unfortunately, none of the projects ever came to fruition."

Less and less interested in fulfilling the desires of others for his artwork, Whelan has become most concerned with expressing his own visions through his paintings. This has been his primary concern over the last decade. "The main thing has been a growing sense of urgency about needing to get more of my personal imagery done," he said, "coupled with a declining lack of interest in realizing other people's visions (that is, illustrating). The chief thing I want my work to do in

Whelan's *Spellweavers* serves as the cover for Melanie Rawn's fantasy novel *The Mageborn Traitor*.

the future is to integrate my work with my life as much as possible, making art an extension of, and reflection of, my human experience. In any event, I still see my work as having a fantasy or SF sense to it, because, artistically speaking, that is my language."

■ Works Cited

"Creative Explorations: An Interview with Michael Whelan," *Hailing Frequencies*, Issue 9, 1993, pp. 1-4.

Lane, Daryl, and William Vernon, *The Sound of Wonder: Interviews from "The Science Fiction Radio Show,"* Volume 1, Oryx Press, 1985, pp. 171-203.

Whelan, Michael, in an interview with Kevin S. Hile for *Authors and Artists for Young Adults*, conducted November 19, 1998.

■ For More Information See

PERIODICALS

Analog: Science Fiction and Fact, June, 1994, pp. 161-68.
Locus, January, 1994, pp. 24, 49.
Publishers Weekly, November 13, 1987, p. 64.
School Library Journal, September, 1980, p. 103.

—Sketch by Kevin S. Hile

Acknowledgments

Acknowledgments

Grateful acknowledgment is made to the following publishers, authors, and artists for their kind permission to reproduce copyrighted material.

SHERMAN ALEXIE. Minor, Wendell, illustrator. From a cover of *The Lone Ranger and Tonto Fistfight in Heaven,* by Sherman Alexie. HarperPerennial, 1994. Cover illustration copyright © 1993 by Wendell Minor. Reproduced by permission of The Atlantic Monthly Press. / Minor, Wendell, illustrator. From a cover of *Reservation Blues,* by Sherman Alexie. Warner Books, 1996. Copyright © 1995 by Sherman Alexie. All rights reserved. Reproduced by permission. / From a cover of *Indian Killer,* by Sherman Alexie. Warner Books, 1998. Copyright © 1996 by Sherman Alexie. All rights reserved. Reproduced by permission. / Adams, Evan, with Adam Beach, in a scene from *Smoke Signals,* photograph. Archive Photos, Inc. Reproduced by permission. / Alexie, Sherman, photograph by Jerry Bauer. © Jerry Bauer. Reproduced by permission.

JENNIFER ARMSTRONG. Martindale, Emily, illustrator. From a cover of *Black-Eyed Susan,* by Jennifer Armstrong. Knopf Paperbacks, 1997. Cover art © 1995 by Emily Martindale. Reproduced by permission of Random House, Inc. / *At the Window,* painting by William Merritt Chase. From a cover of *The Dreams of Mairhe Mehan,* by Jennifer Armstrong. Knopf Paperbacks, 1997. Cover art copyright © 1997 by Superstock, Inc. Reproduced by permission of Random House, Inc. / Armstrong, Jennifer, photograph by Phil Haggerty. Reproduced by permission of Jennifer Armstrong.

MELVIN BURGESS. Waldman, Neil, illustrator. From a cover of *The Cry of the Wolf,* by Melvin Burgess. Beech Tree Paperback Books, 1994. Reproduced by permission of Beech Tree Paperback Books, a division of William Morrow & Company, Inc. / Fiedler, Joseph Daniel, illustrator. From a jacket of *The Baby and Fly Pie,* by Melvin Burgess. Simon & Schuster Books for Young Readers, 1996. Jacket © 1996 by Simon & Schuster. Reproduced by permission of Simon & Schuster Books for Young Readers, an imprint of Simon & Schuster Children's Publishing Division. / From a cover of *Smack,* by Melvin Burgess. Henry Holt and Company, 1997. Reproduced by permission of Henry Holt and Company, Inc. / Burgess, Melvin, photograph. Courtesy of Henry Holt and Company.

CHUCK CLOSE. *Big Self-Portrait,* 1968, acrylic on canvas, 107-1/2 x 83-1/2 x 2" unframed, painting by Chuck Close, photograph. Collection Walker Art Center, Minneapolis. Art Center Acquisition Fund, 1969. Reproduced by permission. / *Lucas II,* painting by Chuck Close. Oil on canvas, 1987. Private Collection. Reproduced by permission of PaceWildenstein. / *Eric,* painting by Chuck Close. Oil on canvas, 1990. G. U. C. Collection, Deerfield, Illinois. Photograph by Bill Jacobson. Reproduced by permission of PaceWildenstein. / *John,* painting by Chuck Close. Oil on Canvas, 1992. Photograph by Bill Jacobson. Reproduced by permission of PaceWildenstein. / *Self-Portrait,* painting by Chuck Close. Oil on canvas, 1997. Photograph by Ellen Page Wilson. Reproduced by permission of PaceWildenstein.

SHARON DRAPER. Ransome, James, illustrator. From a cover of *Shadows of Caesar's Creek,* by Sharon M. Draper. Just Us Books, 1997. Cover illustration copyright © 1997 by James Ransome. Reproduced by permission. / Clapp, John, illustrator. From a cover of *Forged by Fire,* by Sharon M. Draper. Aladdin Paperbacks, 1998. Cover illustration copyright © 1998 by John Clapp. Reproduced by permission of John Clapp. / Draper, Sharon, 1997, photograph. AP/Wide World Photos. Reproduced by permission.

T. S. ELIOT. From a cover of *The Waste Land and Other Poems,* by T. S. Eliot. Harvest Books, 1934. Copyright 1934 by Harcourt Brace & Company. Copyright 1930 and renewed 1962, 1958 by T. S. Eliot. Reproduced by permission of the publisher. / From a cover of *Four Quartets,* by T. S. Eliot. Harvest Books, 1971. Copyright 1943 by T. S. Eliot and renewed 1971 by Esme Valerie Eliot. Reproduced by permission of Harcourt Brace & Company. / *Murder in the Cathedral,* by T. S. Eliot, with John Westbrook as Thomas Becket being murdered at Canterbury Cathedral, performed September 23, 1970, photograph. Hulton-Deutsch Collection/Corbis. Reproduced by permission.

PHILIP JOSÉ FARMER. Di Fate, Vincent, illustrator. From a jacket of *Dayworld Breakup,* by Philip José Farmer. Tor Books, 1990. Reproduced by permission of St. Martin's Press, Inc. / Vallejo, Boris, illustrator. From a jacket of *More Than Fire,* by Philip José Farmer. Tor Books, 1993. Reproduced by permission of St. Martin's Press, Inc. / Stevens, John, illustrator. From a cover of *The Magic Labyrinth,* by Philip José Farmer. Ballantine Books, 1998. Reproduced by permission of Ballantine Books, a division of Random House, Inc. / Stevens, John, illustrator. From a cover of *To Your Scattered Bodies Go,* by Philip José Farmer. Ballantine Books, 1998. Reproduced by permission of Ballantine Books, a division of Random House, Inc. / Farmer, Philip José, photograph by Jay Kay Klein. © Copyright 1976 by Jay Kay Klein. Reproduced by permission.

BARBARA HAMBLY. Whelan, Michael, illustrator. From a cover of *Dragonsbane,* by Barbara Hambly. Ballantine Books, 1986. Reproduced by permission of Ballantine Books, a division of Random House, Inc. / Struzan, Drew, illustrator. From a cover of *Star Wars: Children of the Jedi,* by Barbara Hambly. Bantam Books, 1995. Cover art copyright © 1995 Lucasfilm Ltd. & TM. All rights reserved. Reproduced by permission of Lucasfilm Ltd. / From a cover of *Traveling with the Dead,* by Barbara Hambly. Ballantine Books, 1996. Reproduced by permission of Ballantine Books, a division of Random House, Inc. / Seder, Jason, illustrator. From a cover of *A Free Man of Color,* by Barbara Hambly. Bantam Books, 1997. Cover art copyright © 1998 by Jason Seder. All rights reserved. Reproduced by permission of Bantam Books, a division of Random House, Inc. / Giancola, Donato, illustrator. From a cover of *Mother of Winter,* by Barbara Hambly. Ballantine Books, 1997. Reproduced by permission of Ballantine Books, a division of Random House, Inc. / Hambly, Barbara, photograph by Jay Kay Klein. Reproduced by permission.

VALERIE HOBBS. Weiman, Jon, illustrator. From a jacket of *How Far Would You Have Gotten If I Hadn't Called You Back?,* by Valerie Hobbs. Orchard Books, 1995. Jacket painting copyright © 1995 by Jon Weiman. Reproduced by permission of Jon Weiman. / From a cover of *Get It While It's Hot. Or Not,* by Valerie Hobbs. Avon Books, 1998. Reproduced by permission of Avon Books, Inc. / Hobbs, Valerie, photograph by Jack Hobbs. Reproduced by permission of Valerie Hobbs.

VICTOR HUGO. Bergen, David, illustrator. From a cover of *The Hunchback of Notre Dame,* by Victor Hugo. Puffin Books, 1996. Cover illustration copyright © David Bergen, 1996. Reproduced by permission of Penguin Books, Ltd (London). / Matheson, Hans, in a scene from *Les Miserables,* photograph. Archive Photos, Inc. Reproduced by permission. / Laughton, Charles, in a scene from *The Hunchback of Notre Dame,* photograph. RKO. Courtesy of The Kobal Collection.

PAUL JANECZKO. Leech, Dorothy, illustrator. From an illustration in *Stardust otel,* by Paul B. Janeczko. Orchard Books, 1993. Illustrations copyright © 1993 by Dorothy Leech. Reproduced by permission of Orchard Books, New York. / Janeczko, Paul, photograph by Nadine V. Edris. Reproduced by permission of Nadine V. Edris.

PAUL JENNINGS. McEwan, Keith, illustrator. From a cover of *Unmentionable!,* by Paul Jennings. Puffin Books, 1995. Reproduced by permission of Penguin Books Australia Limited. / McEwan, Keith, illustrator. From a cover of *Undone!,* by Paul Jennings. Puffin Books, 1997. Reproduced by permission of Penguin Books Australia Limited. / McEwan, Keith, illustrator. From a cover of *Covered with Nails,* by Paul Jennings. Puffin Books, 1998. Reproduced by permission of Penguin Books Australia Limited. / McEwan, Keith, illustrator. From a jacket of *Listen Ear,* by Paul Jennings. Puffin Books, 1998. Reproduced by permission of Penguin Books Australia Limited. / Jennings, Paul, photograph from *Magpies,* v. 3, September, 1988.

SEBASTIAN JUNGER. TH.D. DeLange/FPG, photographer. From a cover of *The Perfect Storm,* by Sebastian Junger. HarperPaperbacks, 1998. TH.D. De Lange/FPG Stepback photograph © 1998 FPG. Reproduced by permission of W. W. Norton & Company, Inc., FPG International LLC, and Stuart Krichevsky Literary Agency, Inc. / Junger, Sebastian, photograph by Dan Deitch. © 1997 Dan Deitch. Reproduced by permission of Sebastian Junger and Dan Deitch.

JACKIE FRENCH KOLLER. Edens, John, illustrator. From a cover of *The Primrose Way,* by Jackie French Koller. Gulliver Books, 1992. Cover illustration copyright © 1992 by John Edens. Reproduced by permission of John Edens. / Sayles, Elizabeth, illustrator. From a cover of *A Place to Call Home,* by Jackie French Koller. Aladdin Paperbacks, Cover illustration © 1995 by Elizabeth Sayles. Reproduced by permission of Elizabeth Sayles. / Koller, Jackie French, photograph. Reproduced by permission.

NANCY KRESS. Binger, Bill, photographer. From a cover of *Beggars in Spain,* by Nancy Kress. Avon Books, 1993. Reproduced by permission of Avon Books, Inc. / From a cover of *Beggars and Choosers,* by Nancy Kress. Tor Books, 1994. Reproduced by permission of St. Martin's Press, Incorporated. / From a cover of *Oaths and Miracles,* by Nancy Kress. Tor Books, 1996. Reproduced by permission of St. Martin's Press, Incorporated. / Kress, Nancy, photograph. Reproduced by permission.

MADELEINE L'ENGLE. Steele, Robert Gantt, illustrator. From a cover of *The Summer of the Great-Grandmother,* by Madeleine L'Engle. Harper San Francisco, 1974. Reproduced by permission of Harper San Francisco, a division of HarperCollins Publishers. / Nielsen, Cliff, illustrator. From a cover of *A Wrinkle in Time,* by Madeleine L'Engle. Laurel-Leaf Books, 1976. Copyright © 1962 by Madeleine L'Engle. Reproduced by permission of Dell Publishing, a division of Random House, Inc. / Henderson, Dave, illustrator. From a cover of *A Ring of Endless Light,* by Madeleine L'Engle. Laurel-Leaf Books, 1995. Cover art copyright © 1995 by Dave Henderson. All rights reserved. Reproduced by permission of Dell Publishing, a division of Random House, Inc. / L'Engle, Madeleine, photograph by Thomas Victor. Reproduced by permission of the Estate of Thomas Victor.

JONATHAN LARSON. Performers from the musical *Rent,* photograph. Reuters/Joan Marcus/Archive Photos, Inc. Reproduced by permission. / Larson, Jonathan, 1996, photograph. Archive Photos, Inc. Reproduced by permission.

RICHARD LINKLATER. Hawke, Ethan, and Julie Delpy in the film *Before Sunrise,* photograph by Gabriela Brandenstein. © 1995 Castle Rock Entertainment. All Rights Reserved. Reproduced by permission. / Cochrane, Rory, with Jason London and Sasha Jenson in a scene from *Dazed and Confused,* photograph. Gramercy. The Kobal Collection. / Cast of *SubUrbia*, photograph. Archive Photos, Inc. Reproduced by permission. / Linklater, Richard, photograph. © Will Van Overbeer/Corbis. Reproduced by permission.

HAN NOLAN. Kahl, David, illustrator. From the cover of *If I Should Die Before I Wake*, by Han Nolan. Harcourt Brace & Company, 1994. Cover illustration copyright © 1994 by David Kahl. Reproduced by permission of David Kahl. / Shed, Greg, illustrator. From a cover of *Send Me Down a Miracle*, by Han Nolan. Harcourt Brace & Company, 1996. Cover illustration copyright © 1996 by Greg Shed. Reproduced by permission of Greg Shed. / Lee, Paul, illustrator. From a jacket of *Dancing on the Edge*, by Han Nolan. Harcourt Brace & Company, 1997. Jacket illustration copyright © 1997 by Paul Lee. Reproduced by permission of Paul Lee. / Nolan, Han, photograph by Brian Nolan. Courtesy of Harcourt Brace & Company.

ROBERT PARKER. From a cover of *Promised Land*, by Robert B. Parker. Dell Publishing, 1987. Reproduced by permission of Delacorte Press, a division of Random House, Inc. / Urich, Robert, with Avery Brooks, in a scene from *Spenser: For Hire*, photograph. ABC-TV. Courtesy of The Kobal Collection. / Parker, Robert, photograph. AP/Wide World Photos. Reproduced by permission.

ELIZABETH ANN SCARBOROUGH. Rowena, illustrator. From a cover of *Power Play*, by Elizabeth Ann Scarborough and Anne McCaffrey. Del Rey Books, 1996. Reproduced by permission of Random House, Inc. / Scarborough, Elizabeth Ann, photograph by Paul Boyer. Reproduced by permission of Elizabeth Ann Scarborough.

PAUL THEROUX. McCurry, Steve, photographer. From a cover of *The Great Railway Bazaar*, by Paul Theroux. Penguin Books, 1977. Cover photograph © Steve McCurry, Magnum Photos, Inc. Reproduced by permission of Penguin Books, Ltd (London) and Magnum Photos, Inc. / Ross, Ruth, illustrator. From a cover of *Millroy the Magician*, by Paul Theroux. Ballantine Books, 1996. Reproduced by permission of Ballantine Books, a division of Random House, Inc. / Ford, Harrison (with River Phoenix in background), in a scene from *The Mosquito Coast*, photograph. Archive Photos, Inc. Reproduced by permission. / Theroux, Paul, photograph by Jerry Bauer. © Jerry Bauer. Reproduced by permission.

SUE TOWNSEND. From a cover of *The Queen and I*, by Sue Townsend. Soho, 1993. Reproduced by permission of Soho Press. / From a cover of *Adrian Mole: The Lost Years*, by Sue Townsend. Soho, 1994. Reproduced by permission of Soho Press. / Beavers, Sean, illustrator. From a cover of *The Adrian Mole Diaries*, by Sue Townsend. Avon Books, 1997. Reproduced by permission of Avon Books, Inc. / From a cover of *Ghost Children*, by Sue Townsend. Soho, 1998. Reproduced by permission of Soho Press. / Townsend, Sue, photograph by Tessa Musgrave. © Tessa Musgrave.

MICHAEL WHELAN. *L'Echelle*, painting by Michael Whelan. © Michael Whelan. Reproduced by permission./ *Spellweavers*, painting by Michael Whelan. Cover art for *The Mageborn Traitor* by Melanie Rawn. © Michael Whelan. Reproduced by permission. / *Chanur's Homecoming*, painting by Michael Whelan. Cover art for the novel by C. J. Cherryh. © 1986 Michael Whelan. Reproduced by permission. / *Passage: Verge*, painting by Michael Whelan. © 1988 Michael Whelan. Reproduced by permission. / *Armenia*, painting by Michael Whelan. © 1989 Michael Whelan. Reproduced by permission. / *Weyrworld*, painting by Michael Whelan. Cover art for *All the Weyrs of Pern*, by Anne McCaffrey. © 1990 Michael Whelan. Reproduced by permission. / Whelan, Michael, photograph. Reproduced by permission.

Cumulative Index

Author/Artist Index

The following index gives the number of the volume in which an author/artist's biographical sketch appears.